THE
CONSTRUCTION
OF GROUP
REALITIES

THE
CONSTRUCTION
OF GROUP
REALITIES

Culture, Society, and
Personal Construct Theory

Edited by
Devorah Kalekin-Fishman and
Beverly M. Walker

KRIEGER PUBLISHING COMPANY
MALABAR, FLORIDA
1996

Original Edition 1996

Printed and Published by
KRIEGER PUBLISHING COMPANY
KRIEGER DRIVE
MALABAR, FLORIDA 32950

Copyright © 1996 by Krieger Publishing Company

Library of Congress Cataloging-In-Publication Data

The construction of group realities : culture, society, and personal
    construct theory / Devorah Kalekin-Fishman & Beverly M. Walker.
        p.   cm.
    Includes index.
    ISBN 0-89464-740-7
    1. Social groups.   2. Personal construct theory.   I. Kalekin
-Fishman, Devorah.   II. Walker, Beverly M.
HM131.C7458   1996
305—dc20   93-37579
                                                                   CIP

10 9 8 7 6 5 4 3 2

Contents

PART TWO

APPLICATIONS OF THE THEORY
TO GROUP CONSTRUING

PART THREE

EXTENDING THE THEORY IN
NEW DIRECTIONS

Contributors

Kurt D. Baker
Department of Psychology, Emporia State University, Kansas, USA

Ellen A. Begley
Department of Psychology, Miami University, Oxford, Ohio, USA

Donna L. Brooks
Veterans Administration Medical Center, Little Rock, Arkansas, USA

Bianca De Bernardi
Istituto di Psicologia, Università degli Studi di Verona, Verona, Italy

Pam Denicolo
Department of Educational Studies, University of Surrey, Guilford, Surrey, England

Lothar Duda
Institut für Sozialmedizin, Epidemiologie und Gesundheitssystemforschung, Witten, Germany

Gavin Dunnett
Deceased, formerly of Redcliffe Centre for Community Psychiatry, Wellingborough, Northants, United Kingdom

Franz R. Epting
Department of Psychology, University of Florida, Gainesville, Florida, USA

April J. Faidley
Department of Psychology, Miami University, Oxford, Ohio, USA

Linda Hort
Department of Psychology, Faculty of Applied Science, University of Canberra, Canberra, ACT, Australia

A. Devi Jankowicz
Central and Eastern European Research Centre, Teesside Business School, University of Teesside, United Kingdom

Devorah Kalekin-Fishman
School of Education, University of Haifa, Haifa, Israel

George A. Kelly
Deceased, formerly of Psychology Department, Ohio State University, Columbus, Ohio, USA

Larry M. Leitner
Department of Psychology, Miami University, Oxford, Ohio, USA

Robert A. Neimeyer
Department of Psychology, Memphis State University, Memphis, Tennessee, USA

Harry Oxley
School of Administrative Studies, Faculty of Management, University of Canberra, Canberra, ACT, Australia

Shawn Prichard
Department of Psychology, University of Florida, Gainesville, Florida, USA

Harry G. Procter
Child and Therapeutic Services, Petrel House, Broadway Park, Bridgewater, England

Helen Ross
Centre for Resource and Environmental Studies, Australian National University, Canberra, ACT, Australia

Dusan Stojnov
Department of Psychology, University of Belgrade, Belgrade, Yugoslavia

Peter Stringer
Netherlands Institute of Social Sexological Research, Utrecht, The Netherlands

Laurie Thomas
Centre for the Study of Human Learning, Brunel University, Uxbridge, Middlesex, England

Barbara Tooth
Department of Nursing, University of Wollongong, Wollongong, NSW, Australia

Beverly M. Walker
Department of Psychology, University of Wollongong, Wollongong, NSW, Australia

William G. Warren
Department of Education, University of Newcastle, NSW, Australia

Ulrike Willutzki
Fakultät für Psychologie, Ruhr-Universität, Bochum, Germany

Preface

This book originated in a sense of frustration. The frustration is experienced by many of those individuals who find in George Kelly's psychology of personal constructs (PCP) an inspiring, practical way of understanding themselves and the interpersonal world of which they are both the created and the creator. It arises from seeing Kelly's theory misrepresented in secondary accounts of its tenets and from seeing others reinventing the wheel without acknowledgment of his prior innovations.

In the pages that follow, the contributors highlight an approach to seeing people as social beings, who share ways of making sense of things and differ from others in specifiable ways. As we indicate, this is contrary to how many have interpreted the personal construct perspective. The theory has been criticized as being individualistic, unable to accommodate to recent intellectual trends that emphasize common symbols, particularly language. The contributors to this book share the conviction that this is a misrepresentation of Kelly's position and, further, that the body of work called personal construct psychology has diversified and elaborated on the theory as presented in Kelly's major exposition (Kelly, 1955, reprinted 1991) in interaction with current western intellectual trends. Nevertheless, the roots of personal construct psychology are firmly placed within Kelly's work, demonstrating the conviction of those so sustained that within that tradition lies much of value that has been ignored by these other, more recent perspectives.

The nature of this book typifies much about personal construct psychology at this time. The contributors come from a variety of disciplines. Along with the psychologists that might be expected, there are sociologists, anthropologists, and people with training in education, nursing, philosophy, and management. Many have multiple interests and training, just as George Kelly had (Kelly, 1969). The authors also have come from

xiii

varied national and cultural backgrounds. The traditional domination of representation from the United States and England has been broadened; among the writers are researchers from Australia, Germany, Israel, Italy, and the former Yugoslavia. This spread in the location of work from this perspective reflects not merely a change in who expresses interest in it, but a difference in the way we can now communicate with one another. If computers, e-mail, and fax had not been freely available, this collaboration would not have been possible.

In organizing the papers included here, we eventually resorted to three parts:

1. Implications of the theory for understanding groups;

2. Applications of the theory to group construing;

3. Extending the theory in new directions.

Assigning the papers to one or another of the divisions proved an interesting exercise in construing. We decided on both the sections and the distribution of papers to them only after experimenting with various structures. We relied in part on the stated purposes of the authors themselves in introducing their papers. Still it is possible that the writers interpret their contributions differently. The division should be seen as a matter of emphasis, not as a definitive statement, and particularly not as a commentary on the relative innovativeness of one approach over another.

The empirical papers present a picture of PCP methodology that may be rather surprising to some of our readers. Published research has traditionally been dominated by repertory grid methodology (see Neimeyer, 1982). Yet, at national and international PCP congresses during the eighties and nineties, the preoccupation with grids has in fact been a subject of controversy. Although several studies in this collection have used repertory grids in part (e.g., chapters 10, 11, and 12), qualitative conversational approaches have proved especially useful and often indispensable in applying personal construct theory to samples of people from diverse cultural backgrounds.

The contributions of the editors to the creation of this volume were diverse and cannot readily be prioritized as the ordering of names on the cover of this book might imply. Thus, it was Devorah's (the sociologist's) idea at the time that Beverly (whose principal training is in psychology) was completing a paper on individualism and PCP (Walker, 1990). Who spent more time on which chapter varied both with relative expertise and the inevitable time constraints. It was exciting for both of us to find that with the help of our computers, we could argue our way through to agreement on most of the issues that arose.

Beverly M. Walker
Devorah Kalekin-Fishman

REFERENCES

Kelly, G. A. (1955). *The psychology of personal constructs*. New York: Norton.

Kelly, G. A. (1969). *Clinical psychology and personality: The selected papers of George Kelly*, edited by B. Maher. New York: Krieger.

Neimeyer, R. A. (1982). *The development of personal construct psychology*. Lincoln and London: University of Nebraska Press.

Walker, B. M. (1990, September). *Individualism and personal construct theory*. Paper presented at the Fifth Australasian Personal Construct Conference, Adelaide, SA, Australia.

PART ONE

Implications of
the Theory for
Understanding Groups

INTRODUCTION

Part One, "Implications of the theory for understanding groups," includes five chapters that expand on the social implications of the foundations of personal construct psychology.

The first chapter, by Beverly M. Walker, provides an overview of Kelly's theory with its relevance to the social to the fore. As such, it will be useful to those readers who have only a cursory acquaintance with personal construct psychology either through secondary sources or through reading *A Theory of Personality*, the first three chapters of Kelly's comprehensive work (Kelly, 1963). This chapter, however, also contains suggestions about the contributions that Kellian theory can make to social constructivist perspectives. It explores the distinctive Kellian construction of the individual in context. The chapter elaborates on an earlier paper (Walker, 1990), including some of the material from that presentation that would otherwise not be readily available.

Chapter 2, first published by George Kelly in 1962 in the *Nebraska Symposium on Motivation*, shows that Kelly himself was concerned with the significance of social and cultural factors in personal construing. This chapter gives the lie, more than any other single piece of his work, to the view that Kelly's theoretical perspective is not amenable to applications beyond a narrow clinical setting. Because of the somewhat sexist asides and the naive understanding of the privileges of party members and their children within the Soviet system, the paper might be thought dated, but in other ways the paper is extremely topical. It deals for the most part with his observations of how people of different nationalities make differing senses of things. He focuses particularly on the constructions of the social behind what was then the iron curtain. Reading this chapter at a time when the curtain has to a large extent been drawn back, one is struck by how pertinent his observations are today. Kelly contrasts construing in cultures where people have memories of another way of living

3

with those where they do not. People who have lived through the construction and the destruction of the Berlin Wall, like those who have seen Yugoslavia carved out of the Austro-Hungarian Empire, and then cut up some more, still have to deal with these crucial issues as they struggle to achieve a coherent life. Here we have in personal construct psychology a perspective that has significant things to say, and, more important, to do, about the most monumental issues of our times.

In chapters 3 and 4, traditional Kelly theorizing is applied to people's ongoing experience of society. In addition to demonstrating the utility and general applicability (in Kellian terms, the wide range of convenience) of personal construct theory (PCT), they both illustrate why many of us find this theory of crucial importance to our daily lives. Both papers depart from conventional formats for scientific articles. Dusan Stojnov's chapter arose out of his e-mail correspondence with Beverly Walker, which was carried on until the dissolution of the state of Yugoslavia resulted in the disruption of the computer network route from Belgrade to other networks throughout the world. His letter describes in moving terms one individual's attempt to cope with the overwhelming events thrust upon him. As such it illustrates quite powerfully Kelly's view that while we cannot other than be affected by events around us, by what has happened to us previously as well as at present, still we are not merely "victims of our circumstances." Even in the midst of the horrors of war, there are choices and there are alternative ways of making sense of what is happening, some of which can turn out to be more practical than others. In the extreme circumstances that Dusan has had to brave, what Kelly defined as hostility, "the continued effort to extort validational evidence in favor of a type of social prediction which has already been recognized as a failure" (Kelly, 1955, p. 565), may prove to be the only hope.

Chapter 3 should perhaps have as coauthors the people who contributed to the discussion, the transcript of which forms a large part of the paper. The focus of the discussion by this group was how to characterize personal construct groups. Based on the juxtaposition of various texts, the paper is presented in a format that owes much to literary and philosophical trends that postdate Kelly's life. Such approaches, however, seem to us to fit well with a PCT perspective (see also Mair, 1989; Salmon, 1990) with its focus on contrast and its tolerance of a variety of perspectives. The writers pose questions that actively involve us all—readers and writers—in carrying on our own search for personally meaningful answers through vicarious participation in the group process.

Closing Part One is a chapter in a rather more conventional format, Bill Warren's "The egalitarian outlook as the underpinning of the theory of personal constructs." Warren explicates the basis for reading Kellian theory as inescapably social. Basing his argument on the writings of Kant, Dewey, Sève, and Barbu, he draws parallels between their work and that of Kelly. The human being who figures in personal construct psychology is a meaning-making person who necessarily aspires to take responsibility for his or her own life. Warren shows that the psychological functioning of such individuals can only be sustained in a democratic, egalitarian context. It is, then, the social dimension of the theory of personal constructs that sustains the conception of the person.

REFERENCES

Kelly, G. A. (1955). *The psychology of personal constructs*. New York: Norton (reprinted 1991).

Kelly, G. A. (1963). *A theory of personality: The psychology of personal constructs*. New York: Norton.

Mair, J. M. M. (1989). Kelly, Bannister, and a story-telling psychology. *International Journal of Personal Construct Psychology, 2*, 1–14.

Salmon, P. (1990, April). *Kelly, then and now*. Paper presented at the Second British Conference on Personal Construct Psychology, York.

Walker, B. M. (1990, September). *Individualism and personal construct theory*. Paper presented at the Fifth Australasian Personal Construct Conference, Adelaide, SA, Australia.

CHAPTER 1

A Psychology for Adventurers:
An Introduction to Personal Construct Psychology from a Social Perspective

BEVERLY M. WALKER

> The psychology of personal constructs, rather than being a system in which the study of individual behavior leaves no place for the study of group participation, is one which keeps open vast areas of social relationships to be explored by adventurous psychologists. (Kelly, 1955, p. 179)

Since many who read this book may be coming to personal construct theory (PCT) for the first time or after having only read secondary accounts that are commonly problematic (Walker, 1991), we thought it might be useful to present some of the important aspects of the theory. Those closely identified with the theoretical position should feel free to omit this section, though the later discussion of the relationship between PCT, social determinism and social constructivism, and the meaning of the personal may be of interest. While the aim is to present George Kelly's position as comprehensively as possible, this is not an easy task, a point that can be clearly seen from within the perspective itself.

We are all meaning makers—continually appraising and reappraising the events we encounter in our lives, whether these be the mundane details of our domestic existence or the major theoretical frameworks of our times. The coming to terms with someone's theoretical framework, or indeed anything we attempt to understand, is not carried out in isolation from our understandings of other things we have experienced. The sense we make of things quite obviously has implications for all we say,

7

do, feel, believe, and value, and particularly for our future engagement with those things.

So I come to my attempt to convey something of the nature of Kelly's theory from a perspective, not as a tabula rasa. My assumption is that you also approach this account from a point of view. If a large number of people are interested in this book, as I hope there will be, there are likely to be many perspectives being applied. Then, too, Kelly's theory, while seemingly simple, is quite complex. Because of the limited space available, I will have to be selective, choosing among his important concepts, highlighting some of his metaphors to attempt to facilitate understanding, and using examples of my own devising based on my anticipations of ways you are likely to make sense of things. It won't be easy to make my choice in such a way that my account will make sense within the variety of perspectives I anticipate will be brought to bear on this article.

SOME CENTRAL THEORETICAL IDEAS

The brief account I have given of what my aims are provides a useful illustration of much of Kelly's concerns. This is not surprising because Kelly suggested that if you cannot apply the framework to your own life, to what you do, whether in your private or professional spheres, you should be justifiably skeptical of it. My temptation is to present the ideas without any reference to the specific terms Kelly used to summarize the parts of his theoretical framework, as Rychlak (1981) has done, but part of the function of this chapter is to assist you to gain as much as possible from the papers that follow, all of which use some of the formal theoretical terms.

In the opening paragraphs a variety of words were used interchangeably to refer to what Kelly called *construing*, words like "meaning making," "appraising," "applying a theoretical framework," "ways you are likely to make sense of things," and adopting "a perspective." The sense conveyed is of a process of making differentiations between events, based on ways we have previously discriminated.[1]

Now these ways whereby we discriminate the world are not just theoretical artifacts—they have important relationships to whatever we are and whatever we do. Perhaps your initial exposure to Kelly's theory gives you a feeling of exhilaration at having found at last a perspective that seems to make sense of the things that happen to you and your colleagues, rather than of what you imagine occurs to those who spend long periods of time on therapists' couches. If that is your feeling, you certainly won't approach the rest of this book in the way you would if your reaction had been that the theory is a bit too abstract, just like some of the other theoretical perspectives you've come across before that you didn't want to explore further. Kelly articulates the importance of such expectations when he states the basis of his theoretical position as "a person's processes are psychologically channelized by the ways in which he anticipates events" (Kelly, 1955, p. 46). The processes referred to include those of our self-definition and our relationships with others, as well as the current task of making sense of frameworks such as George Kelly's theory.

Thus, neither you nor I can present a summarizing account of George Kelly's theory that is divorced from our own construing, and neither can we understand each other's accounts in some construct-free vacuum. Life, of course, would be so much simpler if we did approach events directly. Many psychologists have attempted to create such a nirvana in experimental laboratories in the mistaken belief that wishing it to happen will create it. But as Kelly recognized, human beings stubbornly continue to be what they are, meaning-making creatures, even in the face of soundproofed, electrically shielded, and thermally insulated experimental laboratories with someone running around in a white coat to police it all, as Mixon (1971) and Orne (1962) have demonstrated.

In writing about our differing assumptions and frameworks, I'm alluding to another of Kelly's central concerns, that "persons differ from each other in their construction of events" (Kelly, 1955, p. 55), referred to as *individuality*. This proposition needs to be considered in tandem with another of his proposals, *commonality*, which is, "to the extent that one person employs a construction of experience which is similar to that employed by another, his psychological processes are similar to those of the other person" (p. 90). The integral relationship of these two principles is crucial to an understanding of PCT and its location relative to other theoretical frameworks we value or abhor. People are both different from and similar to others.

Some approaches to theorizing seem to stress difference from others, to the detriment of similarity, i.e., individuality at the expense of commonality. This is done by comparing one person to others in idiographic terms or by making individuality or autonomy the goal of effective living as many of the humanistic approaches seem to advocate. Other approaches to psychology and social theory embark on a nomothetic pursuit of general laws to frame all people, emphasizing commonality rather than individuality. Some of these regard human beings as being constituted by nothing but social mechanisms such as language, or determined by social forces in a relatively mechanistic manner. Both these opposing approaches have something of value, but neither extreme in and of itself is satisfactory. As Kelly indicated, in order to understand people both their individuality and commonality are central. Later I will return to the issue of how both individuality and commonality are of equal importance in a personal construct framework. However, there are further Kellian principles illustrated in the account given of my aims.

My assumption is that your exploration of PCT is part of a broader attempt to extend your understanding of people, including yourself. This motivation to make sense of your world is ongoing and inherent, in Kelly's view. Kelly set up somewhat simplified parodies of other theoretical views in attempting to clarify this point, distinguishing his perspective from those of behaviorists who feel the individual is pushed to respond and those like the psychoanalysts who emphasize the pull of specific motives, needs, or drives. For Kelly the motivational emphases that other writers propose are inherent in the person as a given, not something that acts upon the person who is thereby pulled or pushed. It is our nature to ceaselessly pursue meaning-making, whether this be about ourselves, others, the physical world—or George Kelly's personal construct theory.

This is not to say that our pursuit is without direction. Kelly wrote in the choice corollary that our choices are guided by what we anticipate to be the "greater possibility for extension and definition" of our construing system (Kelly, 1955, p. 64) and used the term *elaboration* for both these possibilities. If what you read here about PCT helps you to tie down things that have been puzzling you about yourself or others, or if it sets you off on extending the theoretical perspectives you hold dear to your heart, then this illustrates his view. Alternatively, if you find it does neither of these things, then you're likely to stick this book back on the shelves, muttering to yourself about the waste of trees. What we are presenting hasn't helped you to elaborate your perspective.

This task is not divorced from personal interaction. Both you and I are currently engaged in a further, very central process known as *sociality*. As indicated, I am trying to understand how you make sense of things and am struggling with the puzzle of how to write in such a way that what is said makes sense to you. This is, of course, a difficult task as it is unlikely that we have ever met, and I assume you are a diverse group anyway. But my struggle to relate to you in this way results in what Kelly called the establishment of a *role* relationship. The process of sociality he defined as— "to the extent that one person construes the construction processes of another, he may play a role in a social process involving the other person" (Kelly, 1955, p. 95). My assumption too is that many of you are attempting to establish a role relationship, but in this instance it is more with George Kelly than with me.

Some of you, I suspect, may not be engaged in sociality at all. In fact, in this context you may see it as a waste of time or anathema to proper academic practice. You are approaching these accounts in terms of a set of concepts, a discourse, in postmodern terms, that should be looked at like other such documents as something to be analyzed and criticized in relation to other similar theories and even used in part to justify the views held prior to mistakenly picking up this book. There is nothing wrong with doing that. It is, after all, what most of us were trained to do during university studies. But may I suggest that you might gain a very different understanding of a theoretical perspective, including this one, if you approached it from the starting point of attempting to find out what the creator of the perspective was attempting to do?

And so it is with the relationships we are engaged in on an everyday basis. Relating to our students in ways that involve attempting to under-stand their perspectives is very different from applying the fashionable managerial model to education and seeing students as materials that are processed and eventually form the product output of the university. Kelly is clearly trying to increase awareness of the difference between treating people as objects as opposed to meaning-making individuals, and to a considerable extent, advocating the virtues of the latter. The latter ap-proach, he suggested, could have profound implications for one's own perspective. As Kelly pointed out (see chapter 2), peering at the world through another person's spectacles can permanently affect one's eye-sight. However, he indicated that the treatment of others as objects may be both necessary and useful in some situations. One can't spend all one's time attempting to establish role relationships with every casual relation-ship we experience in the course of our daily lives.

This account of what I am attempting here has been useful to illus-trate many of the major Kellian theoretical principles. However, there are other issues that are important for an understanding of what follows.

Kelly was very much a provocateur. When reading many of the pa-pers he delivered, one finds him using rhetorical devices to jolt his audi-ence into setting aside the ways they currently made sense of many things, inviting them, and challenging them to see things in a different way, at least for a time. As for learning, "we are for throwing it overboard altogether" (Kelly, 1955, p. x); with regard to motivation, "outright repudiation" (Kelly, 1969a, p. 68). He turned accepted givens on their head. For example, instead of seeing behavior as an endpoint, he saw it instead as the posing of a question, a starting point. We act based on our construing of the situation. "If I see this floor as solid then I can walk on it." Kelly wrote of this process in terms of the testing of an hypothesis, "if the world is X, then Y is the result," analogous to the approach scientists use to study the world. It was this process that led him to his well known metaphor of the person as a scientist. Also quite important in the context of this book, Kelly chose to challenge many of the accepted distinctions of our philosophical tradition, such as free will versus determinism, cognition versus affect, subject versus object (Chiari & Nuzzo, 1993).

This provocative strategy of Kelly's illustrates in part what he saw as the philosophical underpinnings of his theoretical position, termed *constructive alternativism*—that whatever we make sense of can always be seen differently. The alternatives may not be very satisfactory, but nevertheless there are possible alternate interpretations. We are not bound to make a differentiation between thinking and feeling, for example, though it is a very pervasive distinction in our culture. What if we see both of these processes as being essentially the same, despite their varying in their ease of articulation and relative diffuseness? What would happen then? The posing of "what if. . . . .?" is an important strategy of Kellian practitioners and theorists. Kelly didn't accept the idea that one theoretical principle had to be discredited before the possibilities for another be entertained. Further, this advocacy of a venturesome approach was not confined to the kinds of theoretical principles we apply at work, but to those we apply to our daily living as well. It also formed the basis of much of Kelly's approach to therapeutic intervention that he developed and wrote about for clinicians and counselors (Kelly, 1955, especially vol. 2). Mair (1977) suggested that the person-as-pioneer/explorer might have been chosen as Kelly's metaphor for the person, with its emphasis on striking out across the prairie into the unknown.

Before moving on to consider the centrality of the social to Kelly's theory, one further central formulation needs to be mentioned. Kelly saw our construing as a system (see chapter 9). Our constructs are related to other constructs, frequently in the form of hierarchical relationships, from the relatively superordinate to the more peripheral subordinate discriminations. In its emphasis on the system we see one of the important differences between PCP and those traditions with which it is sometimes mistakenly linked, cognitive-behavioral perspectives.

THE INTEGRAL NATURE OF THE SOCIAL TO KELLY'S THEORIZING

For Kelly, people are both fashioned *within* and fashioned *of* the complex interpersonal worlds they have inhabited and do inhabit. It may seem curious that a theory labeled *personal* construct psychology should have this focus. That perhaps explains why it has been mistakenly criticized for not seeing people in this way. I'll return to the issue of the title later.

The construct system that we evolve during our lifetime is assembled by and in our interactions with others and develops to a large extent to make sense of ourselves and those others. At the direct interpersonal interaction level, the discriminations we make of events are tested out, with us frequently obtaining the feedback we seek from the explicit or implicit reactions of others (see chapter 6; Walker, 1990). Kelly used the term *validation* to describe this process.

At a broader societal level Kelly adopted the view of culture as a shared system of meanings, providing us with a multitude of preexisting discriminations that our particular language crucially symbolizes. (Such a view contrasts sharply with a perspective that emphasizes culture as material artifacts; see chapter 17.) It is here that role construing is essential. The honing of our construing system benefits from our being able to anticipate how others make sense of the same events. He writes about communities where commonality of construing is extensive. The group's expectancies thus serve as the validators against which one tests out the predictive efficiency of one's construct system. While anticipations of others' construing are commonly relevant, for some sorts of constructs they are crucial, serving as the only validating evidence available, such as our assumption that the earth is a sphere. In the clinical context the therapist is interested in the client's culture as it is this that "has undoubtedly provided him [sic] with much evidence of what is 'true' and much of the data which his [sic] personal construct system has had to keep in systematic order" (Kelly, 1955, p. 688). From Kelly's point of view, one is interested in cultural factors "because *it is validational material for the client*" (p. 689, original emphasis).

Our interpersonal worlds are the focus of much of our construing. And so, when Kelly devised the techniques that have most impressed his followers (if the amount of research it generates is any indication), the repertory test and grid, the elements to be explored were people in the original versions (Kelly, 1955, chapters 5 and 6). It is people on whom we depend to satisfy our needs (Kelly, 1969b) and whom we most crucially need to understand if we are to obtain the psychic necessities of life (Walker, 1993).

Additional evidence in support of the centrality of the social in Kellian perspective comes from a most unlikely area: his defining of important emotions. These emotions were spelled out by Kelly as accompaniments of transitions. In his usual provocative fashion, he took labels commonly used in our culture and in psychology, and redefined them in construct terms. He termed *anxiety* as being an awareness that our present way of making sense of things is unable to cope with that with which we are confronted. He also wrote about our experience when we face the possibility of approaching change to our construing system, using the term *fear* for incidental changes and *threat* for more far-reaching ones. But it is his definitions of guilt and hostility that you should note.

Kelly defined *guilt* as "the awareness of dislodgement of the self from one's core role structure" (Kelly, 1955, p. 565). In volume 2 of *The Psychology of Personal Constructs*, he provided a glossary of key terms but gave no explicit definition of "core role structure." He does define a *core construct* as being "one which governs the client's maintenance processes" (p. 565), and as such a construct essential to one's ongoing existence. However, in his elaboration of guilt he indicated that what he was concerned with was the subset of those core constructs that were used "to predict and control the essential interaction of himself [sic] with other persons and with societal groups of persons . . . One's deepest understanding of being maintained as a social being . . . " (p. 502). In continuing this discussion he makes the point that one's essential maintenance is not merely self-focused.

> We are dependent for life itself upon an understanding of the thoughts of certain other people. The psychology of personal constructs emphasizes the essential importance of social constructions. (p. 503)

He dismissed what he considered to be more superficial meanings of *role*, such as those of a mask or social position, in favor of the relevance of *core role*—"a part one plays as if his [sic] life depended upon it. Indeed, his [sic] life actually does depend upon it" (p. 503).

Hostility is the other emotion that is centrally defined in social terms—"the continued effort to extort validational evidence in favor of a type of social prediction which has already been recognized as a failure" (p. 565). Here, as with his other emotional definitions, Kelly was concerned about describing what was happening from the point of view of the person who was committing the action—i.e., what was happening for that person—rather than describing the effect of such actions on others, as most other definitions of the same terms do. What the hostile person is attempting to do is to make others conform to a view that is out of touch with the social reality, just as Procrustes cut off his guests' legs to fit them into the bed that was too short (Kelly, 1969c; see also Kalekin-Fishman, 1993).

Thus, there is no individual set apart from the social, in Kelly's theory, nor is it a matter of reciprocal determinism that retains the dualist dilemma. Who we are is inextricably bound up with the relationships we have engaged in and continue to be part of. The contrast between the individual versus the social is another of the dichotomies that Kelly aimed to transcend. The person he theorized about was most centrally a person-in-relation (Mair, 1970; Stringer, 1979; Walker, 1990).

SOCIAL DETERMINISM, SOCIAL CONSTRUCTIVISM, AND PERSONAL CONSTRUCT THEORY

So far I have outlined many of the important Kellian themes and perspectives and argued for the importance of the social to the nature of the person. In this section of the paper I want explicitly to consider PCT in comparison with social determinism and social constructivism.

From perspectives that emphasize social factors, Kelly's theory might appear deficient because he doesn't *emphasize* that the important aspects of our being, our constructs, our behaviors, are the outcome of the particular social forces in which we are enmeshed. In this they are correct; it is not one of Kelly's principal emphases. However, that is not the same as saying Kelly doesn't accept that our construing is undertaken within cultural constraints or that it is integrally related to the particular social context in which we are entwined, as I've shown. His paper that follows illustrates this very clearly. Kelly wrote of these constraints as a matrix within which one can (potentially) have choices.

Therefore, a central difference between Kelly's position and a social determinist one lies not in whether we are produced by and in our social fabric, but whether determinism precludes choices, whether determinism and free will can coexist. To illustrate his assumptions he used an example of serving a pie. There are many ways to cut a pie, but some ways simply can't be done if the pie is frozen. Also, if one is serving the pie at a dinner table, social expectations reduce the number of possibilities (Kelly, 1955). It is not the place to debate the adequacy of this solution here. Suffice it to say for present purposes that in some contexts Kelly regards determinism and free will as inseparable, as "opposite sides of the same coin—two aspects of the same relationship" (Kelly, 1955, p. 21). He accepted that our vision is always blinkered, constrained by the choices our cultures acknowledge. Within those constraints, however, there are choices available, though we may not always be aware of them or they may not be viable. Indeed, it is the role of a therapist often to foster appreciation of alternative possibilities.

A further theoretical assumption underlying the criticism of PCP for not centrally seeing constructs as societal or cultural is that it is important to look at the origins of things, including their causes. The argument seems to be that if you know how something came about you can prevent it occurring again; you can change it. Kelly, however, a psychotherapist whose central interest was in change, was disinterested in causes, which he considered to be irrelevant to successful therapy. This lack of concern is further reflected in his seeming disinterest in providing an explicit account of how constructs are formed in early infancy or childhood, despite the fact that many of his examples were of childhood construing.

Kelly's position seems to make a lot of sense. To illustrate, we have a number of important instances relating to the heredity-environment controversy that challenge the need to emphasize the cause of things in order to bring about change. For example, although we know that people have a genetic susceptibility for contracting smallpox, this disease has to a large extent been eradicated in much of our society by environmental intervention. Similarly, phenylketenuria, a genetic disorder entailing an inability to metabolize protein (which results, if untreated, in brain damage), can be controlled by eradicating certain foods from the diet. Knowing the cause of something may be irrelevant to its modification.

Further, the allocation of causes is theory-directed. If a man shoots another, what is the cause? We might locate it in a personality disorder of the person, in the way his mother treated him as a child, in the culture where violence is frequent, in the law that allows people to carry lethal weapons, in the capitalist system that brutalizes those in it, in the immoral behavior of the person he shot who was having an affair with his

wife, in his wife's even more immoral behavior (women after all are supposed to be pure), in the parents of the wife who didn't bring her up the
way she should have been brought up, etc. Constructive alternativism can
readily be demonstrated by examination of so-called causation.

Thus, part of this criticism coalesces into a dispute about whether an
attempt to ascertain the causes of things is useful or not. Kelly did see
construing as socially constrained. However, from the point of view of
changing construing, he felt this issue was of limited significance. Note
the emphasis on *limited* significance. Kelly did not totally ignore these
factors, but their importance for what he was interested in was not overarching for his primary aim of fostering and understanding change.

Kelly's theory has been largely ignored by the recent wave of social
constructivists or constructionists.[2] These theorists (e.g., Gergen, 1985,
1987; Harré, 1984, 1987) share Kelly's focus on the importance of making sense of things, rather than merely reacting to events. It is our interpretations of events that are crucial. For the social constructivist, our
sense-making is inextricably bound to our cultures. Such a view is shared
by many of those influenced by recent literary theories, with language,
the important vehicle of cultural tradition, preeminent (Derrida, 1976;
Hollway, 1989).

It is with respect to Kelly's aim of fostering and understanding
change that we clearly see the advantages of Kelly's position over that of
the social constructivists (and determinists). What so far I haven't emphasized is that, for Kelly, the ways we make sense of things, our constructs, are most usefully viewed as bipolar. By this he meant that our
discriminations of the world inextricably involve contrast; when we
characterize something in some particular fashion (applying a construct
to an element, to use the technical terms), we are also indicating what it
is not. He gives examples such as north having no meaning except in
relation to south, hot relative to cold, dark to light. It follows then that
in order to understand how individuals view the world it is not sufficient
to focus merely on what they say. One also needs to ascertain what they
don't say (Ravenette, 1992). Of course, frequently people provide these
contrasts spontaneously, implicitly aware that by doing so they can communicate their point of view more effectively. But often they do not,[3]
though they might if we asked them. It is questions of this kind that set
interviews from a personal construct perspective apart from other interview techniques. Contrasts are actively solicited, though in such a way
that the ongoing flow of conversation is not impeded. This central focus
on the importance of obtaining contrasts limits, from a personal con-

struct point of view, the utility of free-flowing, uninterrupted, discourse (which forms the basis for some content analysis techniques, as well as some approaches to narrative psychology).[4]

Whereas on first consideration this may seem merely a theoretical or methodological peccadillo, the bipolarity of construing has profound practical implications. It is what enables Kelly to provide an account of change and to elucidate means whereby change may be fostered and its nature predicted. This was clearly central to Kelly's concerns as a psychotherapist, but, as will be illustrated, the implications go far beyond that.

For Kelly, the opposite pole of our construing is our way out; it is the alternative to the current situation as we see it—what Kelly termed our "channel of choice," a potential "avenue of movement." Thus, in situations where our current way of making sense of things fails us, when having tested our construct system we find it wanting in some way, it is this alternative as we see it that we have available to provide the structure and meaning we find so essential to our lives. The breakdown of important relationships is one area where this can commonly be observed. If we can no longer love someone, then our alternative is frequently to hate them. The renegotiation of a relationship that is other than these two stark possibilities often entails a great deal of misunderstanding and animosity, with those caught in the cross-fire suffering along with the chief protagonists. Renegotiation commonly takes considerable time if it is ever to be accomplished.

The power of Kelly's analysis of the importance of bipolarity is demonstrated most clearly in *Europe's matrix of decision*, written in 1962 (see chapter 2). Here he presents his observations of important shared constructs within particular European national groupings. He speculates about what will happen 30 years hence—now. We are in a position to see whether his oppositional analysis has validity. Take his description of a construct he highlighted as being of particular importance to German peoples—idealism versus materialism. He suggested that this axis, which could be typified by the contrast between German scholarship in comparison with simple-minded American materialism, was shared in other European countries also. He indicated there is a long and distinguished history of idealism as being seen to characterize much of what was important in German traditions, an approach that was under challenge from logical positivism and empiricism. But it took a horrific world war, with German idealism in the form of Nazism, to discredit this view. The perceived alternative, materialism, was enthusiastically embraced.

And now, here we are, 30 years later, and what do we find? Materialism has been undermined with the disintegration of the communist bloc, the reunification of Germany, and the world recession. The reactions of ethnic cleansing, national purity and identity, and Nazi-style burning and looting can be seen as a return to the alternative Kelly had articulated. Indeed, Kelly proposed precisely this scenario if some new way of framing the issue could not be found. He expressed his hope for a more fundamental change in central European thinking so that, "instead of slipping back again into the old slot toward fascism the moment the American glamor has worn off, the German mind will conceptualize some new dimensions of national life" (see chapter 2). For many German citizens the latter has indeed been the case; they view themselves more as Europeans concerned with the welfare of diverse cultural heritages rather than as Germans, and they demonstrate and legislate to prevent the acting out of the idealist alternative pole that has brought so much sorrow to Turks, Jews, and immigrant groups, horrifying the fair-minded of the world. But there remain those whose only alternative to the failure of materialism is a return to idealism.

To many of you this illustration of the application of personal construct theory may seem prophetic, or perhaps accidental. But to those who use personal construct psychology in psychotherapy or organizational contexts, it will not seem out of the ordinary. On a smaller scale, it is what they see in their clients on a daily basis. And it is in the operation and implications of bipolarity of construing that we most centrally see the difference between personal construct psychology and recent theoretical trends such as social constructivism or discourse analysis. The problem with such approaches is that they don't provide us with a way forward. They may present us with an analysis of who we are and how we came to be us (and that is of some value), but they don't readily allow us to make predictions about who we will be or might become as a Kellian bipolar analysis invites us to do.

Rychlak (1990) also highlighted bipolarity as the important difference between Kelly's position and that of the social constructivists,[5] but draws different implications from those discussed here. He argued that the social constructivist positions of writers like Rom Harré and Kenneth Gergen presuppose the behaviorist perspectives of old, particularly those mediation-models proposed by people such as Hull (1952). Here we return to the determinist-free will controversy. Within the matrices of construing that our backgrounds have presented to us and our cultures acknowledge, Kelly and Rychlak argue that people are not necessarily victims of their biographies or of their cultures. The shaping processes are limited by our bipolar ways of making sense of life:

> . . . you cannot shape an organism that can think to the opposite of what you are shaping that organism to believe; at least you cannot shape it like you shape a lump of clay, or toss a basketball through a hoop. . . . The person is always in the position of adopting the social norm *or* its opposite. (Rychlak, 1990, pp. 17–18)

WHY IS IT TERMED *PERSONAL* CONSTRUCT THEORY?

So far I have established that the assumption about persons in Kelly's theory is centrally of people in relationships with others. I've also contrasted his position with social determinist and social constructivist positions. There remains the issue of the theory's title.

It perhaps may be easier to indicate what Kelly did not mean when he termed his theory personal construct theory. Quite clearly, he did not mean this to indicate where constructs originally came from, given his emphases on social interactions and the importance of group expectancies, and his disinterest in the practical significance of the origins of construing. Failure to understand this has led, it would seem, to the portrayal of Kelly's theory as fundamentally individualistic (e.g., Henriques, Hollway, Urwin, Venn, & Walkerdine, 1984; Holland, 1970, 1977; Hollway, 1989).

Kelly himself did not discuss his choice of title, although he indicated that the original name was "role theory," thus emphasizing the theory's social nature (Kelly, 1955, p. 179). We must rely on what we infer from the general formulation of the theory, as well as his use of the term *personal* in other contexts to clarify this question.

With regard to his theoretical formulation, it was not the content of individual constructs per se that was of sole interest to Kelly. At least equally important was the construing system, the organized relationships between constructs, which Kelly suggested was characterized by ordinal relationships in that some constructs subsume others. Therefore, it is possible for people to seemingly share a construct, but for that construct to imply very different things for the individuals concerned. Nor is this simply a matter of the relationships between constructs. Kelly argued that any one construct had both a *focus* and a *range of convenience*.

Thus, any one construct has certain events that it is maximally relevant to as well as other events that it is irrelevant to or, so to speak, outside of the range of convenience of the construct. A construct like "good versus bad" has a wide range of application for most people, whereas "likes computers versus hates them" is more limited in its relevance. However, the focus and range of convenience of the latter construct is likely to be more far-ranging for a computer salesperson than it is for a nurse working in a hospital, even if they both use it to make discriminations between people.

The complex and extensive nature of our construing systems precludes the possibility of individuals holding identical systems, despite the sharing of much that is common. Both individuality and commonality are important. While on the one hand our language provides us with many of the discriminations we use in our lives, viewing construing primarily as a linguistic phenomenon may result in the assumption of more similarity than may be the case. As Ravenette (1992) pointed out:

> . . . constructs appear as words only when we try to explore or explicate them; they are not themselves the words. Behind the verbalized construct is a history of personal experiences involving thought, feelings and actions, and patterns of validation and invalidation. (Ravenette, 1992, p. 6).

The verbal formulation of our construing may mask these differences, as this dispute about the interpretation of *personal* exemplifies.

Turning to the use that Kelly made of the term *personal* in other contexts, we find evidence that he used it very differently from those who equate it with *individualistic*. In volume 2 of *The Psychology of Personal Constructs*, the volume in which he outlined his views on clinical practice, he devoted one of the 11 chapters to the appraisal of experience. He organized this chapter under two main headings: *Culture and Experience* and *Personal Experience*. In the first of these he details ways for exploring the client's culture necessitated by the difficulty a person immersed in a culture has in describing that same culture. His discussion is quite detailed and involves issues concerning socioeconomic class (cf. Salmon, 1990) as well as many other societal and cultural features—urban compared with rural, racial, and national extraction; migration; church membership; and so on. In the second part of the chapter, in seeming contrast to the section title of "Personal Experience," he focuses on community background, appraisal of a school, the analysis of a person's current interpersonal relationships, educational experience, domestic relationships, and family history—not the kinds of things that an interpretation of personal as individual would even consider relevant. This idiosyncratic use Kelly makes of the word *personal* is apparently to emphasize that people's interpretations of their culture are important as well as the culture itself. Thus he stated:

> While we have already discussed the analysis of a person's community background as it might be described more or less objectively by various observers, the study of a person's community experience would not be complete unless we attempted to see that background at the neighborhood level through the eyes of the person himself. (1955, p. 716)

Thus, it is not the situation itself, such as the community background within which we function, that determines what will happen, but our interpretation of that situation.

However, there is a further implication of the meaning of personal for a psychology of personal constructs: who needs to take responsibility for these constructs and for the experiments that result from their application (Walker, 1990). We, personally, have this responsibility for our construing. And, if our experiments are not very effective and are leading to dead ends, then it is necessary for us to reconstrue. This may be easier said than done. We are without a doubt operating within constraints, as Kelly's matrix of decision metaphor illustrates. Further, simple reconstrual may not solve the problems—putting food in a starving person's stomach or preventing an enemy bent on maiming another from doing so—but the sense we make of these experiences is within our potential control (see chapter 14 for an elaboration of a similar argument) and may be all we have. As Kelly suggested in his provocative, rhetorical fashion, none of us need be victims of our biographies unless we choose to be. "Freedom of movement is first of all a matter of one's dimensioning of life; no matter how much he pays for railroad fare, one cannot move along a psychological track which for him does not even exist" (1955, p. 694).

CONCLUSION

In this chapter I have attempted to give you a sample of what I think is important about the theory proposed by George Kelly. Readers seeking further introduction might consider reading Dalton and Dunnett (1992), Bannister and Fransella (1986), or Burr and Butt (1992), as well as Kelly's own short account (Kelly, 1970).

Also, I hope the reader can appreciate why this book has been written in the first place: to draw greater attention to this as a social theory, challenging the dualist assumptions contrasting the individual and the social. Its place in the history of psychological thought can be better appreciated as a forerunner of social constructivist accounts, a prior perspective from which these later theoretical positions nevertheless have something to learn.

My aim has not been to convert you to a Kellian position, but to entice you to read further and see whether this perspective has anything to offer you. Enjoyment and fun are very central to PCT for me. It is my hope that you may share these.

ENDNOTES

1. Not surprisingly, the words used might tend to have a cognitive connotation for you as I'm focusing on the understanding of theoretical perspectives, an area that is traditionally viewed as a cognitive process within our culture. It is also something we are trained to be articulate about. However, if another context had been used, such as our relationships with important people in our lives, we would be more likely to use affective words like "felt," and most commonly we might have trouble applying verbal labels to some of the differences we sensed were most significant. For Kelly these are all ways whereby we make sense of things, regardless of whether or not they can be clearly articulated to others or indeed to ourselves. We don't just react to events, we are actively involved in seeing them as like or unlike other things we have experienced, locating them relative to other experiences in terms of their nature, relevance, and importance to us personally. What Western philosophers following in a particular Greek tradition have chosen to distinguish, cognition and affect, Kelly reassembles in his advocacy of the importance of construing (Bannister, 1977).

2. I am using the terms *constructivism* and *constructionism* interchangeably, though I am aware that other authors make distinctions between them (Gergen & Gergen, 1991). In the absence of consensus with regard to their meaning, differentiating here is likely to create diversions that are irrelevant to the current focus.

3. In some cases the alternative can't readily be verbalized or comprehended; in Kellian terms it is submerged. This can be problematic because, among other things, it can prevent the satisfactory testing out of the construct in the same way that a scientist is assumed not to be able to satisfactorily experiment without an alternative hypothesis. Readers are referred to Kelly (1955) for a discussion of this and its implication for psychotherapeutic interventions (e.g., pp. 467–471).

4. This is not to say that these approaches don't have some value. They often provide a context to the ways a person makes sense of things that is too

frequently ignored by simple-minded administrations of repertory grid techniques. It seems reasonable to say that we may miss out on things that are important if we overly structure our interactions. The ongoing changes in our lives can only be appreciated in their context as a narrative allows (Mair, 1988; Runyan, 1984). Indeed, Kelly (1955) himself did this with his self-characterization technique. Because Kelly used his techniques in contexts where there was an ongoing interaction, these difficulties can be overcome if we use them similarly.

5. There are some exceptions such as Lock (1981) who specified certain bipolar distinctions as fundamental in conceptual systems, but his use of them seems to be as a taxonomy to contrast individuals or cultures, rather than as a dynamic of change.

REFERENCES

Bannister, D. (1977). The logic of passion. In D. Bannister (Ed.), *New perspectives in Personal Construct Theory* (pp. 21–37). London: Academic Press.

Bannister, D., & Fransella, F. (1986). *Inquiring man: The psychology of personal constructs*, 3rd ed. London: Croom Helm.

Burr, V., & Butt, T. (1992). *Invitation to personal construct psychology*, London: Whurr Publications.

Chiari, G., & Nuzzo, M. L. (1993, July). *Personal construct theory within psychological constructivism: Precursor or avant-garde?* Plenary paper presented at the 10th International Personal Construct Congress, Townsville, Australia.

Dalton, P., & Dunnett, G. (1992). *A psychology for living: Personal construct theory for professionals and clients*. Chichester: Wiley.

Derrida, J. (1976). *Of grammatology* (G. Spivak, Trans.). Baltimore: Johns Hopkins University Press.

Gergen, K. J. (1985). The social constructionist movement in modern psychology. *American Psychologist, 40,* 266–275.

Gergen, K. J. (1987). Toward self as relationship. In K. Yardley & T. Honess (Eds.), *Self and identity: Psychosocial perspectives*. New York: Wiley.

Gergen, K. J., & Gergen, M. M. (1991). Toward reflexive methodologies. In F. Steier (Ed.), *Research and reflexivity* (pp. 76–95). London: Sage.

Harré, R. (1984). *Personal being: A theory for individual psychology*. Cambridge, MA: Harvard University Press.

Harré, R. (1987). The social construction of selves. In K. Yardley & T. Honess (Eds.), *Self and identity: Psychosocial perspectives* (pp. 41–52). New York: Wiley.

Henriques, J., Hollway, W., Urwin, C., Venn, C., & Walkerdine, V. (1984). *Changing the subject: Psychology, social regulation and subjectivity*. London: Methuen.

Holland, R. (1970). George Kelly: Constructive innocent and reluctant existentialist. In D. Bannister (Ed.), *Perspectives in Personal Construct Psychology* (pp. 111–132). London: Academic Press.

Holland, R. (1977). *Self and social context*. London: Macmillan.

Hollway, W. (1989). *Subjectivity and method in psychology: Gender, meaning and science*. London: Sage.

Hull, C. L. (1952). *A behavior system*. New Haven: Yale University Press.

Kalekin-Fishman, D. (1993). The two faces of hostility. *International Journal of Personal Construct Psychology, 6*, 27–40.

Kelly, G. A. (1955). *The psychology of personal constructs* (Vols. 1 and 2). New York: Norton.

Kelly, G. A. (1969a). Man's construction of his alternatives. In B. Maher (Ed.), *Clinical psychology and personality: The selected papers of George Kelly* (pp. 68–93). New York: Wiley.

Kelly, G. A. (1969b). In whom confide: On whom depend for what? In B. Maher (Ed.), *Clinical psychology and personality: The selected papers of George Kelly* (pp. 189–206). New York: Wiley.

Kelly, G. A. (1969c). Hostility. In B. Maher (Ed.), *Clinical psychology and personality: The selected papers of George Kelly* (pp. 267–280). New York: Wiley.

Kelly, G. A. (1970). A brief introduction to personal construct theory. In D. Bannister (Ed.), *Perspectives in personal construct theory* (pp. 1–30). London: Academic Press.

Lock, A. (1981). Universals in human conception. In P. Heelas & A. Lock (Eds.), *Indigenous psychologies: The anthropology of the self* (pp. 19–38). London: Academic Press.

Mair, J. M. M. (1970). Psychologists are human too. In D. Bannister (Ed.), *Perspectives in personal construct theory* (pp. 157–184). London: Academic Press.

Mair, J. M. M. (1977). Metaphors for living. *Nebraska Symposium on Motivation, 24*, 243–290.

Mair, J. M. M. (1988). Psychology as story-telling. *International Journal of Personal Construct Psychology, 1*, 125–137.

Mixon, D. (1971). Behaviour analysis treating subjects as actors rather than organisms. *Journal of the Theory of Social Behaviour, 1*, 19–31.

Orne, M. T. (1962). On the social psychology of the psychological experiment: With particular reference to demand characteristics and their implications. *American Psychologist, 17*, 776–783.

Ravenette, A. T. (1992). Asking questions within a personal construct framework. Unpublished manuscript.

Runyan, W. M. (1984). *Life histories and psychobiography*. New York: Oxford University Press.

Rychlak, J. F. (1981). *Introduction to personality and psychotherapy*, 2nd ed. Boston: Houghton Mifflin.

Rychlak, J. F. (1990). George Kelly and the concept of construction. *International Journal of Personal Construct Psychology, 3*, 7–20.

Salmon, P. (1990, April). Kelly then and now. Invited address, Second British Conference on Personal Construct Psychology, York.

Stringer, P. (1979). Individuals, roles and persons. In P. Stringer & D. Bannister (Eds.), *Constructs of sociality and individuality* (pp. 91–112). London: Academic Press.

Walker, B. M. (1990). Construing George Kelly's construing of the person-in-relation. *International Journal of Personal Construct Psychology, 3*, 41–50.

Walker, B. M. (1991, July). An analysis of the accounts presented of PCP in undergraduate personality textbooks. Paper presented at the 9th International Congress on Personal Construct Psychology, Albany, New York.

Walker, B. M. (1993). Looking for a whole "mama": Personal construct theory and dependency. In L. M. Leitner & G. Dunnett (Eds.), *Critical issues in personal construct psychotherapy* (pp. 61–81). Malabar, FL: Krieger.

CHAPTER 2

Europe's Matrix of Decision[1]

GEORGE A. KELLY*
Ohio State University

There is something you all should know at the outset of this paper: I have no use for the concept of motivation. Professor Jones was well aware of this last summer when he invited me to come here. We were having coffee together in Copenhagen—at least I remember it as coffee, although Dr. Jones says it was tea. I believe our wives were with us at the time. He doesn't remember that either. At any rate, he remembers that he invited me to come here. At the time, we both found the idea of my having to talk in public about motivation highly amusing. He probably still thinks it is funny, but, after the toil of preparing this paper, I am not so sure I still do. Nevertheless, here I am.

Since that conversation I have pondered on a number of things, including the whimsical possibility of writing such a convincing paper that you would be moved to change the topic of this annual Nebraska conclave to "Snakes in Ireland." How much more to the point it would be if the topic were something like this: "What Is Everybody up to These Days?" or "What in the World Is Mankind about To Do to Itself?" or perhaps this one: "Isn't There Any Other Way of Coping with a Problem Besides Lying Down and Being Treated for It?" A good short title could, I think, be lifted from Hans Fallada's 1932 novel, *Little Man, What Now?* "The Nebraska Symposium on *What Now*"—not bad!

Let us be honest with ourselves—isn't this the persistent question we hope to answer by all our talk about motivation: How can we forecast human behavior when it is left on its own? Not that this is a particularly well-posed question either, for I am sure you could argue, on the one hand, that human behavior is never on its own, or, on the other, that it is always on its own. Nevertheless, what we are trying to get at are the internal predicates of behavior, as contrasted with those external predicates we can more clearly and comfortably envision, such as stimuli or the inescapable logic we assume to be inherent in the way things are.

I. WHAT IT MEANS TO UNDERSTAND MEN
IN TERMS OF THEIR CONSTRUCTS

This paper is essentially a continuation of one I presented in the spring of 1957 as part of the *Syracuse University Symposium on the Assessment of Human Motives*. In that paper—which was published, along with the other contributions, under the editorship of Gardner Lindzey, and is now available in a paperback edition (Kelly, 1958)—I stated my theoretical position under the title, "Man's Construction of His Alternatives."

In my present paper I want to talk about the application of the theory to a specific international problem; the European man's construction of his alternatives. In this way I hope, not only to show how the theory works, but also to throw some light on an important substantive problem. You see, I have brazenly gone ahead with my distortion of the topic of this symposium and am speaking as if it were already "The Nebraska Symposium on *What Now*."

Theoretical Springboard

Before I launch into today's topic, however, I had better sketch some of the more important features of my theoretical position. Motivation is an invented construct. It cropped up a long time ago as a by-product of certain pre-Socratic assumptions about the fundamental nature of things. Once upon a time, there was a division of opinion between the Eleatic School of Parmenides, which assumed that fundamentally objects were solid and inert, and Heraclitus, who wanted to start with the assumption that change was the one inescapable fact of existence. Neither side won the argument outright, but, as far as history is concerned, Heraclitus came out the worse. Atomism, which was a sort of compromise worked out later by Democritus and others, eventually caught hold and, off and on, has pretty much held its own ever since.

The crux of the matter is that if you start with the assumption that whatever the world is made of must be inherently inert, you then have to go ahead and guess that it changes only as force is applied to it. Here you are, saddled with two distinct constructs; objects, and the force that makes them move. As long as you are a materialist—and nearly every-body is, in spite of what he says—there is not much else you can do ex-cept think in terms of primary objects, such as the atoms of Democritus, being pushed around by secondary forces.

Apply this basic thinking to physiology, and you have the notion of a body being actuated by energy; apply it to psychology, and you come up with the notion of a person either being propelled by "motives" in spite of himself, or stuck tight in his fundament. As I say, there is just not much else you can do about it, unless you are willing to go back to about 420 B.C. and start thinking all over.

Well, I suggested in the Syracuse Symposium that we should go back and start over. Suppose we began by assuming that the fundamental thing about life is that it goes on. It isn't that something *makes* it go on; the going on *is the thing itself*. It isn't that motives *make* man come alert and do things; his alertness is an aspect of his very being. Talking about activating motives is simply redundant talky-talk, for once you've got a human being on your hands, you already have alertness and movement, and sometimes a lot more of it than you know what to make of.

There is another habit of thinking that Western Man more or less fell into fortuitously. As long as he was assuming that human beings are pro-pelled by motives, it seemed reasonable to imagine also that the motives give direction to the movement; if they push, they must push in some direction. Now if we could only find out what is pushing, we could pre-dict where everybody is going, as well as how soon he would get there.

So for two thousand years we have been looking for the thing that is doing the pushing, and often trying to define it by the directions it pushes. We haven't found it yet; naturally we haven't found it, but during the centuries we have built up a tremendous lexicon of push and pull terms. Even our language has fallen heir to the design of our quest, and we have committed ourselves to a grammar of motives (Burke, 1945) that controls our speech and channels our thinking about human behav-ior. Now we can scarcely say anything about what a person has done, or is about to do, without using a language form that implies that he has been pushed into it. We are even inclined to think that way about our own behavior, and when we do, it usually means we are in trouble.

But there is another way of accounting for the direction man's behavior takes, besides assuming that it must be imparted by the same forces that make him behave in the first place. We can start by saying that man copes with his environment by construing it into similarities and contrasts. It is not necessary to assume that this is a verbal or conscious undertaking. The associations and distinctions can be made at a very low level of awareness, as psychological research on reflexes has amply demonstrated.

The Personal Construct

The unit form of this construing can be designated as the *construct*, an abstraction of the linkage and differentiation which, inside each man's own tight little world, constitutes a generalized pair of alternatives. The construct, being an abstraction, can be picked up, carried around, and fitted to a great variety of circumstances. If it has a verbal handle on it, so much the better; it is easier to transport. A system of constructs constitutes a ready-made format for future thinking, and for lower order processes as well. To have constructed such a system means that a person has somewhat prepared himself to cope with all sorts of strange things that have not happened yet. But without it he is not free to think, to act, or even to get the gist of what is going on.

When a person can apply a construct to his own behavior, consciously or unconsciously, it opens for him a channel of choice along which he is more or less free to move. But without such a channel his freedom has no dimension, no extent; he cannot even strive toward objectives, nor can he hope for things to come, nor long for something out of reach, for he has no idea of what he is missing, nor even any sense of missing at all. He can no more move about in lines he has not construed than he can use the fourth dimension to side-step a locked door. This is why, throughout the history of the world, men seeking what they supposed to be freedom have struggled heroically to change their masters, but have made only feeble efforts to loosen their chains.

Get some notion of what a person's system of channels is like and you have a rough sketch of the network within which he is prepared to exercise his human right to freedom. Observe the shrinkage of a man's system, and you find yourself a witness to a gradual human enslavement,

enslavement without barbed wire or coercion. It is this enslavement by atrophy of ideas that we sometimes call institutionalized behavior. We are usually thinking about mental hospitals, prisons, and orphans' asylums when we use the term, but the same kind of enslavement can occur in societies and in nations. Understanding a man's construct system is, then, the first, and most important, step in understanding what is commonly known by that vaguest of psychological terms, "motivation." And it is also the first step in comprehending the actual extent of a man's freedom. I was talking about this final step when I presented my Syracuse paper on "Man's Construction of His Alternatives."

Having construed his alternatives, a man still has to make choices between them if he is to commit himself to any undertaking. As a matter of fact, there are two kinds of choices he must make; the selection from his repertory of the most relevant construct to apply to his circumstances, and his choice between the pair of alternatives which that construct presents. There are some psychological principles that govern these choices, but there is no need to expound them here.

This concludes the review of what I said at Syracuse University. It was a theoretical statement, and it was my effort to extricate our thinking from the underlying assumptions upon which the notion of motivation is based, as well as from the deeply ingrained notion of motivation itself.

A Method of Studying Attitudes

This kind of theorizing leads us next, as all good theorizing should, to a methodology, and from methodology to substance, all the while being subject to successive revisions in the light of its outcomes. There are many ramifications of the methodology I am about to describe; ramifications in psychotherapy, in teaching, in negotiation, and in psychometrics. But let me confine myself to one area only; the theory's methodological implications in the appraisal of attitudes having international implications.

It is customary, in studying attitudes, to focus upon certain parameters. We may examine the object or the class of objects embraced by the attitude. We may take account of the attitude's generality across a wide variety of objects. We may judge its consonance with the rest of the attitudinal system and its stability from moment to moment. We may estimate its tendency to express itself in overt action. We may attempt to measure its intensity by estimating the amount of effort that is likely to be mobilized in its behalf. We may note its rigidity in the face of negating experience; and we may appraise its rational status, or look to see how deeply it is rooted in unconscious processes.

All these approaches are similar in one respect; they assume that an attitude is a one-sided affair—a man likes blondes or he does not. The attitude presumably has to do with blondes, and blondes only, which, I am sure some of you will agree, is a pretty one-sided way of looking at things. What in the world does it mean, merely to say that a man likes blondes? Does it mean he likes them rather than hates them, that he likes them better than brunettes, or does it mean he likes them better than doing his own cooking? We suppose there is some dimension along which differentiation is being made, but unless we look for the direction in which the opposite pole lies, we cannot tell what the bewildered fellow has on his mind.

A man says he despises capitalism. Does this mean he is a communist? Or does it mean he favors an economic democracy analogous to the political democracy that was achieved in Western Europe after centuries of struggle and bloodshed? Or can we stretch his statement to mean, on the contrary, that he opposes all forms of government by consent of the governed?

We don't really know what the statement means to the man who made it until we know the issue at stake. One of us might say that, in order to make such a remark, he would have to be a totalitarian of some sort—either a communist or a fascist—because it seems so downright certain that those are the only logical alternatives to capitalism. At least, the fellow must be against human dignity, because we are convinced the capitalism he despises is the natural expression of any society where personal liberties are respected. We may be right, of course—perfectly right; but let us keep in mind that these are the similarities and contrasts of our personal construct system, not necessarily of his. It is by such channels that our flow of thought is facilitated and constrained. But his intellectual efforts may be just as inescapably guided by the ruts worn deep in his way of life, even though they may seem utterly irrational to us.

Personal construct theory approaches attitudes by examining issues. It finds these issues, not so much in man's circumstances, as in his way of making sense out of what surrounds him. Purposeful behavior is a matter of setting up alternatives among his surroundings and, when the time comes, choosing between them. This is not an altogether novel approach;

Mark Twain, in a behavioristic description of an elephant written long before John B. Watson's time, once made use of it (Clemens, 1896).[2]

Seeking Access to an Alien Dimension of Life

How can we use this approach of personal construct theory, in place of the motivational approach, to understand our friend who says he despises capitalism? Before we make the attempt, it is only fair to warn you that it is always hazardous to look at things through another person's glasses, whether he is a Russian, an Eichmann, a Negro, a psychotic patient, or one's own child—perhaps most of all, one's own child. Looking through glasses that are not your own can permanently affect your eyesight. It is much safer to attribute the behavior of other people to their *Motivation*—much safer. Now, you've been warned!

Let us suppose this man we are talking about is a Georgian, a citizen of that ancient little country, now one of the Soviet Republics, that lies just south of the main ridge of the Caucasus Mountains. When he talks about capitalism he undoubtedly has a vivid picture in mind of the privately controlled economic power of pre-revolutionary Georgian landowners—called princes—who held that it was a waste of time and money to teach farmers to read and write.

There is a painting in the world-famed Hermitage Museum in Leningrad that gives poignant meaning to this Georgian's thoughts about capitalism. It depicts a boy in ragged clothes listening furtively at the crack of a school room door. This picture has deep and far-reaching significance to the people of Eastern Europe. It would probably mean something quite different to an American who imagines the only normal response of a boy to school is to play hooky.

The picture is not only symbolic; it is accurately representative. I talked to a man who, as a child, had done just that in his native country of Georgia. But he was soon caught in his delinquency, and the door was slammed in his face. Some time after, his father, touched by the boy's disappointment, managed to save back a sack of grain from the family's meager food supplies, and, taking his boy by the hand, carried the grain to the house of the prince. He told the prince the sack of grain was all he had and he asked if, in return for it, his son could be taught to read and write. The prince called the boy to his desk, showed him how to write his name, and then said, "There, young man; that is all the reading and writing you will ever need to know."

The prince kept the grain, possibly as an object lesson in sound economics. Indeed, one must admit that not many people would consider education a proper form of *capital* investment, particularly for one's last sack of grain. This is not to overlook the fact that there are always some people, even in our own country, who will yell for unrealistic expenditures on education—right up to the last Cadillac.

There was, until a few years ago, a somewhat less defensible practice which land-owners in that part of the world were able to enforce by means of their private control of the capital resources of the agricultural community. Brides were required to sleep with the land-owner before they could be claimed by their husbands. This was not quite as bad as it sounds. There was a way out for the groom, if he happened to be an enterprising young man. He was always perfectly free to give up his farm and look for another landlord—one whom he would be more willing to have sleep with his bride, or one who could be bought off for a price within his means. If he were a really imaginative young fellow he could look for a bride with whom nobody would want to sleep; then he could keep his home, his farm, and have a chaste wife besides.

I don't want to leave the wrong impression about Georgia either; this sort of practice was discontinued after the communist revolution and the advent of a man greatly admired in those parts, a fellow by the name of Joseph Stalin. Moreover, none of this has much to do with American capitalism, for it is obviously not the sort of practice that many American landlords could enforce and survive long enough to brag about it. I am only describing the system of capitalistic free enterprise my Georgian friend has in mind when he says he "despises capitalism." Moreover, I suspect this glimpse of the world through his glasses helps us understand what makes him tick better than would any concept of motivation. But as I warned you before, such surreptitious peeks are likely to affect our own eyesight; so it might be just as well if you forgot what I have just told you.

My other friend, the one who wanted to learn to read and write, also made out pretty well in the end, which goes to show what initiative and gumption will do. He took advantage of the confusion of World War I to escape to America. He is now an author and sculptor, and his writings are full of warmth, humor, and love of this country, with none of the bitterness one might expect (Papashvily & Papashvily, 1945, 1946a, 1946b). He is also a great hero back in Georgia, where we shared some experiences together during a recent visit. His American-born wife, in speaking the next morning of one reception they were given the day before, said it was the first time she had been kissed by a whole town.

A Prelude to Action

The other young men of Georgia also took matters in their own hands. My wife and I visited one of their schools a few months ago, along with the friends I have been talking about. We saw the emphasis upon the fundamentals of education—mathematics, languages, science, etc., just as you have heard it reported. One of the men teachers, overwhelmed at meeting the famous Georgian-American author, whose books he had read, embraced him and said, "You are the only person who ever made me cry."

The next day we visited one of the Pioneer Palaces and saw something of the program that provides for the hours, the days, and the months when young people are not in school. Here, in a program as extensive, as competently staffed, and more lavishly equipped than that of the schools, we saw what would be called "frills" in American education. Some observers have come back from the Soviet Union dismissing the Pioneer program as "something like the Boy Scouts." The comparison is preposterous, and the inference, so frequently made, that Soviet education is confined to good old fundamentals, is completely out of line with the facts.

I am still trying to illustrate the application of personal construct theory, in contrast to motivational theory, to the understanding of human behavior. I am trying to sketch a personal dimension of thought which, simply because it is personal and bears on immediate circumstances, represents so clearly the channel of choice for millions of people in Eastern Europe. The channel has to do with education and, strange as it may seem, I think you will agree it also has to do with the dignity of man, or perhaps you will at least agree that it has to do with the dignity of brides. I am inviting you to examine this principal construct dimension, not from our own point of view or as if it were the channel of choice which must govern our own actions, but from the point of view of those whose behavior we hope to understand.

Look at it. On the one end is the private control of capital and on the other, communism—the first step toward which is regarded as state capitalism, the present stage of the Soviet society. I am sure the line between these poles will remain the visible channel of choice until the people of that country are able to conceptualize their circumstances along other dimensions.

Can we "motivate" these people to go in other directions? I think not. Put pressure on them, put them under extreme conditions of need, jam their families into one-room apartments, deny them Cadillacs, ZILs or Volgas, even take away their spare sacks of grain to support the schools, and you will not shoo them like a flock of chickens into our form of society. They will only sigh and say, "Times are hard, food is scarce, and something may be rotten in the administration. Still misfortune has not completely overtaken us; our children are being educated and our wives are respected. Perhaps we will have to go back to the days of 'capitalism'—but it hasn't happened yet. And anyone who wants to drive us back had better remember Stalingrad!" (Or would they say "Volgograd" now?)

Nothing that I have said should be taken to mean that the Soviet empire is ideologically monolithic. To be sure, one finds a remarkable internalization of the ideological controls, to use Don Marquis' phrase for it. People actually do think in the grooves marked out for them, certainly to a much larger extent than do the people of Czechoslovakia, where there are memories of a different kind of society. There are, again, some other dimensions of Georgian thought which permit a vision of the future not approved by Moscow. Nevertheless, whatever those other dimensions are, the one channel I have described is crystal clear to Georgians and is a key to their behavior.

The Construct as a Daily Way of Life

In delineating this Georgian construct I have dwelt mostly on community behavior, that is to say, the forms of behavior that are either articulated outright by group consensus or simply perpetuated by tacit compliance. But what does the construct mean at the level of everyday "spontaneous" behavior—if I may use a familiar, but relatively meaningless, motivational term. Or, to put it this way, which is better, does this construct have anything to say about what people do when they haven't bothered to go through any complicated process of making up their minds to it? If it does not have anything to do with such everyday individual matters, then our reading of this dimension of Soviet life is probably academic and does not meet the validity criteria that personal construct theory requires. Let us see.

Before entering the Soviet Union my wife and I were more or less aware, as I suppose most Americans are, of the Union's vigorous efforts to put education on a broad popular base, one that is even broader than our own, and not only to permit, but to insure the advanced education of every capable student, regardless of his age, his financial resources, or his formal educational credentials. We knew that some observers have questioned the breadth of this popular base—apart from the fact that the Soviets do not as yet have the total resources comparable to those America has mobilized for the support of education—and we pressed to find out what the restrictions might be. Our observations were mixed and inconclusive on this point, but that the base is very broad, there can be little doubt.[3] I need not go into the detailed ramifications of this complex matter, and besides, they involve dimensions of Soviet life that I cannot, at the present time, unfold to my own satisfaction.

One other fact, which is not so generally known, is that each year the Soviet Union publishes about four times as many new books as the United States—the next most productive country in the publication of this form of literature. With this tremendous publication list they not only seek to satisfy the voracious demand of Soviet citizens for serious reading material, but they make much needed educational materials available for underdeveloped countries. That these educational materials have a communist slant and put the Soviet Union in an unrealistically favorable light, goes without saying. But, more important than this, they constitute tangible evidence abroad of the Soviet Union's commitment to universal education, free of cost to all persons. This commitment stands very close to the center of the Soviet system, more so, I am now convinced, than does any such commitment in our society.

We visited a bookstore in Leningrad a few days after entering the Soviet Union. It was a beehive of activity. Indeed, it was the only instance of merchandising we saw where the demand appeared to be in excess of the supply. We saw no such throngs in the gastronomes—grocery shops—in the department stores, or even at the theater box offices. In the bookstore we observed the types of books being bought. They were serious books, not murder mysteries or comic books such as one sees displayed at most American bookstands. There were books on mathematics, electronics, history, political science, economics, and geography. The bookstores have a practice of accepting used books as partial payment for new ones, with liberal trade-in allowances. Thus it appears likely that a considerable proportion of the new books published each year are read by more than one reader.[4]

It was not an uncommon sight on a Moscow bus, at the end of a working day, to see begrimed laborers reading technical books which, if the illustrations I could see over the men's shoulders were any indication, were quite advanced. When we were in the Moscow airport waiting for the jet plane to take us to Tbilisi, news arrived that astronaut Gagarin was in orbit. During the flight to Tbilisi we received frequent bulletins, concluding with the bulletin that he had safely landed. There was applause and excited conversation, both in the Moscow airport and on the plane. But I noticed that between the flurries of activity two of the men in front of us returned to the books they were reading. One of the books had illustrations of complicated wiring diagrams and pages of mathematical equations. I couldn't see the other one.

Now here we have some observational evidence of the viability of the construct we have been tracing in such detail. The pursuit of learning is not merely a legalized opportunity or a perfunctory ritual, it is a daily fact—a way of life demonstrated by individuals left to the impulse of the moment. It represents a dimension of human freedom which is used, not merely talked about.

Nations and the Shape of Things to Come

In terms of these everyday goings-on one cannot help but draw comparisons between the meaning of education in the Soviet Union and its meaning to those of us who take it for granted, or who take as little of it as is necessary for a college degree. There is no question but that education is a tenet of our political philosophy and an important fact of our economy. It has been so ever since a century ago when Horace Mann uttered his dictum that "Education is the chief defense of the nation," and was accused of being a communist for his advocacy of free public schools. But in addition to this formalized position in America, what part does education play in the way we live? What does it mean, for example, to have our universities rated in terms of their football teams instead of their scholarship?[5] What does it mean in terms of such little things as what one reads on the way home from work, the choice of a television program, or the conversation between two young people in the corner drug store?

To be a valid element in a decision matrix a construct must also have visible implications for the future. So let us ask that question, too. Does all this fascination for book learning betray a weakness in Soviet moral fiber and a fatal inability to envision the solid, neon-lighted values of our

God-fearing economy? Or is it a portent of unfamiliar things to come? And what on earth do you suppose will be the outcome of another thirty years of their society going their way, and our society going ours? These are not detached, academic speculations. They are brutally realistic questions that should not require too much imagination to answer. And, to come back to our central theme, I don't believe these are questions that can be satisfactorily answered in motivational terms.

At this point I feel impelled to reiterate a point which may already be clear enough. I have been talking about one construct dimension of the decision matrix of the Soviet way of life. It is an important one, but not the only one. While it provides a clear enough picture of a road along which Soviet society may now march or retreat, there are other constructs which are important because they channel behavior in other directions, and some that are important because of their absence. A more accurate statement of how the Soviet citizen of the future will live, or what the comparative positions of Soviet and American cultures will be thirty years from now, would certainly require the delineation of more than one of the components of the decision matrices within which the two societies function.

The Dread of Understanding Man Too Well

Now let me do something else, while certain thoughts are fresh in our minds. You will recall that earlier in this paper I invited your attention to the fact that the understanding of human behavior could be threatening. Because of this I suspected that we often employ motivational terms in order to manage human behavior without having to understand it. I suggested, furthermore, that when one comes to understand another person, there are likely to be irreversible changes in his own personality.

It is this imminence of change within ourselves that gives the experience of threat its peculiar feeling quality. There is the sense that our faith is about to be undermined, as, indeed it may well be undermined. For any bold venture into human understanding leaves the wreckage of sacred ideas in its wake. Once we are caught up in this enterprise, the immediate prospect of what we are about to witness may even make us angry, or, if we must avoid the raw experience of anger at any cost, it may lead us to dismiss what we see as merely some evidence of obscure "motivation."

And here is the crucial point of what I am trying to do at this junc-
ture of my discussion of decision matrices: If I have portrayed vividly
enough the Soviet construct of private capitalism *versus* individual opportunity, some of you will personally have experienced the kind of
threat I have been talking about—experienced it right here and now. Perhaps some of you found yourselves apprehensive in the face of the threat
of a new understanding, or was it a shadow of despair that crossed your
mind? Possibly some of you were angry at what you interpreted to be my
lack of faith in the present posture of America, and some equally angry
because the 19th Century promise of this great democracy has been so
widely betrayed by 20th Century abuse of the freedoms it guaranteed.
These were risks I took when I ventured to lift a corner of the Iron Curtain ever so slightly to give you a first hand glimpse of what lies behind.
Finally, some of you may have been simply annoyed that so elusive a matter as human values should be dragged into a scientific symposium. If any
of you has actually experienced these reactions, then you surely must
know by now that it was not just wild speculation when I said that the
prospect of understanding human behavior in other than motivational
terms can be deeply threatening.

Now I must hasten on, for there remains a great deal more to be told
before this paper fulfills its promise to deal with Europe's decision matrices. All that I have said so far has been my effort to disabuse you of any
inclination to think in terms of motives, to paint for you a compellingly
vivid picture of one alien personal construct, and to alert you to the way
your own feelings are likely to become embroiled the moment you decide
to join me in this quest. If you can escape from motivational habits of
thought, and if you can retain both the picture and the stabilizing intro-
spective mood I have tried to create, then what I have yet to say should
make good psychological sense.

II. MATRIX DIMENSIONS

On the morning of June 9th, 1960 my wife and I boarded United
Airlines Flight 610 at the spanking new air terminal in Columbus, Ohio.
We were about to start a journey that would take us around the world
and bring us face to face with people in 37 countries. My pocket was
sagging with a two-inch-thick packet of tickets that were good for one
year, and we were determined not to miss a single day of the adventure

they promised us. The last entry on the last ticket read, "Chicago to Columbus, 5:10 P.M., June 8th, 1961—we had allowed ourselves only seven hours to spare!

Every article in our suitcases had been selected, tested, weighed, and evaluated with the greatest of care, for not only had we to be prepared for arctic cold and tropical heat, but each of us must also stay within the economy class baggage limit of 44 lbs. And, besides, we had to find room within that limit for a typewriter, a tape recorder, and special color films for the camera that dangled around my neck. During the year we were to pack and unpack those bags on the average of every 3.2 days, and take them across an international boundary on the average of every five days. I must admit that our overcoat pockets bulged suspiciously, for there were some additional articles that seemed essential for our undertaking, such as the International Directory of Psychologists, that would have tipped the airport scales over our allowance. Over the great distances we were to fly any excess charges would have wrought havoc on a delicately balanced budget.

This once-in-a-lifetime argosy had been more than a year in the planning. There had been moments when it had all seemed like a child's phantasy; it could not really happen. And there had also been some chilling moments when it seemed that indeed it could not happen, for shortly after the original plans were laid I had an acute coronary attack that immobilized me for several months. But, for once, the p-values, against which all psychologists must gamble their scientific careers, could be ignored. The administrators of The Human Ecology Fund, without whose assistance the project would have been quite impossible, were patient, and time, that persistent meddler in human affairs, decided to play on our side. And so, on that bright June morning, when we mounted the ramp and turned to wave to the members of our family who had come to see us off, we realized at last that this was no dream.

Lemcke's Questions

There had been some intensive psychological preparation for this undertaking. We had prepared ourselves, my wife and I, to ask some provocative questions and, what seemed even more important, to listen in certain ways. Dr. Frances Lemcke, also with the assistance of The Human Ecology Fund, had developed some group discussion procedures which we had pre-tested. We hoped that the use of these procedures would enable us to reach a first approximation of some of the important international decision matrices, as well as to hit upon a more sure-fire way of making such assessments.

Actually, Dr. Lemcke's procedure was only one of six approaches that we came to use, and, while it was relatively informal as psychological procedures go, it was the most elaborate, the most difficult to apply, and altogether the most fruitful. Let me describe it first.

We envisioned small groups, comprising three to fifteen persons, who might be willing to let us influence the course of their conversation for an hour or two. Since we wanted to see how they construed issues, rather than asking them to choose between alternatives we might propose, it was important that the questions with which we initiated the discussion should be more suggestive of a topical area than that they would be precise or objective. Moreover, we wanted as much as possible to put our friends in the position of asking each other questions and of seeking themselves the clarification of each other's responses. The more they interrogated each other the better would be the final statement of the issues as they saw them. After all, it was their system of personal constructs we were seeking to understand, not how they might inadvertently trap themselves within the web of our own dimensional scheme.

There were six lead questions in Lemcke's group discussion plan—the result of nine months' exploration within the American context. In Europe I often took the liberty of altering them somewhat. My entry questions usually ran somewhat as follows:

1. In your country how do people such as yourselves come to choose to become psychologists (philosophers) (psychiatrists) (social scientists)?

2. In each person's life it appears that there are points at which major lifetime decisions must be made. In this country what are the typical personal decisions that people such as yourselves must make, aside from the choice of a profession?

3. Many people in the world today are concerned about the possibility of a major catastrophe—an atom bomb perhaps, a collision of the earth with some celestial body, a devastating earthquake, or something of that sort. Suppose there should be such a catastrophe in this country, destroying perhaps half the population, half the transportation, half the buildings, etc. What would the typical psychologist do?

4. A few months ago I was sitting in a room with three of my colleagues. I allowed myself to have a phantasy about these three persons and

myself. I thought, "Suppose these three individuals were stranded on an ice floe and I were a helicopter pilot sent to rescue them. The helicopter will hold no more than three persons, including the pilot, all four of us are capable of flying it, the ice floe is breaking up, and there is no possibility of making a second trip. What would I do? Suppose the typical psychologist in your country were confronted with a similar problem. How would he go about solving it? If you wish, I can describe each of my colleagues, since I know them well. However, you will have to tell me exactly what you need to know about them.

5. Here is a question involving even more phantasy. Suppose each of us were to be taken to another planet and told that we would be allowed to return to earth only if we chose to be some kind of animal. We know, of course, that certain animals are regarded quite differently in various cultures and that the attributes ascribed to animals often represent important national values. What kind of animal do you suppose the typical psychologist in your country would choose to be?[6]

6. One more question: Suppose about twenty years from now another American psychologist were to come here and ask the same questions of a similar group of your countrymen. How do you suppose the answers might be different after twenty years?

No one could claim that simple categorical answers to these six questions would throw much light on constructs or on construct systems. For this kind of insight it is necessary to probe much deeper in order to develop statements of the alternatives among which the group envisioned its choices being made. For example, to the question about how psychologists in their country came to choose their profession, the first round of replies usually represented some effort to explain the choice in motivational terms. Now I have no particular objection to other people's explanation of their behavior in motivational terms, if those are actually the terms in which they think. But I have serious doubts that many of us actually make our decisions in such terms. I have, instead, the distinct impression that motivational terms injected into this kind of discussion serve only to make one's behavior appear rational, or, if not rational, at least psychological, and therefore, for whatever it is worth, coherent.

Constructs Underlying Occupational Choice

But there were several things one could do to clarify the underlying constructs behind the choice of psychology as a vocation. For example, most of the replies to this question had to do with the person's own choice, rather than the choice of the "typical psychologist." It was appropriate to ask, therefore, against what alternatives was the choice made. What vocational opportunities did the person abandon when he chose to be a psychologist? And on what issues was the decision finally made? What occupations did he see as standing in particularly sharp contrast to the group of occupations he had considered favorably—contrasting occupations especially to be avoided? Could he generalize the similarities and contrasts he had mentioned; that is to say, could he express the theses and their corresponding antitheses? To what extent did the group see this set of constructs operative in the vocational choice of other psychologists they knew?

As I suspect you have already begun to surmise, the wealth of information accruing from this method of inquiry was far greater than one could hope to report in a single paper. Not only did construct dimensions begin to appear, but other things as well—frustrations, compromises, stubborn hopes for the future, disillusionments, despair, conflicts between social groups and between economic groups, impatience with entrenched professors or university policies—all of the overtones of a complex decision matrix. Still, the important outcome of our inquiry was the dimensions themselves—the system of alternatives these persons conceptualized, and therefore the only pathways psychologically available to them. These, by the way, are the ultimate dimensions of human freedom. No others can be of any human use!

Constructs and Personal Freedom

Perhaps at this point I should take a moment to illustrate how personal construct dimensions open up pathways of freedom in what otherwise may seem to be a deadlocked situation. During our visit to the Institute of Psychology in Moscow one of the psychological assistants employed in the Institute was assigned to us as a translator. She was an attractive little girl, very serious, conscientious in her choice of technical words, but quite expressive in her inflection and gesture, and with a manner of relating herself to people that was both open and ingenuous. How had she come to choose psychology as a vocation?

First of all, she did not wish to be a psychologist; her long-standing ambition was to become an actress—a serious actress. But the University of Moscow budgets the support it gives to students according to the faculties in which they study and according to an appraisal of needs of the

Soviet society. In her case she had been unable to secure support for her study of dramatic arts, but, being a bright student, could qualify for support in other fields that were more heavily subsidized. As she examined her objectives more closely she was able to conceptualize a relationship between psychology and dramatics. She proceeded to qualify herself in psychology, completed the psychology curriculum, and found employment in the Psychological Institute.

She had also studied English, both as preparation for a career as an actress and as a skill considered highly valuable in the Soviet Union, especially wherever psychological research is carried on. Moreover, the Institute was downtown on the old university campus, close to the city's theater activities. Having established herself as a full-time research psychologist, with useful language skills and the responsibility for interpreting the ideas and feelings of English-speaking people, she was free to study drama in the evening, also a task of interpreting the ideas and feelings of characters who might not otherwise be properly understood.

At first glance her record might be regarded as no more than the result of a compromise within a rigid system that denied her the freedom she would have liked to have. But it was much more than that; she did not sell so much of her time to the Institute merely in order to earn the money to do what she wanted in the hours that remained. She reconceptualized her objectives, rather than compromised them, and by putting them in a different perspective established a decision matrix for herself that permitted her to move ahead with a minimum of artificial compromise and a maximum of intellectual integrity. She was not merely "putting in hours" and "earning money" in the Institute; she was training herself in the art of interpreting human behavior. Thus she was fulfilling her life rather than subjecting it to economic circumstances. She was no less of a psychologist than the other research workers in the Institute, and scarcely less of a student of the theater, I dare say, than the others who shared her evening classes. She had thought through a dimension of life and, in doing so, had found a measure of freedom in a society where personal freedom is not easy to come by.

And may I say just one more thing while I am about it—just to forestall any tendency some of you may have at this moment to lapse back into motivational thinking. I don't think the intensity of this young lady's motivation, assuming there is any such thing for a person to have, had anything to do with what she was doing. If there had been nothing but a burning desire to be an actress the temptation would have been, not to conceptualize, but to compromise. She would have sold herself to the best-paying job she could find, saved every kopek, hated herself all day long, daydreamed of the stage, and come alive only in those stolen moments she could spend at the theater.

Other Approaches

So far, I have described only one of the approaches my wife and I employed—the Lemcke Series—and, for the most part, I have been speaking of the first question only in that series, the question about vocational choice. Since this first question served mainly to initiate the discussion at a practical level, and generally did not involve as much abstraction as the five subsequent questions, you can readily see that I am having to leave out some of the most important parts of the methodology.

More often than not it was impossible to assemble a group for the kind of discussion the Lemcke approach envisioned. Even when a group was assembled, it was not always feasible to press them into this kind of conversation. In some instances, as in Denmark, for example, it was obvious that the group, assembled around the table in a home and under the most convivial circumstances, was less than enthusiastic about anything that smacked of a psychological inquiry. In some instances I found that we were members of a group that wanted to ask questions about psychology in America or about my own theoretical stand in psychology. Often I found myself limited to what could be learned in a conversation with one or two persons during a half hour's visit across a professor's desk.

As it turned out, we found ourselves using essentially six types of approaches, or combinations of them, depending on the circumstances or the mood of our hosts. The first, and most elaborate, was the group discussion based on Lemcke's questions, which I have already sketched. The second group method, used most effectively in places such as Prague, Warsaw, and Moscow, was a lecture given at the invitation of the local university or academy of science people, and dealing with personal construct theory. These lectures were usually followed by lively discussions lasting until late in the evening. There were also some occasions when I was asked to describe American graduate training in psychology. These naturally led us to problems of decision-making for psychologists and others in similar occupations. Some information could be gleaned from discussions of local research projects, since the laboratory walk is a standard part of any psychologist's visit to another university.

Where friendships developed beyond the formality of the initial visit, the conversation often turned to wartime and immediate post-war experiences. Most Europeans have vivid memories of this catastrophe, for the last war affected civilians in unprecedented ways that are hard for Americans to envision. For most Europeans their recollections of wartime experiences are tightly bound to their construction of life and any discussion of these traumatic events is likely to lead to some kind of effort to structure and evaluate the course of human affairs.

Finally, there was a question I found particularly useful when I was limited to a brief visit with men in their offices, in their laboratories, or at the lunch table. It ran like this: "I am impressed with the rapid changes that are going on in Europe these days. Undoubtedly these are going to have far-reaching consequences in your country as well as in others during the next decade or so. What role do you see psychologists, or the science of psychology, playing in the developments that lie ahead?"

The answers to this question varied greatly from country to country and in ways that seemed reasonably representative of the prevailing decision matrix. In Norway, for example, the young psychologists saw psychology as a major dynamic factor in the new society they believed to be emerging, while in Austria the answer was a flat, "none"—an answer reminiscent of the prewar German intellectuals' disclaimer of any responsible part in the ominous course of events leading up to the Nazi tyranny.

Ways to Listen

As I have already said, as much depended on the ways my wife and I listened as on the ways we posed questions. As a matter of fact, asking and listening must go together, for the act of asking a question attunes one's ear to the sort of answer he expects, and one usually asks his questions in the light of what he thinks he has heard.

Basically, personal construct theory ought to alert one to the implied similarities and contrasts in a respondent's use of terms or in his descriptions of events. If two incidents are described in the same context, one examines both content and syntax to detect, if he can, what the speaker sees as similar between them, and in what way he sees them in contrast with each other. These similarities and contrasts are the traces of the construct dimensions being used. The incidents mentioned are the operations designating the poles of these constructs and hence serve to define them by what is known in logic as the method of extension.

Often the contrasts are clearly implied by the use of introductory phrases in sentences, as, for example, when a sentence is introduced by the phrase, "In *this* country . . . " or "*Our* students are. . . . " It is clear that what follows in the sentence is believed by the speaker to stand in contrast to something he thinks is true in some other country, or of another group of students. Often the speaker is distinguishing between what is true of his country or of his students and what he believes to be true of America or of American students, although the context of the conversation may suggest that he has some other contrast in mind.

Indeed, almost anything that a person chooses to say in a conversation may be regarded in either of two ways; a further elaboration of something that has just been said or of something the presence of his listener implies to him, or, on the other hand, it may be regarded as a statement having salience; that is to say, something that stands out in clear contrast to what has just been said by others, or distinguishes itself from what the listener is believed to represent. To catch the full meaning of what is being said, therefore, one must not limit his listening merely to an absorption of the content or to following a sequence of images, no matter how vivid they may be. He must alert himself to the construct dimensions which serve to conjoin and separate the elements of the conversation. Without such structuring dimensions a conversation would be no more than a kaleidoscopic succession of images.

In an ordinary conversation a speaker will go over and over the same construct dimensions, varying the content, from time to time appearing to change the subject, and approaching the same dimension of thought or feeling, first at one pole and then at the other. One soon senses, if he tries, that the speaker is trying to impress an abstract meaning on his listener by continually shifting its concrete underpinnings. It is up to the listener not to limit himself to stringing these bits of information on his own most convenient axes of reference, but to attempt to abstract from what is being said the true axes of the speaker's system.

There is an axiom often useful in psychotherapeutic interviewing: *The patient may readily change the subject, but only rarely does he change the theme.* In fact, it is by tracing the theme from subject to subject that the therapist gradually distills what is pervasive from what is merely illustrative. This is precisely what one must do in listening to any conversation if he is to detect its underlying essentials. Yet the illustrative material is often so shocking or so dull that the listener becomes preoccupied with it and fails to comprehend what is of central importance.

At a more technical level I might mention listening for the "buts," the "on the other hands," and the "therefores." These are obvious signs of contrasts and linkages. One can look for synonymous usages of terms. He can be alert to compounded modifiers of nouns, chains of modifiers, sweeping generalizations, and name-calling, all of which are common features of propaganda and are therefore likely to carry loose personal meanings which are quite remote from the dictionary meanings of the words used. He can make note of distance-making modifiers; "that versus this," "they versus we," "that class of people," etc. He can be aware of terms that seem to serve more as signals than as conveyors of semantic meanings—"the Germans," "the Nazis," "the Fascists," etc. Here again there may be evidence of a generalization which the person is not prepared to break down into its component parts.

It is often important to watch for artificial breaks in the chain of conversation, for interruptions by other members of the group, for sudden silences, for breaks in a line of discussion to ask the listener a question. There may be sudden blockages in the fluidity of the discussion, or inferential leaps that leave obvious logical gaps in the chain of reasoning, or there may be frantic efforts to disengage from a topic altogether. These are clues to the possibility that the contrasting pole of the construct is threatening and to the fact that the speakers are reluctant to disclose it.

One looks for areas in which discussion is spontaneous and where spontaneity breaks down. He observes constructs where one pole is discussed freely but the contrasting pole is avoided. There are likely to be some matters brought up when one is alone with the speaker which are never mentioned when a third person is present. This is particularly true behind the iron curtain. We were somewhat surprised to discover that constructs underlying such surreptitious conversations are likely to be fairly clearly expressed. In some cases there may be over-documentation of certain conclusions. This suggests that the speaker has some apprehension regarding the antitheses of those conclusions.

Who and Where

In planning this preliminary study of Europe's decision matrices, we had to make some decisions about sampling. We were less concerned with reaching a final statement regarding the decision matrix of a given country than we were about testing the feasibility of the methods derived from personal construct theory. Any final formulation of a particular decision matrix would have to be based on extensive experience within a single country, with proper regard for subcultures, for sizes of samples, and the rate at which patterns were changing. Furthermore, to concentrate on one country alone in our survey, would have led us to become overly involved with the similarities and contrasts between that country and our own. It seemed that only by maximizing the differences between the national cultures we visited that we could hope to get a proper perspective on our method and to determine whether or not it might be expected to reflect major cultural differences.

But we wanted to do something else, too, partly from the standpoint of convenience and partly from the standpoint of methodology. Obviously our most ready access to persons abroad was through our identification with a university and with the discipline of psychology. The fact that my own psychological interests at the present time are largely theoretical also provided a rather broad meeting-ground for conversations with psychologists abroad. Psychologists throughout the world know a good deal about each other, and university people, regardless of discipline and nationality, are likely to sense a common bond among themselves. We, therefore, had what was more or less a ready-made access to universities in general and to psychologists in particular.

But even without this common interest in psychology, it would have been desirable to concentrate the study upon a particular kind of sub-culture. We were not seeking to distinguish the decision matrices of classes, but of national groups. It is to be assumed that the differences between socio-economic classes reflect distinctive differences in decision matrices. Indeed, one of the primary ways in which socio-economic classes are identified by sociologists is in terms of privileges, which are certainly closely related to the freedom of action within a kind of decision matrix. While I believe there is a lot of stereotyped nonsense in the unidimensional way social scientists talk about classes—"upper lower class," "lower middle class," and all that sort of thing, there are, nonetheless, sub-cultural differences worth taking into account. In making our plans it therefore seemed desirable to keep to the same type of sub-culture as we moved from country to country in our effort to become sensitive to national differences.

Now I suspect it may be true that the differences between psychologists from country to country are less remarkable than the differences between other types of sub-culture—merchants, for example, or perhaps miners. From this point of view our methodology is open to valid criticism. But I am not sure we can tell *a priori* what these sub-cultures are in which we may find greater national differences reflected.

There was a third reason for choosing to talk mostly to psychologists. We were trying out a set of psychological techniques and our target was a psychological problem. It was therefore possible to discuss frankly with our respondents just what we were doing and to enlist their comments on the spot. Psychologists tend to be pretty articulate people and we were often grateful for the opportunity to discuss with them just what we were trying to accomplish.

I should point out that our discussions were not limited to psychologists. There were often philosophers in our groups, as well as sociologists, psychiatrists, and individuals from other disciplines, who had a personal ancillary interest in the behavioral sciences. I should mention also the fact that we had very little contact with Americans during our year abroad. We did not mingle with embassy people, with military or technical assistance people, or with tourists, except on rare occasions, and then only briefly. In other words, we concentrated on psychologists and people like them and saw very little of "The American Community" in cities we visited. In some ways, I suppose, this was a disadvantage, but we thought, everything considered, it was best to maximize our contacts with foreign friends.

Altogether, then, our sampling specifications were simple enough: Concentrate on Europe, maximize national differences, and minimize sub-cultural differences by sticking to university communities and talking to psychologists and their friends. We did, of course, have a good many contacts outside university communities and with persons in non-professional occupations. But our very tentative observations in these cases are not part of the study I am reporting.

A Scandinavian Construct

While the differences in national outlook among the five Scandinavian countries (Denmark, Finland, Iceland, Norway, and Sweden) are often surprisingly great, there is one construct dimension which stands out in their appraisal of international affairs. Scandinavians, partly because of their relatively high standards of living and their high level of literary activity, often visit the United States and take a keen interest in comparing their way of life with ours. The Finns, because of the unique system of fellowships for study in the United States operating over the past forty years, are particularly alert to similarities and differences between their society and ours. Their friendship for America runs deep.

This seems to be especially true among university people. While the Finns were defeated in two wars occurring in rapid succession, in one of which they found themselves aligned against us, and while they have been and are still being systematically plundered by the Soviet Union, our erstwhile ally, they have made an amazing recovery. Some measure of that recovery can be attributed to the leadership of persons who had training in the United States.

The Danes and the Norwegians have had particularly close contact with us since the war, and Americans who travel abroad are likely to agree that there is no place in Europe where an American feels more comfortable and accepted than in the homes and on the streets of Copenhagen. The story is somewhat different in Sweden, where local scholars feel they have been cut off from America because of their country's refusal to join NATO. It is painfully different in Iceland where the presence of Americans is regarded as akin to a military occupation. Our activities are deeply resented there, even though they are conceded to be a necessary safeguard against Soviet aggression.

All this contact with America leads Scandinavians to attempt some sort of generalization of the differences they see between their way of life and ours. It is a generalization that appears to arise spontaneously among individuals, rather than following from some official ethnocentric line.

Probably the most shocking thing a Scandinavian sees when he visits the United States is the unbelievable squalor of our cities, towns, and country-side. However he may be impressed with our highways, our universities, and our productive capacity—and he is indeed impressed by these things—he carries away with him a sickening image of the abject hopelessness of the less privileged fourth of our population—of Negroes living in despair, of dilapidated farms, of mental hospitals that look like mismanaged zoos, of fear and violence stalking our city streets, of prisons and courts that have little relation to impartial justice or to the restoration of self-respect, an image of the sick and the helpless being stripped of their dignity the moment they are driven to seek aid. Alongside this he sees profligate spending, arrogant expense accounts of men in private industry, the poor being taunted because of their poverty, and wealth flaunted in the face of the needy. He hears Americans in comfortable surroundings extolling something they call private enterprise in the midst of an economy that has obviously been taken over by corporate enterprise, and he hears of the virtues of self-reliance from people whose fortunes were handed down to them. He wonders why, in a country where self-reliance is regarded so highly, there are so many who seem to have given up in despair and, where equality is so often talked about, there are so many who have no part to play. He concludes that in America it is a disgrace to be colored, to be poor, to be a child without parents, to be sick after you have spent your last dollar on doctor bills, or to be old and helpless.

Almost without exception he is deeply shocked by what he sees, and particularly so because he likes the Americans he meets, and is unfailingly impressed by their courtesy, hospitality, and personal generosity to him. Yet there are few Scandinavians now who do not think of America as the grand contemporary example of extremes of wealth and poverty—not the extremes of a five per cent wealthy against a ninety-five per cent impoverished, but the extremes of a three-fourths self-righteously successful against a one-fourth contemptibly derelict. Against what he sees and hears here the Dane or the Swede cannot help but draw contrasts from his own country and the responsibilities its citizens feel incumbent upon them; for none of the things I have mentioned among his observations could easily be said of a country like Denmark or Sweden, not even if one takes into account a certain amount of poverty to be found there.

I suspect this is a point where I would be well advised to ask you to recall just what it was we were attempting to do. Our task—remember—was, and is, to examine the decision matrices of Europe and to clarify as best we can the construct dimensions in turns of which the people of Europe do what they do and stand prepared to do whatever it is they will do in times of national emergency. The particular construct I have been delineating is not typically an American construct; few Americans see their society, or other societies, in terms of this dimension. And, furthermore, as if it were not abundantly obvious during the last few minutes, may I remind you that looking through other people's glasses is hard on the eyes. Is anyone for changing the topic back to something more academic—such as "motivation?"

Idealism and Materialism

During our visits to university cities it was a simple matter to stop by bookstores in the student districts and observe what books were being displayed and bought. We were surprised in many instances to find what a large proportion were American books. In Helsinki, for example, a rough check indicated that about half the textbooks displayed were

American, with the remainder distributed among Finnish, Swedish, British, and German titles. The topics ranged from science to history and literature. I expressed this surprise to a group of Finnish university people one day and was rewarded by an enlightening reply from these astute observers of world affairs who survive under the shadow of the Soviet Union only by intensive research in political science and keeping their wits about them from week to week.

While Finnish authors are reputed to publish more books in proportion to the population than do those of any other country in the world, except perhaps Iceland, they were, up until the beginning of the last war, greatly dependent upon German textbooks. Like many other people, they looked to Germany as a fountainhead of both science and literature. America, by contrast, was the country where automobiles, airplanes, movie stars, illiterate millionaires, and addle-headed tourists came from. To a somewhat similar extent this axis of German scholarship versus American simple-minded materialism structured the thinking in other countries of Europe as well.

But there has been a curious shuffle since the war. The same construct dimension still holds, but America and Germany have exchanged positions. Now it is the Germans who are the materialistic, money-conscious, crude-mannered, vulgarians of the world, and it is the Americans who are exporting scholarship. German economic growth has been spectacular while American economic growth seems on the point of grinding to a halt. Reactionary voices call America back, not to the dynamics of the nineteenth century but to the status of the nineteenth century, not to the forward look of our pioneers, but the backward look of those who keep talking about them. Since the war we have displayed a strange inability to get things done or to implement any programs comparable to Europe's Common Market. More and more the Germans are making the world's automobiles, the Dutch its medicines, the Italians its business machines.

But when we look at the other pole of this dimension we see something that we can scarcely believe ourselves. America is exporting scholarship as no nation of modern times has ever exported it. American scientific research on a broad front is outdistancing the contributions of other countries. In almost any field you can mention American textbooks are far ahead of those available elsewhere. American artists are exhibiting and performing with exciting new style and competence. America is rapidly coming to mean scholarship and intellectual leadership. This is indeed a switch of images.

Now I have been elaborating considerably on what was actually told me that evening in Finland. This elaboration, however, is based on observations in other parts of Europe and it substantially represents, I believe, an important dimension in the thinking of social scientists in a number of countries—though certainly not in all. Moreover, I doubt if all segments of the societies in which I observed this dimension make the same use of the contrast I have described, or, if they did, if they would all see American scholarship in such a favorable light. Our study is sharply limited to preliminary observations in the kind of sub-cultures we chose to visit.

Nevertheless, I believe we have something important here. So let me go on and describe the remarkable way in which this dimension of thought has guided the affairs of nations during the last decade and a half.

German idealism has always been an important pole of Germanic thinking. While idealism might at first glance appear to be antagonistic to empirical science, it has not always worked out that way in Germany. Indeed it often supported experimentation. The logical positivists of the Vienna Circle, taking their cue from Bertrand Russell of Britain and the American pragmatists, attempted to clean house in German science and sweep out the vestiges of idealism. But German idealism was not to be junked so easily; it was instead about to assume its most grotesque form and plunge the world into a Nazi nightmare.

Germany came out of the war with its idealism discredited, both at home and abroad. How deep this sense of invalidation was is hard to say. But at least it was acute enough on the surface. In the face of such invalidation, then, what was there for the German mind to do? Certainly if one finds his position untenable he must change it, if he is to survive. But how? How do you shift your position, except to move in the most obvious direction from where you stand and along the broadest avenue your mind has been able to pave for itself? For the German, this avenue ran straight from "German" idealism to "American" materialism. What could be more obvious—and with the American occupation forces, from Army sergeants to State Department officials, to show just how it could be done!

But I must point out that such massive shifts are not made along lines that are laid down by strangers from across the Atlantic, or by the immutable logic of the universe, but along lines that are construed by the human mind itself. The idealism the German felt himself forced to abandon was not the Nazism Americans perceived, but the Nazism he himself had experienced. Nor was that idealism some island perched out in natural space, existing independently of what man perceives, it was what the

German experienced it to be in his own generation. And the materialism he envisioned as the alternative now open to him was not the America we experience, but the America he perceived us to be. Hence the shift became what it was. Western Germany, and to a considerable extent Eastern Germany too, has moved toward what they and most of the rest of Europe believed was "successful Americanism!" It has made this move with some misgivings on both sides of the Atlantic, for it was not altogether in the direction of their sober convictions or of what we deeply believe.

That this move may prove to be superficial must go without saying. Indeed, Americans might fervently hope that it is superficial, and that, instead of slipping back again into the old slot toward fascism the moment the American glamor has worn off, the German mind will conceptualize some new dimensions of national life. But we should not expect too much. We must remember that while war and defeat may challenge men to find new pathways along which civilization may move, the suddenness and shock of a great catastrophe too often cause men to turn and run back along old familiar alleys.

One Man's Matrix of Decision

Thus far I have attempted to sketch only two dimensions of European cultural change—one that I have called the Scandinavian dimension of *Humanitarianism versus Opportunism*, and the other that might be called the German dimension of *Ideas versus Wealth*. Rather than going on to catalog other dimensions and trace more complex matrices—which, as you see, takes time—let me show how this simple two-dimensional matrix defines some anxious choices in the life of an individual man and how it channels the destinies of nations in moments when great decisions are made.

A few months before the Berlin wall was put up, my wife and I had the opportunity to make the acquaintance of some young university instructors in Humboldt University, the old and respected "University of Berlin." It happens that this university lies just inside the Soviet sector of the city. Since the war an impressive new university, called the Free University of Berlin, has been erected in the American sector with the generous help of American funds. But one does not construct universities simply by building buildings and recruiting a distinguished staff. In some strange way, quite apart from these important features, each university seems to have its own integrity and character. Humboldt University, though it is now plastered with communist slogans and humming with programs for communizing Latin America, still retains some of its distinction as a center of scholarship. In some of its departments professors are under continual or intermittent harassment, yet are able to carry on in some degree in the old scholarly tradition. In spite of all their handicaps their work stands out in contrast to that in corresponding departments of the Free University where all the gleaming new buildings and equipment are. Psychology is one of those departments.

During one of a number of conversations a young man spoke of the pleasure he and his wife experienced on those occasions when they could leave the darkened rubble-covered streets of East Berlin and take the S-Bahn train over to West Berlin. He expressed himself something like this: "Do you know, even if I were to be offered a position with higher rank and pay in another city of the People's Democratic Republic, my wife and I have agreed that we would turn it down. It would be worth the sacrifice just to be able to retain the opportunity to go to West Berlin when our spirits are low, to walk the wide clean streets, to mingle with the happy crowds, to be caught up in the bright lights, and to look at the endless displays of beautiful things behind big plate glass windows. For us who live in East Berlin it is an exciting privilege just to go over there and breathe the air."

An American, hearing this kind of remark, is likely to feel a lump in his throat and sense a bond of kinship between himself and his new-found friend. I was no exception. After all, there is something about West Berlin that stands for America and its hopes for a war-chastened people, and one cannot help but be thrilled to hear this young man, reared under Nazi tyranny, scarred by combat, starved in a military prison camp, and living in the bleakness of communist oppression, speak of breathing the air of . . . Here he is, a man who, in spite of all that tried to warp his life, has caught a glimpse of that dimension in which all human life seems to pulsate, that dimension so dear to the American heart.

Oppression versus Freedom!

We asked this young man, almost in our next breath, if he was planning to flee the Eastern Sector, something that at that time would have been easy enough to do. The immediate reply was, "No! Why?" The answer, with its overtones, ran something like this: "Well, the rents are very high over there—four or five times as much as we pay. To be sure there are employment opportunities now, but some day something you cannot help will happen. You may lose your position and if you lose your position in Western Germany your financial resources dwindle away very rapidly, very rapidly indeed. Before you know it, you and your wife and your children may be thrown out into the street. That sort of thing happens over there. Medical care is terribly expensive over there. The doctors like to live expensively, and if you can't pay for medical care you don't get it. No, we are going to stay right here. While the pay is poor, and the streets are dark, and you are under continual criticism if someone does not think you are following quite the correct line, still I know this: My family will always have a roof over their heads, I will always have an income, and there will always be free medical care for our children and ourselves, absolutely free—*good* medical care. I remember very well what it was like to be without these things, when children were deserted in the streets, and some starved while others ate. Then I look at my own children, and I know what my decision must be. No, I'm staying here. My family comes first!"

"Oh ho!" you may say. "It's easy enough to see what's wrong with this fellow. He just doesn't have the motivation. All people like him want is security, security! He expects everything to be soft and easy. He thinks the world owes him a living. He's a coward; he's afraid to face up to life. It takes a real man to enjoy freedom and he obviously doesn't measure up."

These comments are, of course, in the language of motivational psychology. They are not the sort of thing one says if he is looking for a glimpse of the world through the other fellow's glasses. They are an outsider's explanation, or, more correctly, a way of dismissing any claim this man may have to validity for the matrix of his decision. The psychology of motivation is like that!

But I have committed you to understanding this man in terms of the psychology of personal constructs. Let us, therefore, look more closely to see if we can detect the principal dimensions of his thought. He has expressed two main ideas, the first, the feeling he and his wife have when they walk the crowded streets of West Berlin, and the second his sense of over-riding responsibility to his family. The second is easy enough to understand in terms of what we called our "Scandinavian dimension of *Humanitarianism versus Opportunism.*" He sees matters in terms of this issue and he chooses for himself the pole of humanitarianism, presumably, of course, with certain personal modifications of the construct.

But what about the first statement? Was it the air of "freedom" that he and his wife were breathing on those walks along the brightly-lit Kurfurstendam—"freedom" as Americans understand it? I suspect it was not, really, just as I am sure it is not for all too many Americans. What

they were breathing was the air of excitement, of glamor, of lavish
wealth, of the endless display of goods—shiny things, soft things, lus-
cious things—the air of the abundance of material possessions. No doubt
they remembered something too, something that happened when they
were youngsters—trumpets and flags, the quickened heart-beat that
keeps time with marching feet, the spectacle of the launching of a thou-
sand-year Reich, the power of brushing away all the villainous adversar-
ies that fouled the path to greatness, the realization that they themselves,
that they were not only Aryan but German. It has been twenty years
now, but who can ever forget the bursting thrill of idealism rising in the
adolescent breast.

But all that is gone now. Nazi idealism has proved itself to be cruel
and wrong, and it has led to bitter reprisals from those who did not share
that dream, just as all great ideals of faith, of hope, and deep conviction
prove to be cruel and wrong when they are held too dearly. Ideals are as
dangerous as they are powerful, and they lead to death and bitterness.
One scarcely dares think of those adolescent moments now, or try to remember how he felt, much less mention such things aloud. So "idealism"
is dead now. It perished with the millions of Jews it slaughtered and is
buried with them in the same mass graves.

As this young man and his wife mingle with the shopping crowds in
the KaDeWe, or stroll among the sidewalk diners at Krantzler's, I am
sure they must hear the echo of distant drums, and sense a rising excitement. I am sure not even that dark ruined tower of the Gedächtniskirche,
left standing high in the center of West Berlin's most brightly lighted district as a stark reminder of evil days, can slow the pulse or draw one's
attention altogether away from the lush splendor of the Berlin-Hilton
Hotel. This time it will be different. It is not the Nazi thrill one should
have now, but the thrill of prosperity—like they are always talking about
in America.

I have, to be sure, taken some liberty here in interpreting the personal experiences of our friends. And while I may be mistaken in some
factual details, our inquiries into the dimensions of European thought
lend strong support for the conclusion that one of the principal axes involved in the German's changing world is that of *Ideas versus Wealth*.

A Premature Conclusion

And now I am near the end of this paper. There were so many things
I started out to say, and so few that got said. I suppose I should have

fulfilled the promise of my title—The Decision Matrices of Europe—by cataloguing more of the dimensions of European thought and by suggesting what the cultural shifts may be if sudden emergencies should arise. I would like to have told you about the French, the wildest free-for-all discussion of Lemcke's questions one could ever imagine, their tolerance of intellectual innovation, their shocking proposals of standards by which to evaluate life. Or the Spanish; I would like to tell you about them, how they gracefully stalked me as a matador stalks a bull, making thrusts, stepping neatly aside, dangling false questions, until at last they were satisfied and let me hear what they were bursting all the time to say. I would like to try to make you feel that personal construct and how it bears upon the ever-approaching choice between Franco-ism and communism, a choice that might have been between Franco-ism and democracy—twenty-five years ago! Most of all, I would like to have told you about the exciting things that are happening to Marxist theory in Poland, and the wisp of hope they hold out for a more tolerant world. But the time is nearly gone, and I want to close with a little incident.

Just a few weeks after our return from the Orient last summer, my wife and I made a second trip to Europe. We met one of our East Berlin friends again. Just a few days before, the Berlin wall had gone up. No more happy walks along the Kurfürstendamm, no more neon lights, no more window shopping! At the moment we talked to him there was still a legitimate way to flee to West Germany, and to take his family with him. He was facing his personal matrix of decision, just as today, or perhaps tomorrow, all Europe, and many other countries of the world as well, face the matrices of decision they have erected for themselves. It was obvious that he was under considerable tension. His voice quivered at times; he sought us out as old friends; he kept looking at us as if there were a question he wanted to ask, but he knew it was one we could not answer for him. For us, of course, with our own type of decision matrix, the choice might have been considerably less difficult. But each man decides within his own matrix. Our talks, on several occasions during those days last August, were warm and friendly, and we spoke briefly of the crisis in his life. But we did not press him to disclose what his decision might be. After all, human decency sets limits to psychological inquiry, and we did not have the heart to probe the anguish of his already troubled mind.

How is it that James Russell Lowell's (1897) poem runs—"Once to every man and nation comes the moment to decide . . . "?

ENDNOTES

1. The experiences upon which this paper is based were made possible by a grant to the writer and his wife from the Human Ecology Fund.

2. "He will leave Bibles to eat bricks, he will leave bricks to eat bottles, he will leave bottles to eat clothing, he will leave clothing to eat cats, he will leave cats to eat oysters, he will leave oysters to eat ham, he will leave ham to eat sugar, he will leave sugar to eat pie, he will leave pie to eat potatoes, he will leave potatoes to eat bran, he will leave bran, to eat hay, he will leave hay to eat oats, he will leave oats to eat rice, for he was mainly raised on it. There is nothing whatever that he will not eat but European butter, and he would eat that if he could taste it."

3. The American Embassy in Moscow interprets the recent policy changes requiring applicants for university admission to have had two years of work experience—except in fields such as science and engineering technology where personnel shortages exist, or in cases of unusual scholarship—to mean that ideological tests are to be used more ruthlessly in screening students. The student strike at the University of Leningrad in support of the Hungarian uprising, caused Moscow no little concern. Still, outside of the disappearance of the leaders of the strike, presumably to spend the rest of their lives raising corn in areas of Asia where rainfall is at a minimum, and trying to remedy the chaotic condition of Soviet agriculture, no conspicuous measures were taken to enforce ideological conformity among students. There may have been, however, more gradual and subtle measures taken that I do not know about.

Regarding restriction of the popular base of higher education, other reports suggest a quiet but systematic elimination of Jewish students from the universities. We ourselves saw nothing that would confirm these reports, and such information as we were able to infer suggested that the main restrictions might be on somewhat different grounds. For example, the promise of occupational productivity within the socialistic system, particularly in skills believed to be underdeveloped, did seem to be extensively used in selecting students. This selection restriction roughly corresponds to our own preferential support for athletes who show promise of making sports page headlines, and for engineering students who have committed their services to large industrial organizations. It was amusing to see how some students circumvent these preferential restrictions, just as they do in this country.

There is nothing that quite seems to parallel our recent large-scale movement toward restricting higher education to students of more than average means, through the sharp increases of student fees in state-supported universities—measures which are intentionally undertaken—and through our growing imbalance of financial resources between the lower third and the upper two-thirds of our population—a development our society has not yet faced up to. The closest Soviet parallel appears to be the class preference given to the children of "workers." This preference was originally said to be justified as a correction constant for the cultural decrement in their measures of intellectual competence. But the term "worker" has come to have a rather limited and meretricious meaning in Soviet society. It is used to refer particularly to factory workers and to those officials who represent themselves as identified with them. Thus what was once an equalizing factor in student selection appears to have become a distorting factor. Whether this distortion is as great as our own growing distortion, which tends to restrict higher education opportunities to the economically more privileged families, is hard to tell. In any case, I suspect the source of their distortion may be harder to dislodge than ours, for theirs has a built-in feature, via communist dogma, that up to now we have not had in our concept of democracy.

What will happen, however, if we decide that our society does not have *democracy* as its central concept, as some leaders are now suggesting, but has instead, *capitalism*, or something of that sort, as its central theme, is another matter. However defensible private capitalism may be, or however broadly we define it, there is nothing in the concept that is likely to serve as grounds for making education equally available to all. We shall have to see how the American society's image of itself develops during the next ten years. And it will be equally important to watch for new developments in Soviet society, too. Such is the central psychological significance of the cold war.

4. This was in Leningrad, of course, which is still Russia's "window to the West." Probably no other city in the Union is as interested in the horizons that lie beyond the drabness that encompasses its daily life.

5. This is not to imply that sports fail to play an important part in Soviet life. One of our group discussions at the Psychological Institute of the Georgian Academy of Sciences had to be cut short because of the intersectional football game scheduled that afternoon. Crowds had begun to gather at the stadium in the late morning, just as they do in an American university town. The Republic of Georgia was playing the Republic of Lithuania, one of the Baltic countries overrun by the Soviet Union and lying some 1300 miles to the northwest. But sports are sports and not a dog-wagging tail of higher education. Nor does one sense the tension when sports are discussed that he senses when the subject of universal education is brought up by a "capitalist" from America.

6. This is essentially one of the questions used by the Spanish psychiatrist, Pigem (1949) in his examination of children.

REFERENCES

Bieri, J. (1961). Complexity-simplicity as a personality variable in cognitive and preferential behavior. In D. Fiske & S. Maddi (Eds.), *Functions of varied experience*. Homewood, Ill.: Dorsey.

Burke, K. (1945). *A grammar of motives*. New York: Prentice-Hall.

Clemens, S. L. (Mark Twain) (1896). The stolen white elephant. In *Tom Sawyer abroad; Tom Sawyer, detective, and other stories*. New York: Harper.

Ditzen, R. (Hans Fallada) (1933). *Little man what now* (trans. by Eric Sutton). New York: Simon & Schuster.

Kelly, G. A. (1955). *The psychology of personal constructs* (Volumes 1 and 2). New York: Norton.

Kelly, G. A. (1958). Man's construction of his alternatives. In G. Lindzey (Ed.), *Assessment of human motives*. New York: Rinehart.

Kelly, G. A. (1961). Suicide: The personal construct point of view. In N. L. Farberow & E. S. Schneidman (Eds.), *The cry for help*. New York: McGraw-Hill.

Lowell, J. R. (1897). *The complete poetical works of James Russell Lowell*. Boston: Houghton Mifflin.

Papashvily, G., & Papashvily, Helen (1945). *Anything can happen*. New York: Harper.

Papashvily, G., & Papashvily, H. (1946a). *Thanks to Noah*. New York: Harper.

Papashvily, G., & Papashvily, H. (1946b). *Yes and no stories*. New York: Harper.

Pigem, J. M. (1949). *La prueba de la expression desiderativa*. Barcelona: Libreria de Ciencias Medic.

CHAPTER 3

Of Cats and Clouds

PETER STRINGER AND LAURIE THOMAS

"It's the Cheshire Cat: now I shall have somebody to talk to."
"How are you getting on?" said the Cat, as soon as there was mouth
enough for it to speak with.
Alice waited till the eyes appeared, and then nodded.
"It's no use speaking to it," she thought, "till its ears have come . . . "

* * *

"A cat may look at a King," said Alice. "I've read that in some book, but
I don't remember where."
"Well, it must be removed," said the King very decidedly . . .

* * *

The Cat's head began fading away the moment he was gone, and, by the
time he had come back with the Duchess, it had entirely disappeared; so
the King and the executioner ran wildly up and down looking for it, while
the rest of the party went back to the game.

Lewis Carroll. *Alice's Adventures in Wonderland*

In the spring of 1980, 12 psychologists, both academic and clinical, gathered over 3 days in a small hotel in the Lake District. The 12—Joyce
Agnew, Don Bannister, Nigel Beail, Gavin Dunnett, Fay Fransella,
Spencer McWilliams, Jonathan Potter, Harry Procter, Anthony Rosie,
Marica Rytovaara, Peter Stringer, and Laurie Thomas—had varying degrees of commitment to the ideas of George Kelly. Their mission was
open-ended: To discuss as a group any aspects of the theory of personal
construct psychology that currently intrigued them. The intentions of the
workshop's organizer (PS) were equally open-ended. Probably he just
wanted to enjoy a stimulating, intellectual conversation in friendly and

picturesque surroundings, though his own current interests in personal construct psychology (cf., Stringer & Bannister, 1979) did make him determined to stimulate a discussion of the "Kellian group" at some stage of the proceedings. Fay Fransella subsequently wrote: "The whole workshop remains in my mind as a fantastic experience. I have never before been involved with a number of people with a common interest in such an unstructured situation for such a long period of time."

A piece of hidden agenda did emerge after the arrangements for the workshop had been made. Jonathan Potter was preparing his doctoral thesis, which came to be called "*Speaking and writing science: Issues in the analysis of psychologists' discourse*" (Potter, 1983). His analyses were to be based both on psychologists' published and unpublished writings and on verbatim transcripts of several scientific discussions among psychologists. We agreed that two of the latter should be the proceedings of the meeting in the Lake District, and later, of its 1981 follow-up in Moonfleet Bay in Dorset.

This chapter pivots on an extract from the transcript of the first meeting. Although the transcript was made as a part of a routine, if unusual, data collection exercise by a postgraduate student, we believe it can serve other functions. It seems to be a rare document in the history and sociology of personal construct psychology: it records the talk, rather than written communications, of a notable assembly of personal construct psychologists. In an earlier introduction to the transcript, Stringer (1985) suggested that a wide range of texts other than journal articles or chapters in books such as this one might be used by personal construct psychologists. We see this transcript as a resource others may wish to use for their own particular purposes—a point to which we return below.

In the context of transcription, and of the focus of this chapter on the construing of a Kellian group (by a Kellian group), the second workshop at Moonfleet included a peculiar, reflexive twist in its proceedings. Once again, there was no explicit agenda—the group for the most part elucidated is own themes for discussion. However, one session of this workshop was, by prior arrangement, devoted to the discussion of two extracts from the transcript of the previous workshop. One of those extracts is reproduced in this chapter. The extract deals with the meaning of a Kellian group. Thus, the transcript of the second workshop includes a discussion by a Kellian group of a record of a prior discussion by a (partially identical) Kellian group of the meaning of the concept "Kellian group." Seven of the Lake District participants were present at Moonfleet, along with four newcomers: Sheila Harri-Augstein, Fraser Reid, Bernadette O'Sullivan, and Norman Todd.

Jonathan Potter has reported analyses of both transcripts in his thesis and in other publications (Potter, 1987, 1988). The transcription was a major exercise. The transcript of the first workshop ran to some 130,000 words; Jonathan shared the task with Anthony Rosie. It was done in a way that was intended to make the end product as easy to read as possible. "It was structured into sentences and punctuated according to the conventions of written English . . . word orders were not changed; hesitations and corrections were not deleted; and for the most part neither were filler words like 'um' and 'ah'. Furthermore, heavy stress was indicated in the transcript by underlining, while laughter and pauses were shown by these terms used in brackets. In this sense the transcript aspires to be as accurate a representation of the audio recording as possible" (Potter, 1983, p. 78). The method did not follow any of the more elaborate conventions of transcription that have been developed. These are more suitable when only fragments of discourse are to be analyzed.

In preparing a section of the Lake District transcript for this chapter, a number of further changes were made, virtually all a matter of punctuation. They had the sole purpose of making the text yet easier to read. The record of the discussion is attributed to fictitiously named persons, though Stringer's sporadic files do contain written permission from a majority of those involved for direct attribution.

We have referred to the transcript, both in its entirety and the section reproduced here, as a "resource." It was clearly that for Jonathan Potter, to help him write a thesis in the social study of scientific knowledge. It could also be treated, intimately, as a part of the (auto)biography of personal construct psychology—material for such reflections as those of Neimeyer (1985). More specifically, one might examine it as a particular example of a highly self-conscious group dynamics process or as empirical evidence of the way in which (some) personal construct psychologists define the construct *group* or fail to define it. One sort of purist might wish to approach the transcript by way of a reflexive glance at a reflexive process: a group looks at group by reflecting upon itself, and so on.

Radically, we should have liked to signpost and bypass the inevitable possibility of these and other alternative readings by offering no more than the piece of transcript as the text of our chapter. But roots are rarely seen or understood. If we capitulate by offering a few of our own separate reflections on what is contained in the transcript, they are intended to be modest and invitational. Our wish, our invitation, is that you now read the transcript, and reread it several times, and produce your own construal of it. Subsequently, you may or may not wish to refer to our reflections. But please, no cheating—do not read the end of the story first! In any case, it is not the end; it is only two beginnings. (There are several other quite different beginnings too. Besides Jonathan Potter, Don Bannister, Fay Fransella, and Fraser Reid also once drafted an interpretation of the transcript.)

First, then, the transcript-extract. It will be followed by reflections, first of Peter Stringer and then of Laurie Thomas. There will be a few remarks on the Moonfleet meeting; and then concluding comments.

TRANSCRIPT EXTRACT

David: Could I take that in the context of a slightly more inclusive question? A question has finally come into my mind about how to think about this group. It has come in a very simple form: like there are many kinds of groups. There are committees, there are encounter groups, there are psychotherapy groups, and seminars and all sorts of things, [**Henry:** Families. **George:** laughs] with a kind of style, their own style of resolving argument, and so on. Now, it just struck me—what the hell would a Kellian group be like?

Frances: We know, we have tried it. [general laughter]

David: We have tried it many times. But this is the first time—which indicates my kind of slowness—that I have actually asked myself the question. [**Frances:** I see.] I think what I have done in the past, and all the groups I have ever been in to do with Kelly, I have sort of not applied Kelly to the group. I mean, I have [**Henry:** That's because you can't.]—the group was about Kelly, but it wasn't of Kelly, as it were. And I think Kelly himself didn't actually amplify that very much. I was interested actually, Paul, when you had the idea of calling this together, as it were. You know, there are two questions in my mind. One is what did you—did you think "Ah, it will be a certain kind of group," because it is about Kelly. And, secondly, do the people here sort of have a picture in their minds of what a Kellian group would be? And whether you do or not, does this group bring a picture to mind; or is it that it is exactly like some other group, the subject of which happens to be Kelly?

Henry: That is precisely why I think that construct theory as Kelly wrote it wasn't very good—it can be done—but it wasn't very good at looking at group process. And that's just the sort of thing—if you get a disagreement in the group, you call that two subgroups. You call that a group construct with the two sets of elements at each end. [**David:** Yes, but Henry . . .]

George: You see, I wouldn't call it a group construct.

David: But you are still not giving me content; and so I will give a bit of my own content.

Frances: Kelly is not sitting up there construing this group [**David:** Yes.] *We* are sitting here, [**George:** He might be!] each construing.

Henry: Absolutely.

David: But with a certain, I keep being . . .

Frances: Or maybe he is . . . [several people talk at once, laughter]

Sam: Is his spirit, is his ghost? . . .

David: I am sorry. Can I give a bit of content to my own question, since nobody gave any content in answer: which is (and it is not very formulated content), it is just—I tried to imagine would a Kellian group be a group in which—it sounds almost like the opposite of what you want, Henry—which did not sort of quite *engage* so completely as other groups tend to. I mean, one of the hallmarks of groups is a committee, is a very engaging group. It keeps defining its topic, it keeps taking votes, it keeps trying to get resolution. At the other end of the scale, even an encounter group, in a way, says "Things have to be confronted. Your feelings about the other person have to come out." A Kellian group would be some weird kind of group where a lot of the time—I don't know—perhaps it is to do with loose construing: you *wouldn't* engage. That is, you would keep throwing out what is going through your mind at the time, but, in fact, wouldn't necessarily debate, resolve, pick up. There would be some inquiry—yes. But inquiry of a kind—I don't know—some sort of easy kind, which was simply to sort of get a bit more knowledge of what it was the other person was saying; but not necessarily to set up a contraposition with it.

Jean: I find that useful, because my paradigm, my problem, is with family therapy. I don't particularly want to take it back into family therapy, but to keep it here: which is, how the hell do you construe a group? I mean, I would think the injunction for the group in a Kellian sense would be "Thou shalt experiment." That would be one way of looking at it. And how the hell do people relate their experiments to each other? I mean, I think there have been experiments going on here which were like soliloquies, and which hopefully they might—or one is validated by hearing the echo back of what you have already said. That is one kind of experiment, but a narcissistic one basically. And my hope is that somehow, by looking at that now and here, that it might help me. Anyway, to take that problem of *coincidental* experimentation going on; and how these relate to each other, deny each other, validate, or what the matter is.

Henry: In order—that's what I have wanted to do. I have come along and said: 'Well look, why don't you take the credulous approach with me really, instead of just saying that's a load of crap straightaway?' [Louis: Can I . . .] That's all it is, an experiment. Please listen for five minutes.

Frances: We have listened.

Louis: Um.

George: I, I . . .

Frances: What we haven't had is feedback from you to our comments. It seems to me . . .

Louis: Can I just pick up on David's point? [Frances: It is like a one-way system.] I think it relates to what you are saying. I have been involved in a group for a long time—a fortnightly group for about 6 years now—which has a really very nebulous sort of process in it, where everybody says, everybody is agreed that they are never going to understand what the group is about; or that there is never going to be really any agreement content. And yet the group as a resource is seen—is really quite valued by most of the people that come. And they come intermittently: they will come for a bit and then go away. Really, I hadn't thought about it as a Kelly group, until you coined the phrase; but there is something there which—and this relates to your group construct—it seems to me that, although each person is remaining individual, they are contributing to something which is a resource out of which everybody is taking different things. [**Frances:** Um, right.] It is very difficult to formulate. And what I feel you wanting to do is to insist that what is there is yours, in a sense, rather than . . . You see, your point about—I can't remember how you put it—the experiment being, er, [**Frances:** Coincidental.] coincidental. It seems to me that each can be playing out their own experiment [**Frances:** Um. **Mary:** Um.] with the help of the group resource, without insisting that other people play the same game as you are playing. And I think . . .

Jean: That is exactly the issue that has been lying between you.

Henry: But I think I am being misunderstood, if you think I am not agreeing with that. [**Louis:** Um. **Mary:** Um. unsure.]

Arthur: I think at the Utrecht conference there were six of us who got on very well together. And we did this—we really were experimenting with each other for the week. And one of the things that came out from it was an incredible series of absolutely loose construing. And it was so loose that going home was physically quite a problem. It was quite a problem to get on the bloody train. [general laughter] It was quite amazing. And we contacted each other about a week or a fortnight later, just to see how far the tightening up process had gone on. [**Louis:** You did get home?] If we got home. And that to me was the most valuable thing about that week. And that seems to me to be one of the concomitants of a sort of Kellian grouping.

Jean: Could you say a bit more about how you see the notion of resource? [pause]

Louis: Ha. Well I could, but I would make just the kind of—I mean, yes, it seems to me that people—I don't think it has to be totally loose—but it goes through. This is why in a sense, really, it seems to me that the group goes through, or the resource that the group generates goes through the sort of process of loosening and tightening.

Henry: Absolutely. [pause] You got empirical evidence for it in your study, haven't you, that the whole group goes through it?

Louis: Now, I don't think—I don't think that the construing of the individual is necessarily synchronized with the structure of the resource. That's . . .

David: Yes. Can I—take—I am thinking of particular *forms* that such a group would be; of a kind where people could throw in, very quickly, could throw in *form* for the experiment [inaudible], a form which the group would readily pick up and run through and then move on. And I think one of the ways—because that's kind of like getting some degree of commonality in the form of the experiment. And I think one way in which this group has failed a bit is that we haven't been able to do that. If I can give an example—and I don't want to—I really don't want to start arguing about whether [tape ends]

David: [tape continues] . . . killed it, by quite wrongly cutting on Mary's attempt to find a title, by finding a title for her which was a nonsense title; [Louis: But in fact . . .] and I apologize for that. What I am getting at: if you take—you know, I have also worked regularly in a group that meets fortnightly. And one thing we have found after—and I hadn't thought of it as a Kellian group, I always call it a men's consciousness raising group [laughter] but one of the things I have noticed that we are developing and getting very adept at—and it is to do with, I think, essentially with the notion of *people's experiments*—is quite quickly, as it were, one or the other will think of a form for a quick experiment, you know. And it can be thrown in; and there almost seems to be an agreement that you never resist a form, you know, even if that doesn't particularly [Louis: Um, um, um.] attract you. That is not an issue. You simply go in with it because it is an experiment. That is, in a sense, what the group has realized—is that you don't know what the, whether the experiment is good or bad, or whether the form is going to act, until after you have done it. You may decide after you have done it [Louis: Um, um, um.] that it wasn't a great deal of help. It doesn't matter. But that decision cannot be taken in advance.

Louis: I think that is interesting. Because I think the group made a decision not to go along with that form. I mean, I consciously had decided I was not going to name my form [David: Yes.] yesterday evening [laughs].

David: Why?

Louis: Because I wasn't going to get that involved in this group at that stage. [**David:** All right, now . . .] And I couldn't—I wasn't going to give a pseudonym, and I wasn't going to actually give a title to it.

Henry: That's a good illustration of why I want to use the word *family*. And everyone will groan again, okay—but the point is that when a group does begin to negotiate, when it begins to have a history, it becomes something different. It begins to function like a family; and that's what your group has become. And that's the distinction that I want to make all the time. *Yet* at the moment we are still loosely related, we are still functioning as individuals, we haven't got to know each other sufficiently to really anticipate [**David:** But . . . **Louis:** Um.] in a very complemental way.

Paul: I think it is inaccurate to just put that on it. Because what we are like, if we are like anything, is something quite close to a family with a lot of visitors; some are relations and some are total strangers. And if you want to find an analogy for the state of the group, there isn't actually the proper nuclear family within it, but there is some kind of approximation to it. [**Henry:** Yes. **Frances:** inaudible. Several talk at once.]

Louis: The only time that most families come together is at a wedding or a funeral. I don't know if that is . . . [general laughter].

David: Yes, that dreadful Sunday tea, where Aunt Annie and her friend came, [**Louis:** Right.] that buggered everything up!

Frances: Did you feel that your experiment was a failure?

David: A failure in the sense, yes, of not being accepted. But something intrigues me about that, about what Louis was saying, which is—which also says something about where we are at—which is that you saw it, and it is quite reasonable to see it so, that you either had to, in a way, either had to take part or kill the experiment. Or . . .

Louis: Or opt out. I, you see [**David:** Or opt out, yes.]—in the kind of group that I am talking about, I would have opted out of that, [**David:** That's right.] and nobody would have taken any notice.

David: That's right, now that's what I am getting at here . . .

Louis: Now I felt yesterday, if we had started going around, [**David:**

Yes. **Mary:** Um, hum.] it would have been absolutely imperative—I mean, I would have had to make an issue of opting out.
Whereas in that other group it would have gone around and
people would have picked it up and there would have been no
feeling that you had to go. And when it stopped, it stopped.
And nobody would have turned round and said, You haven't
given a title yet. [David: Yes, that's right.]

Frances: But I was going to say . . . [David, inaudible. **Louis** laughs] as
well . . .

David: But it is interesting that people didn't, you know—I felt—looking back on it, I now feel an incomplete and undeveloped understanding, because that is the way in fact in which these . . .

Frances: Yes, but that is your experiment [David: . . . form experiments.] and I was going to opt out for a totally different reason, totally different. I just could not. I had given up. I was too
tired. My head was buzzing. And in no way, I saw, could I come
up with a title. [David: Yes, well, that's alright.] In no way did
I have the strength to tighten. [David: Right, but] I probably
didn't want to, but I was going to opt out for a totally different
reason.

David: But—fine—but what I am getting at is the difference between
opting out personally and the group saying "We will not have
the experiment." I mean, the two are really two rather different ways of handling it. Because a form offered can work in the
sense that it runs round everyone who is interested in putting
their bit into the resource created by that experiment. And it
simply doesn't matter that some opt out, for all kinds of reasons. Or . . .

Frances: I think there would have been pressure in this group not to opt
[George: Yes.] out.

David: The group has a kind of understanding that you are going to
have to kill the experiment if you opt out; because even if you
opt out, somehow you have done something that is part of the
experiment, you know—that is you have said something about
yourself. You know, it is kind of like the question of freedoms
and constrictions. [pause]

Henry: When you say the group has an understanding, I am not sure
that—he was saying that the reason he didn't want to do it was
for purely personal reasons: he didn't want to tighten. In other

words, a personal construct theory analysis of why you didn't do it. I would say that we have to say more than that; we have to look at the whole role structure of the group, the way it is beginning to develop and the fact that that was a piece of process that went on, which was bidding for leadership of the group, and saying "I am going to structure the next half-hour."

Frances: But I don't like being rejected like that. [**David:** We don't like . . . **Louis** laughs] And I have a personal . . .

Louis: And I don't like role theory. [some laughter]

Henry: Yes, well, I don't want to use the word *role*, but that was the one . . . [several people talk at once. **Sam:** I feel like a crab, and I don't want to be a crustacean. laughter]

David: You know, in a way—is part of what we are talking about, this notion of an ideal Kelly group, what would it be like? One of the things must be that whether you are in the group at a given point or not was entirely optional. That is, that group members are—that is, one understanding between some groups, like committees or encounter groups, for instance, is that all members are present all the time. [**Louis:** Yes, um.] I don't mean just physically present, but are *psychologically* present. Would a construct theory group, in fact, have a kind of understanding, or common constructs,—that there is no reason why all members should be psychologically present all the time? So . . .

Sam: We are all free to construe the situation, however we choose.

David: Yes, if in fact you have gone into reverie [**Louis:** But in . . .] or whatever, that is not to be challenged; it is to be simply accepted as the way the thing was at the time.

Paul: I can't think of a Kellian group in the way that you are. Though I am not, you know, trying to invalidate it at all. It seems to me that you are talking about the rules of the Kellian group. [**David:** Um.] And I, going back to your original question of how I conceived this group, and how I saw it before it happened, I think I saw it in the terms in which I have seen other groups, and *would* want to see other groups in the future: which is simply as being a set of constructs. And these constructs are not in any simple way the constructs that are held by each individual. They are a set of constructs that are, as it were, pushed up into the air—I mean, I think of it very physically—by people talking to one another. And the group had a Kellian reality for me in the first hour that it met, which I also found a very peculiar hour, and in many ways a very empty hour. But at the same time I saw the group there in a Kellian kind of way, as a set of construings. And I will carry it away in that way, and I would hope that other people did the same, quite honestly. I mean the—this is my perspective, admittedly—its success as a Kellian group, in the way in which I would want to see it, is that people do take away that set of constructs and identify it, for the sake of economy—or sort of cognitive processing and all the rest of it—as the set of constructs that were thrown up by the construings of particular people in a particular place at a particular time.

Henry: Yeah, that's the sort of thing—I mean, the typical sort of thing that you get in human behavior, or whatever you want to call it—is that in different contexts people will do different things. Now, it might be that me and you, George, argue about something, okay, and you are defending so and so and I am attacking it. It might be that next week somebody is attacking your position and I will come in and I will really defend your position. [George: Um.] You know, because I have taken away the entire set of alternatives that has been generated by this group and I then use it. And I have become bigger as a result of being with this group.

Paul: I am not interested—sorry, just to come back in an egocentric way—that does not fit what I said. I am not terribly interested in what happens to you or what is happening to you, and that's why I am just going back to where we started in this bit of the discussion. You and George are really not terribly interesting.

Henry: Yes, well, I was just trying to illustrate what you are saying.

Paul: Well, it doesn't illustrate what I am trying to say from the point of view of a Kellian group. [Henry: Um.] Because the set of constructs that constitutes a Kellian group for me—I was going to say superordinate to it—it is not just superordinate to it. It is in a different realm of discourse from what is happening— well, not totally different realm of discourse—but it is at a different level from what is happening between the two of you. That's why I think it is very unprofitable to start talking about a Kellian group in terms of what's happening between two people, because one very quickly gets locked into that way of seeing the group.

Henry: I don't see how you can separate them. You are talking about group constructs, or whatever you call them, as being up there in the air. You literally went like that [gestures]. And I don't think they are up there. I think they are between us. I think they are very concrete. They are acts.

Paul: Yes, but they are not between you and George.

Henry: That was just an example. [inaudible. Mary and Louis try to speak]

Paul: You had to talk about you and George. I am sorry, George, you are looking slightly anxious [laughter]. What you are not talking about is you and George in the context of other people. Maybe because it is actually quite a clumsy thing to talk about. Louis was pointing this out yesterday: that these more systemic things are quite clumsy things to get into. But that's how one would do it for me, from a Kellian viewpoint. [**David:** Is . . .]

Louis: Um, I was, um—it is quite important. This idea of it being up in the air—certainly this group I am talking about talks like that. It [laughs] talks as if the resource was up there in the air. And people contribute to it, almost literally, [general laughter] and they sort of throw things up there. And what is seen—it is really totally different from this business. I mean, people are not—they no doubt are—and you know there are group dynamics going on, but they are not the concern of the group. The group is concerned with the . . .

Frances: Do you mean that there is an agreed agenda, somewhere, an agreed issue? An agreed . . .

Louis: No, it's very difficult. There isn't an agreed agenda; there [**Frances:** I don't mean physically, I mean implicit agreement.] is a dynamic agenda. That, I think, I find that a difficult concept, because there isn't agreement at the beginning.

Frances: Well, I find yours almost impossible, you see, so I am trying to negotiate a . . . [**Louis:** Well it's . . .]

David: I am sorry, Louis. Does it help if we try and—I mean, I am very intrigued by this, because actually my notions of a Kellian group are actually, you know, tightening a bit [some laughter]. I have tried to tighten that for the moment, if you like, into a group rule. I am not suggesting, like, we have to have this rule, or something like that; I am just in my own way trying to go from loose to tight a bit. And if I read you right about what you are saying, this notion of a thing in the air, and the particular reference that Paul was making to George and Henry, it is almost like there is a—if we tighten it into the formal group rule, the rule would read something like the opposite, say, of some of the rules in some encounter groups and so on, [**Louis:** Yes.] which is if there is a strong personal challenge engagement going on between two people in the room then that becomes, for the time being, the agenda and must be resolved and met. Whereas the group rule in this imaginary Kellian group, with almost that little cloud in the air—there would almost be that that must *not* be the case, that would be really—the rule would be the opposite way around. That's not, somehow . . .

Louis: Yes, but. Again, that's interesting. When that kind of stuff really gets in the way, the group stops being the group and deals, in a sense, deals with that. But it is not dealt with in the context of the intellectual job. It's dealt with at—it is almost the equivalent of pairing. Even if the group stays together, it sort of goes away and deals with its group problems and comes back and gets on with the content job. And it's very interesting too. I have never really taken it to pieces properly.

David: But it comes back to some very *loose* engagement. [**Louis:** Yes, ya.] That, in fact—it seems to me that the point of this metaphor, as it were—I hope it is a metaphor [laughter] [**Louis:** It is when it drops . . . **George:** I sort of have this vision of sort of balloons dropping out of them. **Mary:** It is a sort of . . . [lost in general laughter and comments]].

David: What I was going on to say is that somehow the group would be loose, in the sense that—in a curious way there would be little engagement between people. And it seems to me that this metaphor points that out, because the engagement is with the cloud out there, and almost like you are looking up at that. And although you are all throwing into it, and things are echoing through it and so on back to you, the actual degree of kind of taking hold of each other, you know, across the group, is sort of—to the extent that it does that, it is ceasing to be, this, this kind of . . . I mean, I don't even know that I like the sound of a Kellian group [some laughter. **Frances:** That's why they never lasted.] Yes. I am very sort of, you know—I have just realized that all the hundreds of groups I have been in as some sort of construct theorist, I have never actually said to myself: All right, what the hell is the group going to be like if it tried to be reflexive, and tried to apply the theory to itself?

George: And, surely, what Henry is trying to do, if I got it right, is make some sort of explanation of what the hell that is up there.

Frances: I keep seeing Kelly's Cheshire grin up there, [laughter] as he looks down on you.

Henry: I am—I was lost from where you . . . [**David:** We have to have a picture of Kelly.]

Mary: No, no; it is just the grin in the air.

Frances: Just the grin and the glasses.

David: Yes, the cat's gone.

Paul: It will slowly fade . . .

Henry: I am feeling a bit lost and bewildered ever since you [Paul] came back at me, and I am not sure what that was about. I mean you sort of came back quite sort of strongly, and I would like to know what that's about.

Paul: Well I..

Mary: Isn't it another dyad again?

Frances: Yes.

Paul: Well yes, I don't want to get locked into that dyad, once again. I was trying to answer David's question. But I did it illustratively, by referring to the quite, er, powerful interchange that occurred earlier on, at the beginning of the discussion about what's happening in this group.

Frances: Is it to do—I am still trying to understand this notion of what's up there (apart from Kelly's grin)—that you see the group as attempting to form a construct about what we are about. And so people throw in their own experimental notions about what that construct seems to be. And part of it is right, and someone else comes in with another bit, and when—in the end you form some sort of central notion [**Louis:** No.] contributed to by all the . . . Sort of a commonality construct?

Louis: I don't—it's—I mean, the more I talk about it, the more rubbish it is going to become actually. [some laughter] But what it seems to me is that everybody stays true to their own experiment, stays basically interested in making sense of it to themselves. And in doing so, it does have a sort of encounter, you know. People really do talk out of their gut about the things. And because they are in the same room at the same time and listening to each other, they relate. But there isn't any attempt to produce a consensus. [Frances: No.] There is an attempt to pool experience, or pool related experience; that is, in such a way as each person is sort of creating their own pattern.

Frances: I see a common pool, actually. You don't each throw up your little bit. There is an attempt to relate your bit to other people's. Isn't it?

Sam: There is an attempt to subsume other people's constructs and so to [Frances: And so form commonality?] construe them. Not just to be them, but to make sense of them. And as that evolves, it seems like commonality will tend to evolve along with that. Not fully and totally, but there will be some commonality, because as we attempt to construe each other's constructions we tend to construe more similarly. At least we are construing more similarly if we are construing the same thing.

Louis: Well, also real differences are recognized, but don't get in the way. [Frances: Um. Sam: Ya.] So that it doesn't continuously move toward commonality. [Sam: More liable to commonality . . .] I think what—the throwing is almost literal. I think you let the stuff into the group; but you don't retain it, it is not yours anymore. It becomes public in a real sense, in that you are not worried what other people do with it.

Frances: Ah. Well, I don't agree with you there. It depends how superordinate it is; [Henry: No, I don't either.] it depends how superordinate it is for you. I think that you can be concerned with what other people do with it.

Louis: Yes, I am trying. It is difficult. I am—they are concerned with it for you; but if they can use it in another way, [George: That's fine.] it's fine. And if it contributes, if the use they make of it is not what you make of it, that is still a useful resource then to the group.

George: Well, it could equally be threatening. It depends if it is a very core construct to you. If someone, then, uses it in a way that makes you feel as if you are going to have to change it—I mean, that is . . . [**Mary:** Yes.]

Sam: Or a way which contradicts it, too. I mean . . . [**Mary:** You learn, because no longer does it reflect back on you.]

Louis: But also, I think, you can opt out. [**Mary:** You can always let go of it. **George:** Can you let go of something like a core construct?] I think one of the most important characteristics is this business of not having to listen part of the time, or always sort of moving in and out as it becomes . . . I would not say this is a Kelly group at all, just that it is one way of operating.

Sam: I think there is a way in which, even though we do put something out publicly, we still, we still hold a certain attachment to it, in speaking of it metaphorically in the sense of the way we were talking about what Kelly meant by hostility, and how upset we were that Wiggins, or whatever it was, [**Louis:** Right.] came along and totally changed that around. And in a sense we are taking Kelly's role, and saying: No, no; that's not what I meant; you are really doing a disservice to my construct to look at it that way. [**Louis:** Right, right.] Certainly if you want to look at it that way, okay; but that's not my—that's not what I said any more, because I think we just totally just . . .

Louis: I am suggesting that if you do that you disown it. It isn't your construct any more [**Frances:** Um. Several people talk at once]

Henry: You seem to be separating two things and saying that, um right—you are saying that there are certain things that sort of *impede* the group development, that are separate from the development itself.

Louis: The group does not develop. No, that's not true actually. [several people talk] No, I am going to give it up. [laughter and several people talking]

David: I think it might become clear if we could like take it to its extreme [inaudible], Louis. But I was trying to think of, like, taking the sort of notions that we are playing around with: like kind of looseness, engagement, throwing into a pool, staying with the notion that both Jean and you put forward, that a group is about an experiment. But there are, kind of, experiments within experiments, aren't there? Your experiment doesn't have to be the same as my experiment; even though, if you like, the design is allowing both our experiments to proceed. If we took that right to its extreme, I was trying to think—I had actually got to a totally silent group, which was actually quite [inaudible]. Suppose you had, I don't know, six people sitting round, and they all lean back and look at the ceiling—and somehow that seems essential [laughter]—and kind of, as things drift through their minds, they speak them out. Now, in a way they may occasionally hear what somebody else is saying, because they are, or maybe not, throwing things out and occasionally hearing bits of what someone else is saying. But you *are not* pushing to extreme, you are not making any attempt to connect up. That is, you are saying that, if somehow a connection had been made—that is, if what I am now saying is somehow bounced off, inside me, that's fine. What I am not going to do is *engage* the other person with the connection.

Jean: But, you know—but we have all done that. We did it when we were about 3. Because it is exactly the description of 3-year-olds playing together.

David: Ah, ha.

Jean: Which is called—what do they call it—a collective monologue.

Paul: It is not unlike a Quaker meeting as well. [several people talk at once]

Henry: It is still a group. You can't say that it is not a group.

Frances: But when we attempt to construe that . . .

David: Oh no—but I—alright, I am intrigued by what you have just said. Maybe the answer is that 3-year-olds actually have figured out what a Kellian group . . . [general laughter]

George: On that note we have to have lunch.

PETER'S REFLECTIONS

You have now read the transcript. I hope that you have read it several times over. The repeated exercise should have underlined one of the basic propositions of personal construct psychology: there is no one way of

construing, even a part of, the world. There is no "correct" way of reading or interpreting the transcript.

The transcript could be analyzed as a historical document. It contains information about the ideas, at a particular point in time, of several
of the best-known personal construct psychologists. It could be treated
sociologically—for example, as a piece of the discourse of social science.
We might be interested in how social scientists talk to one another. Because the transcript is of a group discussion, the dynamics of interaction
between its members could be analyzed. From the perspective of personal
construct psychology, a more reflexive approach would be suggested:
How does a group of personal construct psychologists, as a group, reflect
upon the notion of *group* in terms of personal construct psychology?

You may read the transcript as you will. But there is one reading, at
least, that I would contest. It is not legitimate to treat the transcript as a
test of whether personal construct psychology, or a group of personal
construct psychologists, can provide a satisfactory, or definitive, rationale
of the concept *group*. This is an important disavowal because it has been
argued in the past that personal construct psychology is irredeemably individualistic. The proponents of that argument might wish to leap on the
transcript as evidence of their case: A group of personal construct psychologists is palpably incapable of producing a definition of the concept
group in terms of personal construct psychology. The reflexivity of the
failure makes it all the more damaging.

As a matter of record, it was quite simply not the goal of the
Lakeland group to produce anything approaching a definition of the personal construct psychology concept of "group." At the beginning of the
transcript David makes it clear that the participants are being *invited*
(not challenged) to think about what a Kellian group would be like.
Their endeavors are experimental, a form of inquiry, but they are not
designed to confront compelling ideas or to resolve conceptual issues
once and for all.

Frances rejects a more personalized version of the group as its own
test bed: "Kelly is not sitting up there construing this group." Not only
does the group not have to satisfy our external, idealized version of what
a personal construct psychology group ought, in its own terms, to be able
to achieve, but it does not have to measure its activities against its perception of what the author of the theory might have thought. There is no
question of trying to "satisfy" Kelly. He is, anyway, a Cheshire cat. He
is a continually elusive topic of discussion for the group, rather than de-

fining it through his ideas. If he is observing the group from "up there," it is with a sardonic grin.

The Lakeland group rejects the self-conscious, precious idea that they are, or could be, the epitome of a personal construct psychology group. Nor do they see themselves as typical, or a model for, everyday groups. More simply, they are a personal construct psychology group if each of the members is construing in terms of personal construct psychology; that is, if the members are consciously interrogative, experimenting, reflexive, creative, constructive, self-determining, and actively choosing.

As reader of the transcript, you can direct your attention both to the historical group—the psychologists who happened to meet in the early 1980s in the Lake District—and to the concept of *group* that they worried. In either case, it is possible to see the group as an "ideal" Kellian group (historically, it may not have been ideal, but it was certainly representative in an unusual way); or as a typical group, explicated in Kellian terms (reflexively, for the historical group); or as a particular group, the activities of which are interpreted in terms of personal construct psychology. As a reader of the transcript, I feel the third of these interpretations is the only one that is consistent with the viewpoint of the group members themselves, though that does not make it decisive.

The actors in the transcript clearly have problems with the concept of group and with the role of individuals in a group. (Are the terms *individual* and *collective* perhaps less problematic for psychology than *group* or *relations*?) David, whose involvement with personal construct psychology had been longer and more extensive than that of any of the participants, says more than once that he has never "applied Kelly to the group." None of the participants gives the impression of ever having been reflectively involved in a group as a personal construct psychologist. Henry even goes so far as to say that personal construct psychology is deficient in its failure to provide a rationale for group processes. Louis denies that the present group could be seen as a personal construct psychology group. Does some of the difficulty come from the familiarity of a number of the discussants with therapeutic groups, which are at the service of individuals?

The opposition between group and individual arises, inevitably, at several points in the discussion. Individuals are seen at one point as being the potential enemy of the group: They can choose to "kill" the group's experiment. In an open and creative atmosphere, one individual can, by veto or noncollaboration, frustrate the goals of a group.

Louis, who was inclined to opt out of a part of the Lakeland group's proceedings, at one point proposes the group as a resource for individuals. The group is reduced to a means for supplying the purposes of individuals. Henry is pleased at the prospect of becoming "bigger as a result of being with this group."

While Jean accepts that a Kellian group would basically engage in experiments (that is, rather than try to produce definitive resolutions), she cannot see how they might avoid being narcissistic and coincidental—the experiments of individuals who happen to be thrust together for a while. Toward the end of the transcript she produces the arresting, but depressing, metaphor of group activity as a collective monologue, 3-year-olds playing together.

But these rather negative or instrumental views of the group are also actively counteracted in the discussion. Both David and Arthur see the group as a particular means of encouraging successively loose and tight construing. Their expression of this notion places the emphasis not on advantages that might accrue to the individuals involved, but on the value of the process as such.

David and Paul propose a group as a set of constructs rather than as its members. That is to say, a group is composed of the totality of constructs of its members rather than of the individuals in the group. The construals of individuals, or of dyads, are at a fundamentally different level than those of the group as such.

This attempt to define group in terms of constructs is backed up in two ways: by exclusion and metaphorically. In the first case, David insists that a group seen through personal construct psychology would not be an encounter group or a committee, or anything in between. In the second case, Paul and Louis, between them, produce the notion of a group as a cloud of constructs, exuded into a space that is independent of the actual members of the group. There may have been interpersonal engagement that led to the constructs, but the constructs, as an expression of that engagement, can proceed independently. The group has a silent existence of its own, as a summary of everything that preceded. The group exists by virtue of being construed as a group—reflexively or by others; it is not a collection or sum of individuals, individually construed.

Consensus or commonality between individual members of the group is thus irrelevant to the possibility of group construal. A pooling of individuals' repertory grids can reveal any similarity or commonality in their constructs, but it cannot give more than a one-dimensional view of those individuals as a group. (However grid-ridden much of personal construct psychology may have been, the transcript shows how unnecessary that was.) Groups are neither necessary nor sufficient for the emergence of collectively shared constructs, though, of course, in practice we would expect group members to have constructs in common. But as soon as we focus on or compare individual members of a group, we are making them superordinate to the group. Much of the discussion in the Lake District was attempting to articulate a viewpoint in which individuals and groups coexist, without being reduced to one another, as different levels of analysis.

For that reason, the discussion showed remarkably little interest in group dynamics. David takes pains to stress the lack of engagement he would expect in a Kellian group. When Henry, who preemptively at the beginning of the transcript had dismissed the value of a construct theoretical approach to group process, later tries to reduce group process to (sets of) dyadic interaction, he is firmly rebutted. Louis suggests that group dynamics are not the concern of the group, as such. It may take time out now and then to discuss and resolve issues of individuals' interaction with one another, but at such moments it is not concerned with itself *as a group*.

LAURIE'S REFLECTIONS

On first reading the transcript I felt deflated. It did not seem to offer the rich search for the meaning of a "Kelly group" that I felt had taken place in the Lake District. However, on rereading it a number of times, I found myself reconstructing the original experience and developing and systematizing certain themes and ideas.

I started with the idea that I could literally cut up a photocopy of the transcript into small items, which could then be categorized to yield elements and constructs. This idea of a group grid was rapidly revealed as impossibly naive, as was the idea that the transcript could yield individual grids that overlapped in various ways. While it is quite fruitful to construe a group as a set of overlapping construct systems, the transcript, and even the totality of the original activity, does not contain the evidence needed to describe the group in this way. This would require much more time and more powerful and systematic methods (Thomas & Harri-Augstein, 1985; Harri-Augstein & Thomas, 1991). Approaching a group in this way can easily fall into an error analogous to trying to capture the beauty of butterflies in flight by killing them and pinning them out artistically on a board. What the iterative sorting of the items from the transcript did was to enable me to identify a number of themes, topics, and processes. The themes and topics formed the content of the group activity. The processes revealed how the group and the members were going about constructing and pursuing this activity.

I was fascinated to see how a group of people thoroughly involved in personal construct psychology (PCP) would together construe a Kellian group and how they would go about this group activity. How reflective would they be? Would the group be and act as they felt a Kellian group would be and act?

My conclusions are "yes" and "no." By and large the group's ideas about a Kellian view of group activity illuminated my reflections of how the group went about its activity, but there were and are a lot of loose ends. However, at a metalevel the PCP approach was shown to both encompass and distill aspects of group activity not often confronted. This was done without excluding or seriously inhibiting other constructions of group activity.

My construing of the group is not strictly a function of the sequence of events in the transcript. I was obviously running a number of parallel themes simultaneously. The patterns of meaning that I brought to each theme and that I developed during and after the activity were greater than and different from everything that was said. Some of what was said I recognized, but had not incorporated into the patterns of meaning I retrospectively valued and upon which I worked. Rereading the transcript raised my awareness of this selectivity and led me to reflect constructively upon it.

My reconstruing and reflection could currently be in terms of seven themes.

1. *George Kelly is Watching*. An overall impression is that the group and its members were monitoring its activity from a general, but quite well-articulated point of view. This is captured by the metaphors of the grin of the Cheshire cat, George Kelly as Cheshire cat, Kelly sitting up there construing the group, the cloud, the resource, and the Kelly picture.

2. *The Inquiring Group*. There is a strong, but rather nebulous, feeling never fully expressed of the group as a living entity that is seeking meaning. This is more than merely the aggregate of a set of inquiring men and women. Having felt the group as more than the sum of its

parts, one can identify certain self-organized group processes that articulate it and give it a living structure. "Anything" can be suggested and tried out so long as the group accepts or at least tolerates it.

3. *The Group as a Shared Construction.* Another overall idea is of the group as a construction or set of constructs. Within this general idea were three related but separate constructions:

   (a) The group is a set of common or shared constructs.

   (b) The group is transient, being depicted in certain superordinate constructs that are unique and specific to that set of people, concerned with that realm of discourse, in that time and place.

   (c) The group is itself a process of change and development: It lives so long as ideas, perceptions, and feelings are negotiated, reconstructed, and reformulated. This adds to and goes beyond the PCP sociality corollary.

4. *The Idea of Group as a Multifaceted Resource or Cloud in the Air.* Yet another metaphor implied that the group was something separate from and larger than its individual members. This was the notion that comments were not information exchanges between members; rather they were contributions to a resource or "cloud" up in the air. Members could select from this cloud and construct and reconstruct their own meanings (thoughts, perceptions, and feelings). They seemed to share a metaphor that implied that by contributing in the group the member "part-clones off things" from their individual resource of personal meaning, which thereby becomes public property. They part-clone it because the original personal meaning is larger and different and remains their own property. This group property itself can be part-cloned off by any individual and reconstructed to become incorporated into their personal individual meaning; from whence it may again be part-cloned into the group resource. There is a freedom in this metaphor that is different from many descriptions of group process.

5. *The Group as Arena for Experiment.* A theme that relates to theme 2 (the idea of an inquiring group) is that of the group as an arena for experimenting.

   There is a strong, ongoing theme that construes the group as both an opportunity for individual experiments and as a semicoherent entity that can propose and undertake experiments that are more complex than and different from these individual experiments.

So there are three aspects of experimenting:

(a) As an arena for individual experiments. These individual enterprises use the group as an arena for experimenting. The reactions of others are treated as evidence or results.

(b) As an arena for individual experiments in which the group is treated as an observer of the experiment. Others' comments are treated as alternative views or evaluative commentaries.

(c) Group experiments are different. They are explicitly negotiated and participated in to produce evidence or results. Then as a separate, additional process, the group reflects on what it has learned from the experiment.

6. *The Group as a Pattern of Processes in Time.* There is an ongoing commentary by the group on its own processes and on the processes members would expect to find in Kellian groups. These processes can be clustered under three headings. First, there are comments concerned with what are we doing. These can be variously seen as identifying the topic of concern to the group, i.e., as indicating a realm of discourse; formulating a purpose for the group to pursue, i.e., as giving the group a directionality or intentionality that may even be formulated as a task or related set of tasks; and seeing the need for an agenda, or to identify a hidden agenda. This may imply separate topics to be taken in an agreed order or priority.

Then there is discussion of the terms on which individual members take part in the group. Again this activity is varied, but it includes expecting to be able to opt out for certain periods without disrupting the group process: contribute what one chooses when one chooses; attend but stay silent; offer commentary, evaluation, and feedback; and experiment in an exploratory and tentative manner.

Finally, there is negotiation of the rules of group activity. This activity is quite varied, but it takes the form of questions or suggestions such as: What kind of a group is this? What is relevant? What can or cannot be said? and What can be done?

7. *Construings That Lie Outside the PCP Paradigm.* Some contributions seem to be formulated in terms that lie outside of personal construct theory. This does not mean that the themes, topics, and processes are unacceptable within a Kellian group. Quite the contrary, any topic is acceptable; however, there are certain ways of construing these topics, and languages for discussing them, that appear to run counter to the

PCP approach. Some of them are: family, relatives, and visitors; role structure and leadership; group dynamics—dyads, etc.; crabs and crustaceans; and people "relating" one to another.

MOONFLEET BAY

In the absence of space to reproduce here a transcript of the Moonfleet discussion, any remarks on it will, necessarily, be more one-sided and less invitational than in the preceding two sections.

The meeting at Moonfleet was in no formal sense a follow-up to the workshop in the Lake District. It was simply a restaging of the original open-ended mission, with an overlapping, but not identical, cast. But one deliberate cross-reference was made. As explained in the introduction to this chapter, participants had been given two extracts from the Lake District transcript (one of which is that reproduced here) and were invited to devote a morning session to discussing them. We will restrict ourselves to just a few observations on that discussion—each of which reflects on its sheer difficulty.

There was considerable reluctance on the part of the original participants to engage with the transcript. The first 20% or so of the discussion was taken up by various forms of avoidance behavior. They seemed to be shy or nervous in front of the four newcomers—not in a general sense of course, because the Moonfleet workshop was already well underway—but as though they had suddenly been laid bare, from a most unflattering view. The original participants gave technical criticisms of the transcript, which seemed to mask feelings that it reproduced their thoughts quite inadequately. David, who had been possibly the most talkative in the Lake District, insisted that he could simply remember nothing of what had been enacted there, even with the script in front of him.

Implicit attempts to kill this experiment, recalling a similar piece of business in the Lake District group, were only fended off by three of the newcomers, together with one of the original participants who had made no contribution at all to the discussions as transcribed. (The fourth of the newcomers, by contrast, was and remained openly hostile to the whole exercise, feeling that a nonparticipant could not hope to construe the transcript.) Two of the newcomers became particularly energetic in pursuing their reflections on the transcript. They had clearly read it carefully and thoroughly and were able to make a wide range of interpretive remarks. They seemed much better able than other participants to construe for themselves a meaningful task that morning.

One particular way of avoiding the demands of what was intended to be (in part) a reflexive view of a group discussing the concept *group* was by referring to some of the original group dynamics, and in particular by engaging in self-justification when there had originally been a measure of disagreement or conflict. This ploy was doggedly followed by one participant and, in spite of an expressed lack of sympathy from the rest of the group, consumed a significant portion of the discussion.

The hoped-for hyperreflexivity was ultimately not achieved because of the emergent artificiality of the exercise. While in the Lake District there were no objections to an outsider (Jonathan Potter was uniquely not identified as a personal construct psychologist) tape-recording the workshop for his own purposes, at Moonfleet the initiative to have the transcript extracts discussed was seen as staged, outside the wishes or control of the group. Reflexivity was not allowed to occur spontaneously. Attempts to justify and rescue the faltering exercise halfway through, in terms that were external to the interests of the rest of the group, only made matters worse.

But let us end on a more positive note, by quoting David as the light dawns, some two thirds of the way through the Moonfleet discussion.

David: Yeah. I am wondering if we are being a bit unfair to the text or not. I mean, I hadn't noticed it—but in fact you can—I had got a bit, you are quite right, locked into just trying to look at the text, as if I was seeing it for the first time. And I know it is still sticking with the example, which you rightly pointed out is well explicated. But just reading on I find there is a lovely *resumption*. And what fascinates me is that it is almost like in a group. I started to wonder. This missing thing, of course, from any text is what all—what everybody was thinking about while they were not—while they were being silent, while they were not the bit in the text. And I think one of the sort of clues you get to that is the—that suddenly a dialogue is taken up again, as if there had been nothing in between, as it were. And looking at page [79], you suddenly get [. . .], there's a long discussion been going on about the Cheshire Cat grin of Kelly up there, and so on. And that goes on and on. And then suddenly—and Paul says "and it will slowly fade"—which is still talking about that—and then suddenly Henry comes in: "I am

feeling a bit lost and bewildered ever since you"—that's Paul—
"came back at me. I am not sure what that was about." You
sort of come back quite sort of strongly; and he is referring
back to that quite *strong* declaration earlier: "I would like to
know what that's about."

Paul: Well I, and two dots [laughter].

David: And then Mary comes in very nicely with this reflexive bit here:
"Isn't it another dyad again?" In other words, trying hard to
hook Paul into what he has been trying to escape from, which
is: "well yes, it is just like—it is not George and Henry, now it's
Paul and Henry." Or, Frances says "yes"—sort of, "I'll vote for
that." [laughter] Then Paul sort of realizes the danger, and says
"Well yes, I don't want to get *locked* into that dyad, once
again" and tries to pull it away: "I was trying to answer David's
question"—and so on. But what rather fascinates me is this
sort of—you could almost cut—I mean the sequence here is the
true chronological sequence. But one wonders if you couldn't
cut it up, and actually put the parts together so it would read
much more logically. That is, that the true discussion is actually
broken up and could be reassembled out of chronology into argument.

REFERENCES

Harri-Augstein, E. S., & Thomas, L. F. (1991). *Learning conversations.*
London: Routledge.

Neimeyer, R. A. (1985). Problems and prospects in personal construct
theory. In D. Bannister (Ed.), *Issues and approaches in personal construct theory* (pp. 143–172). London: Academic Press.

Potter, J. A. (1983). *Speaking and writing science: Issues in the analysis
of psychologists' discourse.* Unpublished PhD thesis, University of
York.

Potter, J. A. (1987). Reading repertoires: A preliminary study of some
techniques that scientists use to construct readings. *Science & Technology Studies, 5,* 112–121.

Potter, J. A. (1988). What is reflexive about discourse analysis?—The
case of reading readings. In S. Woolgar (Ed.), *Knowledge and*

reflexivity: New frontiers in the sociology of knowledge (pp. 37–52). London: Sage.

Stringer, P. (1985). You decide what your title is to be and (read) write to that title. In D. Bannister (Ed.), *Issues and approaches in personal construct theory*. London: Academic Press.

Stringer, P., & Bannister, D. (Eds.). (1979). *Constructs of sociality and individuality*. London: Academic Press.

Thomas, L. F., & Harri-Augstein, E. S. (1985). *Self-organized learning: Foundations of a conversational science for psychology*. London: Routledge.

CHAPTER 4

A Personal Construction of War in Yugoslavia:
Transition as a Way of Life

DUSAN STOJNOV

Psychology Dept,
University of Belgrade,
Belgrade,
Yugoslavia.
28th November, 1992

Dear Beverly,

Threats are not easy things to face, so I feel awkward writing to you in this way about threats. But when, like me, you live in a country that maybe exists or maybe doesn't, which is in the middle of a very bloody civil war and yet officially it is not, when you do not know if you are actually living in the biggest concentration camp since World War II or not—well, then, I'm afraid there are not many subjects left for me to share with you. All that remains is an ever-growing awareness that my neat little construct system, so carefully nurtured for the past 30 years, does such a poor job in the anticipation business that I must consider replacing it with a brand new one. I just have to get a little advice from you.

I was reading Rom Harré's *Social Being* the other day and it contains a very interesting chapter called "People in Groups." It is about possibly one of the most important philosophical issues in the theory of the social sciences: the metaphysics of the groups in which human beings associate. The controversy can be stated simply in the following way: Do groups of

human beings in interaction with one another have properties that are
different in any causally significant way from the aggregate of the properties of the individuals concerned and their interactions with each
other? Of course, possible answers can be grouped around two contrasting poles. On the one hand, extreme collectivism advocates the position
that each human being is wholly constituted as a social person by collective properties that are not of themselves made up of the properties of
individuals. On the other hand, extreme individualism holds that each
individual is wholly autonomous and could exist as a person totally independently of the collectives to which he or she belongs.

My attention was attracted to this chapter in particular because I see
before me politicians, reporters, and scientists attempting to explain the
war that is enveloping those people who used to live together in Yugoslavia. One obvious similarity in the way all of them construe this situation
is a very consistent inconsistency in using the individual or the social
realm in their explanations. Despite differences in the *content* of their
prognostications, in strikingly similar ways they begin with collective
properties, continue with individual ones, and finish on one side or the
other of this metaphysical division. Well, consistency was never a building block of successful politics, and I am painfully aware of that now, but
I was very surprised when I noticed the same controversy engaged in by
all those psychiatrists, psychologists, sociologists, and historians being
interviewed on TV, writing for the papers, or giving lectures at the universities.

What was not a surprise was to find that Harré suggests that both
extreme positions—collective and individual—fail to give complete and
useful accounts of the metaphysics of human groups. Either they deny
the autonomy or creativity inherent in the individual human being, or
they fail to appreciate that many of the important properties characteristic of fully developed and individuated persons are dependent upon
that person being part of a collective. It was interesting to see how he
further develops a range of possible (and hopefully superordinated) alternatives trying to resolve the failures and controversies of the opposing
extreme positions. Particularly striking was his elaboration of a general
theory of institutions, with two sorts of elements, social practices and
people. But with people as elements one must distinguish personal identity ("the individuality of a single human being") and social identity
("the person type or status occupied as of right and constitutively by that
person"). Although the text began to sound more familiar after using the
word elements, I was not so sure that I was following and understanding

clearly enough to pursue further reading. So I have turned my modest mental capacities to elucidating for myself the importance of the relationship of personal and social identity, which intuitively looked to me to be the key point for understanding the complicated metaphysical issue.

As you might have guessed, I haven't been able to resolve that little problem that has been bothering distinguished scientific minds for the last couple of centuries. However, at one point I remembered that sentence that our common favorite psychologist mentioned on the very opening page of his first chapter of the Old Testament for all PCPers: "Man might be better understood if he were viewed in the perspective of the centuries rather than in the flicker of passing moments" (Kelly, 1955, p. 3). Also a little later he wrote that "time provides the ultimate bond in all relationships" (p. 6).

So this was something to start with. If time provides the ultimate bond for all relationships, it certainly must provide at least a little bond for the relationship between the individual and the collective. And it certainly does. But what a bond it seemed in my imagination!

On page 7, Kelly said: "There are some parts of the universe which make a good deal of sense even when they are not viewed in the perspective of time. But there are other parts which make sense only when they are plotted along the time line. Life is one of the latter." And at that point I realized that a lot of the problems confronting individuals in my country at present can be construed as a clash of different time cycles plotted along the very same time line.

In his work on dissipative structures such as his book with Stengers *Order Out of Chaos*, Prigogine referred to the capacity of open systems to exhibit clear self-organizing tendencies that increase with their complexity. But if they face environmental turbulence that exceeds their assimilative capacities, they go into temporary cycles of disorganization, out of which emerges a structural transformation. If this transformed system successfully survives validational evaluation, it will then, through a transitional period of dissipation, accommodate the perturbing challenge and reorganize on a more subordinated level. I do not have to convince you of the strong similarities that exist between Prigogine's work and Kelly's ideal of dimensions of transition. Both have helped me to elaborate a personal construction of war in Yugoslavia more abstractly.

If we can apply the same constructions to the processes of collectives, such as nations, as we can to individuals, and if they show satisfactory levels of predictive validity demonstrating their viability, then where is the problem between the individual and the collective? In my humble opinion, it lies in the different time cycles reflecting the transitional periods for both persons and societies. So, if I am not capable of resolving a problem, might I add a little something to it?

Much has been said and written about dimensions of transitions in the PCP literature. For the sake of clarity and the airmail rates I will focus only on one of them—threat. We all know well enough the unpleasantness that accompanies the awareness that a major part of someone's construct system faces thorough and imminent revision. Stated in different terms, it means that someone has to change a large portion of, or indeed their entire, personal identity in a reasonably short time in order to accommodate events that occur outside their control and that so often trivialize and marginalize the precious long-term projects we refer to as our lives. This is not an easy task as every therapist, no matter what his or her psychological orientation, knows without doubt. The availability of a stable and structured self-identity permits continuous and coherent self-perception and self-evaluation in the face of the slow process of becoming, in the ever-changing flux of life events. Maintenance of someone's identity becomes as important as life itself because without it the individual would be incapable of proper functioning, risking loss of the very sense of reality. This is probably the reason why a good therapist can get a hundred bucks for a session. Helping a client cope with painful and threatening transitions in order to reconstrue their personal identities, ending successfully and reasonably quickly a transition which, through dissipation and through questioning a lot of the predictions and hypotheses we take for granted, leads to a new phase of life pregnant with meaning, not chaos.

So far, nothing new. But what if the transition doesn't get resolved in a reasonably short time? What if it goes on to become a way of life? That is exactly what happens when two transitional cycles, unmatched on a timeline, occur at one and the same time. The cycle of the individual and that for the nation or society are in opposition. I agree and I support the theses of the importance and existence of both personal and societal/social identities. But I also am forced to recognize their differing duration: If you cannot profitably view humanity in the flicker of the passing moments, even less can you nations. Their duration often lasts a couple of centuries (or even millenia) longer. So what happens to the individual when his or her nation faces a period of transition so comprehensive and brutal that it becomes amputated from the rest of the world and thus may avoid serving as a model for even more comprehensive transition and eventual reconstruction?

Well, this is exactly the topic of this letter to you. Looking at what is happening around me has made me construe and reflect on some of the threats and transitions among individuals induced by the longer lasting transitions of collectives. Actually, I think the major problem lies in the fact that the transition of a nation or society can last much longer than the average individual transition, and that it can occupy the greater part of an individual's life. In a way, a societal transition can also be constructed as a sort of individual transition, but the important difference is that it is mainly out of the control of the person and his or her therapist to influence the national leaders and politicians to reconstrue their superordinates. So, it seems that in times like these you have to accept the inevitability of living with a personal construct system with the lowest predictive capabilities possible. And this is what you get when you pyramid down this abstract and academic discussion: There are so many ifs. . . . . .

- If the war doesn't reach Belgrade, I will defend my PhD in December.[1]

- If our passports are still valid throughout Europe, I will try to get to the next EPCA (European Personal Construct Association) conference.

- If there is enough electricity with the oil embargo through the winter, maybe we should buy some extra food and freeze it for a rainy day.

- If the prime minister stays, there might not be so many cutbacks and my wife will not lose her job.

- But if the war comes, and Belgrade faces air attack, is it better to go to the cellar and stay put, or to try to run away to the countryside?

These are, believe it or not, minor dilemmas, although they can have drastic outcomes. If you make the wrong choice, you lose a great deal. Probably the best example is the guy next door, who carefully calculated that he could sell his two-room flat in the center of Belgrade for the same price he would have to pay for a five-room flat in the suburb. So the poor fellow arranges the deal, gets the money for his apartment, loads his family and literally everything he possesses into a big truck, and on the agreed date goes to a suburb to enter his large new flat. To his horror, he discovers that the owner had, just a couple of hours before, had to take in five members of his own family—Serbs from Bosnia who had just run

away from Sarajevo and had no place to stay—so he calls the whole deal
off. My friend returned to his original neighborhood, with his family out
on the street. He rushed back to his one old apartment only to find out
that the new owner had already moved in and had no intentions of can-
celling the deal and taking back his money. With more than 400,000
refugees from Sarajevo in Belgrade who came in the last couple of
months, his all-too-typical transition of finding a new home could last
the rest of his life.

Now, no matter how uncomfortable and overwhelming they feel, I
will try to show you some of the major dilemmas. These arise from a
clash of different or concurrent realities. The challenge they pose is to
decide who to believe and to determine which reality to accept as a more
probable one from the vast array of realities imposed by TV, newspapers,
radio, and word of mouth. Indeed, what is one supposed to do when
nailed down by several concurrent realities, all of which are in opposition
to one's own construing, and each and every one an ultimate threat?

You could say that any person in that sort of dilemma could try on
some of those realities for size, and check their predictive validity, i.e.,
their viability. But our person could face the same problem again. The
opportunity to check their validity does not lie on the individual's time
scale. To assess the value of different political options or directions offered to a nation or a country, one might have to wait more than a couple
of years, since nothing eventuates overnight. You do not have to distort
a negative validation outcome, but be totally open to it. And if, after 20
or even 40 years of steadfast belief and hard work you realize that you
have opted for the wrong alternative, life does not give you another
chance, enough time for a second try. This is what has happened to many
of the idealists who believed in Yugoslavia, who believed in communism
and intercultural marriages. A lot of them became hostile. Others accept
that it was all wrong from the beginning—and they are willing to reconstrue and start a life again with brand new beliefs, political orientations,
and choices—in their late eighties. But alas, you cannot turn the clock
back. So it all sounds very depressing. And what might be the best alternative?

The only thing I have come up with so far is refusing to live with
threat as a way of life. That is a sort of reconstruction, although it might
be regarded as a shift or a slot rattle as well. The idea is not to believe in
anything too predictable, anything optimistic, or anything good that can
help. It is better to live with the belief that everything bad is possible and
to begin to erect a new structure and construe things you had previously

met only in your nightmares. To accept that exhibitions in museums are not dedicated to famous painters, but instead to photographs of cities that do not exist any more. To watch headless bodies and eyeless heads scattered all over the newspapers and TV. To witness so many young people wandering around without arms or legs, with empty looks on their faces. To avoid reacting with a chill when you read that a couple of dozen newborn children in Banja Luka died because oxygen bottles did not arrive in time to save them. To accept that the crime rate is rapidly rising and that nobody is safe and sane any more. Even walking through the street can be a dangerous undertaking when guns start shooting from the pub next door. And to believe that this is all for your good, and that all that is said and done is the only possible choice.

At one time, I thought that I was misjudging politicians; maybe they are not all the same, maybe they differ in that there are good guys and bad guys—as everywhere. But, unfortunately, I was sitting next to one of the main leaders of the political opposition in Serbia, and he was supposed to be a good guy. I was trying to share some of my worries about destinies and the threats of individuals, ordinary people in this high-level international game. "People?" he said smiling graciously. "You know, people are just like cattle. You use a pitchfork and move them in one direction—and they go there obediently. When you need them to go to the other side, turn them and use the fork again. That is what you do with people. You just need a sharp fork and strong hands, and they will follow." I still do not know if he noticed any sign of my disappointment when I muttered, to myself more than to him, that I still prefer cattle theories to pitchfork theories. But I was sure that he knew somehow that he won't gain a new vote from me.

Well, I just cannot take this kind of frame of mind anymore. I simply am incapable of construing the sorts of things I've mentioned here as everyday affairs, and most especially the idea that this was the one and only alternative left for us. And I made a decision, a decision at a very high level of cognitive awareness, that *I want to be hostile*! Hostile in my beliefs that this is not the only alternative, that there must be another way; that there is enough sense and reason left in politicians and leaders to say that it is wrong; that we still value particular lives more than national interest; and that there are some people with similar construct systems to mine who share my idea of basic human principles, believing in trust and tolerance, people who do not accept the dangerous challenge of arranging different nationalities, ethnic groups, and religions into hierarchies. As Varela stated in Watzlawick's book *The Invented Reality*, the first consequence of constructivist epistemology is tolerance. I just cannot bypass the idea of construing the world (although my part of the world is not very significant or important to the rest of the world, it is the sole world in which I live) without a place for tolerance in it. Unfortunately, the system I cultivated so carefully for the last couple of decades could not offer me anything but hostility in the end.

So, as you have seen, dear Beverly, the only things I can share with you at the moment are my threats and my actively chosen hostility. If you can subsume my choice and agree, at least partly with me, it will help a little. If your attitudes differ, and you have some alternatives to offer, recommend them to me please, and I will start considering them immediately. As you see, time is a precious thing. I think I have to plan what I am going to do with the rest of my own lifetime very carefully.

Love,
Dusan

P.S. I just heard that the United Nations have decided to "close the sky" above the war zones in Yugoslavia—no flights will be permitted. I will be very interested to find out how they are going to explain this to the birds.

ENDNOTE

1. Dusan successfully defended his Ph.D. dissertation and subsequently wrote to Beverly on January 4, 1993: "I MADE IT! I AM A DOCTOR! IT IS NOT THE MOST IMPORTANT THING, BUT THE TURMOIL IS OVER! NO MORE EXAMS! NO MORE FEARS AND ANXIETIES! I HAVE SURVIVED!"

CHAPTER 5

The Egalitarian Outlook as the Underpinning of the Theory of Personal Constructs

WILLIAM G. WARREN

This chapter discusses two themes by way of exposing the social and psychosocial dimensions of Kelly's (1955) theory of personal constructs. It aims with this discussion to contribute to a refutation of the view that personal construct theory is only or merely a theory of the isolated individual.

The first theme addresses the extent to which both optimal psychological functioning and effective psychotherapy, as Kelly (1955, 1962/ 1979, 1963/1979) envisaged them, require and assume a particular social context. This context is one that is characterized by a high degree of freedom, by flexibility, and a tendency for members of that society to judge others as being of equal intrinsic worth to themselves and to display a nonexploitative attitude to other people and the world. This last context has been called a *democratic* context, and the mental outlook (or mentality or character structure) both emerging in that context and necessary for its continuance has been identified as the *democratic mentality* (Barbu, 1956, 1971) or, more generally, the *egalitarian* outlook.

The second theme arises from Sève's (1978) comment that every *psychology* is underpinned by a *philosophical anthropology*, a view of human nature. As it has developed as a domain of inquiry, philosophical anthropology is both descriptive and critical. Its significance is seen in the fact that Immanual Kant had made the question "What is Man?"[1] one of four fundamental questions of philosophy, a question that either invites an answer or is left implicitly answered in any attempt to state a comprehensive psychology. Of course, an answer to the question might well be that it has no definitive answer; yet such a response, which is a typical answer from the existentialist camp, remains an answer. Moreover, the answer to or the reframing of this fundamental question thrusts at the very essence of social life, and Kelly (1955) devotes some specific attention to it, just as his more general writing has implications for it.

Thus, the present discussion examines personal construct theory against these two themes to show the substantial social dimension of the theory. Such discussion aims to contribute directly to the main aim of the present volume and at the same time offers a useful integration of personal construct theory with other work in social theory and social psychology. In turn, this goes toward redressing the problem of integration that Neimeyer (1985) had highlighted, but without opting for an alliance with any particular school of psychology.

These two themes are taken in turn and drawn to several conclusions by way of completing the present discussion.

THEME ONE: THE EGALITARIAN OUTLOOK

Barbu (1956) examines the type of mental outlook that characterizes individuals living, respectively, under democracy, nazism, and communism. The context of his discussion is an attempt to build a common ground between psychology and sociology, a ground that would be fertile for an understanding of the democratic and totalitarian ways of life. He develops the thesis that democracy is a pattern of life characterized by flexibility and a sense of ease, totalitarianism by rigidity and stress.

His thesis is based in the belief that to properly understand democracy we must look not to the external, procedural apparatus such as elections, universal suffrage, fixed terms of office of rulers, and so forth. Rather, we should see democracy in terms of a frame of mind or mental outlook characterizing individuals who live in democratic societies.

Democracy promotes a democratic mentality that he characterizes in terms of four concepts, the four cardinal sociopsychological concepts of democracy: *individuality, the critical mind, objectivity*, and *leisure*. While he admits to some arbitrariness in the singling out of these four, he argues that these concepts have regularly been closely associated with the democratic evolution of civilization, and that they are borderline concepts between sociology and psychology.

Individuality refers to the capacity and the self-determination to shape and integrate experience. It suggests a uniqueness in that shaping and integrating. What is implied is a recognition of one's difference from others, despite the similarities with them, and the ability to recognize boundaries between self and other. In a totalitarian society, by contrast to a democratic one, individuality is discouraged in favor of a stress on sameness. Further, the insecurity and fear associated with the recognition of one's difference and aloneness issues in an instability within the personality and the development of a high need to integrate with the group. Fromm (1941) refers in this respect to a "fear of freedom" issuing in three defensive reactions of which *authoritarianism* is the most socially significant; the others are *automaton conformity* and *cynicism and destructiveness*

Critical-mindedness refers to the individual's capacity to take action based on personal judgment, after weighing propositions for him or her self. It relates to the dominance of the intellect, of reason—substantive or critical—as contrasted with decisions based on emotion. Critical-mindedness suggests that decisions are based on a habit of deliberation, on a concern for logic or noncontradiction, on free and open dialogue and discussion. By contrast, again, totalitarian society encourages adherence to doctrine, whatever the tortuous maneuvering required in an argument or attempt at dialogue. Here, criticalness can only be an internal criticism concerned with understanding the catechism; the doctrine or dogma as such remains beyond criticism.

As a feature of the democratic mind, objectivity is the process of looking at the world as it is, rather than how one would like it to be or how some doctrinal position says it is. The objective mind can balance points of view and try to put itself in the place of another. The objective attitude is the opposite of a mystical or magical attitude; it can tolerate ambiguity and uncertainty and is not driven to find final or ultimate answers. There is no inconsistency here with an existentialist position that might reject the idea of objectivity because what is involved is always an attempt. The essential otherness and ultimate unknowability of another is not in question. Objectivity, as here conceived, is thus distinguished from *objectivism*, which is a claim to some privileged position in relation to absolute knowledge or ultimate truth.

Finally, leisure refers to a sense of ease, of being able to do things without a mind to their usefulness or immediate practical outcome. Leisure is essential to the operation of critical-mindedness, which implies time, time free of pressures, to reflect and speculate. Freed periodically from the pressures of life, or operating in a social system characterized by an absence of pressure, the individual is able to see aspects of life that are obscured by the daily exigencies of life.

Barbu (1956) indicated a general view of the nature of the democratic outlook as follows:

> That type of personality is democratic which shows enough flexibility in its inner organization, in its attitudes, feelings, ideas and action, to understand other personalities as "others" and not as its own projections, to cooperate and to construct a way of life on the basis of free exchange of experience with others; that type of personality which is flexible and free enough to avoid its rigid integration with the culture-pattern of its own group. (p. 106)

He avoided the question of whether a democratic outlook creates the democratic pattern of culture and social life or whether that culture and life create the personality. His thesis is the more modest, descriptive one that the democratic way of life expresses itself in the personality type he has delineated.

Now, the democratic personality may be taken as expressing in the political realm part of the features of a more general type, the *egalitarian* type. Barbu (1956) himself indicated that a synonym for what he has in mind is the *liberal personality* (p. 106). He notes also how both his democratic personality and the liberal personality stand in opposition to what Adorno et al. (1950) called the *authoritarian personality*.

Egalitarianism can be considered in general terms as having a clear position with respect to how people are to be regarded and how they are to be treated. This is that others are to be regarded as equals, as having equal worth and value in their own right as fellow human beings. In respect of treatment, they are to be treated as one would treat oneself and expect to be treated. Alternatively, equality of regard might lead to unequal treatment of unequals. Thus, a notion of equality of opportunity arises under which those who need more are given more in order to overcome some individual or social disadvantage.

Historically, while the ancient Greeks discussed equality, egalitarianism has its origins in 17th-century thought. Both Hobbes (1651/1947) and Locke (1690/1960) accepted that people were naturally free and equal in respect of rights. They developed theories about political authority that showed how a claim to superior right—as in the case of a ruler or ruling group—might be justified. In the 18th century, a theory of human nature was added to the idea of equality of rights and freedom. This found expression in a number of thinkers, but Rousseau (1762/1916) was to give it force and Kant (1785/1940) a philosophical integrity, insisting that persons be treated as ends not means.

Contemporary egalitarianism is rooted in these ideas and the tradition they delineate. It is best thought of as an articulated, consistent set of interrelated ideas and principles that is summarized in terms of the two points noted above. First, the term egalitarian expresses a belief that each of us should regard others as having worth and rights equal to our own. Second, it implies that others should be treated in a fashion that respects that worth and those rights.

Thus, we have a twofold conceptualization of the egalitarian outlook. As a general social theory it is a normative position stressing equality of worth and regard, rights and freedom. As a psychological outlook it is characterized by flexibility and the features of the democratic mind offered by Barbu (1956). The last is clarified by contrast with the type of outlook described as the authoritarian personality (Adorno et al., 1950) or the closed mind (Rokeach, 1960).

Now, Kelly's (1955, 1963/1979) respect for the ideas of John Dewey supports the present thesis that personal construct theory has an implicit theory of an egalitarian outlook and a democratic society underpinning it. As Kelly (1955) noted, Dewey's "philosophy and psychology can be read between many of the lines of the psychology of personal constructs" (p. 154).

Dewey (1916/1966) had no doubt that democracy was the ideal form of social organization, democracy conceived in terms that are analogous to our earlier characterization. Dewey (1916/1966) saw democracy in the existence and acceptance of more numerous and varied points of shared interest within a wide range of different interests. He stressed freer social interaction and continuous change and suggested that democracy is more than a form of government, "it is primarily a mode of associated living, of conjoint communicated experience" (p. 87).

Beyond this circumstantial evidence, Kelly (1955) himself identified the origins of his image of the person in the "democratic political inventions of the eighteenth and nineteenth centuries" (p. 4). Further, in a discussion of communal living, he distanced personal construct theory—or at least its vision of personal integrity—from that "group acculturation" that characterizes an extreme nationalism or that leads to a blind loyalty to a doctrine, as opposed to loyalty to facts and to humanity (p. 1175). Again, in a more directly political observation, he was critical of what he saw as the closed-mindedness of the then Soviet Union, characterizing it by analogy to a disturbed person, as a "disturbed nation."

Elsewhere it has been argued (Warren, 1992) that the idea of optimal psychological functioning or mental health, as discussed in personal construct theory, requires a social context being described here as democratic or egalitarian. That is, in order for the type of balanced or perspectival construing (Landfield, 1980) that enables optimal functioning to occur, or mental health to be instanced, an open society is essential. In totalitarian society, meanings are fixed and categories hardened, not by the individual but by the system.

In the authoritarian outlook, preemption reigns. The cycle of circumspection-preemption-control (the CPC cycle) in which the person first considers a range of possible options, then narrows the options to a single dichotomous option before choosing a pole of that dichotomy, proceeds in a distorted fashion. In this last society, there is no, or a very limited, multidimensionality in the initial consideration of a situation and there is a drivenness about limiting the already narrow range of options. As Kelly (1955) noted:

> The preemption of issues characterizes "the man of action." He is likely to see things in what may appear to his associates to be an oversimplified manner. He consolidates all the possible perspectives in terms of one dichotomous issue and then makes his choice between the only two alternatives he allows himself to perceive. Yet, because he tends to do this in times of emergency, he may, on such occasions, be accepted by his associates as a leader. (p. 516)

The interesting relation of "leaders" and "men of action" to historical totalitarian regimes like nazism aside, there is an indication here of a distorted CPC cycle in social organization that is not democratic. If impulsivity is defined as a characteristic foreshortening of the CPC cycle (Kelly, 1955, p. 526), then construing in totalitarian society can perhaps be seen as an impulsivity to close on an acceptable construction, that is, acceptable to the ruling or dominant ideology.

Again, a second cycle emphasized by Kelly (1955), the creativity cycle, also implies that degree of encouragement and flexibility that will exist in democratic society. The creativity cycle starts with loosened construction and ends with tightened and validated construction. If this cycle is in evidence, then the individual is seen to be actively engaged in developing new ideas—new constructs and new elements that are not tightly related to existing constructs or elements. He or she is able to pose unusual, possibly preposterous, solutions to old problems to challenge traditional thinking. However, in totalitarian society, the tightening of constructs will not be relinquished in this cycle. The individual will not be encouraged to move beyond the most rigid assignment of elements within a limited construct system and tightening will proceed in the absence of, or with minimal, validation.

In each case, the foreshortening of the CPC cycle and the premature and relatively fixed tightening in the creativity cycle lead to an opposite outlook to that being offered here as an egalitarian outlook. Indeed, this relation between optimal functioning and egalitarian outlook has been noted by others. Epting and Amerikaner (1980), for example, draw attention to the significance of Frenkel-Brunswick's (1949) concept, intolerance of ambiguity, in relation to that style of construing that is literalism, which they see as disrupting optimal functioning. Again, there is a similarity between the type of construing operating in nonoptimally functioning individuals and that going on in the type identified by Adorno et al. (1950) as the authoritarian personality. Finally, we might note Kelly's (1962/1979) observation of "the personal construct as a dimension of freedom in human interaction" (p. 198); that is, a freedom *to*.

Thus, it can be argued that personal construct theory is based on a position that to be fully operational as a scientist there must be no restriction on the individual in terms of the range and nature of constructs employed. Moreover, for the individual to function optimally, there must be no impediment to the full operation and repetition of the CPC and creativity cycles. That is, there must be both a freedom *from* and a freedom *to*. This implies a democratic social organization and an egalitarian outlook as here conceived. Moreover, as Rychlak (1991) noted, the cultural milieu does not merely have an impact on the individual who is somehow its receptacle. Rather, as Kelly (1955) argued, the individual is an active participant in what is a two-way relation that is culture and society making:

> Personal construct theory [understands] cultural similarity, not only in terms of personal outlook rather than in terms of the impingement of social stimuli, but also in terms of what the individual anticipates others will do, and in turn, what he thinks they are expecting him to do. . . . People belong to the same cultural group, not merely because they behave alike, nor because they expect the same things from others, but especially because they construe their experience in the same way. (p. 93)

THEME TWO: PSYCHOLOGY AND ITS IMAGE OF HUMAN NATURE

Philosophical anthropology derives from Kant's question "What is Man?" This question is concerned with issues of capacity or essence, perhaps with some concept of an ultimate human nature. It contrasts with sociology, which is concerned with what humankind in groups actually *does.*

The notion that every psychology is underpinned by a philosophical anthropology was expressed most forcefully, if as a criticism, in the context of a recognition of a shortcoming in Marxism; viz., that it lacked a psychology (Sève, 1978). That Marxism should be thought to need a psychology, indeed, that psychology could be important at all within Marxism, is already a controversial issue and one beyond present interests. The issue was well canvassed by Sève (1978), and a case is made that Marxism can and should develop a theory of the individual. His discussion raised the problem in the context of Marxism addressing a broad social level and issuing not in a speculative view of human nature, but in a scientific anthropology. He goes on to consider the relation of this to a theory of personality. In this discussion he observed that:

> albeit unconsciously, all psychology, even the most positivist looking, rests on a *philosophical* belief, belief in man, in the theoretical validity of the concept of man. Marx's fundamental discovery is that what exists, theoretically speaking, is not man but social relations. (Sève, 1978, p. 70)

Sève went on to attempt to rescue Marxism from the charges that it cannot have and does not need a psychology; as indicated, this is beyond our present purpose. What is of interest is the observation that every psychology is underpinned by a concept or image of man. Philosophical anthropology links the different sciences of human action (psychology, sociology, biology) and coordinates them through the prism that is philosophy as a critical enterprise. It seeks to address Kant's question directly, and insofar as it is a critical exercise—in addition to its analytic, synthetic, and speculative perspectives—it has disclosed a number of images.

Various concepts/images of man have been suggested since the early days of modern inquiry in this domain. Rawley (1966) elaborated those of the founder of modern philosophical anthropology, Max Scheler (1874–1928), who noted five such images: *Homo religiosus, Homo sapiens, Homo faber, Homo creator, Homo Dionysius. Homo religiosus* portrays us as creatures living in awe of a supernatural being who leaves us to work out our salvation from a sense of guilt; man is a sinful creature fallen from God's grace. *Homo sapiens* is the Greek image that stresses reason; we are above all else rational animals. *Homo faber* is the tool maker; that which differentiates us from other animals is our inventiveness in relation to making implements by which to operate on the environment—the most sophisticated instrument being language. *Homo creator* is the originator of meaning and values, responsible for the world we create. *Homo Dionysius* is the image of human beings driven by an impulse to live, to go with the flow of experience guided by nothing save an inner sense of having a limited life to squander in enjoyment.

There are other images beyond these, but the point is made in disclosing these classic ones. Whatever view we take of the individual will be underpinned by some such image of the species; we will have an explicit or implicit view of the nature of human persons, perhaps of human nature or essence.

Indeed, the failure to recognize underlying images led in the 1970s to attempts to disclose the manner in which psychology operated in terms of an image that reinforced the status quo. Brown (1973) and Brown, Galen, and Henley (1974), among others, drew attention to the manner in which psychology was not socially neutral. It constructed the female in terms of restrictive stereotypes; delineated normality and intelligence in a fashion that discriminated against certain social, ethnic, and racial groups; understood cure as adjustment to the given state of affairs, which may in fact be oppressive and corrupt; and was generally unquestioning and conservative. Psychiatry, too, came under a similar attack for similar reasons (Boyers and Orrill, 1971). Further, in other political regimes, psychology and psychiatry have been found equally malleable to different official positions (Lauterbach, 1984).

The status quo being supported in the West rested on an image of persons in psychology drawn from the dominant Liberal-Rational tradition; that is, an image of man the rational, a being motivated by rational self-interest who was to be left relatively alone to pursue his or her interests in as free an economic environment as was possible (Carroll, 1974). The assumption was that the interests being pursued would be primarily those of work or vocation in which qualities of "perseverance, energy, thoroughness, honesty, thrift, self-reliance, and common sense" would be to the fore (Carroll, 1974, p. 12). In the philosophy underpinning the other power block, the image was of man the malleable, a being who was always and only molded by external circumstances. This was drawn from the Marxist-Socialist tradition (Carroll, 1974).

The underlying image of persons in the social context best known to us is seen in the dominant psychologies, psychoanalysis and behaviorism. Psychoanalysis regards people as victims of instinctual forces to which the person is blind, and it treats the person as someone to be interpreted for, by another who has privileged information. Behaviorism regards the person as a machine to be treated by personal and environmental manipulation. Indeed, behaviorism proper, as a theory of mind, rejects the idea that there is any underlying human nature, any domain of mind at all. Yet, there is in behaviorist learning theory and in behavior therapy the implicit view of the nature of persons just indicated.

Psychology, then, either implicitly or explicitly works with an image of man, a view of human nature; at least all large-scale psychological theory does. If this is explicit, then it is open for scrutiny and debate, and its social and political consequences are able to be more easily examined. If it is hidden or implicit, then a particular psychology may function for a long time in a fashion that conserves particular etablished interests. The controversy over intelligence is a case in point (Kamin, 1974), though the realizations behind the development of radical psychology and antipsychology are equally instructive.

Even endeavors to derive a psychology from Marx's historical materialism, Marx's allegedly scientific, as contrasted with the then dominant philosophical, anthropology he attacked, will produce some vision of a collective: Man might give way to men, but an image of men remains to inform any psychology of this particular individual that might be derived from it. Such a psychology may reject abstract notions of a human essence and derive an understanding of the individual from a study of the real relations of social labor. Rather than, at present, the psychology of work being a special and advanced area of inquiry, a so-called applied psychology, psychology will start with the study of work. Yet, even in the elevation of this activity there is a statement that answers the anthropological question. Indeed, that Marx did in fact escape the influence of Hegel and did expound a genuinely nonspeculative concept of man is questionable (Bloch, 1983; Fromm, 1941).

Whatever the ultimate resolution of these last issues—and there are important matters for psychology in the discussion they open up—an articulated anthropology would seem to be preferable to an implicit one. Thus, a view of the social, in essence or in action would be exposed within psychology. Equally, the significance of interactionism, of all psychology being grounded in the social context as emphasized in the person-in-situation perspective, would be properly centered for psychology rather than being controversial (Carson, 1989; Pervin, 1985).

Now, in respect of this, the second theme concerning the image of man, personal construct theory is quite open; there is a clear concept of human nature in personal construct theory. Moreover, this is built on an optimistic view of humankind that contrasts with the pessimistic concept underlying the authoritarian outlook.

The statement of Kelly's (1955) theory began with an indication of its point of departure, its basic assumptions, which included a view of the person:

> When we speak of *man-the-scientist* we are speaking of all mankind and not merely a particular class of men who have publicly attained the stature of "scientists." We are speaking of all mankind in its scientist-like aspects, rather than all mankind in its biological aspects or all mankind in its appetitive aspects. Moreover, we are speaking of aspects of mankind rather than collections of men. Thus the notion of *man-the-scientist* is a particular abstraction of all mankind and not a concrete classification of particular men. (p. 4)

This observation demarcates a sociological from an anthropological perspective. It expresses a view about what mankind is like in some essential way, rather than about what this or that group of people are observed to do or how they collectively behave. It identifies a feature, a central and important feature, of humanness as contrasted with a particular characteristic of people. In elaborating this feature Kelly (1955) draws an analogy with the shift from a Catholic view of the relation of the person to God with the advent of a Protestant view. In this last shift, a view of a particular class of individuals serving as mediators of God's message to the world, viz., the priests, is challenged by a view of God mediating the message directly to all people via the Bible, which was open to all to understand. Analogously, *all* people have this inherent capacity to inquire, which is the essence of science; there is no privileged class of scientists. Where such a class comes to exist, science can come adrift from its origins in the day-to-day concerns of ordinary people to know something of their world. In this way, living science is separated from formal science, and the type of crisis discussed by Husserl (1954/1970) arises; science loses its moral dimension.

There is also an analogy to Freud's position here. The critical question for Freud was how a creature driven by aggressive and narcissistic impulses (a philosophical anthropological observation) could be expected to have a harmonious social life (a sociological issue). Marcuse (1955) reframed this problem by juxtaposing the two antagonistic concepts of *eros* and *civilization*, arguing that a freeing up of libidinal energy would not mean the collapse into barbarism that Freud feared. However, for personal construct theory there is no essential antagonism. The anthropological point that our essence lies in inquiry, in meaning making, does not conflict with the most harmonious social life, at least in an open society.

Yet, Kelly's (1955) concept of the person does not attempt to state a fixed human nature. Consistent with the broad tradition of thought that is existentialism, personal construct theory sees the self as a process of construction and reconstruction. The self is not a substance but a lived relationship. To borrow Shearson's (1980) terms, the human situation is one in which the individual strives endlessly for meaning, and construing is done in a fashion that most elaborates the individual's field in encounter with others. Elsewhere, Kelly (1963/1979) argued that without an important focus on psychotherapy within psychology, the nature of persons cannot be fully understood. It is the discussion of those extraordinary moments in a life that constitutes psychotherapy, when deeper insights into the nature of man are provided (Kelly 1963/1979, pp. 214–215).

Finally, we might return to the type of issues raised by Sève (1978) and ask an analogous question to the one he asked. That question was whether existentialism could provide a psychology for Marxism. He concluded that it could not. Elsewhere it has been suggested that as personal contruct theory was silent as to the origins of our constructs, it may offer a psychology for Marxism (Warren, 1985, p. 264). If this last suggestion is to prove fruitful, however, it will require a reading of Marx less inclined to the hard-line materialist and deterministic position and more inclined to the humanistic and voluntaristic, which allows a two-way interaction between the economic base and the superstructure. Whatever the resolution of this issue, to the extent that it is worth taking up, there is, again, a social dimension and an implication for thoroughgoing social analysis in personal construct theory.

CONCLUSIONS

At the outset, the discussion has suggested two conclusions. First, the psychology of personal constructs assumes a social life in which the egalitarian outlook is prevalent. In turn, optimal psychological functioning and the most efficacious operation of the important cycles of change ensure a continuing operation of a democratic way of life.

To conclude the contrary would be to ignore the manner in which individuals operate in and on the world. People seek to make sense of that world for themselves, despite efforts by others to make sense of it for them. It would also be to ignore the requirement that for optimal psychological functioning there must be in place a system of social relations and an underlying mentality that encourages flexibility, a sense of ease, and so forth.

There is in personal construct theory, then, and aside from its specific corollaries that deal with interpersonal interaction, a deep level of social concern and significance. A particular type of social situation and a particular type of outlook is both prerequisite for and kept alive by personal construct theory as a psychology of the inner outlook.

The second conclusion is more straightforward, namely, that personal construct psychology has an underpinning view of human nature. This is a view of the human person sharing more general characteristics of the species, the chief of which is the inescapable need to make meaning. The human animal is first and foremost a meaning-making animal. The social dimension is here addressed at an even deeper level. There is an ontological level of interest that says something about human beings as such. In this connection, personal construct theory is aligned with the grand schools of psychology, all of which have an explicit or implicit theory of human nature. In so far as this is true, there is again a focus on the level of interaction that constitutes the social. Thus, when one moves beyond the specific sociality and commonality corollaries, there is an even richer domain of reflection that takes us beyond, just as it situates, the individual.

Before closing the present discussion, there is another conclusion implicit in much of our discussion. This resides in a question, and in a corollary to it. The question is to ask whether we have instanced anywhere in the world the democratic type of society; the corollary is to ask how personal construct theory stands in relation to the sociocultural context in which it grew. Without a response to this question, personal construct theory might fail to meet the type of criticism raised by radical psychology against mainstream psychology as it had established itself in the Western democracies. It might be accused of serving to legitimate the status quo or the particular political system in which it was nurtured. In the case of personal construct psychology, this would mean legitimating the status quo of the United States of America and, then, perhaps of a special part of that country. The democracy that personal construct psychology implied would be argued to be merely a particular historical form of social organization labeled only by its supporters as democratic.

Indeed, Holland (1981) drew attention to the manner in which developers of personal construct theory have failed to notice the pervasiveness of ideologies and how personal construct theory has been caught up in a social-theoretical context. Yet, he distinguished what is done in the name of personal construct theory and what Kelly (1955) urged on us. The former may well reflect a particular orientation, but a return to Kelly (1955) discloses a reflexivity that encourages us to look beyond the theory, and thus beyond any particular social-political orientation.

Now, writings of the social critics in the post-World War II period draw attention to the impacts of advanced technology and the social-psychological context it creates. In such a context, a flight from thinking—from meditative thinking to mere calculative thinking—is observed (Heidegger, 1968). There is a concern that false needs are constructed and satisfied, such that real human needs go unmet, indeed unrecognized (Marcuse, 1964). More generally, there is a concern that the individual does not know what is going on and has to be awakened (Ellul, 1965). Moreover, this critique bites across ideological divides, indicting both the industrialized East and West.

It would be difficult to conclude there is an extant social system that encourages the egalitarian outlook that is argued here to be the underpinning of the theory of personal constructs. Equally, it would be unfair to conclude that personal construct theory was merely a product of a particular form of social organization and that the democracy it implied was the particular form of society in which it developed. That it was influenced by such a system must remain beyond question, but the reflexivity of the theory and its invitation to find it ultimately something we go beyond marks it as a critical enterprise in which we can "discover our capacities for radical reflection and social criticism" (Holland, 1981, p. 29).

Thus, as the theory of personal constructs is elaborated, so too is a more critical social position elaborated. Indeed, to conclude by returning to the two traditions of Western thought previously alluded to—Liberal-Rationalism and Marxist-Socialism (Carroll, 1974)—it can be suggested that egalitarianism and personal construct theory imply Carroll's (1974) third: *Anarcho-Psychologism*. The image here is of man the individual, and the nonrational aspects, the deeper, darker side of our nature, are highlighted. Carroll's (1974) exemplars of this tradition are Stirner, Nietszche, and Dostoevsky who, he argued, paved the way for Freud's work, for our interest in inner psychological man, and for existentialism. At the level of social life, the interest is in what we can learn about group life and from the perspective of the outsider, from the values and outlook of individualist types like the artist. This tradition mounts a powerful critique of the idea of objective knowledge, of the image of the person as *Homo economicus*, and of ideology.

Thus, the type of egalitarianism underpinning personal construct theory is exposed as bringing this theory well within the tradition that includes such different but related positions as existentialism, phenomenology, and anarchism. In these positions and in this tradition there is a fundamental social dimension underlying personal construct theory.

ENDNOTE

1. It is difficult to avoid the use of the term *man* when discussing anthropology, particularly when referring to historical figures; it is also convenient to use this word when alternatives read less well. Whatever term is used—Man, man, persons, individuals—it is used to include all human beings.

REFERENCES

Adorno, T. W., Frenkel-Brunswick, E., Levison, D. F., & Sanford, R. N. (1950). *The authoritarian personality*. New York: Harper and Row.

Barbu, Z. (1956). *Democracy and dictatorship: Their psychology and patterns of life*. London: Routledge and Kegan Paul.

Barbu, Z. (1971). *Society, culture and personality*. Oxford: Blackwell.

Bloch, M. (1983). *Marxism and anthropology*. Oxford: Oxford University Press.

Boyers, R., & Orrill, R. (1971). *Laing and anti-psychiatry*. Harmondsworth: Penguin.

Brown, P. (Ed.). (1973). *Radical psychology*. London: Tavistock.

Brown, P., Galen, M., & Henley, N. (Eds.). (1974). *The radical therapist*. Harmondsworth: Pelican.

Carroll, J. (1974). *Breakout from the Crystal Palace*. London: Routledge and Kegan Paul.

Carson, R. C. (1989). Personality. *Annual Review of Psychology, 40,* 227–248.

Dewey, J. (1966). *Democracy and education*. New York: The Free Press. (Original work published 1916).

Ellul, J. (1965). *The technological society* (J. Wilkinson, Trans.). London: Jonathan Cape. (Original work published 1954 in French).

Epting, F. R., & Amerikaner, M. (1980). Optimal functioning: A personal construct approach. In A. W. Landfield & L. M. Leitner (Eds.), *Personal construct psychology: Psychotherapy and personality* (pp. 53–73). New York: Wiley.

Frenkel-Brunswick, E. (1949). Intolerance of ambiguity as an emotional and perceptual personality variable. *Journal of Social Psychology*, *18*, 108–143.

Fromm, E. (1941). *Marx's concept of man*. New York: Frederick Unger.

Heidegger, M. (1968). *What is called thinking?* (F. D. Wieck and J. G. Gray Intro. and Trans.). New York: Harper and Row. (Original work published 1954 in German).

Hobbes, T. (1947). *Leviathan* (M. Oakshot, Ed.). Oxford: Blackwell. (Original work published 1651).

Holland, R. (1981). From perspective to reflexivity. In H. Bonarius, R. Holland, & S. Rosenberg (Eds.), *Personal construct psychology: Advances in theory and practice* (pp. 23–30). London: MacMillan Publishers.

Husserl, E. (1970). *The crisis in European sciences and transcendental phenomenology: An introduction to phenomenological philosophy*. (D. E. Carr, Trans.). Evanston, IL: Northwestern University Press. (Original work published 1954 in German).

Kamin, L. G. (1974). *The science and politics of I. Q.* New York: Wiley.

Kant, I. (1940). *Fundamental principles of a metaphysics of morals* (T. K. Abbott, Ed.). London: Longmans, Green. (Original work published 1785).

Kelly, G. A. (1955). *The psychology of personal constructs*. (Vols. 1 and 2) New York: W. W. Norton and Co.

Kelly, G. A. (1979). In whom confide: On whom depend for what? In B. Maher (Ed.), *Clinical psychology and personality: The selected papers of George Kelly* (pp. 189–206). Huntington, New York: Wiley. (Original work written in 1962).

Kelly, G. A. (1979). Psychotherapy and the nature of man. In B. Maher (Ed.), *Clinical psychology and personality: The selected papers of George Kelly* (pp. 207–215). Huntington, New York: Wiley. (Original work written in 1963).

Landfield, A. W. (1980). The person as perspectivist, literalist, and chaotic fragmentalist. In A. W. Landfield & L. M. Leitner (Eds.), *Personal construct psychology: *Psychotherapy and personality.* (pp. 289–320). New York: Wiley.

Lauterbach, W. (1984). *Soviet psychotherapy.* Oxford: Pergamon.

Locke, J. (1960). *Two treatises on government* (P. Laslett, Ed.). Cambridge: Cambridge University Press. (Original work published in 1690).

Marcuse, H. (1955). *Eros and civilization.* New York: Beacon Press.

Marcuse, H. (1964). *One-dimensional man.* London: Routledge and Kegan Paul.

Neimeyer, R. A. (1985). Problems and prospects in personal construct psychology. In D. Bannister (Ed.), *Issues and approaches in personal construct theory* (pp. 143–171). New York: Academic Press.

Pervin, L. A. (1985). Personality: Current controversies, issues, and directions. *Annual Review of Psychology, 36,* 83–114.

Rawley, E. W. (1966). *Scheler's phenomenology of community.* The Hague: Martinus Nijhoff.

Rokeach, M. (1960). *The open and closed mind.* New York: Basic Books.

Rousseau, J. J. (1916). *The social contract* (H. J. Tozer, Ed.). London: George Allen and Unwin. (Original work published 1762).

Rychlak, J. (1991). The missing links of artificial intelligence: Predication and opposition. *International Journal of Personal Construct Psychology, 4,* 241–249.

Sève, L. (1978). *Man in Marxist theory and the psychology of personality* (J. McGreal, Trans.). Hassocks, Sussex: Harvester. (Original work published in 1974 in French).

Shearson, W. W. (1980). *The notion of encounter.* Ottawa, Canada: Canadian Association for Publishing in Philosophy.

Warren, W. G. (1985). Personal construct psychology and contemporary philosophy: An examination of alignments. In D. Bannister (Ed.), *Issues and approaches in personal construct theory* (pp. 253–265). London: Academic Press.

Warren, W. G. (1992). Personal construct theory and mental health. *International Journal of Personal Construct Psychology, 5,* 223–238.

PART TWO

Applications of the Theory to Group Construing

INTRODUCTION

Part Two, "Applications of the theory to group construing," includes eight papers that apply personal construct theory (PCT) to learning about how groups share construals.

Kelly defined the range of convenience of his theory, the boundaries that the approach usefully addresses, most centrally to be "problems of interpersonal relationships" that arise because people participate in groups (Kelly, 1955, p. 11). Part Two opens with chapters on groups that have traditionally been considered part of the purview of PCT. In chapter 6, Robert A. Neimeyer, Donna L. Brooks, and Kurt D. Baker review psychological research of the last 20 years on why people form, develop, and maintain friendships. Then they describe their own research in which personal construct psychology contributes to a deeper understanding of these processes. Focusing on the effects that people have on one another in face-to-face contact, they define friendship as "a voluntary, typically reciprocal form of relating based on mutual preference" (see chapter 6). Providing situations for dyadic contacts, they have explored the types of constructs that develop among friends and have made some discoveries about the evolution of constructs, as well as about kinds of commonality. The study used the methodology of repertory grids to show connections among the functions, structures, and complexity of constructs in friendships.

In a chapter that has grown out of many years of research, Harry G. Procter presents a model for analyzing the the family construct system along whose streets and avenues members steer their actions. This model serves the therapist as well as the researcher interested in tracing the dynamics of family functioning. Procter has found PCT especially suited to exploring and understanding generosity, care, and thoughtfulness that are likely to characterize much of family life as well as the more highly publicized pathologies. On the basis of his work, Procter finds that it is

123

possible to revise and extend Kelly's choice corollary to account for the centrality of mutual concerns. This, in his view, is the basis of an ethical psychology that " . . . could fill the moral vacuum of society in its present state." His conclusion in chapter 7 suggests an interesting extension of the sociological conceptualization of the family as an agent of socialization.

Helen Ross applies personal construct psychology to elicit construals shared by a community. Her interest in personal construct psychology arose in connection with a central problem of Australian public policy— supplying appropriate housing to the indigenous Australians. In chapter 8, Ross describes how she adopted a personal construct approach to explore aboriginals' descriptions of their lifestyles and the significance of shelter for them. Here personal construct psychology was enlisted to enhance impressions she gathered as a participant observer in an aboriginal camp. In the one case, rep-grids and orthodox statistical tools were used to elicit constructs. In the second, Ross elicited narratives, which she content analyzed to examine underlying constructs. The paper leads to conclusions about the relative usefulness of each analytical strategy.

Specific educational environments are investigated by Kalekin-Fishman and De Bernardi. In chapter 9, Devorah Kalekin-Fishman assumes with personal construct psychology that all those involved in organizations are agents. She focuses on the children for whom, educators would probably say, schools are run. Examining how the school organization is construed by pupils, she analyzes their constructs as the key to the kinds of relationships children establish, the modes of action they adopt, and their evaluation of what goes on. Clearly, the degree to which pupils' construals clash or converge with those of teachers and administrators is crucial to how the school organization develops over time. The holistic approach to the construction of organizations has practical uses.

In chapter 10, Bianca De Bernardi examines the effects of school organization on teachers and on their construals. The test case is teachers' constructions of IQ, the theories that teachers use for judging their pupils. Analyses of lay theories of IQ have generally taken as their point of departure statistical tests of validity and reliability applied to the form and content of the tests, as well as to the testing procedures. Here, De Bernardi makes it clear that the issues cannot be resolved by these or by attributions of good or bad will. In her investigation of the constructs of groups of teachers who participated in in-service training courses in the north of Italy, she demonstrates that teachers' constructions of intelligence may have only a distant relationship to the standardized grasp of the construct. Teachers' judgments were based on personal modes of construing mediated by institutional constraints.

The last three papers in this section, those by Tooth, Denicolo, and Jankowicz, explore construals of professions in organizations of different kinds. The locales are England, Australia, and Poland.

The vicissitudes of socialization into the service professions are nicely captured in chapter 11 by Barbara Tooth, who investigated members of different mental health professions. While there are forces that seek to overcome professional differences by introducing a conception of the "generalist" mental health worker, groups that have undergone distinct types of training seem to become "more committed to establishing [their] uniqueness" and the uniqueness of their services. By exploring constructions of training and construals of professional-patient relationships, Tooth discovered that the mental health professionals are more alike than many of them realize. In her opinion, the field should be viewed as a "culture." On this basis, it will be possible to reframe definitions of the mental health professions.

In chapter 12, Pam Denicolo shows that the rep-grid is a useful tool in facilitating courses of staff development. The staff she describes were instructors in adult vocational education, teachers whose task is to prepare students for a world of work undergoing dynamic change. Course participants were called upon to adopt more flexible approaches to teaching and learning and to formulate new curricula and new types of course delivery. To these ends, the staff had to reorganize as a team. When the reorganization was impeded by unexpected difficulties, different forms of the repertory grid helped open the eyes of staff members to the sources of their difficulties and to the array of choices that were available to them. The investment of effort and expertise in compiling the grids, administering them, and clarifying respondents' intentions proved deeply rewarding in the long run. Solutions to some of the problems were found through systematic construing. Subsequently, when new problems arose, the teachers could use the grid effectively on their own.

In chapter 13, A. Devi Jankowicz introduces us to some unexpected differences in the interpretation of basic skills that today separate peoples far more effectively than does mere distance. Acquiring management efficiency is a major challenge for societies formerly governed by a communist regime and currently acting to gain entrance into the world market. In some of the countries of the former Eastern Bloc, programs have been instituted for acquiring the necessary knowledge. Yet, as Jankowicz discovered, the construction of what makes for efficiency, like the construal of knowledge and of teaching, is often quite different in Western and Eastern Europe. Jankowicz had first hand experience of the contradictions involved when he introduced Polish administrators to the knotty problems of management as understood in the United Kingdom. His own Polish background enabled him to grasp the diverse interpretations and intentions of Polish manager-candidates, even as he attempted to convey what many Westerners would assume to be objective principles of management. The epistemological dilemmas that resulted for the parties involved are presented.

Taken together, the studies included demonstrate both the diversity of approaches that can be used from a personal construct perspective, as well as a diversity of applications, of which those here are but a sample. We hope they may stimulate you to extend the range of convenience of the theory even further.

CHAPTER 6

Personal Epistemologies and Personal Relationships:
Consensual Validation and Impression Formation in the Acquaintance Process

ROBERT A. NEIMEYER, DONNA L. BROOKS, AND KURT D. BAKER

Why do people form friendships, and how are such relationships developed and maintained over time? Remarkably, despite the obvious centrality of friendship and other forms of intimate relationships in our lives, social psychology was relatively silent on such questions until quite recently. When questions about human relationships were addressed at all, they were typically limited to inquiries about correlates of attraction following an initial encounter with a real or fictitious other or to a search for the determinants of some static relational state, such as marital satisfaction. Such a focus is not so much incorrect as limited, especially in its ability to illuminate the essence and structure of our long- and short-term relationships with other people over time (Duck, 1986). This situation is rapidly changing, however, and psychology has begun to restore human relationships to the central position in research that they have long occupied in our lives.

In this chapter, we attempt to make a modest contribution to this effort. Working from our grounding in personal construct theory (Kelly, 1955/1991), we first review the results of a constructivist program of research into friendship formation that has spanned more than 20 years, beginning with the early work of Duck (1972) on personal constructs in the acquaintance process and progressing through our subsequent extensions of this model. Following this historical overview, we then present a recent study reflecting our current fascination with the subtleties of impression formation and attraction between pairs of prospective friends interacting across time. In view of the complexity of human relationships, we do not claim that the model we are espousing represents an exhaustive or comprehensive treatment of intimate relationships, although we believe this constructivist research program has proven productive in illuminating some critical dynamics of developing dyads.

DEFINITIONAL BEGINNING

So far, we have been using the terms *relationship* and *friendship* as if their meanings were self-evident, and to some extent this may be true. Certainly, all of us are participants in a living web of human interconnectedness, which joins us directly or indirectly with an indeterminately large number of others. But precisely because this relational field is so broad, including quite different kinds of relating, it may be helpful to be more precise about what we are and are not concerned with in this chapter.

Traditionally, social psychologists have considered two people to be in a relationship to the extent that they have impact on each other or are interdependent with each other such that a change in the state of one causes a change in the state of the other (Kelley, Berscheid, Christensen, Harvey, Huston, Levinger, McClintock, Peplau, & Peterson, 1983). In accepting this definition, we are adopting a focus on the processes entailed in encounters between pairs of individuals rather than within larger groupings such as social organizations, work groups, societies, or the like. Moreover, our definition of relationship implies some form of at least occasional face-to-face or other direct, bilateral communication between interactants (e.g., pen pals), excluding from the present discussion our relationship to God, the President of the United States, or a deceased loved one. But even with these definitional restrictions, the concept of relationship is quite broad, encompassing client/therapist, employer/employee, collegial, marital, familial, and many other kinds of dyads that vary in their frequency of contact, level of intimacy, reciprocity, and formality.

Within this broad field of relationships, friendship is distinguished by its being a voluntary, typically reciprocal form of relating based on mutual preference, with the goal of satisfying primarily socioemotional, rather than instrumental needs of the interactants. Although constrained in some respects by social norms and customs, it has been characterized as the least programmed or predefined of any important relationship (Suttles, 1970). For many reasons, understanding how individuals develop satisfying, affectively close relationships is an important area of study.

A CONSTRUCTIVIST THEORY OF FRIENDSHIP FORMATION

The cornerstone for a constructivist model of friendship formation was laid in Kelly's (1955/1991) basic theory of personal constructs. In keeping with his conceptualization of people as incipient scientists, he viewed individuals as constructing informal personal theories to render experience interpretable and, to some degree, predictable. But despite the individuality inherent in Kelly's position, he was equally careful to draw attention to the social embeddedness of our construing efforts. In fact, 2 of the basic 11 corollaries in his theory address the broader social field within which individuals negotiate in their "effort after meaning" (see chapter 1 for an extended discussion). In the commonality corollary, he stressed that the similarity of two individuals should be understood fundamentally as an expression of the similarity in their constructions of experience, rather than as a result of the similarity in the background events of their life per se (1955/1991, p. 63). This starting point for a social psychology was elaborated in Kelly's (1955/1991, p. 66 ff.) sociality corollary, which stressed that individuals establish a genuine role relationship with one another only to the extent that they attempt to construe one another's construction processes as the basis for their social interaction.

The social dimension of personal construct theory is expressed in another respect as well, namely, in its focus on construing interpersonal rather than impersonal events. As Kelly (1955/1991, p. 122) noted, "Among the kinds of events in the world which one seeks to anticipate optimally, people and their behaviors are particularly salient." Thus, much of our psychological effort is directed toward interpreting and predicting the outlooks and actions of others with whom we are involved in a social process. The constructions of others are also important because, as Kelly (1955/1991, p. 123) stated, "The expectancies which are common to [a] group actually operate as the validators against which the individual tends to verify the predictive efficiency of his system." Particularly in the case of social phenomena, the outcomes we use to validate our systems are so elusive that often the only evidence available consists of the opinions and expectations of others. Is a student who is failing a certain course best construed as lazy, stupid, rebellious, or depressed? Is this the way "normal" married couples interact? Which political party can do the most for the economy? Kelly (1955/1991, p. 123) noted that even the most concrete physical phenomena (e.g., the sphericity of the earth) are ordinarily not subject to direct validation by individuals, but instead are interpreted in ways that are consistent with the constructions of a community of observers. This emphasis on consensual validation as a primary criterion for the validation of knowledge characterizes many forms of constructivist psychology (Neimeyer, 1993).

Building upon Kelly's (1955/1991) foundation, Duck (1973b) constructed a preliminary model for the development of close relationships, with a special focus on friendship formation. In contrast to models of the acquaintance process that emphasized physical characteristics of interactants (e.g., attractiveness) or their circumstances (e.g., propinquity) as determinants of relationship development, Duck (1977) posited a process of "inquiry, hypothesis, and the quest for validation" as central to interpersonal attraction. Thus, while he acknowledged that situational factors might be responsible for the initial encounter of two people, he sought to understand the psychological processes by which two individuals filter the pool of prospective friends, deepening and extending certain relationships while winnowing out others.

For Duck (1973a), as for Kelly, people garner validation for their constructions largely through seeking support for them in a social context. Because people assess the validity of their interpretive systems by comparing them with those of others, Duck proposed that individuals are attracted to others whose constructs are similar to their own. Thus, on the basis of the sorts of relatively superficial information available to interactants about one another in an initial encounter (e.g., appearance, casual remarks), individuals hypothesize about the existence of deeper commonalities at the level of their personal construct systems. The discovery of such commonality at progressively deeper levels validates the constructions of both partners, offering a background against which each can extend his or her understandings into new, previously unelaborated areas.

The theory's central hypothesis, that pairs of friends will evidence greater construct similarity than pairs of unacquainted persons, has been supported in a number of cross-sectional (Duck, 1972; 1973a) and longi-tudinal studies (Duck & Allison, 1978; Duck & Spencer, 1972) using repertory grid technique to examine the construct systems of relational partners. This effect has been observed in adolescent (Duck, 1975) and college (Duck, 1973a) populations, and has been shown in both male and female same-sex friendships (Duck, 1973b). But a distinctive aspect of Duck's model is that the type of similarity considered important by interactants will vary systematically as a function of level of acquain-tance, as partners seek validation at deeper levels of their construct systems across time. Accordingly, Duck and Spencer (1972) and Lea (1979) have shown that possession of similar psychological constructs (e.g., when both partners tend to evaluate people in terms of their being caring vs. insensitive) differentiates advanced friendship pairs from nominal pairs, while commonality in the use of more superficial interac-tional dimensions (e.g., viewing people as talkative vs. quiet) or physical constructs (e.g., evaluating people in terms of their being fat vs. thin) does not.

ELABORATING THE MODEL

Our own work represents an extension of this basic constructivist paradigm. In our initial study (Neimeyer & Neimeyer, 1977), we sought to test one additional implication of the filtering model, namely, that in-dividuals would construe friends, as opposed to acquaintances, using more superordinate, personality-descriptive dimensions. This hypothesis was supported by a textual analysis of free-form descriptions of both types of figures by 34 university students in an international housing co-op. In addition, we found that participants tended to form more com-plex, differentiated constructions of friends than of acquaintances, and to form less ambiguous, more polarized impressions of those individuals with whom they tended to have deeper, more disclosing relationships. Thus, at least on an individual level of analysis, participants seemed to be construing others in qualitatively different ways as they developed more intimacy with them, in keeping with Duck's model.

Functional Similarity

While this initial investigation was compatible with the filtering model, its focus on the perceptions of only one member of a relational pair precluded a genuine analysis of the role of commonality in construing between partners, which was fundamental to Duck's earlier theorizing. For this reason, our next pair of studies (Neimeyer & Neimeyer, 1981) made use of actual dyads and employed both longitudinal and cross-sectional designs to examine the process of friendship formation in initial acquaintance and established relationships. In particular, we attempted to extend Duck's model of friendship development by positing a second aspect of social-cognitive comparison, beyond construct similarity per se. For Duck, *construct similarity* referred to commonality in the content of the constructs individuals used to structure their interpersonal worlds. For example, both Bob and Al may tend to view or schematize acquaintances in terms of their being trustworthy versus untrustworthy, fun versus boring, or tense versus relaxed. From Duck's perspective, they would be regarded as similar to the extent that they used similar dimensions in interpreting their social experience. It is worth noting, however, that they may apply these dimensions quite differently to particular people in their shared lives. For instance, Bob may see certain mutual acquaintances as trustworthy, fun, and relaxed, while Al might view these same figures as untrustworthy, boring, and tense. In this case, despite a high degree of construct similarity between Bob and Al, these constructs might function quite differently for each in organizing their social worlds. *Functional similarity*, then, refers to the extent to which two individuals actually apply constructs similarly to particular elements of experience, given at least some background of shared dimensions of meaning.

On the basis of the consensual validation argument, we expected that functional similarity would also be positively related to interpersonal attraction because relational partners should find in functionally similar others support for the application of their personal constructs. We therefore hypothesized that functionally similar dyads would report more mutual attraction than would functionally dissimilar dyads in the course of initial acquaintance. As a laboratory for studying the acquaintance process, we conducted an Interpersonal Transaction (IT) group (cf., Landfield, 1979; Neimeyer, 1988) with 10 previously unacquainted college students, who met weekly for 2 hours over a period of 5 weeks. Each group meeting provided for a series of very brief (4-minute) dyadic interactions among all group members, each of which focused on a leader-assigned self-disclosure topic (e.g., things I enjoy and things I dislike; ways people understand me and misunderstand me). Group members rotated from one interaction partner to another until everyone had a chance to discuss the topic for the meeting with each of the other participants, yielding a total of 45 different dyadic groupings. In this way, the IT procedure rigorously controlled the frequency, duration, and content of interaction without sacrificing the reality of face-to-face encounters among participants.

In the first session we administered repertory grids to each participant as a means of sampling the salient constructs they used to construe friends and family members in their lives. Following the 5 weeks of interaction, we reassessed participants, asking them not only to evaluate each other group member on their own (i.e., the rater's) initial constructs, but also to rate each other group member on his or her own constructs. The number of times that two participants (e.g., Al and Bob) rated each of the other group members (e.g., Carl, Donna, etc.) on the same poles of these construct dimensions was tallied to produce the index of functional similarity. Attraction was measured by the number of positive construct poles on which each rater placed each of the other participants. As predicted, members of dyads demonstrating greater levels of functional similarity perceived one another as more attractive, despite their similar relational histories with each member of the IT group.

The results of this study suggested that functional similarity played a significant role in the context of the early weeks of acquaintance, but it remained to be seen whether it had any continuing relevance to friendship selection at more advanced stages of relationship. For this reason, we used sociometric procedures to identify 10 undergraduate college students living in the same dormitory for the past year, who nominated one another as friends or acquaintances, respectively (Neimeyer & Neimeyer, 1981). All students then completed an assessment of functional similarity as in the previous longitudinal study, except that ratings were made on standardized lists of constructs divided equally into physical, interactional, and psychological groupings.

Extending Duck's rationale, we predicted that friends would construe others in the group more similarly (i.e., would show high functional similarity) relative to acquaintances. Furthermore, we hypothesized that acquaintances would display the greatest similarity in construct use at the level of physical constructs, somewhat less along interactional dimensions, and least of all along psychological constructs. Finally, we expected friends to have greater functional similarity than acquaintances along psychological, but not necessarily more physical constructs. All predictions were confirmed, pointing to the continued relevance of commonality in construct application to friendship selection or maintenance in more established relationships.

Having established that functional similarity in construct application is related to interpersonal attraction at both early and later stages of relationship development, we became intrigued with the possibility that the absence of such consensual validation in construct application could help predict relationship failure in the future. Moreover, we began to consider that higher levels of consensual validation of each partner's social reality could represent not only a cause, but also an effect, of continued interaction. This accorded with Stephen and Markman's (1983, p. 17) view that social comparison of one's constructions with the perspective of others "bonds relationship partners in an emerging, interdependent epistemology," leading to a convergence in their constructions over time. We therefore designed a longitudinal study of two mixed-sex groups of 20 previously unacquainted noncollege adults, who participated in an extended form of the Interpersonal Transaction (IT) group format used in our earlier study (Neimeyer & Neimeyer, 1981).

The resulting study of the social ecology of the two IT groups allowed us to test two primary hypotheses. First, we reasoned that the development of a shared epistemology should increase across the 5 months of weekly interaction. That is, as participants gained more knowledge of one another's outlooks in the course of the dyadic disclosure exercises, they should show greater convergence in their construing of other group members. In addition, in keeping with the predictions of the filtering model, this trend toward increased functional similarity should be qualified by the success of the relationship. In particular, failing relationships should be marked by lower levels of such commonality in construct application than successful ones. This view of relationship disruption as a consequence of the discovery of inadequate commonality in construct content or application struck us as a useful tool for constructing a taxonomy of different relationship trajectories (Neimeyer, G. J., & Neimeyer, R. A., 1985).

As in the previous study using the IT group structure (Neimeyer & Neimeyer, 1981), we elicited personal constructs from each group member prior to the group using a role construct repertory test comparing important figures in the life of the respondent. These dimensions were then used following the 4th and 18th weeks of interaction to rate each of the other group members, as previously described. Similarly, the attractiveness of each group member to each of the others was measured by the percentage of positive construct poles assigned to the other on the rater's grid. This allowed us to discriminate two broad classes of relationships in terms of their success over time: developing relationships, in which both members of a given dyad showed increasing attraction to the partner over time, and deteriorating relationships, in which at least one member reported a decrement in attraction.

In keeping with our hypotheses, deteriorating relationships were found to have lower levels of functional similarity than developing relationships, although commonality in the construing of other group members was found to increase for both groups from the 4th to the 18th week of interaction. Moreover, a post hoc analysis revealed that deteriorating dyads were characterized by especially low levels of commonality at week 4 of the IT group. This prompted the speculation that consensual validation was particularly critical early in the acquaintance process when the potential friendship was in its formative stages. This is consistent with the position that relationships can tolerate greater levels of dissimilarity after a period of initial bonding and development.

Beyond this, however, the significant increase in functional similarity was noteworthy, especially since it occurred for both developing and deteriorating dyads. One way to account for this is to recognize the interdependence of knowledge among those individuals who share a common social context, regardless of their levels of attraction to one another. This is consistent with Berger and Luckmann's (1967) classic argument that social knowledge is organized on two levels, the societal and the intimate. According to this view, all active members of a social group share in the construction and validation of a common *social* reality, but successful relationships (such as friendships) add to this the development of an intersubjective intimate reality that is unique to that partnership. In our study (Neimeyer & Neimeyer, 1986), this could have been reflected in the finding that, while both developing and deteriorating dyads showed a movement toward social consensus over time, after 18 weeks the deteriorating dyads had barely attained the level of functional similarity shown by the more successful dyads after only 4 weeks of interaction.

Structural Similarity

As we were conducting this series of studies on the role of functional similarity in relationship development and breakdown, we were also considering the implications of a broader Kellian formulation of the organization of personal construct systems for future research using the filtering model. From Kelly's (1955/1991, p. 39) perspective, "Not only do men [sic] differ in their constructions of events, but they also differ in the ways they organize their constructions of events." He therefore took pains to discuss ways in which individual constructs formed part of a larger implicative network of meaning, the organization of which varied from one person to another. Yet in terms of previous constructivist work on friendship formation, we noted that Duck had concentrated on similarity in construct content, and we had examined the way in which both partners' constructs function to organize their perceptions of others. Neither of us, however, had explored systematically the role of similarity in construct system structure in the development of relationships.

We therefore designed a further study to examine the role of structural similarity in interpersonal attraction (Neimeyer & Neimeyer, 1983). While construct system structure can be analyzed in an indefinitely large number of ways using available computer programs (Bringmann, 1992; Sewell, Adams-Webber, Mitterer & Cromwell, 1992), we chose to focus on a measure of construct differentiation in view of the long tradition of research on differentiation or cognitive complexity using repertory grid technique. Our choice of measures was the functionally independent construction (FIC) score, which refers to the number of independent dimensions or clusters of dimensions elicited by the repertory grid (Landfield & Cannell, 1988). Simply stated, more differentiated grids consist of constructs that are used in an essentially uncorrelated pattern in rating elements, whereas undifferentiated grids consist of highly redundant construct dimensions. Thus, construct systems can be viewed as ranging from structural complexity at one extreme to structural simplicity at the other.

Interestingly, Duck (1972) had briefly experimented with a similar measure in an early study of friendship formation. He administered repertory grids containing mutually known figures as elements to a group of 10 friends and 10 acquaintances and discovered that the friends evidenced greater similarity in the structure of their construct systems (as measured by a principal component analysis) than the comparison group. Duck interpreted this finding as indicating "the normative effect of group membership on construing processes" (1972, p. 233), although no direct evidence supported this interpretation. Instead, he argued for this conclusion because "the types of intricacies yielded by the statistical analysis are [not] likely to be directly perceptible by individuals" (1972, p. 234). As a result, despite this encouraging finding, he excluded structural properties of construct systems from his subsequent research on the acquaintance process and instead focused on similarity in construct content.

In spite of Duck's conclusion that structural similarity between friends was probably a consequence rather than a cause of their relating, we felt that his data were equally consonant with a consensual validation argument. That is, structural similarity in terms of the complexity of social construing could be accommodated into an expanded filtering model as a third aspect of social cognitive comparison, complementing comparison at the level of construct content and function. One way to clarify the direction of influence between structural similarity and friendship formation would be to regulate closely the interactions among members of a small group in an effort to hold constant what Duck had referred to as "the normative effect of group membership on construing processes." If structural similarity proved to be associated with attraction within this carefully controlled group, it would argue indirectly for a consensual validation interpretation, since the influence of group membership per se would be equal for all group members.

To test this rationale, we conducted a study of 20 noncollege adults participating in two 20-week IT groups, using the same procedures employed by Neimeyer and Neimeyer (1986). FIC scores were computed for grids completed at sessions 4 and 18 (using other group members as elements), and attraction at these same sessions was operationalized in terms of the construct positivity scores described above. We then trichotomized dyads on the basis of their similarity in construct system structure at these two points in the acquaintance process and compared them for the level of mutual attraction shown at each of the two sessions. Results indicated that although groups classed by structural similarity could not be discriminated at session 2, by session 18 members of high structural similarity dyads reported more mutual attraction than did members of medium- or low-similarity dyads. These results gave qualified support to a consensual validation model, suggesting that structural similarity could emerge as a relevant filter in friendship formation at more advanced stages of acquaintance. However, Duck's (1972) reservations concerning the perceptibility of structural similarity may be well founded, at least during the initial stages of acquaintance.

INTEGRATIVE FIELD STUDY

In combination, the research programs conducted by Duck and the Neimeyers reviewed above established the relevance of commonality in construct system content, function, and structure to the course of friendship formation. In keeping with a constructivist model emphasizing consensual validation of social hypotheses as one important process in relationship development, mutually attracted partners display greater similarity in the constructs they use to organize social experience, in the way they apply these constructs to mutually known acquaintances, and in the overall complexity of their social schemata. Moreover, at least at the level of the functional application of such constructs to others, members of interactive groups tend to converge in their interpretations of social reality, with those interactants having the greatest initial similarity in their construing of others attaining still higher levels of convergence and mutual attraction, and those having the greatest initial discrepancy in construing being most likely to experience relationship deterioration over time. Finally, there is at least some support for a refinement of the filtering model, hinting that content and functional similarity may become relevant filters early in the acquaintance process, while social comparison at the level of structural similarity may be possible only at later stages of relationship development.

While promising, this model of friendship formation required replication, especially in naturalistic settings. In particular, it seemed important to assess the implications of the model in a more comprehensive study that would consider several aspects of similarity simultaneously and that would examine their relationship to attraction in a real world context. The need to measure several similarity variables in the same study arose not only because content, functional, and structural similarity had never been compared directly in the personal construct literature, but also because many other investigators in the broader field of social psychology had studied other aspects of interpersonal similarity as predictors of interpersonal attraction, producing a large, if contradictory, literature (Berscheid, 1985). In particular, decades of research (particularly in highly artificial laboratory contexts) had indicated that commonality in attitudes, values, and personality contributed to attraction to real or hypothetical others, although few studies had compared the redundancy or distinctiveness of these types of similarity, and none had studied their relationship to attraction at different stages of relationship development (see Neimeyer & Mitchell, 1988, for a review and critique of this literature). We therefore designed a longitudinal, naturalistic study that included the simultaneous assessment of several facets of similarity deriving from both constructivist and social psychological research programs.

Much of the ambiguity in the larger literature seemed to derive from the unspoken assumption that there were no important differences be-

Table 1. Levels of psychological similarity, in order of hypothetical accessibility for social comparison during the acquaintance process.

Level	Definition	Representative study
Attitude similarity	Personal likes and dislikes in food, entertainment, etc.	Baron & Byrne (1981)
Construct similarity	Content of personal constructs used to interpret others	Duck (1977)
Functional similarity	Application of constructs to mutually known others	Neimeyer & Neimeyer (1981)
Personality similarity	Basic traits or qualities of a person; temperament	Blankenship et al. (1984)
Value similarity	Personal standards that guide social behavior	Newcomb (1961)
Structural similarity	Differentiation or complexity of construct system	Neimeyer & Neimeyer (1983)

Note: Strictly speaking, attitude, value, and personality could be assimilated more completely into a personal construct framework by a use of more theoretically consistent terminology. Thus, attitudes could be seen as relatively peripheral constructions of events, while values and personality could be viewed as expressions of core role structure. However, we have preserved the more common terminology here, both to promote communication with researchers in the broader field and to respect the rather different ways these concepts have been operationalized in the literature.

tween attitudes, values, and personality structures, so that similarity between interactants on all of these dimensions was discussed as if each was interchangeable. In our view, however, it seemed more plausible to posit a hierarchical view of psychological similarity with respect to attraction, with subtypes varying in their accessibility for purposes of social comparison (see Table 1). In this expanded interpretation of filter theory, relatively more superficial levels of similarity (e.g., in attitude and construct content) should be more readily perceived, and hence should influence attraction at earlier stages of the acquaintance process. Deeper levels of similarity (e.g., in values, personality, and construct system structure) should require longer periods to infer, and hence should be associated with attraction only after considerable information about the partner has become available. Among other things, this conceptualization implied that the various types of interpersonal similarity would display at least modest stability over time (otherwise, it would not make sense to regard them as sources of information about the future of the relationship; Aron & Aron, 1986). The model also led us to hypothesize that similarity at more superficial levels would be associated with increasing mutual attraction over time, rather than relational ambivalence or deterioration, whereas commonality at deeper levels would be less clearly related to relationship development in the early weeks of acquaintance. Finally, the model predicted that similarity between partners at more superficial levels would predict attraction early in acquaintance, whereas only deeper level similarities would contribute to the prediction of attraction after several weeks of interaction. This hypothesis complements that concerning relationship development above because it concerns the variance in mutual attraction accounted for by similarity measures at a given point in a relationship trajectory rather than the overall course that a relationship takes over time.

We conducted an 8-week longitudinal study to test the viability of these predictions. We began by assessing 70 undergraduate college students using established scales to measure their attitudes (e.g., preferences in pastime activities, musical tastes), personalities (e.g., their level of introversion/ extroversion), values (e.g., in political and religious domains), and personal construct systems (at the level of both content and structure).[2] We then assigned them to same-sex, same-race dyads with partners with whom they were previously unacquainted and instructed them to interact with each other at least 2 hours per week in any way they chose (e.g., talking on the phone, having lunch together). These contacts were unsupervised, but were monitored by the participants themselves using an interaction diary. Attraction was measured by a validated questionnaire after the first and eighth week of interaction, when similarity measures were readministered (Neimeyer & Mitchell, 1988).

As predicted, we found that each of the similarity subtypes showed significant stability over the course of the study, with similarity at the level of construct content being the least stable and commonality in construct system structure being the most stable. However, the modest magnitude of the correlations (.37 to .50) reinforced the view that relational similarity represents a changing interpersonal process rather than a simple juxtaposition of static partner attributes (cf. Duck & Sants, 1983).

To test our hypothesis about predictors of various relationship trajectories, we divided dyads into those that were *developing* (both partners increasing in attraction over time), *deteriorating* (both decreasing), and *ambivalent* (one increasing and one decreasing). This represented a refinement of the earlier Neimeyer and Neimeyer (1986) classification system. As suggested by our model, similarity at the level of attitudes distinguished developing from deteriorating dyads, with ambivalent dyads being intermediate in this comparison. Contrary to expectations, however, similarity in construct content was not associated with relationship success. Likewise, analyses for personality, value, and structural similarity were not predictive of relationship trajectory over the 8 weeks of interaction.

Finally, we performed regression analyses on pre- and postinteraction attraction scores, using levels of interpersonal similarity as predictors. In conformity with the expanded filtering model, attitude similarity emerged as a predictor of attraction after the first encounter, accounting for 16% of the variance in the mutual attractiveness reported by members of each dyad. Similarity in construct content, however, failed to contribute to the equation. Following extended acquaintance, commonality in the structure of participants' construct systems proved to be the strongest predictor of attraction, supplemented by similarity at the level of personality. Together, these two grounds of potential social comparison accounted for more than 30% of the variance in attraction, indicating that they functioned as substantial predictors of relationship success or failure. When predictor variables were factor analyzed prior to entry into the regression formula, broadly similar results were obtained, with the factor representing structural similarity and value similarity predicting later, but not early, attraction.

In summary, this longitudinal field study demonstrated that the effects of interpersonal similarity on friendship development could survive the transition from the relatively regulated context of the laboratory or IT group to the essentially unconstrained context of naturalistic interaction. Moreover, results of the research were accommodated by our expanded filtering model, with initial similarity in the theoretically more accessible area of attitudinal comparison predicting early attraction and a developing relationship trajectory and attitudinal dissimilarity predicting early disliking and relational deterioration. However, following 8 weeks of interaction, commonality in superficial attitudes no longer predicted attraction and was instead displaced in importance by similarity in more basic personality and especially construct system structure. The most significant discrepancy between results and theoretical expectations concerned the failure of similarity in construct system content, measured according to Duck's criteria, to contribute to the prediction of attraction at either week 1 or week 8 of interaction.

CONSTRUCTION OF ACCOUNTS: NEW DATA ON
IMPRESSION FORMATION IN THE
ACQUAINTANCE PROCESS

The constructivist account of relationship development foreshadowed by Kelly, outlined by Duck, elaborated by Neimeyer and Neimeyer, and supported in a series of studies across a period of nearly 20 years, offers a theoretically focused and empirically grounded portrayal of the acquaintance process, emphasizing the role of social comparison and validation as one important process guiding friendship selection and maintenance. Moreover, as Duck and Montgomery (1991, pp. 8–9) recently have argued, an approach that allows one to posit different layers of similarity that are engaged at different points in the course of interaction encourages the researcher to devise much more revealing and sophisticated methods for illuminating the process of relationship development over time. In general, then, this vein of constructivist research has been progressive, both extending Kelly's original prototheory of personal relationships with its emphasis on commonality, and contributing to social psychological research on the similarity/attraction phenomenon.

In spite of this success—or perhaps because of it—we began to experience misgivings about the adequacy (or rather the comprehensiveness) of this personal construct model by the mid- to late 1980s. As Duck (1985) acknowledged, the model was not so much incorrect as limited in its implicit view of attraction as essentially a one-sided venture. While social comparison at many different levels may permeate much of our relating, particularly during the initial development of friendships, this clearly is not a process that takes place only within the heads of each individual involved. Instead, such comparison is embedded in a broader and more public "languaging" or negotiating about the views of the participants, the opinions of others, and the emerging nature of the relationship itself. Yet our own research on friendship formation had given scant attention to the subtle processes of impression formation in this social context beyond occasional measurements of attraction of each partner for the other. In many respects, this constriction of focus to the relatively private phenomena of social comparison and validation struck us as ironic and unfortunate given the potentially much broader contribution that personal construct theory could make to an understanding of (1) the self as socially situated, (2) the strategic management of personal identities in various relationships, (3) the negotiation of both intimate and nonintimate relational trajectories, and (4) the origin and function of relationship disturbance (Neimeyer, R. A., & Neimeyer, G. J., 1985).

For all of these reasons, we began to think about dilating the focus of our previous research to capture more of the complexity of real-life encounters (Neimeyer & Mitchell, 1988). Some guidance in this effort was provided by other constructivists who had grappled with similar problems in the contexts of their own research programs. For instance, Wilkinson (1982) had criticized the tendency of researchers to isolate variables in laboratory settings that imposed artificial constraints on subjects, losing sight of the social settings in which relationships ordinarily developed. She also had pointed out the limitations arising from a preemptive focus on the degree to which subjects like one another as their sole account of the evolving nature of their relationship. Wilkinson (1981) claimed there has been a massive conceptual oversimplification in the research deriving from attempts to study the impressions individuals form of one another independently of their relationships with one another. Instead, she argued that the two are inseparably linked and should be studied as such. Thus, it seemed important to somehow integrate attention to the individual accounts given by each partner in a developing relationship with the salient public dimensions of that relationship as revealed in their interaction.

Further guidance in the extension of our efforts was provided by the impressive program of research conducted by constructivists in the field of communication (see Applegate, 1990, for a review). In particular, it seemed likely that the exploration of friendship development could be enriched by a closer consideration of what an individual's personal view includes and how the elements of that view are organized (Crockett, Press, Delia, & Kenny, 1974). The measurement of various aspects of the complexity of narrative descriptions of others by investigators in this tradition offered one methodological point of entry into this area (Burleson & Waltman, 1988). A focus on the highly individual activity of impression formation within relationships seemed all the more appropriate in light of the abundant evidence that the construction of private explanations or interpersonal accounts is a prominent feature of virtually any developing or declining relationship (Harvey, Weber, & Orbuch, 1990).

Finally, a focus on impression formation or account making in a relational context seemed uniquely appropriate to a broader constructivist research methodology. This approach attempts to provide some structure to research efforts, but with a minimum of interference with the subject's own processing of her or his own experience. Constructivists maintain that if we are attempting to study persons who actively interpret reality in their own terms, then their own account of those terms is the only acceptable primary source of data (cf., Viney, 1988). It is the individual's own accounting of the situation that is significant. The ideal study, then, would interfere with its participants less, study them in natural social situations, and give maximum credence to their own phenomenal accounts as compared with other sources of data. By using this methodology, patterns found in one case may be found in others; hence, it is possible to look for similarities in processes between people.

On the basis of these considerations, we attempted to design a study that carried over some of the procedures of our earlier research program while introducing new methods that revealed different aspects of the personal and interpersonal processes entailed in friendship formation. We therefore retained our naturalistic, longitudinal research design with its emphasis on the measurement of attraction at various stages of acquaintance (Neimeyer & Mitchell, 1988). Similarly, we maintained our interest in discriminating relationship trajectories distinguished by their levels of success or failure (Neimeyer & Neimeyer, 1986). However, rather than focus on similarity at various levels as a predictor of outcome of relationship development, we focused on the process of impression formation within each dyad as revealed by the structure of each partner's account of the other. We assumed this approach would enable us to detect shifts in the process of impression formation across time in tandem with more public data on the topography of each dyad's interactions.

Specifically, we planned to test the following hypotheses:

1. Individuals who are more attracted to their partners over 8 weeks of initial acquaintance should form impressions of them that are relatively more differentiated or complex, and also more abstract, than other individuals in less mutually attractive relationships. This prediction reflects Duck's (1977) concern with a movement toward deeper levels of construing across the course of successful relationship development and also our early research on differentiation and abstractness in impressions of friends versus acquaintances (Neimeyer & Neimeyer, 1977).

2. In contrast to ambivalent and deteriorating relationships, developing relationships should be construed in more complex and abstract terms and should also be characterized by interactions that are qualitatively different (e.g., more intimate and disclosing) than less successful rela-

tionship trajectories. This hypothesis represents a preliminary attempt to integrate attention to the private account of each partner's impressions with more public data on actual encounters between partners over time (cf., Wheeler, Reis, & Nezlek, 1983).

3. With the exception of a greater male preference for more rule-governed mutual activities with their partners (e.g., participation in a sporting event), male and female acquaintances will rate their interactions as similar in quality and will develop similarly complex and abstract impressions of their same-sex partners. This prediction is implicit in the constructivist account of friendship formation that is discussed above, which posits the same basic processes in the motivations, if not the topography, of male and female friendships. However, sex differences in relational patterns are important to examine in view of the larger social psychological research tradition that has attempted to document sex-specific modes of relating (e.g., Jones, 1991).

METHOD

Participants

Undergraduate volunteers (19 men and 62 women) from Memphis State University agreed to participate in a project presented as a study in friendships. Participants ranged in age from 17 to 54 years old ($M = 23$); 20% were African-Americans, and the remaining 80% were Euro-Americans. Those participants enrolled in a psychology class were eligible to receive extra credit for their participation in the study.

Materials

The Rochester Interaction Record (RIR; Wheeler, Reis, & Nezlek, 1983; Wheeler and Nezlek, 1977) is a self-report measure that requires immediate recording of one's interactions with specific others on a number of qualitative and quantitative variables. This measure was chosen because it provides a method of monitoring naturalistic interactions, soliciting quantitative indices of the number of interaction partners in a given social encounter, length of the contact, and types of activities involved in the encounter. It also provides ratings of intimacy, satisfaction, self- and other-disclosure. Advantages of the RIR include (1) its assessment of a variety of social behaviors, (2) the specificity of the ratings on a number of discrete dimensions, (3) the fact that each record represents only one social event, minimizing aggregation problems and other difficulties that can arise from the use of global, retrospective summaries, and (4) the potential for comparison with a partner's rating of the same interaction.

Ratings of intimacy, satisfaction, self- and other-disclosure were made on seven-point Likert-type scales, ranging from "a great deal" of self- and other-disclosure and "pleasant" degree of satisfaction to an absence of disclosure or satisfaction with the encounter. Lower scores on the RIR qualitative variables reflect more positive ratings. The RIR is considered a reliable measure, with intraclass correlations in the range of .76 to .84 between independent ratings performed by the interactants (Reis, Nezlek, & Wheeler, 1980; Wheeler & Nezlek, 1977; Wheeler, Reis & Nezlek, 1983).

The Impression Diary (Wilkinson, 1981, 1982) was completed by each participant each week. As a minimally structured idiographic assessment, the Impression Diary simply required all participants in the study to record their impressions of their partners and their basis for these impressions on a weekly schedule. These accounts were then analyzed using the scheme devised by Crockett and his colleagues (1974) for scoring the cognitive complexity of written narratives describing other people. In the present case, this required identifying and counting the number of constructs each impression included. The degree of complexity or differentiation consists of the number of constructs in the description; the higher the score, the more cognitively complex the narrative is taken to be. A fuller description of this scoring procedure has been provided by Burleson and Waltman (1988). Interrater reliability correlations for complexity scores commonly exceed .90 (e.g., Delia, Clark, & Switzer, 1974; Delia, Kline, & Burleson, 1979; O'Keefe & Brady, 1980), and empirical evidence suggests that Crockett's measure is largely independent of extraneous influences like verbal ability and intelligence (see Applegate, 1990; O'Keefe & Sypher, 1981). In the present study, reliability in scoring constructs was established between the three raters prior to scoring of the participants' diaries. Correlations between raters for number of constructs were .97, .98, and .98.

Finally, constructs drawn from the Impression Diary were also scored for their degree of concreteness or abstractness on the basis of Applegate's (1983, 1990) scoring system. Abstract constructs were those referring to the partner in terms of dispositional, personality descriptive dimensions (e.g., ambitious, sensitive, intelligent), while concrete constructs referred to physical characteristics, roles, or behaviors of the partner (e.g., tall, member of a fraternity, quiet). As with our scoring of impression complexity, reliability was established between the three raters prior to scoring of abstract and concrete constructs drawn from the participants' diaries. Correlations between the raters for abstract constructs were .93, .97, and .97. Correlations between raters for concrete constructs were .82, .94, and .91.

The Acquaintance Description Form (ADF; Wright & Bergloff, 1984) is a self-report person-perception questionnaire of 65 statements comprising 13 five-item scales. For each item, participants indicate on a 6-point Likert-type scale either the degree of applicability or the probability of occurrence of the statements about a designated target person, in this case the assigned interaction partner. The subscales entitled Voluntary Interdependence and Person-qua-Person are summed to provide a measure of attraction or friendship. Numerous reliability studies of the ADF have yielded test-retest correlations that are consistently around .85 or higher. Similarly, Cronbach's alpha is .82 or higher for all scales (Wright, 1985).

Procedure

Participants were randomly assigned a same-sex/same-race partner, with the only constraints in pairing being that they must be mutually unacquainted at the beginning of the study and be approximately the same age. Of the original 81 participants, 8 did not complete the study, and data for only 1 member were collected for three dyads. The result was 35 dyads (27 women, 8 men), matched according to the sociodemographic variables of sex, race, approximate age, and general level of education.

The length of the study was 8 weeks. Individuals were required to interact with their partner for a minimum of 2 hours per week, including at least one contact of 50 minutes or more. This time frame was selected to approximate naturally occurring friendship patterns as closely as possible. In three separate studies, Nezlek, Wheeler, and Reis (1983) found that same-sex contact was the most common type of social event experienced, and the average length of interactions between friends across the studies was approximately 50 minutes. No restrictions were placed as to the location or time of day of the interactions, but an interaction was defined as any encounter with the partner in which the two attended to one another and adjusted their behavior in response to one another. Interactions exceeding the 2 hour per week minimum were left to the discretion of the participants.

Participants completed the RIR following every interaction with their partner that lasted more than 10 minutes. The Impression Diary was completed on a weekly basis, regardless of the number of interactions that had occurred. The records were collected on a weekly basis to encourage contemporaneous monitoring of interactions. Additionally, each participant completed the ADF twice during the study, once immediately after meeting the partner and again at the completion of the entire study.

RESULTS

Individual Level of Attraction

A Pearson correlation was computed between participants' ADF attraction scores within dyads at weeks 1 and 8 to assure that partners' scores were independent of one another and could therefore appropriately be analyzed on an individual basis. The correlations were .14 at week 1 and .24 at week 8, neither correlation being statistically significant. Thus, analyses on an individual level were conducted as planned.

To examine the individual correlates of attraction across the course of acquaintance, the distribution of participants' ratings of their partner on the ADF for weeks 1 and 8 were divided into three levels of attraction, which were labelled "maximally attracted," "somewhat attracted" and "minimally attracted." ADF scores were available at weeks 1 and 8, so that the first rating was labeled "initial attraction" while the second rating was labeled "final attraction."

For assessment of initial attraction, no differences were found among maximally attracted, somewhat attracted, and minimally attracted individuals in total amount of time spent with the partner, number of concrete constructs used in the impression diaries, or number of abstract constructs used. Likewise, at the final assessment of attraction, a one-way analysis of variance (ANOVA) yielded no significant difference between maximally attracted, somewhat attracted, and minimally attracted individuals in the total time spent with partner or number of

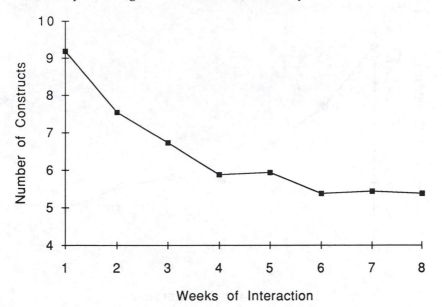

Figure 1. Changes in number of abstract constructs in partner impressions over time

concrete constructs used. However, as hypothesized, a significant difference in number of abstract constructs in impression diaries was found [$F(2,72) = 3.62$, $p = .03$]. Individuals who were more attracted to their partners after 8 weeks of interaction used more abstract constructs ($M = 2.59$) in their impression diaries than those who were less attracted to their partners($M = 1.87$).

Relationship Trajectory

A significant main effect for time was found for impression complexity [$F(7,322) = 6.29$, $p = .001$]. Week 1 differed from weeks 2 through 8, and week 2 differed from weeks 6 through 8 at $p < .05$ (see Figure 1). Contrary to expectation, impression complexity decreased over time rather than increased.

Similarly, a significant main effect for time emerged in the number of abstract constructs used in impression diaries [$F(7,322) = 6.56$, $p = .001$], although no comparable effect was observed for the number of concrete constructs. Week 1 differed from weeks 3 through 8 and week 2 differed from weeks 6 through 8 in the number of abstract constructs

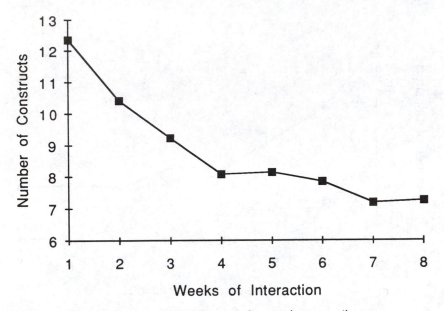

Figure 2. Changes in complexity of partner impressions over time

used. Again, contrary to prediction, the number of abstract constructs used to construe partners seemed to decrease rather than increase over time (see Figure 2).

In order to discriminate more and less successful relationship trajectories, a change score was computed for each individual, reflecting the difference between the ADF attraction score at weeks 1 and 8. Following our usual procedures, dyads were then classified into three relationship types on the basis of the agreement between the partners' change scores. Those dyads in which both partners showed an increase in attraction over time were designated as "developing" relationships ($N = 14$), those in which both partners showed a decrease were considered "deteriorating" ($N = 10$), and those in which one partner showed an increase while the other showed a decrease were labeled "ambivalent" ($N = 11$).

A 3 (type of relationship) by 8 (time) by 4 (RIR variables: intimacy, satisfaction, self- and other-disclosure) MANOVA was used to analyze differences among developing, ambivalent, and deteriorating relationships on the RIR qualitative variables across time. There were no significant interactions, but main effects for type of relationship [$F(2,46) = 5.70$, $p = .006$] and time [$F(7,322) = 33.63$, $p = .001$] were found. Because there was no main effect for the RIR variables, the ratings were collapsed to yield an overall mean quality of interactions score. Follow-up analyses indicated that developing relationships ($M = 2.99$) differed from deteriorating relationships ($M = 4.24$) in their ratings of intimacy, satisfaction, and self- and other-disclosure. Ambivalent relationships were intermediate in this comparison ($M = 3.58$) and could not be distinguished from either of the other groups. Thus, relationships characterized by growth or decline in attraction across time showed clear qualitative differences in the course of their development.

A series of one-way ANOVAs was used to assess differences between the three relationship trajectories in the total time spent with the partner, total number of concrete constructs used, and total number of abstract constructs used. Significant results were found only for the total number of abstract constructs used [$F(2,69) = 7.18$, $p = .002$]. Members of developing relationships ($M = 57.14$) differed significantly from those in either ambivalent ($M = 42.27$) or deteriorating ($M = 35.95$) relationships in the number of abstract constructs used. The more abstract construing of relational partners in developing relationships conforms to predictions, suggesting that potential friends do attempt to formulate deeper level impressions of one another across the course of their relationship.

Sex Differences

Differences in men's and women's activity preferences were assessed using analysis of variance. In keeping with our expectations, male dyads engaged in more sports activities ($M = 1.13$) than did female dyads ($M = .19$) [$F(1,35) = 5.86$, $p = .021$]. However, no differences were found between the sexes in preference for other activities. Similarly, when repeated measures ANOVAs were used to analyze gender differences in complexity of relationship impressions over time and in number of abstract and concrete constructs, no differences between men and women on these measures were found.

DISCUSSION

As predicted, individuals who were maximally attracted to their partners at the end of the study formed more abstract impressions of them than did those individuals who were minimally attracted to their partners, although no such effect was evidenced early in their acquaintance. This finding is congruent with our general filter theory of relationship development, with its emphasis on a shift toward more abstract, psychological bases of evaluation of partners as friendships progress. This finding was reinforced by our analyses at the dyadic level, which indicated that developing relationships differed from deteriorating relationships in two important respects. At an interactive level, developing relationships were characterized by significantly more disclosing, intimate, and satisfying encounters over time than were deteriorating relationships. At a cognitive level, partners in developing relationships used a greater number of abstract constructs in formulating impressions of their partner than did those in either deteriorating or ambivalent relationships. Thus, it appears that the attempt of partners to construe one another in genuinely psychological, rather than simple behavioral terms, is associated with successful relationship trajectories, whereas the tendency to maintain more concrete impressions of the partner is associated with more negative outcomes. Whether more abstract construing of one's relational partner is a cause or a consequence of mutual attraction cannot be answered definitively on the basis of this preliminary study.

Overall, men's and women's same-sex relationships, at least within the framework of this naturalistic study, emerged as more similar than different. Although the topography of their interaction differed (with male partners devoting more time to sports activities than female dyads), the meaning of their relationships did not differ on qualitative dimensions concerning the intimacy, mutual disclosure, or satisfaction with their interactions. This is congruent with the emerging view that, despite differences in form, male and female friendships serve similar functions (Ashton, 1980; Caldwell & Peplau, 1982; Jones, 1991).

Perhaps the most intriguing finding of the study was unexpected, namely, the tendency for complexity in impressions partners formed of one another to decrease rather than increase over time. While this could represent a kind of cognitive consolidation in partners' views of the relationship with increasing acquaintance, this trend could also reflect the effects of repeated testing. Complexity was scored from the diaries that the participants completed each week. Because there were no time limits imposed on participants when they produced their diaries, it may be that over time they simply became habituated to the task and wrote briefer impressions for this reason. This possible methodological confound could be tested in future research by comparing participants who wrote weekly diaries without constraints with those who were either constrained as to amount of time they spent, or who completed the diary on a less frequent basis.

CODA

In keeping with broader trends in the social sciences, social psychologists have shown greater willingness over the last decade to step out of the controlled environment of the psychological laboratory and to begin to direct their theoretical and empirical efforts with greater consistency to the problems and possibilities offered by a fuller engagement with human life. The now robust study of personal relationships reflects this trend.

Within this broad and occasionally diffuse literature, research inspired by personal construct theory has made a consistent and theoretically focused contribution. Grounding his model in Kelly's image of the person as scientist, formulating social hypotheses and attempting to validate these against the data of ongoing experience, Duck originated a program of research on the way in which individuals enlist developing friendships to support them in this epistemological effort. In general, the data produced by several studies of friends and acquaintances reinforces this view, suggesting that the existence of sufficient commonality in the content of prospective friends' construct systems at progressively deeper levels functions as a relevant filter for further development of the relationship.

Our work represents an effort to extend and refine this basic constructivist model. As we have reviewed above, a good deal of evidence converges to indicate that similarity in the function and structure of acquaintances' construct systems also facilitates the development of relationships, whereas dissimilarity in these dimensions is associated with eventual relationship deterioration. Moreover, it seems likely that social comparisons at the levels of construct system content, function, and structure operate as relevant filters at different stages in the acquaintance process, with less accessible features of partners' construing (e.g., in the structural complexity of their systems) coming into play only at more advanced levels of acquaintance. This expanded filtering model articulates with—and renders more coherent—the often atheoretical and contradictory research on similarity and attraction, in which comparisons between interactants in terms of their attitudes, values, and personalities are too often used interchangeably and imprecisely, to the detriment of a more integrated understanding of the role of social comparison in the development of close relationships.[3]

Finally, our recent attempt to broaden the focus of a constructivist account of friendship formation to include interactants' own accounts of the quality of their interactions and the impressions they construct of one another suggests fruitful new directions for research. In particular, it illustrates the potential value of integrating research on the more public, interactive dimensions of friendship formation with a focus on the private processing of the relationship by the individuals who constitute it. Taken together, these complementary approaches offer a more refined picture of interpersonal attraction in naturalistic, longitudinal encounters; of developing versus deteriorating relationship trajectories; and of possible sex differences in relationship patterns. We are optimistic that constructivist research of this kind can contribute to a fuller understanding of the many interwoven strands that make up the fabric of our lives with others.

ENDNOTES

1. Of course, from the standpoint of a broader constructivist analysis, a discussion of the meaning and function of such relationships could be quite relevant. For example, in the case of our continuing relationship to loved ones who have died, Klass (1993) has documented the palpable sense of presence and continued interaction parents experience toward their deceased children. In our view, these are not necessarily pathological phenomena, but potentially viable ways that individuals and families sustain a sense of meaning and identity in the face of ineffable loss. Landfield (1988) has provided a general personal construct model of real and hypothetical validating agents that is compatible with this perspective. Our project in the present chapter simply is more focused in its attempt to elaborate and test a model for the development of contemporary relationships with actual others.

2. Ideally, we would have preferred to measure functional similarity as well, yielding a comprehensive assessment of the filtering model. However, this would have necessitated the administration of yet another repertory grid at multiple points in the study, one having standardized constructs that permitted a construct-by-construct comparison of ratings. Because the assessment burden borne by participants was already quite heavy, we decided to forego this ideal design in order to avoid the larger attrition we feared might result.

3. Here we stress the possible relevance of social comparison in construing to close relationships in general, rather than friendships only, although friendships have been the focus of this chapter. That is, we believe that the processes of consensual validation of construct system content, application, and structure are likely to be associated with relational satisfaction in other intimate contexts as well, such as marital or family relationships, at least with older children. For example, G. J. Neimeyer (1984) found that similarity in cognitive complexity (i.e., structural similarity) predicted marital satisfaction in a group of 20 couples, while their absolute levels of cognitive complexity were unrelated to their levels of marital distress or happiness. Likewise, Harter, Neimeyer, and Alexander

(1989) conducted a multifaceted assessment of the ways in which 47 family triads (consisting of mother, father, and adolescent son or daughter) construed their family relationships. Among other findings, we discovered that functional similarity in construing other family members significantly predicted relational satisfaction, although the individual with whom similarity was important varied as a function of the person's position in the family system. For example, the adolescents' sense of the family as adaptive, cohesive, and communicative was related to their functional similarity with both parents, while the mothers' satisfaction was predicted only by their convergence with their spouses. The fathers' satisfaction, on the other hand, was predicted only by functional similarity with their adolescent children, and in general, their happiness with the family experience was far less dependent on developing a joint epistemology with family members than was true for mothers or children. Findings like these, and those of other researchers of family construct systems (see Feixas, 1992, for a review) demonstrate that while commonality at various levels of construing may remain relevant to a broad range of close relationships, the assumptions of symmetry and reciprocity that characterize friendship may not hold in other settings.

REFERENCES

Applegate, J. (1983). Construct system development, strategic complexity, and impression formation in persuasive communication. In J. Adams-Webber & J. Mancuso (Eds.), *Applications of personal construct theory* (pp. 187–206). Toronto: Academic Press.

Applegate, J. (1990). Constructs and communication: A pragmatic integration. In G. J. Neimeyer & R. A. Neimeyer (Eds.), *Advances in personal construct psychology* (Vol. 1, pp. 203–232). Greenwich, CT: JAI Press.

Aron, A., & Aron, E. N. (1986). *Love and the expansion of self*. Washington, DC: Hemisphere.

Ashton, N. (1980). Exploratory investigation of perceptions of influences on best-friend relationships. *Perceptual and Motor Skills, 50*, 379–386.

Baron, R. A., & Byrne, D. (1981). *Social psychology: Understanding human interaction* (3rd ed.). Boston: Allyn & Bacon.

Berger, P. L., & Luckmann, T. (1967). *The social construction of reality*. Harmondsworth: Penguin Books.

Berscheid, E. (1985). Interpersonal attraction. In G. Lindzey & E. Aronson (Eds.), *The handbook of social psychology* (pp. 413–484). New York: Random House.

Blankenship, V., Hant, S. M., Hess, T. G., & Brown, D. R. (1984). Reciprocal interaction and similarity of personality attributes. *Journal of Social and Personal Relationships*, 1, 415–432.

Bringmann, M. (1992). Computer-based methods for the analysis and interpretation of personal construct systems. In R. A. Neimeyer & G. J. Neimeyer (Eds.), *Advances in personal construct psychology* (Vol 2, pp. 57–90). Greenwich, CT: JAI Press.

Burleson, B., & Waltman, M. (1988). Cognitive complexity: Using the Role Category Questionnaire measure. In C. H. Tardy (Ed.), *A handbook for the study of human communication* (pp. 1–36). Norwood, NJ: Ablex.

Caldwell, M. A.; & Peplau, L. A. (1982). Sex differences in same-sex friendship. *Sex Roles*, 8, 721–732.

Crockett, W., Press, A., Delia, J., & Kenny, C. (1974). Structural analysis of the organization of written impressions. Unpublished manuscript, University of Kansas.

Delia, J., Clark, R., & Switzer, D. (1974). Cognitive complexity and impression formation in informal social interaction. *Speech Monographs*, 41, 299–308.

Delia, J., Kline, S., & Burleson, B. (1979). The development of persuasive communication strategies in kindergarteners through twelfth-graders. *Communication Monographs*, 46, 241–256.

Duck, S. W. (1972). Friendship, similarity and the reptest. *Psychology Reports*, 31, 231–234.

Duck, S. W. (1973a). Similarity and perceived similarity of personal constructs as influences on friendship choice. *British Journal of Social and Clinical Psychology*, 12, 1–6.

Duck, S. W. (1973b). *Personal relationships and personal constructs: A study of friendship formation*. London: Wiley.

Duck, S. W. (1975). Personality similarity and friendship choices by adolescents. *European Journal of Social Psychology*, 5, 351–365.

Duck, S. W. (1977). Inquiry, hypothesis and the quest for validation: Personal construct systems in the development of acquaintance. In S. Duck (Ed.), *Theory and practice in interpersonal attraction* (pp. 379–404). New York: Academic Press.

Duck, S. W. (1985). Attraction, acquaintance, filtering, and communication—but not necessarily in that order. In F. R. Epting & A. W. Landfield (Eds.), *Anticipating personal construct psychology* (pp. 87–94). Lincoln, NE: University of Nebraska Press.

Duck, S. W. (1986). *Human relationships*. Beverly Hills: Sage.

Duck, S. W., & Allison, D. (1978). I like you but I can't live with you: A study of lapsed friendships. *Social Behavior and Personality, 8,* 43–47.

Duck, S. W., & Montgomery, B. M. (1991). The interdependence among interaction substance, theory, and methods. In B. M. Montgomery & S. Duck (Eds.), *Studying interpersonal interaction* (pp. 3–15). New York: Guilford.

Duck, S. W., & Sants, H. K. A. (1983) On the origin of the specious: Are personal relationships really interpersonal states? *Journal of Social and Clinical Psychology, 1,* 27–41.

Duck, S. W., & Spencer, C. (1972). Personal constructs and friendship formation. *Journal of Personality and Social Psychology, 23,* 40–45.

Feixas, G. (1992). Personal construct approaches to family therapy. In R. A. Neimeyer & G. J. Neimeyer (Eds.), *Advances in personal construct psychology* (Vol 2 pp. 217–249). Greenwich, CT: JAI Press.

Harter, S., Neimeyer, R. A., & Alexander, P. C. (1989). Personal construction of family relationships: The relation of commonality and sociality to family satisfaction for parents and adolescents. *International Journal of Personal Construct Psychology, 2,* 123–142.

Harvey, J. H., Weber, A. L., & Orbuch, T. L. (1990). *Interpersonal accounts*. Cambridge: Blackwell.

Jones, D. C. (1991). Friendship satisfaction and gender. *Journal of Social and Personal Relationships, 8,* 167–185.

Kelley, H., Berscheid, E., Christensen, A., Harvey, J., Huston, T., Levinger, G., McClintock, E., Peplau, L., & Peterson, D. (1983). *Close relationships*. San Francisco: Freeman.

Kelly, G. A. (1955/1991). *The psychology of personal constructs* Vols. 1 and 2. New York: Routledge.

Klass, D. (1993). Solace and immortality: Bereaved parents' continuing bond with their children. *Death Studies, 17,* 343–368.

Landfield, A. W. (1979). Exploring socialization through the interpersonal transaction group. In P. Stringer & D. Bannister (Eds.), *Constructs of sociality and individuality* (pp. 133–152). New York/London: Academic Press.

Landfield, A. W. (1988). Personal science and the concept of validation. *International Journal of Personal Construct Psychology, 1,* 237–250.

Landfield, A. W., & Cannell, J. E. (1988). Ways of assessing functionally independent construction, meaningfulness, and construction in hierarchy. In J. C. Mancuso & M. L. G. Shaw (Eds.), *Cognition and personal structure* (pp. 67–90). New York: Praeger.

Lea, M. (1979). Personality similarity in unreciprocated friendships. *British Journal of Social and Clinical Psychology, 18,* 393–394.

Neimeyer, G. J. (1984). Cognitive complexity and marital satisfaction. *Journal of Social and Clinical Psychology, 2,* 258–263.

Neimeyer, G. J., & Neimeyer, R. A. (1981). Personal construct perspectives on cognitive assessment. In T. Merluzzi, C. Glass & M. Genest (Eds.), *Cognitive assessment.* New York: Guilford.

Neimeyer, G. J., & Neimeyer, R. A. (1985). Relational trajectories: A personal construct contribution. *Journal of Social and Personal Relationships, 2,* 325–348.

Neimeyer, G. J., & Neimeyer, R. A. (1986). Personal constructs in relationship deterioration: A longitudinal study. *Social Behavior and Personality, 14,* 253–257.

Neimeyer, R. A. (1988). Clinical guidelines for conducting interpersonal transaction groups. *International Journal of Personal Construct Psychology 1,* 181–190.

Neimeyer, R. A. (1993). An appraisal of constructivist psychotherapies. *Journal of Consulting and Clinical Psychology, 61,* 221–234.

Neimeyer, R. A., & Mitchell, K. A. (1988). Similarity and attraction: A longitudinal study. *Journal of Social and Personal Relationships, 5,* 131–148.

Neimeyer, R. A., & Neimeyer, G. J. (1977). A personal construct approach to perception of disclosure targets. *Perceptual and Motor Skills, 44,* 791–794.

Neimeyer, R. A., & Neimeyer, G. J. (1983). Structural similarity in the acquaintance process. *Journal of Social and Clinical Psychology, 1,* 146–154.

Neimeyer, R. A., & Neimeyer, G. J. (1985). Disturbed relationships: A personal construct view. In E. Button (Ed.), *Personal construct theory and mental health: Theory, research, and practice* (pp. 195–223). Beckenham, England: Croom Helm.

Newcomb, T. M. (1961). *The acquaintance process.* New York: Holt, Rinehart, & Winston.

Nezlek, J., Wheeler, L., & Reis, H. (1983). Studies of social participation. In H. Reis (Ed.), *Naturalistic approaches to studying social interaction.* San Francisco: Jossey-Bass.

O'Keefe, D., & Brady, R. (1980). Cognitive complexity and the effect of thought on atittude change. *Social Behavior and Personality*, 8, 49–56.

O'Keefe, D., & Sypher, H. (1981). Cognitive complexity measures and the relationship of cognitive complexity to communication. *Human Communication Research*, 8, 72–92.

Reis, H., Nezlek, J., & Wheeler, L. (1980). Physical attractiveness in social interaction. *Journal of Personality and Social Psychology*, 38, 604–617.

Sewell, K. W., Adams-Webber, J., Mitterer, J., & Cromwell, R. L. (1992). Computerized repertory grids: Review of the literature. *International Journal of Personal Construct Psychology*, 5, 1–24.

Stephen, T. D., & Markman, H. J. (1983). Assessing the development of relationships: A new measure. *Family Process*, 22, 15–25.

Suttles, G. (1970). Friendship as a social institution. In G. J. McCall (Ed.), *Social Relationships* (pp. 295–325). Chicago: Aldine.

Viney, L. L. (1988). Which data-collection methods are appropriate for a constructivist psychology? *International Journal of Personal Construct Psychology*, 1, 191–204.

Wheeler, L., & Nezlek, J. (1977). Sex differences in social participation. *Journal of Personality and Social Psychology*, 35, 742–754.

Wheeler, L., Reis, H., & Nezlek, J. (1983). Loneliness, social interaction, and sex roles. *Journal of Personality and Social Psychology*, 45, 943–953.

Wilkinson, S. (1981). Personal constructs and private explanations. In C. Antaki (Ed.), *The psychology of ordinary experience of social behavior* (pp. 205–220). London: Academic Press.

Wilkinson, S. (1982, May). *The exploration of identity: Understanding of self and other in developing relationships*. Paper presented at an interdisciplinary symposium on Representing Understanding, London.

Wright, P. H. (1985). The Acquaintance Description Form. S. Duck & D. Perlman (Eds.), *Understanding personal relationships: An interdisciplinary approach* (pp. 39–62). Newbury Park, CA: Sage.

Wright, P. H., & Bergloff, P. (1984, June). *The Acquaintance Description Form and the study of relationship differentiation*. Paper presented at the Second International Conference on Personal Relationships, Madison, Wisconsin.

CHAPTER 7

The Family Construct System

HARRY G. PROCTER

My intention over several years now has been to develop a psychology of the family that would prove useful both at the level of description and as a guide to action for therapists and researchers and for people in general as they struggle with their own family experiences (Procter, 1978, 1981, 1985a, 1985b). This approach has been developed further by Dallos (Dallos and Procter, 1984; Dallos 1991) and Feixas (Feixas, 1990a, 1990b, 1992; Feixas, Procter, & Neimeyer, 1993). This paper will devote itself to examining the central, organizing concept within this approach, the family construct system. The justification for continuing to develop this approach, amidst so many contenders, is particularly its integrative capacity (Neimeyer & Feixas, 1990), allowing knowledge from different models to be drawn into a single and consistent theory. It also proves to be extremely practical for both therapists and researchers in the way it generates therapy and research procedures (Procter, 1985a, 1985b; Feixas, 1992; Feixas, Procter & Neimeyer 1993; Procter & Pieczora, 1993). Finally, it emphasizes ethical as well as psychological aspects of family dynamics and therapy.

The family construct system as a concept came to me all at once one day while I was engaged in my doctoral research on families. While there are similar concepts in the literature—my forbears are Laing and the British psychoanalytic school as well as Kelly himself—I think it is an idea that is packaged slightly differently and is more elaborated. It therefore leads to alternative implications in its utilization.

The basis of the approach is Kelly's *Psychology of Personal Constructs* (1955). Kelly's work constitutes an achievement still too unrecognized within the fields of psychology and psychotherapy. He offered an elaborate psychology based on emphasizing the unique system of constructs that each of us evolve in our lives. The family construct system is an extension of this concept to cover inter- or transpersonal systems of construction.

In a field where dualistic separations are made between the subjective and the objective, between the individual and the social, and between psychology and physiology, Kelly's approach is a potentially unifying framework that builds bridges between the dualities. Kelly's notion of construct itself manages, tightly, to unite the formerly disparate concepts of choice from the area of action and ethics, and difference from the area of perception and cognition. Constructs range from being high-level precepts formed within someone's life experiences and struggles, such as "my wish to be a loving and compassionate person to others" versus "being uncaring and selfish," right down to a recognition of a particular color, pitch, or smell at a sensory level.

At the sensory level, constructs are likely to be much more common between different people; red and orange, sweet and sour, heavier and lighter are behaviorally, and probably experientially, similar for each of us. Nevertheless, these already exist in the unique semantic context of our personal construct system in which the higher level (superordinate) constructs influence their meaning and use. Apart from these very basic discriminations, structured by the way our bodies are built, constructs evolve within and may have their origins in the social (micro and macro) culture and grouping in which we live (Procter & Parry, 1978). From our earliest experiences our parents and teachers select, label, and punctuate the data presented to us, influencing the way we see and value things. It may be that commonality between different constructs is highest for the most subordinate and superordinate construing and our individuality and uniqueness show mostly in the midrange of ordinacy, giving an inverted U shape (see Figure 1).

Our constructs evolve within and govern our daily experiences and actions. For example, a construct that evaluatively discriminates between male and female as a result of an abusive experience is a person's way of making sense of that experience, but it will also then structure the way they see others and will govern the way they behave toward the others around them. This construct will be shaped by views held about men and women in the belief system and knowledge base of the person's language, culture, religion, and family system.

We can extend the notion of construct beyond the personal to the social, for example, to a discrimination made within the ideology of a political party. This is negotiated within the interactions and conversations of the members of the party but also becomes a "badge" or a con-

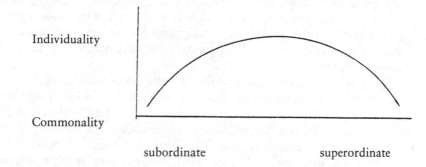

Figure 1. Individuality and commonality plotted against ordinacy

struct that defines the identity of a member of the party. There will be many such constructs and within the party the members will vary according to the meaning and place of the constructs within their own unique system of construction. The same applies to families. We are born into and continue to exist in a changing system of specific relationships. Those most significant and enduring constitute our family, the arena in which our individuality and commonalities are negotiated and evolved. Each family necessarily evolves a unique construct system that structures the family members' perception of their lives and provides a rationale for their actions. It governs their interactions.

The family construct system can be seen as a system of streets and avenues along which the members are free to move independently or contingently as they take up different positions (Procter, 1981). While there is freedom to move within the system and to elaborate and revise it over time, the system itself is imposed on the members; they are not free to change the dimensions themselves at any point in time. Some families will have a much more extensive set of conceptual positions available to them than others, and the freedom with which members can change within the system will also vary. At times of difficulty and stress, the rigidity and tendency to polarize into more extreme and exaggerated views tends to increase.

Each of these streets is a family construct available to all the members. We are taught ways of looking at the world, events, each other, problems, and outsiders by the people who rear us (and of course this is a two-way process from the start as we influence them reciprocally). We also select what we want to accept, or such selection is made by the particular set of constructs we are using at the time. This choice may be just as colored by the positions other members are taking and our loyalty to or disapproval of them, as the intrinsic logic of the choice itself. Thus, it is common to observe in families people identifying and contra-identifying with each other; for instance, a daughter who consistently takes up a belief and style at variance to her parents, whom she perceives as bigoted and old-fashioned.

Early in life and during childhood and young adulthood we are likely to be most influenced by those we love and fall in love with. We will fall in love with someone because they seem to be likely to occupy and elaborate some position within our system of shared meaning. This position may be occupied or not. The lover is attractive because they seem similar to someone, real or idealized, in our system, or because they represent a contrast or opposite to such a position. A core construct sets up the distinction. An example might be, "my fiance is reliable (no previous occupant) versus chaotic (like mother)." Having initially identified someone through similarity, new constructs defining differences will then begin to emerge as a relationship is negotiated. Likewise, initial difference may change to similarities being later identified.

As a relationship develops, we negotiate constructs that begin to characterize who I am, who you are, what our relationship consists of, who they are, and what you and I ought to do in such-and-such a situation. At the core of important relationships we could talk of shared I-thou constructs, following Martin Buber (1937). "You are my baby, my pride-and-joy who has arrived after a difficult and stressful pregnancy. I am your darling mother who loves you." For the baby: "You are that beautiful smiling face with a sweet voice (although sometimes cross!) who makes me warm and satisfies me." When she is not there: "Where is my darling mum? This is a terrifying room. I want her."

Of course, it is not always so positive. We may systematically disassociate from constructs offered. We may fail to get our cherished understanding through to our loved ones. Consistent misunderstandings arise and the family construct system becomes fragmented with inferentially incompatible subsystems. Thus, a couple argues for years, never agreeing to differ, in the light of the wife's Christian position and her husband's atheistic/scientific assumptions. The most enduring constructs applied are likely to be those formed in the family origin of each partner, although these are likely to become coherent in the light of family core constructs, to quote Feixas' (1990a) adaptation of Kelly's fragmentation corollary.

The family construct system at this point in time is a heuristic concept. This means that it leads to new ideas, that it is capable of appearing in different incarnations. It can be defined and illustrated in a variety of different ways according to our purpose—therapeutic, methodological, conceptual, or didactic. It is thus loose and permeable but can be tightened to illustrate, for example, the particular construing held by the members of a family in difficulty (e.g., see Figure 8). This then allows us to test hypotheses flowing from the picture so built up, and later assessment allows therapeutic change to be measured. I assume it is useful to consider that such an entity exists within the life of a family and will set out to describe and investigate it in various ways. We can use various methods to point toward what it may be like. Some of these methods are presented later.

The model of the family construct system being proposed here applies the view that Kelly had of the personal construct system to the construing system shared between several people. This simplifies theorizing a great deal. In this view constructs are constructs, not particularly personal or social. It does not mean the members all agree or construe in the same way. They may occupy different regions of the system, and a construct of one person may not be available to another member. I may fail to grasp construing in my wife, my sister, my son all my life. But in this view, all the constructs tend to link in systematically into a wider construct system. The individual's construing is thus systematically related and the overall family construct system is rooted in a culturally imbued belief system.

Is it justifiable to make a theoretical leap like this? Is it not nonsense to say that constructs are ever anything but personal—mine or yours? I believe it is justifiable. This step may be harder to accept for personal construct theorists than, for example, sociologists of knowledge. I do not wish to deemphasize the importance of the individual that, in a sense, the whole of Kelly's venture stands for. Psychology should be about individuals—us—people who have experiences, who make sense of the world in a unique personal way and who make choices in the light of this. It is precisely this aspect of Kelly's psychology that keeps me using it and that is so important politically in the struggle against the depersonalization of psychoanalytic, behavioral, and medical thinking. But extending the theory need not and should not deemphasize these Kellian values. In fact, it allows these to be accessed by social scientists, family researchers, and therapists often working within a much more arid view of human beings. It is a justifiable theoretical step because it simplifies. In science, as the law of parsimony states, if two phenomena, for example hypnotic and psychotic hallucinations, can be explained according to one principle, then that is better than having two separate and unrelated explanatory principles. A purely individualist construct theorist, if such exists, either has little to say about sociological and family-systemic processes or simply reduces these to the addition of many individual actions. This step improves our theorizing by making construing more fundamental and develops a position more unifying within a wide range of social-scientific concerns. To achieve this but maintain within it a satisfactory psychology, and as I hinted earlier, a physiology of the individual (Procter, 1988), is to me an exciting development that should help us to achieve a wider and deeper understanding of ourselves.

DYNAMICS OF THE FAMILY CONSTRUCT SYSTEM

To discuss the dynamics of our family construct system, we must first home in a little more on the nature of the construct. To me this notion of Kelly's has the same looseness but ability to be defined as the family construct system itself. I have already mentioned the construct as a choice, as a discrimination, and as an avenue of movement. It can be symbolized also as a scale or a dimension as the repertory grid tends to emphasize. To me it is a deep concept, and this depth comes from its dialectical nature. It is living and creative. It is the heart of mental life. Kelly's originality in bringing this "archaic" dialectical thinking into the center of a modern psychological theory was a brilliant move. It flows directly, perhaps through Dewey, from Hegel's *Science of Logic* (1812/1968). Any idea here is, if you like, fundamentally unstable and poses its opposite. This is the case in the theory and in everyday thinking and conversation. The moment I state something, or think it, its exceptions, its limitations, and its loopholes arise. The stream of consciousness as we experience it may proceed to develop and flow according to this principle. As we converse together, we will bring to each other elements, events, and examples of our experiences that validate, extend, or attempt to disabuse us of agreements so far attained. As we assemble a certain domain of experience together, new construing will occur to one or the other of us to throw the events or ideas into new perspective. This conversation will be structured or governed by the construing at a more superordinate level on which we agree or systematically differ. This latter aspect is likely to be unconscious, as far as the participants are concerned.

The systematic constraints on a conversation may be available to another family member, however, whose contributions and considerations at this higher level of concern prove to be central. While mother and father covertly but systematically differ about the significance of Derek's problem behavior, Derek himself is engaged in a project of attempting to expose the partiality of their positions as he sees these. If his contributions have become too heavily disqualified by them, he may seek progressively more indirect and metaphorical ways to comment. In Kellian terms we may operate, in interaction, at different "levels of convenience," as well as in different ranges. Such interaction is likely to be encountered commonly in clinical situations such as parent-child or marital conflict, and it demonstrates a particular type of fragmentation in the family construct system.

Thus, in the ongoing conversation of which family life consists, we trade or refuse to trade ways of construing. We justify and validate our construing and agree or disagree about the significance of events. In this and out of this certain enduring constructs will be sustained that allow us to continue relating to each other. This is the family construct system.

Within it we will be taking positions. I basically see things in contrast to the way you do, and I will assemble evidence for the validity of my view. Alternatively, I agree with you and you agree with me in contrast to how they see things (parents, in-laws, the Conservatives, our son Jim, and so on). We may disagree and pretend we don't (cf. pseudomutuality; Wynne, Ryckoff, Day, & Hirsch, 1958). We may fight when we actually agree. We may only fight when Derek is present to reduce our apparent extreme disapproval of his behavior. We may struggle to invalidate the other's position in order to shore up our own shaky position. This seems to help to reduce the guilt.

Belinda, admitted to hospital to detoxify from heavy alcohol misuse, sees herself as the victim of cruelty and injustice on the part of her daughter, mother, and boyfriend. In turn, Belinda's mother indignantly attacks her, desperately attempting to validate the shared family construing of herself as loving and giving. This construct governs their interaction when together but leads them to fight each other from symmetrical positions. This reduces to "I'm not as bad as you—what you did in 1958 proves it." Belinda came into hospital, but all the family drink heavily. Belinda's alcoholism is a taboo subject with John, her boyfriend, but when they came to see me together, "Belinda is better than John" is shared amicably by both. The evidence: John drank a whole bottle of whisky yesterday. "Yes I did," says John, his tail between his legs. Meanwhile, daughter hates Gran and John, but loves and cares for her Mum, "the poor helpless alcoholic." "It's Gran and John's fault she's like this," she says.

In this rigid but shifting and developing dance, the family members live out their lives in ways that make sense to them according to their own position in the construing. Each one's actions and choices are contained in the here-and-now context of the others' latest contributions and are constrained by the dimensions of meaning that are operating across the group. It is potentially a highly creative process that is harnessed during the natural (or therapeutic) change or problem-solution that groups, thankfully, demonstrate ubiquitously.

The opportunity for a new family construct system appears when two partners begin to relate rather than remain acquaintances. They may begin to define the relationship as friends, lovers, carer/sufferer, and so on. One may see the other as a friend and the other sees the first as a nuisance, but choice or circumstances keep the two in contact. Then, other positions will be filled in with figures, alive or dead, and their significance will be negotiated and struggled over. "Your Mum," "your ex," "our child," "my work," "your church," and so on become positions modified by their holders, perhaps idealized if vacant. Positions may be suspended: "We don't want children; we do not share the notion of us as parents." Then, when a child unexpectedly arrives: "We love her; we never thought we wanted a child. Peter is a wonderful father, aren't you?" Peter grins contentedly.

Many of the processes so easily ascribed solely to individuals are, on closer reflection, very interpersonal. One of these is learning. Groups learn and partners learn together as the family construct system is progressively revised, refined, and elaborated. A fund of knowledge is held in common. This may be inaccessible as a member enters a role in a new system—school, new partner's family, becoming divorced. My ability to be confident and have a relaxed sense of humor and the associated fund of attitudes and anecdotes that I may feel in my family depends on the validating approval and reciprocal repertory of family members. I go away to college in a foreign country. The way of being I normally experience when relating to my family is unusable. I feel isolated and lonely. I may need to learn a whole new way of being. This becomes possible as new relationships develop. Family constructs will again be evoked and utilized as intimate relationships with new people are negotiated.

Therapy provides an opportunity for the group to learn as the temporary construct system of the therapist-cum-family is enabled to facilitate the construction of a new set of perspectives. The same is just as true within systems when conversations with a parent, a friend, or an advisor are facilitative. Ideally, the family will go on increasing its knowledge and sets of options. Flexibility, permeability, and the opportunity to try out different possibilities will be maintained. Complementarity will exist and construing will be accessible to different members.

When a system reduces through separation and loss, a member experiences more than the personal loss of the departing one, painful though that is. The construct system can suffer a catastrophic constriction and fragmentation, leaving large areas of construing unavailable to the surviving members. Because of the shared constructs, the lost one's knowledge and voice should be accessible to the others, but a great deal of work searching through the memory, going through the lost one's ways, sayings, and interactions, may be necessary.

This approach allows us to enter the world of mechanisms of defense that psychodynamic and related approaches readily ascribe to families (e.g., Laing, 1967, 1972). Identification and contra-identification were mentioned earlier. A part of the construct system occupied by the lost member may be introjected back into the remaining members' system. This may happen gradually or quite suddenly, as for example when the farmer's son steps into his father's shoes, taking on his ways and attitudes when the old man dies. Construct theory allows such processes to be understood within a different epistemology to analytic theory, avoiding the latter's objectivist concern with perceptions as distorted views of reality. It is also possible to define these processes operationally and measure them, for example, with the repertory grid (Procter, 1978, 1985b, 1993).

DISPLAYING THE FAMILY CONSTRUCT SYSTEM

The family construct approach allows us to see patterns in families, but using the family members' own dimensions rather than ones imposed from outside. Having said this, it also allows us to define and operationalize professional dimensions of meaning that can be used in family research. Thus, family construct systems will vary in their permeability (ability to take in new ideas), looseness (shifting meanings), and complexity (variety of perspectives contained within the system). These could be used for researching families with particular mental health problems and patterns of violence and abuse as well as families with positive characteristics that allow their members to thrive.

As mentioned earlier, the family construct system is a heuristic concept. Thus, rather than leading to one methodology, it generates methodologies for researching family construing. Depending on one's purposes, the family's views of any particular issue or type of element can be investigated. A selection of possibilities will be presented here. The reader is also directed to Procter (1978, 1985a, 1985b), Feixas, Procter & Neimeyer (1993), Feixas (1992), and Neimeyer (1993).

A very simple tool, valuable as an interviewing method, is the perceiver-element grid (PEG) in which the rows give the members' views of each person in the family and the columns show how each is viewed by all the others, including themselves. Figure 2 gives the PEG for the four members of Peter's family. This grid is summarized from repertory grids given to all four members, but such a grid can be constructed in an interview simply by asking the members how they see themselves and others ideally at a particular point in time or in a specific situation. It provides a lot of information and, as an initial entry into a family, is preferable to information based on an imposed category system explicitly or implicitly arising from the therapist's or researcher's dimensions.

Collecting this information is a structured conversation, the family members being given ample opportunity to check, revise, and elaborate the data so far collected. Grids also output a number of diagrammatic forms that are useful for capturing family construing. Figures 3 and 4 show element and construct linkage diagrams. Figure 3 shows an exam-

| | | Elements | | | |
		Mother	Father	(Peter)	Brother
Perceivers	Mother	placid, happy, quiet, doesn't like football	unhappy, temper, likes football	placid/happy	placid/happy
	Father	sad, argumentative, shy, proud	sad, argumentative, modest	sad, argumentative, shy, modest	proud, sociable, happy, talkative
	Peter	hard to please, warm, loving, babyish	cold, not loving	warm, shows feeling	cold, not loving
	Brother	depressed, introvert, gentle	extrovert, rough, not clever	depressed, introvert, gentle, not generous	extrovert

Figure 2. Construing in Peter's family (from Procter 1978)

ple of a construct system. Each of these are constructs that correlate as shown by the arrows (the arrowheads also show which other constructs are most highly linked with a construct). Computer calculations of the correlations were performed on a grid given to all members of the family. We can see how in this case constructs are clustering together; the letters in brackets refer to members of the family from whom the constructs were elicited: father, mother, Nigel, and his sister. One can see how the constructs from the different family members are clustered, each having their own unique word for them. This illustrates nicely how it is not just a collection of individuals that are construing entirely in a unique way, but that there is an overall system they are all part of.

Figure 4 shows how the elements (each member's view of each of the others) are linked. Significant levels of perceived similarity (e.g., father's view of mother and sister) and commonality (e.g., mother's and sibling's view of father) can be seen. Mother's view of father (M-F), mother's view of herself (M-M), Paul's view of himself (P-P), and father's view of mother (F-M) are correlated. The figures at the bottom are isolated and are different from the main cluster: Paul's view of his mother (P-M) and his view of his father (P-F).

Useful diagrams can also be drawn of the family construct system by looking at perceived similarity as seen by each member and the overall pooled perceived similarity (Figure 5). Mother (M) sees herself and her husband (F) as identical (double line) and orthogonal to the identified patient, Henry (P), and her other son (S). Henry (P) sees all family members as being different from each other. The others see Mother (M) and Father (F) as being significantly similar. Father sees much similarity in but distinguishes himself from both children.

Figure 6 gives the actual agreements (as demonstrated by significant element correlations on a pooled family grid) that the members as perceivers have about each member and about the family members pooled together. Again in Henry's family, perceived similarity between parents is accompanied by their actual agreement, perhaps supporting Kelly's commonality corollary that people are characterized by their construing and resemble one another if they construe in a similar way. These results were extracted from the family grid, a method that can be examined further in Procter (1978, 1985b, 1993).

Figure 7 shows a graph in which two main factors are plotted against each other. The lines represent the emergent poles of constructs. Elements outside the box are significantly loaded on the factors. The data are drawn from a pooled family grid in which the four members' percep-

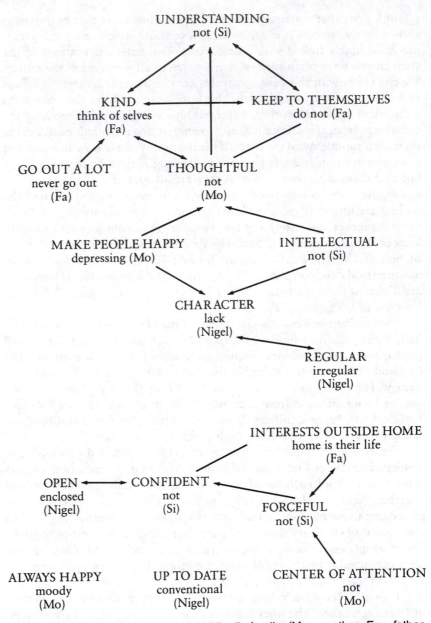

Figure 3. Clustering of constructs in Nigel's family (Mo = mother, Fa = father, Si = sister)

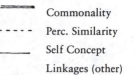

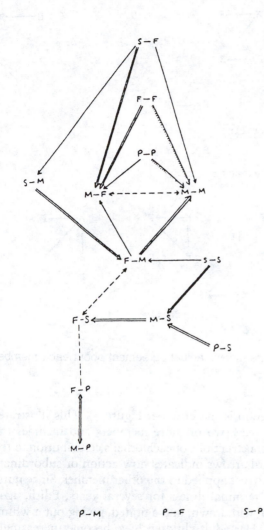

Figure 4. Linkage and cluster of elements in Nigel's common family grid

tions of themselves and each other are put together. Views of father (aggressive, argumentative) cluster in the left bottom quadrant. Peter's brother (S) is contrasted to father (quiet and placid). Peter himself (depressed) is contrasted to the unoccupied (idealized?) positive left upper quadrant (sociable, confident).

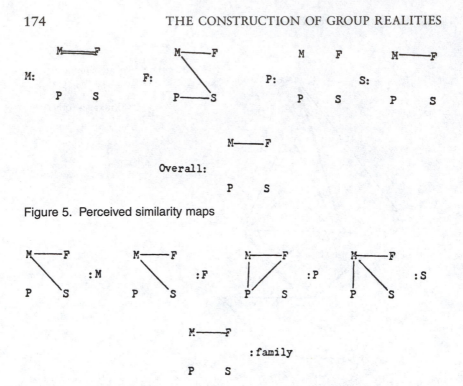

Figure 5. Perceived similarity maps

Figure 6. Commonality maps (shows actual agreement about each member and the family)

Another kind of diagram is the bow tie (Figure 8). This illustrates the recursive process between two or more members and includes the members' perceptions or constructions of each other's contribution to the interaction. The downward arrows indicates how action or subordinate choices flow from the construct applied to the other member. Since nursing her husband through terminal illness for several years, Edith, aged 71, has become depressed, withdrawn, and agitated, giving out a whimpering sound of self-pity. Her adult children have become increasingly impatient with her, feeling she is not helping herself enough. They confront her, asking her what is the matter. The diagonal arrows show how the evidence of the other's action confirms, validates, and justifies the construction held.

Apart from being a useful tool in therapy, the bow tie illustrates how constructs are shaped and maintained within interpersonal interaction within the family. Constructs are an aspect of interaction and function to maintain it in certain patterns, not just intrapsychic factors in the

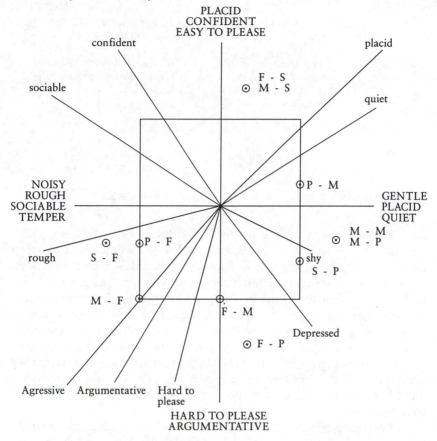

Figure 7. Elements mapped on two constructs from Peter's Commom Family grid.

mind of the individual. Alterations in the action or shifts in the construing lead the whole construing system to drift (as constructs are revised), shift into a new configuration, or occasionally to oscillate between two patterns.

EPISTEMOLOGICAL ISSUES

The concept of the family construct system as outlined in this chapter leads to implications similar to but different in important ways from other constructivist approaches currently popular in the family therapy

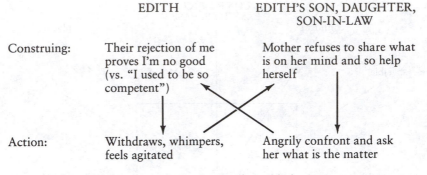

Figure 8. Construing process in the family of an elderly person

field. Radical constructivism (Kenny & Gardner, 1988; Mahoney, 1988) talks of an objective world being a myth. While I would want to assert that no direct knowledge of the world is possible—it is always seen through the spectacles of constructs—Kelly's original assertion (1955) that the external world exists (and that we are gradually coming to know it better) remains fundamental for me. We are not free to simply dream up a different set of events from those that occur, although the construction we make of them is all we can know. Only one set of events ever happens objectively; there is no ambiguity in events in themselves as they occur in space and time. We are unassailably associated with our physiological and social realities. I cannot prove this, but it remains axiomatic to my position.

   Construing systems can change and develop astoundingly. Human beings can reframe the most appalling situations, deepening their resilience and understanding in the process. But our systems have developed in a particular context that we are not free to wish away. In particular, people live in situations of gross social, sexual, and ethnic inequality. It is important not to allow the constructivist component of our approach to ignore this.

   I believe it is important to clarify this as it leads to important implications at practical and political levels. It shows in my daily practice in that, in spite of my emphasis on construction, I am interested in the objective evidence that family members use to bolster their arguments. While we can argue about the significance of events of the previous Tuesday night, the fact is that certain events did occur, certain words were spoken. Either 8-year-old Dianne was sexually abused by her uncle or she was not, although I may never get to know exactly what transpired.

Thus, within our constructivist position, the truth and lies can be spoken, although events cannot affect people except through the way they are construed by them.

This analysis, starting with Kelly with the person, allows the construing underlying gender inequalities to be drawn out and demonstrated to the researcher and to the family members themselves. Many families, influenced by the discourses of the surrounding culture, develop gender construing to the disadvantage of women. However, this is not inevitably the case. In an earlier generation of my own family, women came to be regarded as strong and men as weak, partly because of sibling-order effects (three older sisters and two younger brothers). This, then, reverted not only in response to wider sociological influences, but also as a strong reaction to the previous construing within the dynamics of the subsequent generation.

TOWARD AN ETHICAL PSYCHOLOGY

Kelly puts choice at the center of his psychology. Choice is axiomatic to our position. Unless a psychology does this, it cannot begin to address ethical issues that are central in family life (Boszormenyi-Nagy & Spark, 1973) and social intervention. These cannot be reduced to psychology or, worse, physiology. We need to continue to elaborate a constructivist ethics, and in a broader sense bring ethics properly into the realm of psychology.

To the extent that it explains human action in terms of individual advantage (hedonism, self-actualization, reduction of dissonance), any individual psychology ultimately is a view of people as selfish. Even Kelly's choice corollary—we choose to define, extend, and elaborate our construct systems—could be seen as falling into this trap. And yet human beings are commonly not necessarily selfish but also altruistic, at least as far as the benefit of their immediate family and friends are concerned. This could be interpreted cynically, of course: "They only look after their context so they may survive."

By extending the construct from the personal to the social, we can begin to build a much more satisfactory view of the ethical nature of action and interaction. The choice corollary is now extended to say that we decide on actions because they seem to elaborate our shared, mutual construct system. This is seen quite literally in the form of gifts of all kinds (material gifts, acts of generosity, care, thoughtfulness). A psychology putting genuine altruism at its core will make a welcome change from the implicit Skinnerian ethic that has imbued so much of our 20th-century culture and values and underlies the abusive and violent society that characterizes so many countries in the post Judeo-Christian world.

Introducing an ethical psychology into the culture could fill the moral vacuum of society in its present state. Psychology as an ethical subject in schools (of course, experientially) would be of intrinsic interest to children (perhaps explaining the tremendous popularity of soap operas that illustrate the everyday struggles and dilemmas of family situations). There is a serious need for this as a preventive measure instead of relying solely on therapeutic methods after mental health problems, abuse, violence, needless separation and divorce, crime, and other problems have broken out in families. The family construct approach as an example would contribute by encouraging pupils to think multilaterally about their families rather than tacitly encouraging a validation of only their own immediate wishes and needs as promoted by the ideology of so much individual counseling and psychotherapy. Psychotherapy has entered the culture in a big way, and the idea of solving problems in confidential one-to-one work (this should of course remain available) can encourage privacy, secrecy, and coalition against other family members, often destabilizing families and perpetuating family difficulties. This ideology can ultimately be traced to an individualist emphasis in its basic assumptions.

Of course, I use the word *family* in a very broad sense, and it is very much part of the values of constructive alternativism that society should allow many forms of small living groups to thrive. But hopefully the concept of the family construct system will help to reestablish the importance of the intimate groups we live within—cultures at the microsocial level that are so important to us in terms of our psychological well-being and that are potentially such rich resources of knowledge and creativity.

REFERENCES

Boszormenyi-Nagy, I., & Spark, G. (1973). *Invisible loyalties: Reciprocity in intergenerational family therapy*. New York: Harper and Row.
Buber, M. (1937). *I and thou* (R. G. Smith, Trans.). Edinburgh: Clark.
Dallos, R. (1991). *Family belief systems, therapy and change: A constructional approach*. Milton Keynes, UK: Open University Press.

Dallos, R., & Procter, H. G. (1984) *Family processes: An interactional view*. D307 Social Psychology Course, Milton Keynes, UK: Open University Press.

Feixas, G. (1990a). Approaching the individual, approaching the system: A constructivist model for integrative psychotherapy. *Journal of Family Psychology, 4*, 4–35.

Feixas, G. (1990b). Personal construct theory and the systemic therapies: Parallel or convergent trends? *Journal of Marital and Family Therapy, 16*, 1–20.

Feixas, G. (1992). Personal construct approaches to family therapy. In R. A. Neimeyer & G. J. Neimeyer (Eds.), *Advances in personal construct psychology* Vol. 2 (pp. 217–249). Greenwich, CT: JAI Press.

Feixas, G., Procter, H. G., & Neimeyer, G. J. (1993). Convergent lines of assessment: Systemic and constructivist contributions. In G. J. Neimeyer (Ed.), *Constructivist assessment: A casebook* (pp. 143–178). New York: Sage.

Hegel, G. W. F. (1968). *Science of logic* (A. V. Miller, Trans.). London: Allen and Unwin. (Original work published 1812).

Kelly, G. A. (1955). *The psychology of personal constructs,* Vols. 1 and 2. New York: Norton. (2nd Edition 1991, Routledge and Kegan Paul).

Kenny, V., & Gardner, G. (1988). Constructions of self-organising systems. *Irish Journal of Psychology, 9*, 1–24.

Laing, R. D. (1967). Family and individual structure. In P. Lomas (Ed.), *The predicament of the family* (pp. 107–125). London: Hogarth.

Laing, R. D. (1972). *The politics of the family*. New York: Random House.

Mahoney, M. J. (1988). Constructive metatheory II: Implications for psychotherapy. *International Journal of Personal Construct Psychology, 1*, 299–317.

Neimeyer, R. A. (1993). Constructivist approaches to the measurement of meaning. In G. J. Neimeyer (Ed.), *Constructivist assessment: A casebook* (pp. 58–103). New York: Sage.

Neimeyer, R. A., & Feixas, G. (1990). Constructivist contributions to psychotherapy integration. *Journal of Integrative and Eclectic Psychotherapy, 9*, 131–148.

Procter, H. G. (1978). *Personal construct theory and the family: A theoretical and methodological study*. Unpublished PhD thesis, University of Bristol.

Procter, H. G. (1981). Family construct psychology: An approach to understanding and treating families. In S. Walrond-Skinner (Ed.), *Developments in Family Therapy* (pp. 350–366). London: Routledge and Kegan Paul.

Procter, H. G. (1985a). A construct approach to family therapy and systems intervention. In E. Button (Ed.), *Personal construct theory and mental health* (pp. 327–350). Beckenham, Kent: Croom Helm.

Procter, H. G. (1985b). Repertory grid techniques in family therapy and research. In N. Beail (Ed.), *Repertory grid technique: Application in clinical and educational settings* (pp. 218–239). Beckenham, Kent: Croom Helm.

Procter, H. G. (1988, June). The family construct approach and psychosomatic research. Paper presented to the Seventeenth European Conference on Psychosomatic Research, Marburg, West Germany.

Procter, H. G. (1993). Die Untersuchung von Familien [An investigation of families]. In J. W. Scheer & A. Catina (Eds.), *Einfuehrung in die Repertory Grid-Technik: Band 2. Klinische Forschung und Praxis* (pp. 72–85). Bern (Switzerland), Göttingen, Toronto, Seattle: Verlag Hans Huber.

Procter, H. G., & Parry, G. (1978). Constraint and freedom: The social origin of personal constructs. In Fransella, F. (Ed.), *Personal Construct Psychology 1977* (pp. 157–170). London: Academic Press.

Procter, H. G., & Pieczora, R. (1993). A family oriented community mental health centre. In A. Treacher, & J. Carpenter (Eds.), *Using family therapy in the 90's* (pp. 131–144). Oxford: Blackwell.

Wynne, L. C., Ryckoff, I., Day, J., & Hirsch, S. (1958). Pseudomutuality in the family relations of schizophrenics. *Psychiatry, 21,* 205–220.

CHAPTER 8

Construing Across Cultures:
Aboriginal Australians Construe
Their Housing and Histories

HELEN ROSS

The purpose of this paper is to provide illustrations of ways the psychology of personal constructs can be applied to understand those coming from differing cultural traditions. Kelly (1955) supported a view of culture as being essentially a shared system of meanings, though he devoted only a few pages to elaborating how culture fits within his personal construct theory. Such a view of culture with shared meanings, providing patterns for behavior, now has wide acceptance (Geertz, 1973; Keesing, 1981; Schwartz, 1980). In these comments on culture, Kelly did not attempt to distinguish construing that is individual from that which is cultural. He acknowledged both shared and individual construing, and he acknowledged that social processes influence individual construing.

METHODS FOR CROSS-CULTURAL INQUIRY
INTO CONSTRUING

Research into the construct systems of other cultures is an exercise in cross-cultural communication. With his sociality corollary, Kelly emphasized that one need not actually adopt or share the constructs of another person (or culture) in order to understand them, but must be capable of construing what they are construing: "to the extent that one person construes the construction processes of another, he may play a role in a social process involving the other person" (Kelly, 1955, p. 95).

181

Clinical psychologists, for instance, do not need to think like their clients so much as be able to see things from their clients' points of view.

The relative neglect of the group and cultural dimensions in personal construct psychology research cannot be blamed on methodology so much as on Kelly's highly individual orientation and the interests of later practitioners. A lack of useful methods has, however, hindered this type of research. Kelly's versions of the repertory grid method, and the many adaptations since (see, for example, Bonarius, Holland, & Rosenberg, 1981; Epting, Suchman, & Nickeson, 1971; Fransella & Bannister, 1977; Landfield & Epting, 1987; Stewart & Stewart, 1981), work superbly with individuals but less well with groups.

Kelly saw constructs as being organized into systems. He did not intend that the study of personal constructs should be concentrated mainly at the most basic level, that of the dichotomous constructs elicited when three elements are compared, yet this has occurred owing to the popularity of the repertory grid and its amenability to sophisticated mathematical analysis (see Fransella & Bannister, 1977; Kelly, 1955, pp. 267ff.). Kelly was as interested in the content of constructs (1955, pp. 219ff.) as in their application to elements, and he foresaw other ways of exploring the organization of personal constructs besides mathematical identification of correlations and clusters in completed grids (1955, p. 331). Among the naturalistic ways he suggested for eliciting constructs are conversations and character sketches (1955, pp. 328ff.). Further methods are described by Landfield and Epting (1987, chapter 2).

A variety of what I will term *naturalistic* methods have been advocated especially, but not exclusively, for use with less-verbal members of western societies; for instance, children, deaf people and those with mental disabilities (see Bell & Bell, 1989; Fransella & Bannister, 1977, pp. 54–55; Hayhow, Lansdown, Maddick, & Ravenette, 1988; Landfield & Epting, 1987; Neimeyer, 1981; ten Kate, 1981). These methods have included analyzing essays, conversations, stories, children's drawings and discussion of models. Kelly emphasized that constructs need not be verbalized and could be inferred from observation (see also chapter 16).

The organization of construct systems has been made easier to study through variants of Hinkle's implications grid and applications of his technique for exploring the nature of hierarchies in construing (*laddering*), described by Fransella and Bannister (1977). Consequent to Hinkle's thesis, some authors use the term *pyramiding* to distinguish downward from upward exploration of construct relationships through a hierarchical construct system (see Landfield & Epting, 1987, pp. 64ff.), while others use the term *laddering* for both upward and downward directions (see Stewart & Stewart, 1981, p. 23).

Anthropologists, who are similarly interested in appreciating the worldview of others, combine observation and linguistic analysis in particular to explore how members of other cultures conceptualize objects and events. A typical method is to explore the hierarchical organization of conceptual and linguistic categories (Spradley & McCurdy, 1977). The linguistic approach is analogous to personal construct psychologists' analysis of conversations or stories. Psychologists could learn from anthropologists' willingness to combine their verbal and nonverbal methods of collecting information. Indeed, Kelly and other clinicians expected to use specific techniques such as character sketches or repertory grids in combination with discussions with their clients and observation of their behavioral cues (see also Landfield & Epting, 1987, p. 64)

When one is studying cross-culturally, the content of the other culture's constructs should be of primary interest. Methods are needed that allow constructs to be elicited from individuals, but compared among group members. Methods that explore the hierarchical organization of constructs are also necessary, as well as those that investigate the social and situational uses of constructs. Formative influences on patterns of construing, and relationships between construing and behavior patterns, require investigation, using methods from sociology, anthropology, and social psychology repertoires alongside adapted personal construct methods.

In accordance with Kelly's sociality corollary, the first priority in cross-cultural methods must be to promote effective communication between the construing parties. The greater the cultural differences between researcher and researched, the less commonality is likely between them at the beginning of the process. This makes the communication task more difficult for both parties. It is sometimes forgotten that both parties contribute to the communication. Apparently, skilled anthropologists often turn out to have very perceptive and communicative informants. A highly sophisticated method from the researcher's academic culture may appear to assist the researcher's side of the transaction, but does not necessarily provide an effective vehicle for communication if it is too unfamiliar to enable the members of the other culture to express themselves comfortably and freely. As Mair (1989, p. 4) put it; "too much technicality can impoverish the story being told."

The more structured variants on repertory grid methods—those in which constructs are elicited through structured comparison tasks, and constructs are matched to elements to complete a matrix (grid)—are eth-nocentric and class-biased in many respects. Many cultures do not cus-tomarily follow the modes of discourse and inquiry necessary for the completion of a grid such as asking and answering questions and making direct comparisons. Few anthropologists would attempt a structured sur-vey in the field for this reason. Landfield and Epting (1987, p. 22) also query the assumption that survey questions mean the same to all respon-dents. The methods of eliciting constructs by comparing triads or pairs of objects are even more foreign to the discourse of many cultures. Re-course to the anthropologists' toolbox, referred to as *participant obser-vation* (including various forms of observation such as interviewing and conversation), makes eliciting and sharing the constructs of members of another culture far more practicable and less intrusive.

Another crucial consideration in cross-cultural research is the flexi-bility of the researcher's own construct system to appreciate and accom-modate the construct systems she or he is about to learn (sociality corol-lary). This is a matter of personal outlook, but reading, guidance, and prior experience in cross-cultural encounters can presumably assist in de-veloping such openness to constructions in the other culture.

This paper shares my experiences in exploring the construing of Aboriginal Australians. The first study was of Aboriginal construing of housing (Ross, 1987) and illustrated ways in which relatively structured methods can be devised for cross-cultural study. The second study was of the cumulative impacts of resource developments such as mining, roads, and tourism and was conducted using communication methods chosen by the Aboriginal people concerned. Through oral history and free inter-views, they explained how they construed their history. These methods, variants of conversation analysis, are relatively unstructured. Together the studies illustrate possibilities for construing the construing of others across cultures, by means which make verbal (and nonverbal) communi-cation between the researched and the researcher possible.

ABORIGINAL HOUSING STUDY

Before embarking on this study, I had been struck by the way in which Australian governments were prescribing new forms of housing for Aboriginal people, entirely according to their own construction of the problems. No one was bothering to find out how Aboriginal people con-strued their present forms of shelter versus the more Western forms offered. Research in other cultures (Duncan, 1981; Lloyd, 1979; Rapoport, 1977; Turner, 1976) had long shown that forms of housing are related integrally to culture, and that forcing people into forms of housing that were incompatible with core cultural norms could be extremely debilitating both individually and culturally (Rapoport, 1980).

I chose the task of exploring how Aboriginal people construed their housing, and how their housing suited their lifestyles. I wanted to identify both individual and group similarities and differences in construing related to housing. I conducted the study in a remote town of about 1,000 people in northwest Australia that had an unusual variety of forms of Aboriginal housing. These ranged from simple camp dwellings built by their occupants from canvas and scrap metal, to intermediate forms of shelter with some services, to conventional public housing provided to non-Aborigines and Aborigines alike. At the time of the study (1980–1981), Aboriginal people comprised about 80% of the town's population, varying seasonally according to the employment available on surrounding cattle stations.

The study required me, a non-Aboriginal Australian, to be able to construe Aboriginal people's construing of housing (see Kelly's sociality corollary). In accordance with the triangulation approach to social research advocated by Webb, Campbell, Schwartz and Sechrest (1966) to compensate for the imperfections of any single method, I considered it vital to use more than one method to study Aboriginal people's construing.

The first of these methods was the anthropologists' staple, known as participant observation. Participant observation is really a toolbox of methods, including intimate involvement with a community (usually living in) and whatever combinations of unstructured and structured observation and interview techniques suit one's purposes and opportunities. Listening to and joining in conversations, for instance, and observing everyday incidents and behavior, helps one to understand one's research topic in cultural context to a degree impossible with more structured social science research methods. I lived in a camp on the edge of the town for a year and participated in the other residential groups' activities from this base.

From the beginning, participant observation helped to establish my credentials as a person prepared to see matters from an Aboriginal point of view and able to present this point of view to government. My accessibility assisted Aboriginal people to construe and reconstrue my purposes. They took some months to test out various role expectations derived from their previous experiences, eliminating missionary, nursing sister, linguist, and government before reaching an understanding of my research purposes that more or less approximated my own. Living in the community also promoted essential rapport, so people were prepared to open up to me far more readily than to a visitor. This rapport and tolerance was vital when it came to my survey (see below), which required my breaching Aboriginal conversational norms by asking direct questions. I also needed constant conversational practice to gain an ear for heavy Aboriginal accents, to learn to speak Kriol (the northern Australian creole language) fluently, and to learn enough of an Aboriginal language (Jaru) to show willingness and to appreciate how Aboriginal conceptual systems are structured in language.

Observation enabled me to note the behavior patterns that accompanied constructs, and thus to understand much more of the meaning of each construct, and the organization of constructs, than could be verbalized. For instance, economic constructs concerning reluctance to pay rent and bills have to be understood in the cultural context of kinship norms. The subtleties of Aboriginal kinship behavior had to be observed in different situations; they could not have been asked in an interview. The norms provide for a wide circle of kin to have access to all of an Aboriginal person's goods and cash. This was ecologically and economically efficient in a hunter-gatherer society, ensuring the best sharing and least wastage of foods, but the norms of reciprocation have become overextended and inequitable in a town situation. The owner or tenant of a large or well-located house finds herself host to all comers, who may eat the cupboard bare while spending their own cash on entertainment or consumer goods, leaving the host to meet the bills. Many houses were described as too big, meaning that the space invited more guests than the host found manageable. One antidote to the excessive financial demands of kin is to have a tiny or inconveniently located dwelling, so that relatives stay elsewhere, and indeed this solution was not uncommon (Ross, 1987).

The first 9 months of my year in the town were spent exclusively on familiarization, on participant observation, and in developing a structured method for eliciting constructs for use within a sampled survey. The stages of developing this method, trying out different lines of questioning, supplemented my participant observation data and the later data from the survey. For instance, economic constructs loomed large in my exploratory methods, but were less well represented in the survey. I attributed this to imperfections in both my research methods. Insufficient dwellings likely to elicit economic constructs were included in my survey, while my social location among people who were particularly adamant about economic constructs made these show up strongly in the participant observation methods. An anthropologist relying purely on participant observation data would have been tempted to generalize from her own social circle, whereas a psychologist relying entirely on a survey would not have realized the underrepresentation of a salient construct caused by the survey design, let alone understood the meaning of the construct in terms of its behavioral implications in the kinship system.

It took 9 months to design and pretest the structured survey and three months for the interviewing and content analysis. The sample was designed to include equal numbers of adults randomly drawn from four residential groups, aiming for four cells of 20 people each for analysis of variance comparisons. These targets were not met exactly as it proved valuable to interview some extra campers, and the number of non-Aborigines fell short. Equal numbers were not essential for the main forms of analysis used. The groups were

1. Campers who built their own rudimentary dwellings (known as humpies or tents) and shacks on vacant land around the town (27). These were totally unserviced. Water had to be fetched by hand and there were no sanitary arrangements.

2. People in dwellings intermediate between the camps and public housing in terms of size, standard, and services (21). Ten were from Redhill, a camp that had obtained land tenure and had houses with wide verandas built to the people's own design. It had a limited and unreliable water supply—one tap for 50 to 100 people. The other 11 lived in old single or three-roomed metal shelters on the government-built reserve, with shared ablution blocks and one tap outside each house. (The houses were due for replacement.) These subgroups were treated separately in the eventual analyses as there were some interesting social and construing differences among their members.

3. Aboriginal people in conventional three-bedroom public housing (20).

4. Non-Aboriginal people in the same types of public housing (17).

Interviews were held at people's homes in two sessions of approximately an hour each, owing to the length of the schedule. Either Kriol or English was spoken. Aboriginal assistants were present at most of the

Kriol interviews to help with the content analysis. Aboriginal interviewees were paid in cash, and non-Aboriginal interviewees were recompensed with an Aboriginal artefact.

Two personal construct questions formed the main part of the survey, one eliciting constructs pertinent to the full range of housing options and locations available in and near the town and the other a group grid based on supplied constructs. These were accompanied by questions collecting personal and family data (such as sex, household compositions) and scales on traditionalism and previous experience of housing. A rating scale question was included.

Technique 1: Elicited Constructs

This method was the outcome of several months of experimentation. The methods of eliciting constructs by asking people to compare triads or pairs of objects (referred to in the literature as elements; see Fransella & Bannister, 1977, chapter 3; Kelly, 1955; Landfield & Epting, 1987, chapter 2; Stewart & Stewart, 1981, chapter 2) were tried using both photographs of houses and verbal labels as elements. These foundered as few of the traditionally-oriented people were able to verbalize comparisons between elements, though they could describe each element individually. In Aboriginal conversation it is impolite to ask complex direct questions, and many Aboriginal people can become tongue-tied by the breach of etiquette. When the direct question was of an unusual type for their culture, as in the comparison task, it was even more difficult for many to respond. (Aboriginal people would use an indirect mode of questioning, such as making a comment followed by a silence inviting the other to open up discussion if they wish. Such leading questions could not be used validly in a survey.)

A pyramiding technique (Fransella & Bannister, 1977, pp. 42–52; Landfield & Epting, 1987, pp. 64ff.), however, proved very successful. The first construct given by most people in the pretesting of eliciting methods was a general evaluative one (good/no good or I like it/I don't like it). Preempting this response by asking whether the person would like (evaluative construct) living in (behavioral guideline) each house or living environment (element) proved an excellent basis for exploring why the person made their evaluation through elaboration down the person's pyramid of relevant constructs.

The question is shown in Table 1.

The five types of dwellings (used as elements) were the full range of

Table 1. Question Used to Elicit Constructs

Question	Yes/no	Why?
Would you like living in . . .		
(i) *a humpy? (or a tent)*		
(ii) *a shack?*		
(iii) *a house like a Reserve house, but not necessarily on the Reserve?*		
(iv) *a house like a Redhill house, but not necessarily at Redhill?*		
(v) *a state house (public housing)?*		
(vi)–(x) *a corresponding list of the locations at which these types of dwelling are available*		

options available locally and were familiar to all of the respondents. A humpy (called by some a tent) is a self-built successor to traditional bark dwellings, now constructed out of combinations of scrap iron and canvas. These are the dwellings that give a third-world image to Aboriginal living conditions, but have certain climatic and social advantages to their occupants that non-Aborigines have been slow to appreciate. A shack is a self-built metal shed, a little more permanent than a humpy. Variations (iii) and (iv) referred to the intermediate types of dwelling and (v) to the public housing. It was necessary to separate each type of dwelling from its typical location for the purposes of this question to avoid confounding constructs applicable to the location or social environment with those applicable to the design of the dwelling.

Experimentation showed that the phrase "living in" the house was far more productive than asking directly about the house. This phrase emphasized the experience of houses rather than visual features. It produced responses within a comparable common range of convenience, whereas the alternative phrasing tried ("Do you like the dwelling?") produced sets of constructs that defied any comparison. (For instance, there were many comments on minor design features such as roof guttering which, on probing, turned out to have no social or psychological significance for the respondents.)

The question "Why would you like/not like living in it?" invited the pyramiding steps. Most people responded with a series of constructs, giving the emergent poles only. (A basic construct has two poles: the emergent pole and its contrast.) Some people continued giving constructs spontaneously for a number of steps. All were encouraged to offer constructs as far as possible with probing until their constructs on that dwelling or location were exhausted. Note that in this technique, people were pyramiding from the evaluative construct "like (or dislike) living in it" rather than the element, the type of dwelling concerned.

Some illustrative contrasting constructs, given by two individuals about living in their own and in a contrasting type of dwelling, are presented in Table 2.

Content Analysis

Each person's evaluation of each type of dwelling and location was recorded, and their constructs were coded into the content categories shown in Table 3 by a panel of three, the researcher and two Aboriginal assistants (see Stewart & Stewart 1981, p. 49). Each group's constructs under each category were recorded on card indexes showing any grammatical linkages between a person's constructs (such as where a space and crowding construct was followed by an explanatory negative social construct). These formed the basis of detailed descriptions of how each residental group construed each dwelling and location and what they meant by each construct category. For instance, both campers and non-Aborigines emphasized privacy, but they had slightly different conceptualizations of it and different expectations as to how to achieve it. Interpretation of this descriptive content of the constructs formed the majority of my report (Ross, 1983, 1987). Explanations of each type of construct drew on the participant observation data as well as the responses to the question.

Statistical Analyses

The number of constructs occurring in each coding category (e.g., shelter, positive social) and against each element was counted, then converted to a percentage of that person's total number of constructs to control for the wide variation in numbers of constructs given. In turn, these percentages had to be converted to arc sine values (see Winer, 1971), to compensate for the variances within each group of subjects being correlated with the means.

The percentage of a person's constructs in each category (e.g., shelter) was taken as an indicator of the importance of that category to that

Table 2. Examples of Two People's Constructs in Relation to Two of the Dwellings

Humpy (tent)	Public housing

Elderly married male camper

- Very good you know, narrow humpy (general and evaluative)
- Enough for me, my wife and three dogs (space and crowding - inside dwellings)
- Little humpy enough (space and crowding inside dwellings)
- Want a little bit of a light, electric light, enough to see the place dark time (facilities)
- And pipe running down, save me from carting [water]. Me and Nellie get tired la arm (facilities)

- If I living in this one I might fall down (safety)
- All right for somebody got good eye, young people (general)
- Only [I like the idea of] bathroom, toilet,—light (facilities)

Woman with children, living in public housing

- No good humpy (general and evaluative)
- Strong wind (shelter)
- And people sneaking round, drunken people, take your tucker (negative social)
- You can't make your tea and sugar and things last (storage)
- Very open. When big whirlwind come around he'll just lift em up, break him (design)
- You can't have dry fire for cooking (coded shelter because emphasis is on rain)
- What about water, bathroom and toilets? (facilities)

- We like to stay in state house (general, evaluative)
- Because we've got little kids and all that (care of others)
- Got toilet close up when they get up middle of the night (facilities)
- They go bogey [to wash], got a bathtub just here (facilities)
- Not like if we living outside, got no water, kids can't hardly have a wash, toilet and thing (facilities)

Note: Coding is given in round brackets. Researcher's additions essential to clarify the speakers' meanings are in square brackets.

Table 3. Coding Frame Used for Content Analysis of Constucts

Category	Description
Information	Purely informative statements, not interpretable as constructs
General and evaluative statements	Variants on liking/disliking, willingness to live somewhere if one had to, being accustomed to a certain standard of living
Shelter	Heat, cold, wind, rain
Facilities	Water, showers and toilets, kitchens, electricity
Space and crowding	Inside dwellings
Neighborhood space and crowding	Crowding among dwellings or overload of people in the neighborhood
Privacy	
Economics	
Positive social	Kinship, friendship
Negative social	Fights, disturbance, theft
Location	Access to town and its resources, desirability of sites
Mobility	Having to move around for employment
Owning	Having one's own dwelling or room (psychological rather than technical ownership)
Design features and construction materials	Verandahs, floor surfaces, strength of construction, fences and gardens, potential for modification
Maintenance of houses	References to repairs, cleaning
Care of others	Children, elderly, visiting relations
Health	
Safety	
Storage	
Quietness	
Activities	References to domestic activities (sleep, cooking, childrens' play), hunting and gathering, prospecting for gold
Attachment to places	Often as traditional land or on account of long residence there

Note: More than 30 categories were used initially. Those listed above represent the collapsed categories used in the descriptive analysis.

person. For example, someone who gave a high percentage of shelter constructs was assumed to consider shelter important. The participant observation data corroborated this assumption.

Discriminant analysis, a method that identifies differences among groups of subjects according to their scores on the variables supplied, was used to identify how the four residential groups differed in their use of categories of constructs. The strongest differences were found between non-Aborigines and Aborigines, who differed in terms of their emphasis on the built features versus the social aspects of houses. The Aborigines who lived in public housing differed from those who lived in intermediate houses or camp dwellings in their willingness to trade the facilities available with a house (such as bathrooms and kitchens) against attachment to particular living locations. In turn, the Aborigines living in the camps, and the two subgroups living in intermediate houses (who were very similar in their cultural values but chose very different combinations of dwellings and living environments) differed with respect to social control and personal well-being.

Discriminant analysis was used again to identify the types of constructs associated with liking or disliking each type of dwelling and living environment. Other statistical analyses used were the ranking of each residential group's categories of constructs according to the mean frequency given to each type of construct by each group (cf., Stewart & Stewart, 1981, p. 47), cross-tabulations among personal and household variables and constructs used, and results from a rating scale measure. Differences among the residential groups were dominant, and the few gender, age, and other differences that were statistically significant were of little theoretical interest.

Technique 2: Group Grid with Supplied Constructs

The most common method of adapting the repertory grid to work with groups is to supply constructs as well as elements so that a number of people can complete the same grid. This does not contradict the principle that constructs should be each individual's own so long as each individual understands each construct and it means much the same to each person (Fransella & Bannister, 1977, pp. 56–57). The supplied constructs should thus be part of each individual's repertoire. In practice, supplied constructs may be part of, but not equally central to (organized similarly within), each person's construct system. A group grid is useful for showing how group members use constructs in relation to elements and may be essential in certain contexts (as Denicolo's work in chapter 12 illustrates), but does not substitute for the rich picture gained when constructs are elicited directly from individuals.

A group grid using supplied constructs was also used in this study but proved far less enlightening than the method using elicited constructs described above. Twelve constructs that were used very commonly by participants in my pilot studies were selected to be supplied so that the interviewees could complete a repertory grid (see Table 4).

The people were asked to sort 11 photos of dwellings (four camp dwellings, three intermediate houses and four public houses) according to each of the supplied constructs in turn, on a 5-point scale. Pretesting showed that in this case, photos worked more successfully than verbal labels. The scaling was achieved by placing the photos in five positions on a vertical board.

Despite its length, everyone enjoyed carrying out the task. The results were disappointing, however. The constructs were so highly intercorrelated as to be uninterpretable. I attribute this to the particular combination of dwellings, constructs, and number of points on the sorting scale. There were vast differences among the houses, which could only be accommodated clumsily on the 5-point scale (the greatest number of points that most traditionally oriented people could handle). People thus made only minor variations in the ways they sorted the photos on each construct, resulting in the high intercorrelations. While discussing the sorting task spontaneously, a number made comments that showed they were approaching the task objectively rather than subjectively. For instance, campers would comment that a particular camp dwelling was good for hot weather, but when forced to scale it against state houses (public houses), would only give it a rating of 2 to 3 to the state house's 5. The different scaling invited by the social and locational constructs was insufficient to break this pattern. (Stewart & Stewart, 1981, pp. 30–32 give useful advice about choosing elements and constructs so as to avoid this type of intercorrelation.)

After corrections were made for unequal numbers in each group, the grid was analyzed using an analysis of variance. This was statistically significant but not particularly informative. Its main point of interest was interaction effects that showed that each residential group was capable of making finer discriminations about its own type of dwelling than about others. For example, the campers could differentiate among the four camp dwellings, whereas the other groups could not.

The task was valuable as a methodological exercise, showing that

Table 4. Design of the Group Grid

Supplied constructs	Dwellings										
	A	B	C	D	E	F	G	H	I	J	K
Good to live in											
for rain											
for hot weather											
for facilities											
for room inside											
cheap to live in											
among your own people											
for nuisance from people											
to look after											
for location											
strong											
for feeling happy											

Sorting scale: construct applies 1 (least) to 5 (most).

Dwellings:

Camp dwellings		A-C	humpies
		D	shack
Intermediate dwellings		E	Redhill house (campers' design)
		F-G	Reserve houses (Government supplied)
State (public rental) houses		H	(oldest) - K (newest) houses

traditionally oriented Aboriginal people can carry out such a complex task if it is designed with care and one has sufficient rapport. In terms of the results it produced, I would have to call it a comparative waste of time.

SOCIAL IMPACT STUDY

The second study was designed to develop methods of social impact assessment within the new paradigm of political or community development approaches to social impact assessment. This paradigm reacts against the technical, positivist approach to social impact assessment in which an expert is deemed to know best, and the perceptions of the people affected by a proposed development are discounted as subjective and therefore not valid. The political paradigm holds that development decisions are made on political rather than objective grounds, and that affected communities must have an equitable role in this political process. Moreover, their predictions of potential impacts, based on their own values and experiences, have a major role in the shaping of the impacts (Ross, 1989, 1990). For instance, local attitudes about employment will affect whether people are for or against a new factory, and those with a positive outlook on the new development are in a better position to adjust to the social changes it brings.

The case study was undertaken as part of a large research project among Aboriginal communities in the midst of a regional development boom involving mining, tourism, and the decline of the cattle industry in which they had formerly been employed (Coombs, McCann, Ross, & Williams, 1989; Ross, 1991). Members of a community of about 300 people and five of its satellite outstation communities were invited to share in the development of a research method and the making of an impact assessment from their own point of view. They chose oral history as a research method, which I supplemented with participant observation.

The project was designed to be under community control, but I soon found that the elders construed the appropriate form of control in a different way than the colleagues who were advising me on approaches to social impact research. They saw their control of the study as being based in trust and their familiarity with me as a person who would respect their wishes, and they rejected the formal mechanisms that Aboriginal communities elsewhere had begun to insist on. Their form of control relied on their cultural norms, not ones imported from non-Aboriginal society.

For this study I lived for 4 months (over two periods in late 1986 and early 1987) in a staff house on the edge of the community, not with a family as I had in the previous study. I recorded some 45 tapes of oral histories from members of the communities, supplemented with numerous interviews and small group discussions and observations. Visits to traditional country and former places of residence were an important part of the method, enlightening for the features people chose to show me. The people also communicated most freely when at the location they were discussing. They were invited to talk in English, Kriol, or their

Aboriginal language, Kija. A trained Aboriginal language worker from the community school assisted me and translated from tapes where necessary.

In effect, the people were recording through me how they construed their history since white encroachment into the area a century before and how they construed the events as having had an impact on their society and culture. A historian, Cathie Clement, went to great lengths to search for corroboration of the oral histories in the archives, finding very substantial support for the Aboriginal versions of events. The result (Ross, 1989; Ross & Bray, 1989; Clement, 1989) is a more complete history of the region than has been available so far from non-Aboriginal written sources.

Aboriginal construing of the history and impacts differed from popular non-Aboriginal beliefs in many ways. The former takes a long-term view of history, seeing the events of a century or decades ago as more recent and important than the non-Aboriginal population, which is largely unaware of the massacres that accompanied the 1886 gold rush, the establishment of pastoral stations, and the telegraph line between the goldfields inland and the northern port. They accompany this long-term historical view with a vision for the future. Their social and cultural goals—caring for their traditional country, reestablishing rights of residence on their country, socializing children and young people more strongly in traditional cultural values and knowledge, and gaining equitable decision-making rights with non-Aborigines—are mainly concerned with overcoming the social and environmental impacts they have experienced.

Whereas well-meaning non-Aboriginal people have tended to portray Aboriginal people more or less as passive victims of white settlement, the Aboriginal accounts emphasize their own roles in the shaping of events. Historians concur that Aboriginal violent resistance in this region was among the strongest in Australia. The oral histories emphasize Aboriginal initiative in spearing lone travelers, followed by massive retaliations that wiped out many of their number. Humorous reconstructions are made of how their forebears must have interpreted their first sightings of white men, horses, bullock carts and flour.

Before in this country they used to shoot blackfellas, and blackfellas used to murder white people, got a buggy (with a cart) when they used to come across here. They used to see em coming along, they reckon "that's the big water snake coming along the road" (the cart tracks looked as though they

belonged to the mythical rainbow serpent). They used to go across with a
spear, wait in the road. They used to kill em. One white bloke shoot em
one, another bloke spear em white man, all that used to be before, all over
this country, in the hills. (Frank Budbaria in Ross & Bray, 1989, p. 2)

Again contradicting popular non-Aboriginal views of race relations,
many of the people were at pains to emphasize individual differences in
the treatment of their ancestors by settler families or policemen. Kindly
actions were reported at length. One outstation group was keen to have
the pastoralist family with which they had been associated restored to
local historical knowledge through our written record, because only
those families that had kept diaries or had prominent descendants to
publicize their activities in the regional history remain generally known
among the non-Aboriginal population.

Seen in terms of personal construct theory, this study involved eliciting the organization of constructs and events (construing) rather than
particular constructs. The method was one in which the Aboriginal participants could talk to me in their own way, and thus structure and communicate their material in the ways most comfortable for them. Given
the recognition that impacts are experienced according to how they have
been construed (Ross, 1990), it would be valuable to explore the role of
construing in people's selection of strategies to deal with anticipated impacts.

CONCLUSIONS

These studies illustrate relatively structured and unstructured possibilities for exploring the construing of another culture with respect to a
chosen topic. They show that a rich variety of constructs can be elicited
and their organization and meaning explored effectively.

Construing the constructions of others is made easier, richer, and
more valid by using more than one method. Just as a clinical psychologist
would always use any psychological tests in combination with discussion
with the client and observation, and never alone, the cross-cultural researcher would be wise to use participant observation alongside repertory grid methods. The variety of interviewing, observation, and conversational opportunities involved in participant observation assists in the
interpretation of constructs elicited more formally and helps to build up
essential rapport. The eliciting method used in the housing study shows

that a structured question can work if it matches the way people think and talk and if sufficient care is taken with pretesting. It shows how constructs can be elicited from individuals, yet compared among groups. It also demonstrates new ways of analyzing the content of constructs, both qualitatively and quantitatively.

The conventional group grid used in the same study is of interest in demonstrating that a formal task can be accomplished in an Aboriginal interview. This would surprise most researchers experienced with Aboriginal people of northern and central Australia. Its success on this criterion was again thanks to careful pretesting and the good rapport gained through participant observation. It was, however, the least useful method in terms of assisting me to construe the construing of Aboriginal people about housing, and the least economical when one considers results against the time taken over the task.

The less structured method used in the social impact study illustrates the advantages of construing the construing of others through their chosen means of expressing themselves rather than ours. Our tendency as researchers is to pursue the structured methods often preferred in our research cultures, which facilitate our side of the construing process but not necessarily our subjects' ease of communicating their views to us. Particularly where we are trying to communicate across cultures, there is a strong argument for our encouraging the communication to take place on the other's or on mutual terms.

The role of language must be remembered in cross-cultural study. We tend to overlook the adequacy of our own language to convey the intricacies of our constructs, although we often refer to having trouble "putting something into words." People are able to convey their constructs most richly in their first language; even if the researcher learns this language, or has a translator, the vocabulary may be restricted or the concepts untranslatable. This is another reason for using observation alongside methods reliant on language.

It is doubtful whether I could have engaged Aboriginal cooperation in my personal construct survey had I attempted it as a newcomer to the community. It should be possible to explore constructs entirely through participant observation, if necessary.

Ultimately, the ability to construe the constructions of another culture also relies on personal qualities. Experience, immersion in the culture, and appropriate methods count for a great deal, but one's own construct system must be flexible enough to permit the appreciation of alternative views.

The flexibility to take a cross-cultural and interdisciplinary approach is inherent in personal construct psychology. A fresh selection of problems for study and a greater repertoire of methods for group use are necessary to develop the theory and its empirical use in group and cultural directions. I hope the ideas offered in this chapter inspire others to extend the use of personal construct psychology in cross-cultural study.

REFERENCES

Bell, R. C., & Bell, S. (1989). *Self-characterisation in children's drawings: Some links between PCT and the work of Winnicott and Milner.* Paper presented at the Eighth International Congress on Personal Construct Psychology, Assisi, Italy.

Bonarius, H., Holland, R., & Rosenberg, S. (Eds.), (1981). *Personal construct psychology: Recent advances in theory and practice.* London: Macmillan.

Clement, C. (1989). *Historical notes relevant to impact stories of the East Kimberley.* East Kimberley working paper no. 29. Canberra: Centre for Resource and Environmental Studies, Australian National University.

Coombs, H. C., McCann, H., Ross, H., & Williams, N. (Eds.), (1989). *Land of promises: Aborigines and development in the East Kimberley.* Canberra: Centre for Resource and Environmental Studies and Aboriginal Studies Press.

Duncan, J. S. (Ed.), (1981). *Housing and identity: Cross-cultural perspectives.* London: Croom Helm.

Epting, F. R., Suchman, D. I., & Nickeson, C. J. (1971). An evaluation of elicitation procedures for personal constructs. *British Journal of Psychology, 62,* 4, 513–518.

Fransella F., & Bannister D. (1977). *A mannual for repertory grid technique.* London: Academic Press.

Geertz, C. (1973). *The interpretation of cultures.* New York: Basic Books.

Hayhow, R., Lansdown, R., Maddick, J., & Ravenette, T. (1988). PCP and children. In F. Fransella & L. Thomas (Eds.), *Experimenting with personal construct psychology* (pp. 199–209). London: Routledge & Kegan Paul.

Keesing, R. M. (1981). *Cultural anthropology: A contemporary perspective*. New York: Holt, Rinehart and Winston.

Kelly G. A. (1955). *The psychology of personal constructs*, vol. 1. New York: Norton.

Landfield, A. W., & Epting, F. R. (1987) *Personal construct psychology: Clinical and personality assessment*. New York: Human Sciences.

Lloyd, P. (1979). *Slums of hope: Shanty towns of the third world*. UK: Penguin.

Mair, J. M. M. (1989). Kelly, Bannister and a story-telling psychology. *International Journal of Personal Construct Psychology*, 2, 1–14.

Neimeyer, R. A. (1981). The structure and meaningfulness of tacit construing. In H. Bonarius, R. Holland, & S. Rosenberg (Eds.), *Personal construct psychology: Recent advances in theory and practice* (pp. 105–113). London: Macmillan.

Rapoport, A. (1977). *Human aspects of urban form*. Oxford: Pergamon Press.

Rapoport, A. (1980). Cross-cultural aspects of environmental design. In I. Altman, A. Rapoport, and J. F. Wohlwill (Eds.), *Human behavior and environment*, vol. 4 (pp. 7–46). New York: Plenum.

Ross, H. (1983). *Australian Aboriginal perceptions of dwellings and living environments*. PhD thesis, University of London.

Ross, H. (1987). *Just for living: Aboriginal perceptions of housing in northwest Australia*. Canberra: Aboriginal Studies Press.

Ross, H. (1989). *Community social impact assessment: A cumulative study in the Turkey Creek area, Western Australia*. East Kimberley working paper no. 27. Canberra: Centre for Resource and Environmental Studies, Australian National University.

Ross, H. (1990). Community social impact assessment: A framework for indigenous peoples. *Environmental Impact Assessment Review, 10*, 185–193.

Ross, H. (1991). The East Kimberley Impact Assessment Project. *Interdisciplinary Science Reviews, 16*, 313–324.

Ross, H., & Bray, E. (1989). *Impact stories of the East Kimberley*. East Kimberley working paper no. 28. Canberra: Centre for Resource and Environmental Studies, Australian National University.

Schwartz, T. (1980). Where is the culture? Personality as the distributive locus of culture. In G. D. Spindler (Ed.), *The making of psychological anthropology* (pp. 417–441). Berkeley: University of California Press.

Spradley, J. P., & McCurdy, D. W. (1977). *The cultural experience: Ethnography in complex society*. Chicago: Science Research Associates.

Stewart, V., & Stewart, A. (1981). *Business applications of repertory grid*. London: McGraw-Hill.

ten Kate, H. (1981). A theoretical explication of Hinkle's implication theory. In H. Bonarius, R. Holland, & S. Rosenberg (Eds.), (1981). *Personal construct psychology: Recent advances in theory and practice* (pp. 167–175). London: Macmillan.

Turner, J. F. C. (1976). *Housing by people*. London: Marion Boyars.

Webb, E. J., Campbell, D. T., Schwartz, R. D., & Sechrest, L. (1966). *Unobtrusive measures: Nonreactive research in the social sciences*. Chicago: Rand McNally.

Winer, B. J. (1971). *Statistical principles in experimental design*. New York: McGraw-Hill.

CHAPTER 9

Organization as a Constructed Context

DEVORAH KALEKIN-FISHMAN

In the course of this chapter, I examine the possibility of tracing connections between individuals and social forms. The basis for the analysis is the construal and the construction of organizations. It would seem that the theory of personal constructs can help us to understand organizational processes better and to find ways of improving educational organizations by enlisting the inclinations of the actors participating in them.

Organization is a construct that has many applications. It is the act of arranging as well as the fact of being arranged. It is at once process and state. Moreover, in both these aspects, organization is inherent in both groups and individuals.

Concrete organizations are the means for carrying out most of the tasks of modern society. People regularly meet in organizations and act in them according to their construals of social reality. Whatever the function of an organization, it necessarily transmits general lessons about itself as a social form. Schools are organizations specifically set up for the purpose of teaching, i.e., for helping people gain information about the world. Commonly, information is thought of as knowledge of school subjects, yet to know the school as an organization is no less significant as learning. It is an experience that undoubtedly adds to pupils' knowledge about culture and social groupings.

But, as is true of all instruction, the type of learning, its quantity, and its expression in behavior are shaped by the foundations on which the individual builds. And when people learn about organizations, they build on the networks of construals they have collected in earlier encounters

203

with social formations. In those encounters, people have already become familiar with the elements of organization they expect to have replicated and with the modes of organizing those replications. These processes are examples of how organization consolidates in psychological functioning. This insight, however, is only a preliminary step.

ORGANIZATION IN INDIVIDUALS AND INDIVIDUALS DOING ORGANIZING

According to personal construct theory, organization characterizes human beings. First of all, it is a metaconstruct that governs a person's way of being in the world (Kelly, 1969). This perception accords with philosophical assertions that people are by nature organized for liberty and programmed for autonomy. That is to say, people become themselves only through exercising the freedom that makes them human (Habermas, 1984; see also chapter 5). Paradoxically, freedom is practiced by forcing the human and material environment to submit to organization (Kelly, 1955).

The principle of organization makes it possible for people to anticipate new situations and their outcomes. Every given experience is organized for translation into constructs themselves organized in a kind of ground plan that enables the individual to recognize successive replications of an event. To anticipate a situation as capable of bearing a particular type of interpretation and subsequently to test the interpretation in "real time" is the ongoing process of organizing experience through reflection. Furthermore, people's actions construct their participation to accord with the replication they anticipate. Because perception-cognition-affect are inseparable, construals provide a basis for acting.

In effect, for the person-scientist that Kelly predicated, construing is a kind of minimal sampling. This is done with the help of dichotomies: descriptors and their implied contrasts (Rychlak, 1990). Basically, the application of constructs is limited to a certain range of convenience by the construed boundaries of an individual's life experiences. Still, because it is a dynamic process, the construction of a new situation is not completely determined by anticipation. Successive construals prepare the individual for experimenting in situated actions. The validity of the anticipations is tested. From the findings, the outcomes of a given test, a person learns lessons that may extend her constructs' range of convenience.

People construe in order to cope with reality and coping involves actively construing the essential parameters of events and their configurations. In many areas of living people order their constructs according to preference in relatively complex hierarchies so as to construe the qualities of events comprehensively. Decisions on action are based on a perception that related constructs cohere. When the hierarchical arrangements are not compatible (see chapter 17), a person may become aware of the problematic nature of his or her psychological functioning.

Moreover, construing events entails a constant fine-tuning of the self. While construing, the person organizes and reorganizes the set of core constructs we interpret as the self. The core constructs govern organized access to what we construe as our inner reality. Thus, because of the supreme personal investment in anticipations of many cardinal situations, action also turns out to be a test of one's personal validity.

The search for adequate validation is the theme of daily life. People tend to fuel the search for alternative ways of constructing reality with the help of partial validations from their environments. In a sense, it may be said that in construing and constructing reality, people "satisfice" (i.e., accept the best available reward) in order to go ahead with the business of living (Simon, 1957). In Kelly's view, the mature personality will be capable of adopting alternative constructs when necessary, so as to open the way to different ways of anticipating. This is, in short, doing practical science in order to enhance understanding (Kelly, 1958; Walker, 1991).

Being organized and doing organizing is a way of making one's predictions come true and achieving the actualization of self (Maslow, 1954). This type of activity is not restricted to face-to-face interaction. It is part of the composite behavior of social organizations. How persons with their highly intricate inner organization contend with socially regulated organizations is an engaging study.

PERSONAL CONSTRUCT THEORY AND SCHOOL ORGANIZATIONS

As noted above, educational organizations have particular responsibility for transmitting knowledge. The ways in which social configurations, or organizations, are construed and constructed in schools are, therefore, of unique significance. Traditionally, analyses of school organizations relate to the normatively defined needs and points of view of professionals. It is quite commonly assumed that in order to know what schools are about, one has to examine the conscious decisions of principals and teachers. This approach ignores the message of personal construct theory, namely, that all the participants in an organization are agents and that their input into a given social configuration through action in situations contributes to shaping it.

It is also the message of research in educational administration. Leadership styles have been presumed to have crucial effects on teaching and learning (e.g., Smyth, 1989). In this paradigm, effective administrators are those that design and execute programs, act rationally, and above all impose their authority on subordinates. However, the gap between this description and the stormy realities of school life has led a number of researchers to question the approach.

In an analysis of the weaknesses of the conventional construction of leadership, Angus (1989) stated that these models of authority perpetuate a myth that effectiveness is attained through power. In his view, school principals are agents who are likely to act in different ways depending on the situation. In some cases, school heads may act in a way that demonstrates leadership, but not always (Angus, 1989, p. 86). Other participants in the school organization are also capable of acting as leaders if suitable conditions arise. The actions of children, as well as those of teachers, are likely to have an effect on organizational processes. Hence, the ways in which they all interpret the school organization are significant.

This view of leadership accords with Kelly's construction of the person. It therefore stands to reason that the comprehensive question about how schools transmit sociocultural forms can usefully be operationalized as one of how all agents in an organization construe educational institutions. Along with this, it is of interest to extrapolate the ways in which such actions are likely to affect the organization. Since we cannot foretell which construals will have the greatest influence, we assume that the construals of all agents have to be considered factors in effecting change. Administrators would do well to examine the probabilities.

In this chapter I look at children's reflections on schools as organizations and I trace some implications of their construals on the active construction of life in schools. The milieu I will be examining is the Israeli state school system. First, I sketch some of the rudiments of the state educational system. Then I present data from interviews with children and draw some conclusions about uses for children's personal construals and constructions of the school organization.

ISRAEL'S SCHOOL SYSTEM

Until the foundation of the State of Israel in 1948, schooling was a scarce resource in the country. Overall, only about 30% of the children of school age had access to a systematic education (Nardi, 1945; Tibawi, 1955). The state schools that had flourished under the Ottoman Empire and, after 1918, under the British Mandate, catered to a relatively limited number of students. For the most part, children who did attend school were enrolled in educational institutions maintained by diverse religious establishments or in schools sponsored by the consulates of European countries.[2]

Among the earliest laws of the new state was the Law for Compulsory Free Education (1949), which obligated parents to register their children aged 5 to 14 for schooling. The Law for State Education (1953) asserted that the state was responsible for providing universal education (Medzini, 1979). Over the last 40-odd years, successive acts of legislation have provided for compulsory education to the age of 15 and free education to the age of 18. Laws outline support for state-religious schools so children can be taught according to the religious beliefs of their parents. Provision for instruction in the mother tongue (Arabic or Hebrew) is also made. Schools are allocated to residential areas according to the density of the population, are graded according to the children's ages, and are suited to special interests and talents. Completion of schooling is marked by examinations and evaluation on the national level. In the course of time, the Ministry of Education and Culture went so far as to publish guidelines for regulating school behaviors. These are prefaced by a recapitulation of the moral basis for school regulations (Kalekin-Fishman, 1993).

The official explanation for consolidating control is that only in this way can the public be certain that the system will suit the needs of the community and be sensitive to the changing demands of society. Because the Israeli system is highly centralized, schools are usually characterized as relatively impermeable structures, driven by well-formulated goals and objectives. Among others, the prevailing view is the basis for assessments of educational events.

PUPILS' CONSTRUALS OF SCHOOL AS AN ORGANIZATION

As noted above, the structure of the Israeli school is embodied in the succession of legislative enactments and official regulations that relate to children's behaviors, the school's moral commitments, and criteria of evaluation. How the construals of the school organization proposed by children diverge from the official construction will be shown in this section.

The analysis that follows is based on the responses of students to questions that touch on the school as an organization. The respondents were children from 36 state-secular educational frameworks: elementary schools and junior and senior high schools in which Hebrew or Arabic was the language of instruction. The data were part of a research project on school culture. Interviews were held with students, and school situations (in class and during recess) were observed. Teachers and other members of the school staff were also interviewed, and school documents were scrutinized. The general aims of the project were to analyze patterns of behavior and sets of expectations that characterize different role incumbents in schools.

This paper grew out of a serendipitous discovery. In analyzing the data that were collected, we discovered a phenomenon that led us to look again at how construals permeate the construction of organizational reality. The various actors who were interviewed and observed (principals, teachers, students, and maintenance staff) described the same school in different ways. Frequently, they suggested construals of their school that were quite removed from the consensus on what constitutes an educational organization. Most varied were pupils' construals of their schools. We decided to focus on the constructions they supplied in interviews.

All together 288 pupils were interviewed. More than half of the interviewees expressed the view that school was a unique type of organization—a place for learning—although there were different perceptions of what learning meant. Of the interviewees, 139 identified their schools with other organizations. I will focus on their analogies in this chapter. Since constructs are necessarily grouped, I was able to adopt Ravenette's (1992) recommendation that researchers examine constructs in configurations rather than focusing on each and every construct separately.

Some of the students talked about school as an industrial plant, others related to it as if it was a military organization, and still others described it in terms that one might use for a political party or for informal associations such as the family or a sports team. Each of these constructions rules out the official definition of the educational institution as it rules out the other ways of construing. From the interviewees' style of expression as well as from the content, it was possible to extrapolate their intentions in regard to school behaviors, their moral commitment, and the criteria they used to evaluate organizational events.[3]

School as a Workplace

A favored construal was that of school as a place of work. Many children ($n = 54$) defined their school as a "factory for marks." In this construction, the pupils interpreted themselves as part of the production process, and in some cases as no more than the raw material. For them, therefore, learning was elaboration of the raw material, and the principal responsibility was that of the educator-experts who plan and design the production process, define conditions of entry, and formulate criteria for adequate performance. Marks were not a felt student goal, but rather the product of the learning process. Pupils who spoke in this way construed the teachers as if they were forepersons on the factory floor, the principal and those involved in administration as a board of directors, and their own parents as the consumers.

This structure indicates extreme pupil dependency on the one hand and alienation on the other. On the production line, in classrooms, pupils are isolated from one another. The best maneuver is to submit oneself to routine. Pupils who interpret the school in this way cannot judge themselves apart from what is being done to them. If there is personal meaning to the experience of school, it is grasped only in retrospect. The pupils then are freed of moral commitment. The final value of the pupil-product, just as in the case of all raw material, was taken to reflect the qualifications and the talents of those who have carried out the actual work. If the production process is well aligned, the pupils will be able to succeed. And success will make it possible for them to demand a high return in the job market in terms of prestige, property, or power. They are already able to excuse failure, however. The principal and the staff will be faulted.

School as a Military Organization

Twenty junior high school pupils pointed to the army as the model for school as an organization. There was an impressive consistency between popular anecdotes of how recruits are conscripted and treated in the military and the construals of the way schools are run. Entrance into

post-elementary education with its unfamiliar facilities and forced encounter with new classmates and strange teachers was described as boot
camp. In this light, the ideology of ethnic and social integration that
makes claims for army service as complementary education was highly
suitable to school.

The pupils who spoke in this way described the schools using military terminology. They carried on conversations liberally embellished
with current army slang, i.e., punning acronyms. Some of them com-
plained about being forced, as in the army, to "hang out with all kinds."
A more polite way of putting it were comments such as, "It was a shock
to find myself sitting next to a kid from downtown." To their minds,
school, like the army, had strict laws that regulated every hour in their
lives. They felt like the end of a rigid chain of command: the principal
commands those in administrative positions, who supervise the teachers,
who rule the pupils. Still, as in the Israeli Defense Forces, pastoral care
and consideration were perceived to be a fundamental component in
teacher-pupil (officer-soldier) relationships.

The salient behavioral principle was a kind of cynical resignation to
checks. Obedience and fear of deviance were construed to be inviolable.
These pupils construed every school duty as imperative, and they were
reticent about expressing personal opinions. Their descriptions of school
showed a pledge to conformist thinking and regulated behavior.

School as an Annex to the Home

Some of the children (n = 40) spoke of school as an extension of the
family. Like a family, a school class can be a complete society in itself.
The children who responded in this vein talked of themselves as related
by simulated blood ties. They described the class as a closed social unit
with responsibilities for one another. These children saw themselves as
sharing beliefs and values, and they viewed the class as having collective
responsibility for the behavior of all of them in school and out.

Here are a few typical statements of children who related to their
classes as if they were groups of kin: "Kids in the class have to help one
another. . . . Kids in the class have to give up their individual interests for
the good of all of us. . . . Classmates are mates after school as well. . . .
We're like sisters and brothers, and that's why there is no competition
among us . . . ," and so on.

Children for whom the class was like a family repeatedly referred to
the ways in which they shared the experience of time. They had the same

daily schedule, similar profane agendas, and common celebrations and festivals. They had parties "of our own on Friday evenings," and they shared rites of passage. Pupils who operated according to this construal were part of a compact group distinguished by intensive interaction. They tend to feel they are sanctioned unfairly just because they are so close. In their eyes, the teacher had a nurturing function; she was obliged to provide affection, to reward them on the basis of particularistic criteria, and, moreover, to reinforce the (kinship) ties among the classmates.

School as a Sports Turf

Some of the adolescents among the interviewees ($n = 12$) construed school as headquarters for appropriately organized sports. These interviewees were ardent soccer fans who rode motorbikes and looked forward to driving cars. Their objectives were to fit in with social frameworks that were quite distant from school. They judged their classmates according to their capacity to live up to the style of life of a sports team, including adoration for a peer as captain. They denigrated their teachers because they did not understand the rules of the game. They ignored the principal, except when punished for some misdeed.[4]

School as a Social Institution

Although none of the schools involved in the research belonged to the state-religious system, a few students ($n = 8$) talked about their school as if it were part of the religious establishment. They reflected on morality and lauded the school's allegiance to tradition. They also expressed concern about "decadence." Two boys talked about their school, a selective urban school, as if it were a political organization. They mentioned processes of decision making and pointed out types of decisions that were made and the ways in which they were implemented. They described events that had taken place in school as legal or illegal and described people as rulers or ruled. They also related to ideological matters such as "the good of the school" or "the good of the pupils."

SIGNIFICANCE OF STUDENTS' CONSTRUALS FOR UNDERSTANDING EDUCATIONAL ADMINISTRATION

In the above, I have presented perceptions of organized interaction, moral commitments, and technologies that were described or implied by students of different schools. The students' constructs express their construals of themselves as they act in the organization as well as of the kinds of behaviors expected from other participants in the organization. The constructions indicate pupils' anticipations of what is likely to happen in school and of what is not so likely to happen. They also indicate the kinds of action pupils who share a particular organizational construal are likely to adopt. Pupils who construe school as a kinship group anticipate situations that will be quite different from those anticipated by pupils who construe school as a military organization. Pupils who construe school as an industrial plant anticipate situations widely different from the situations that are likely to take place in playgrounds or on sports fields. They construe different systems of relationships and invest different levels of energy in the school experience. They will react differently to school events and will interpret validation and nonvalidation in different ways.

Students evolve systems of constructs that suit their needs by sampling the variety of organizational frameworks and situations with which they are acquainted (see Kelly, 1969, p. 10). It is apparent that pupils reach school equipped with conceptualizations based on their samples of such experiences. By means of their constructs, they interpret the significance of encounters in diverse situations, construe the organizational context, and act and react according to their construals. The interaction of systems of constructs of different kinds creates organizational reality. Since the constructs cited embody competing cultural anticipations (Bochner, 1982, p. 27), their encounter may well create friction. Furthermore, by acting out the implications of their constructs, pupils oppose every effort to abrogate or revoke their right to agency. The mechanisms of control and the range of techniques that the institution has in hand attempt to be strong enough to prevent constant confrontation with restructuring by the pupils.

From the above analysis we may conclude that pupils who are part of a school framework are not simply learners of formal lessons. They experience school as an organization. Their construals of the organization are of decisive importance to an understanding of the school's functioning and to the ways in which schools contribute to societal functioning. Careful analyses of systems of constructs are likely to clarify the gaps between how the principal thinks and how his/her subordinates see organizational affairs and what the construals of each group imply. Since the realization of an organized system of personal constructs combines necessarily with action, the construal of a context changes it at one and the same time.

If principals are not aware of what can happen, they are likely to find themselves either struggling against the inevitable or swept along by an unarticulated current of change. As personal construct theory suggests, however, processes can be tempered if adults in the school organization use their experience to comprehend alternative constructions of the reality they share. To the extent that sociality is achieved (see chapter 1), participants in the organization, including school principals, will be more adept at keeping abreast of change and even of leading it.

School staffs will do well to develop sensitivity to the constructions of their pupils. Thus, they will increase their capacity for sociality, and for the possibility of participating in the pupils' world or worlds. As noted above, the principals of schools are agents who have the capacity to act as leaders from time to time. It is important to remember that agency is not exclusively theirs. All the members of an organization have access to agency. Pupils' construals have an impact on educational frameworks. There is good reason to suspect that the impact of personal constructs on organizational life is especially great in educational organizations, because they are not restrained by clear goals of profit and loss.

It is commonly said of educational organizations that they carry out a social mission. The significance of the mission is disclosed by their potential to achieve change and to influence environmental changes for the common good. The approach suggested here points up difficulties in realizing the mission that are usually overlooked. At this point, we can only hint at new ways of construing and anticipating the evolution of school organizations. The empirical and theoretical challenge that awaits us is that of exposing the many types of construals, so as to detail how organizations that deal with education combine to confront organizations in other societal institutions.

Combinations of methods such as observation, depth interviews, and analyses of everyday talk will enable researchers to trace the complex trends of change that are initiated when systems of constructs of different groups meet in schools. By mapping replicative patterns of behavior and by exposing and decoding constructs, the researcher in educational administration can aid actors to understand the changes that are taking place. Research based on the psychology of personal constructs can help school administrators discover new horizons of the life-world (*Lebenswelt*; see Habermas, 1984), and trace new forms of organization. Once they understand the processes, they will be able to harness the active strength of systems of personal constructs to realize valuable social objectives.

ENDNOTES

1. This chapter is a revised version of the keynote address at the Inaugural Conference of the European Personal Construct Association, April 22, 1992.

2. This was a practice that spread under the Ottoman Empire. The empire developed a system of capitulations that in effect released the government from responsibility for foreigners. Under this system, foreign consulates were authorized to protect their citizens and to provide services. Foreign citizenship was, therefore, an advantage for residents of Palestine, and for their children

3. The approach described here is based on Burns, Baumgartner, and Deville (1985, p. 284). They suggest defining frames of reference by means of "times and places for applying rules, groups of actors, roles, aims, rights, commitments, forces and opportunities for action, together with algorithms that govern social action."

4. For elaborations of the behavioral implications of construals see Kalekin-Fishman (1980, 1987, 1991).

REFERENCES

Angus, L. (1989). "New" leadership and the possibility of educational reform. In J. Smyth (Ed.), *Critical perspectives on educational leadership* (pp. 63–92). London: Falmer.

Bochner, S. (1982). The social psychology of cross-cultural relations. In S. Bochner (Ed.), *Cultures in contact: Studies in cross-cultural interaction* (pp. 5–44). Oxford: Pergamon.

Burns, T. R., Baumgartner, T., & Deville, P. (1985). *Man, decisions, society: The theory of actor-system dynamics for social scientists*. New York, London, Paris, Montreux, Tokyo: Gordon & Breach.

Habermas, J. (1984). *The theory of communicative action*. Volume One: Reason and the rationalization of society. Boston: Beacon Press.

Kalekin-Fishman, D. (1980). *Time, sound and control: Aspects of socialization in the kindergarten*. Unpublished doctoral dissertation, University of Konstanz, West Germany.

Kalekin-Fishman, D. (1987). Performances and accounts: The social construction of the kindergarten experience. *Sociological Studies of Child Development: A Research Annual, 1,* 81–104.

Kalekin-Fishman, D. (1991). Latent messages: The acoustical environments of kindergartens in Israel and West Germany. *Sociology of Education, 64,* 209–222.

Kalekin-Fishman D. (1993) What kind of school is this? *Studies in Educational Administration and Organization, 19,* 71–92 [Hebrew]

Kelly, G. A. (1955). *The psychology of personal constructs.* Vols. 1 and 2. New York: Norton.

Kelly, G. A. (1958). Man's construction of his alternatives. In G. Lindzey (Ed.), *The assessment of human motives* (pp. 33–64). New York: Holt, Rinehart & Winston.

Kelly, G. A. (1969). In whom confide: On whom depend for what. In B. Maher (Ed.), *Clinical psychology and personality: The selected papers of George Kelly* (pp. 189–206). New York: Wiley.

Maslow, A. H. (1954). *Motivation and personality.* New York: Harper & Row.

Medzini, M. (Ed.), (1979). *Collection of official publications in the history of the state: Documents, laws, announcements, accords.* Jerusalem: Ministry of Defense. [Hebrew]

Nardi, N. (1945) *Education in Palestine: 1920–1945.* Washington, DC: Zionist Organization of America.

Ravenette, T. (1992, April). Abstract for workshop on *Interviewing: The use of drawings in the elicitation of personal constructions.* Inaugural Conference of the European Personal Construct Association. York, England.

Rychlak, J. F. (1990). George Kelly and the concept of construction. *International Journal of Personal Construct Psychology, 3,* 7–20.

Simon, H. (1957). *Administrative behavior: A study of decision-making processes.* New York: Free Press.

Smyth, J. (Ed.), (1989). *Critical perspectives on educational leadership.* London: Falmer.

Tibawi, A. L. (1955). *Arab education in mandatory Palestine.* London: Lozac.

Walker, B. M. (1991) Values and Kelly's theory: Becoming a good scientist. *International Journal of Personal Construct Psychology, 5,* 259–270.

CHAPTER 10

How Teachers Construe Pupils' Intelligence

BIANCA DE BERNARDI

Intelligence is a psychological construct with a long history. One of the earliest and best known explorations of the meaning of intelligence was a symposium on *Intelligence and Its Measurement* that was published in the *Journal of Educational Psychology* in 1921. Fourteen "experts" on intelligence were asked to define it. The results were diverse and difficult to relate to each other. Intelligence was portrayed as a comprehensive construct composed of various kinds of abilities, such as reasoning abstractly, responding in a clear and truthful way, adapting to new environmental situations, knowing how to acquire new abilities, and learning to take advantage of experiences. Recent studies of experts have found similar results. Snyderman and Rothman (1987) gave 661 psychologists, educationalists and teachers a questionnaire. They found that a variety of traits were considered distinguishing characteristics of intelligence, but there was little agreement on their relative importance. The level of agreement varied from over 90% for characteristics such as thinking, abstract reasoning, problem solving ability, and capacity to acquire knowledge to a minimum of 19% for a trait such as motivation to success.

From the theoretical view, there has been a move away from the assumptions made earlier in the century of a unitary concept of intelligence to a description of it in terms of a particular set of abilities. The former position, exemplified by Spearman (1927), explored the relationships between ability measures and established via factor analysis a general factor termed "g." General intelligence was assumed to underlie every kind of ability, but was most representative of the reasoning processes producing inferences, analogies, relations, etc. By contrast, the later theoretical

217

perspective demonstrated a number of parallel abilities that were narrower in scope than general ability, including verbal fluency, reasoning, etc. Typified by Thurstone (1938), this perspective also used factor analysis. This latter approach was pushed to its extreme by Guilford's (1967) taxonomic structure-of-intellect model, which proposed 120 independent intellectual factors.

Further theories and models have been developed, but the conviction persists that there remain important features that have not been accounted for. However, experts are not the only ones who develop and use theories of intelligence; the "person on the street" also uses constructions to help confront everyday reality in an economical way, without wasting mental effort.

For this reason it is usual to distinguish between explicit and implicit theories of intelligence. Explicit theories are the formalized accounts of intelligence presented by psychologists; implicit theories are those everyday conceptions and representations made by all of us (Sternberg, 1985a). Such representations have very important functions in individuals' lives. Their aim is to accelerate and simplify sociocognitive adaptation to everyday reality. If this were to be accomplished only through strictly scientific reasoning and thinking, it would occur only after the expenditure of much energy and time. Their origin usually lies within a social context where systems of beliefs, traditions, and convictions are well established. Individuals accrue experience within a social context; they observe, they come into contact with already existing prior knowledge, they get information they then elaborate and modify, if necessary, on the basis of their own cognitive structures and already acquired knowledge. In this way they build up a personal, more or less coherent, system of beliefs, sufficiently well established to become almost totally resistant to change (Carugati, 1990). Implicit theories, therefore, are founded on these personal ideas and social representations. For this reason, Sternberg, Conway, Ketron, & Bernstein (1981) observed that they do not have to be invented by researchers as is the case for explicit theories, but only discovered because they preexist in people's minds.

For a long time, however, the importance of implicit theories of intelligence has been underestimated by researchers, despite the utility of learning how people value their own intellectual abilities in everyday life situations as well as the abilities of others. Further, it appears that explicit theories originated from experts' implicit theories, which were then verified by objective experimental data (Sternberg, 1985a).

Since the 1980s, in connection with assumptions about implicit theories of intelligence, there have been a number of studies carried out with adult subjects, both experts and laypersons (e.g., Calegari, 1990; Carugati, 1990; Fry, 1984; Mugny & Carugati, 1989; Sternberg et al., 1981; Sternberg, 1985a, 1985b, 1990). Other research has focused on a developmental analysis of the same phenomena, using children and adolescents as participants (De Bernardi, 1991; Dweck & Bempechat, 1983; Nicholls, 1978, 1980, 1984a, 1984b, 1990; Nicholls & Miller, 1984; Yussen & Kane, 1985). These studies varied both in their aims and the methodologies used.

A comparison between experts' and laypersons' conceptions of intelligence was indeed the focus of a large-scale investigation carried out by Sternberg Conway, Ketron, and Bernstein (1981). The aim was to explore behaviors considered to characterize either intelligence, academic intelligence, everyday intelligence, or unintelligence. The results showed typifying prototypes for each type of intelligence that were fairly similar to each other. Further, the prototypes provided by experts and by laypersons did not differ substantially, though they were not identical. The experts considered motivation to be important for academic intelligence, while laypersons placed more emphasis on the sociocultural aspects of intelligence (Sternberg, 1990).

Given the focus of the present research, the studies of Fry (1984) and Sternberg (1985a) are of particular interest. In both cases the participants were either teachers of various school levels or of diverse subject areas. Differing conceptions of intelligence were obtained within levels and subject area, though they were not substantial.

Sternberg (1985a) noted particularly the characteristics ascribed to the very intelligent pupil. The art teachers stressed the importance of knowledge and the ability to use it in the evaluation of alternatives, the business professors emphasized logical thinking, and the philosophy professors the abilities considered essential to analyze and create philosophical arguments, whereas the physicists focused on precise mathematical thinking (Sternberg, 1985b; 1990).

Fry (1984) found that the prominence of different characteristics varied as a function of the grade level taught by the teachers. Primary school teachers attached greater significance to social competence features such as popularity, helpfulness, respect for law and order, and so on. By contrast, secondary school teachers stressed verbal abilities, especially verbal fluency and energy, whereas college teachers highlighted cognitive variables as the most important aspects of students' intelligent functioning. The implications of these results are far-reaching if we assume that these implicit theories of intelligent functioning are integral to the evaluation of competence and intelligent behavior at differing school levels. Further, they can greatly influence the nature of the teachers' educational behavior toward their pupils. In other words, as Dweck and Bempechat (1983) indicate, teachers' ideas on pupils' intelligence would determine educational interventions and especially attitudes toward their pupils. Significant too is the fact that teachers' behaviors have important implications for whether pupils develop a self-image as an intelligent person or as someone who is not very intelligent. Teachers' implicit theories and the resulting behaviors would also be relevant to the development of pupils' goals and expectations of school achievement.

In view of the potential practical significance of these issues, the present research aimed to investigate how teachers of different school levels and in different teaching areas construed high intelligence and lack of intelligence. A second aim, integral to the first, was to see how pupils lying between these two extremes would be construed in comparison with the extremes.

The framework in which I have chosen to investigate these constructions of intelligence is that of George A. Kelly's personal construct theory. Kelly (1955) stated that each person forms theories and evaluates hypotheses to anticipate and control events. He also pointed out that people develop systems of personal constructs that are unique to each individual. The conversational techniques considered integral to personal construct psychology (PCP) are very efficient tools in the exploration of the worlds of human beings (Salmon, 1980, 1986; Salmon & Claire, 1984; Shaw, 1979, 1980; Thomas & Harri-Augstein, 1985). They allow the personal involvement of both parties, researcher and subject, in analyzing the nature of events. This collaboration between participant and researcher allows greater awareness of the parties' own constructions of reality and, consequently, a greater ability to control or, if necessary, to modify both their own theory and ensuing behaviors. For this reason I regard this theoretical and methodological approach as extremely useful and productive; my concerns encompass both the achievement of the aims of the research and the potential benefits for the individuals participating.

The research was carried out in two stages. Different research tools were used in each stage.

Teachers of different subjects from nursery, primary, and middle schools in northern Italy took part in the research. This was important because different types of professionalism are required of teachers at each of these school levels.

The nursery school provides a three-year course for children ages 3 to 6. Although attendance is not compulsory, nursery school is attended by almost all the children in this age group. Sections made up of a maximum of 30 children are only rarely homogeneous for age. In the course of a teaching day, two teachers take turns in each section, with a period of overlapping duty. Most teachers carry out educational activities in all fields of the curriculum: the linguistic-expressive, the logico-mathematical, and the socio-environmental.

The primary school provides a compulsory 5-year course for 6- to 10-year-old children. By law (#148, 1990), teaching in modules is required in the Italian primary school. The arrangement is that for every two classes there are three teachers. Each of them has responsibility for only one subject (either language, mathematics, or social studies). Teachers may work either singly or as a team in the same class, following the teaching plan agreed on by the whole team. This mode of teaching is rapidly taking the place of situations in which only one class teacher is present throughout the day and teaches all the subject areas.

The middle school provides a compulsory three-year course for 11 to 14 year olds. Together with the primary school, it represents a complex educational system whose formative aim is to promote the acquisition of basic skills. Each subject is taught by a different teacher and allowed a specific slot in the daily schedule.

STAGE 1

During Stage 1 of the research, we interviewed 62 teachers; 12 were from nursery school, 30 from primary school, and 20 from middle school. Care was taken to choose the primary and middle school teachers so as to represent the different subjects taught in these schools. We were interested in discovering (a) what constructs teachers used to characterize the concept of intelligence and which constructs were shared by teachers who taught at a given level or were peculiar to them; and (b) how teachers characterized pupils they had met during their teaching experience on the basis of intelligence and school achievements.

The research tool used at this stage was characterization. The use of characterization recalls the method of self-characterization, which is probably one of the most original and productive tools of investigation devised by Kelly (see Bannister & Fransella, 1971/1986). Characterization, however, is different from self-characterization as it requires the subjects to describe another person rather than themselves. The main reason for using this tool is my belief that characterization, by contrast with closed questions, allows subjects to express something that is significant for themselves. At the same time it helps them to analyze more deeply their own construction of reality.

Each teacher was asked to describe the features which, according to their personal experience, are characteristic of a very intelligent pupil and those that are characteristic of a pupil who is not very intelligent. They were asked to complete the following sentences:

> I think X is a very intelligent pupil because. . . .
> (in Italian: X è, secondo me, un allievo molto intelligente, perché. . . .)
> I think Y is not a very intelligent pupil because. . . .
> (in Italian: Y è, secondo me, un allievo poco intelligente, perché. . . .)

About half the teachers were asked to complete both sentences. The remaining teachers were asked to describe either the very intelligent pupil or the one who is not very intelligent. Although this was a convenient way to elicit bipolar constructs, only half the respondents were asked to give both characterizations. This was done to boost the likelihood of eliciting constructs that were especially suitable for the description of one or the other of the types of pupils. By asking a teacher to describe either the very intelligent one or the one who is not very intelligent, I was able to elicit more focused constructs while preventing the teacher from being influenced by her earlier description.

A superficial analysis of the protocols disclosed disparity in the levels of content complexity among the interviewees. The number of identified characteristics varied considerably from protocol to protocol, regardless of school level and subject taught. The number of traits supplied varied from 2 or 3 to as many as 20 characteristics. In some of the protocols, the characteristics cited all belonged to the same universe of content while in others the traits noted belonged to different categories of meaning.

The variation we were concerned about in the interviews did not lead to any meaningful differences in the responses. True, many of the teachers who were asked to describe both types of pupils did tend to describe the second type using the same constructs they had supplied for

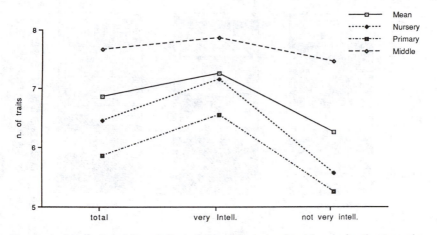

Figure 1. Means of traits elicited at the different school levels for the two elements and in total

the first. But, in terms of content, the responses of those who were asked to characterize either the intelligent or the not so intelligent pupil were very similar. In both cases, fewer constructs were supplied for the pupil who is not so intelligent. Here are some of the details about the distributions.

The average number of characterizations (Figure 1) elicited from the whole sample was 6.8. The mean number of constructs characterizing the intelligent pupil was 7.2 and that for the not very intelligent pupil was 6.2. When we looked at the number of constructs according to school level, we discovered that the lowest means were those of the teachers from primary school (5.8, 6.5, and 5.2 respectively). Nevertheless, as can be seen in Figures 2 and 3, there is a great deal of individual variability.

The number of characteristics supplied for the very intelligent pupil was fairly similar over the three school levels with a mode of 4 in the nursery school and 3 in the primary school. The distribution of the responses of teachers in the middle school was bimodal, with modes of 4 and 11 characterizations and a wider range of between 2 and 20 characteristics.

For the not very intelligent pupil, about half the nursery school teachers supplied only 2 traits and the others supplied from 7 to 12 traits. About 30% of the primary school teachers supplied 3 traits and

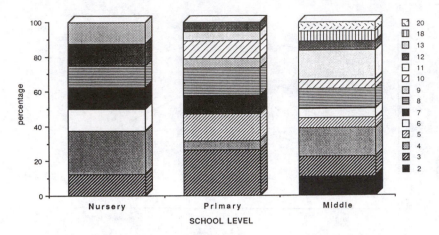

Figure 2. The very intelligent pupil: distribution of numbers-of-traits at the different school levels

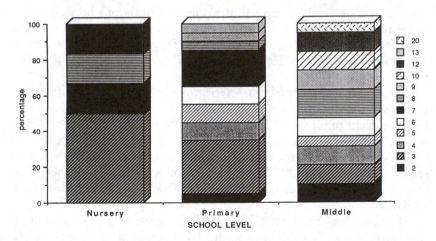

Figure 3. The not very intelligent pupil: distribution of numbers-of-traits at the different school levels

20% supplied 7 traits. The range of responses by teachers from the middle school was from 4 to 11.

Two independent judges carried out a content analysis of the characterizations in order to isolate the constructs. Despite the variety in the responses, it was possible to sort the constructs utilized in describing

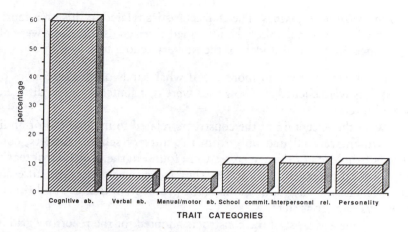

Figure 4. Percentages of trait categories

both the intelligent and the not very intelligent pupil according to categories of characteristics (see Figure 4). The areas that were distinguished were the following:

1. *Cognitive abilities.* About 60% of all the traits cited in the protocols related to this category. Among the responses of the teachers from the primary and the middle schools, the frequency was even higher.

2. *Interpersonal relationships.* The characteristics making up this area (about 10% of the total number) were mainly elicited from the nursery and middle school teachers; only very occasionally did they appear in the primary school teachers' protocols.

3. *Personality.* The traits making up this area of content appeared in the protocols of every school level and represented about 10% of the identified categories.

4. *School commitment and involvement.* This area represented under 10% of the total number of elicited constructs. For the most part, this area was important to teachers in the primary and middle schools. Nursery school teachers who mentioned traits of this kind interpreted this area as involvement in the planned activities.

5. *Verbal abilities.* The constructs related to this category were only about 5% of the total number of supplied characteristics, but they were mentioned by all the teachers interviewed.

6. *Manual/motor abilities.* The characteristics related to this area represented fewer than 5% of the identified characteristics. They were all elicited from the protocols of the nursery school teachers.

I will now analyze in more detail what kinds of characteristics or constructs were elicited and how they were distributed over the different school levels.

With the exception of the constructs related to manual-motor abilities, which were elicited only from the nursery school teachers, constructs from each of the categories were found in the protocols of teachers from all three levels. However, they sometimes concerned different abilities, and the distribution among the protocols of teachers at different levels was not consistent.

In Table 1 is a list of the constructs adopted for the repertory grid in stage 2 of the research (see pp 229 ff.), with the source of each construct indicated. The constructs shared by all the teachers are indicated by a star (*). Most of them refer to the category of cognitive ability or to that of verbal abilities. Examples are: can/cannot spot the essential elements in every situation, finds original and divergent solutions/gives repetitive solutions, and shows well-organized exposition/fragmentary exposition.

Some of the characteristics related to motivation and school commitment were also shared. These included: motivated/unmotivated, always concentrates [on schoolwork]/often absentminded, and curious/seldom asks the reason why.

Other constructs were peculiar to one school level. In their characterizations, the great majority of the nursery school teachers (^) supplied characteristics related to manual abilities that were not found in the protocols of teachers for the other school levels. They referred to these as either excellent or poor. The primary school teachers (+) supplied a series of traits relating to the cognitive abilities disclosed in reading and writing. They made comments such as "understands very complex written and oral texts/understands only very simple texts." Only the middle school teachers (#) supplied constructs related to different cognitive abilities such as "precise intuition/poor intuition" as well as constructs from the area of personality such as "has his/her own ideas/repeats other people's ideas."

Some constructs were shared by teachers of two distinct school levels. Both nursery school and primary school teachers (^+) referred to the elaboration of information in a personally relevant way (e.g., "refers to his/her knowledge/refers almost exclusively to his/her experience").

Table 1. The Constructs Supplied in the Repertory Grid

+#	Is interested in studying	/ Has little interest in studying
#	Remarkable theoretical abilities	/ Poor theoretical abilities
^#	Refers almost exclusively to his/her experience	/ Refers to his/her knowledge
*	Finds original and divergent solutions	/ Gives repetitive solutions
*	Unfavorable and unstimulating family environment	/ Favorable and stimulating family environment
*	Has an excellent memory	/ Has a poor memory
+#	Passively follows the others	/ Has initiative
^#	Sought after by his/her classmates	/ Rejected by his/her classmates
+#	Learns and memorizes easily	/ Learns and memorizes with difficulty
*	Can spot the essential elements in every situation	/ Cannot spot the essential elements
^	Gifted	/ Not very gifted
+#	Always gives pertinent answers	/ Often answers haphazardly
+	Understands very complex written and oral texts	/ Understands only very simple texts
+#	To learn s/he needs to have reinforcements and explanations	/ Learns without outside help
*	Expresses him/herself precisely and articulately	/ Expresses him/herself imprecisely and inarticulately
+#	Mechanical and confused performance	/ Creative and speedy performance
^#	Disagreeable	/ Liked by all
*	Unmotivated	/ Motivated
+#	Committed to school activities	/ Not very committed to school activities
+#	Knows how to derive procedures and apply them	/ Does not know how to derive procedures and apply them
^#	Active	/ Lazy
+	Knows how to compose a text efficiently	/ Does not know how to compose a text efficiently
+	Reads with difficulty	/ Reads fluently
^+	Lacks experiences lived in a significant and intense way	/ Has lived many experiences in a significant and intense way

Continued on next page

Table 1—*Continued*

*	Expresses him/herself in an original and detailed way	/	Expresses him/herself in a stereotyped way
+#	Can see the funny sides of things	/	Lacks sense of humor
+#	Excellent ability to elaborate information in a personally relevant way	/	Poor ability to elaborate information in a personally relevant way
+#	Able to choose the right procedure in problem solving	/	Chooses at random
*	Often absentminded	/	Always concentrates
*	Seldom asks the reason why	/	Curious
#	Can analyze and synthesize promptly	/	Cannot analyze and synthesize
^#	Willing to help and friendly towards his/her classmates	/	Finds it difficult to establish relationships with his/her classmates
+#	Needs time to learn	/	Learns quickly
+#	Critical	/	Uncritical
*	Fragmentary exposition	/	Well-organized exposition
*	Understands readily and quickly	/	Understands with difficulty
*	Knows how to communicate and listen	/	Does not knows how to communicate and listen
+#	Connects concepts in a mechanical and repetitive way	/	Can find links in an original and "unconventional" way
+#	Accurate	/	Haphazard
^	Excellent manual and motor abilities	/	Poor manual and motor abilities
#	Prompt intuition	/	Poor intuition
#	Repeats other people's ideas	/	Has his/her own ideas
+#	Conscientious	/	Not conscientious
^#	Isolated	/	Blends with the group

Nursery school teachers and middle school teachers (^#) shared constructs about interpersonal relationships. Among them were "sought after by his/her classmates/rejected by his/her classmates" and "willing to help and makes friends easily/finds it difficult to establish relationships with his/her classmates." Primary school teachers and middle school teachers (+#) shared an interest in constructs related to cognitive abilities, commitment to school, and personality. Examples are: excellent/poor in personal reelaboration, knows/does not know how to ab-

Table 2. The Elements Supplied in the Repertory Grid

Element	Characterization
E1	A very intelligent pupil
E2	A not very intelligent pupil
E3	A pupil successful in everything
E4	A pupil successful in the logico-mathematical field, but with linguistic difficulties
E5	A pupil successful in the linguistic field, but with difficulties in the logico-mathematical field
E6	A mediocre pupil
E7	A pupil with learning difficulties
E8	A pupil succeeding best in practical activities

stract principles and to apply them in different situations, is involved/not involved in school activities, has initiative/passively follows the others.

Some of the construct labels were typical of individual teachers, but the areas referred to were the same as those cited above.

We also asked participants to describe different kinds of pupils they had taught during their career on the basis of both their level of native intelligence and their school achievements. Most respondents suggested a small number of types. These are shown in Table 2 together with the two elements supplied for the characterizations. Only a few of the nursery school teachers found it difficult to define these types. They stated that it was almost impossible to assign young pupils to a type that would remain fixed over time.

STAGE 2

In the second stage of the research, respondents were 160 teachers from the province of Verona, about one third of whom had taken part in stage 1 of the research as well. Among the respondents there were: (a) 20 nursery school teachers, (b) 80 teachers from primary schools, and (c) 60 people who teach in middle schools. The primary school teachers included class teachers as well as specialist teachers from each of the areas of instruction referred to above: language, logic and mathematics, and social studies. The middle school teachers also represented three different areas: language (including foreign languages), mathematics and science, and technical studies.

The teachers were given a repertory grid with elements the same as those we had presented in Stage 1. We also supplied constructs from among those that were elicited in the first stage (see Table 1). The order of presentation was randomized to avoid any undue influence on the rating of the constructs. In one third of the constructs, the pole presented first was the one that had served teachers to describe the not very intelligent pupil. A few adjustments had to be made to suit the level of teaching. For example, the construct "reads fluently / reads with difficulty" was omitted from the grid presented to the nursery school teachers because it was not applicable to their pupils. Teachers were asked to complete the grid and evaluate each element on every construct using a 5-point scale.

Computer analyses were carried out on individual grids as well as on the grids grouped according to school levels and subject areas. For the latter we decided to work with a mean grid. Because the constructs as well as the elements had been supplied, we were able to calculate the mean rating for each element on each construct for the groups separately. We chose this because we were interested in getting an idea of how the group as a whole construed the elements. We used the FOCUS program, one method for providing a cluster analysis, and the MGRIDS program (Tschudi, 1988, 1989) to extract the mean grid for school-level homogeneous groups. These grid transformations have enabled us to highlight the ways in which teachers at different school levels construed the intelligent pupil in relation to the other types of pupils included as elements in the grid.

The FOCUSed mean grid of the nursery school teachers showed three element clusters. The first comprised elements 1 and 3 (a "very intelligent pupil" and a "pupil successful in every subject"), with a matching score of 95. The second consisted of elements 5, 8, and 4 (a "pupil successful in the field of language, but who has difficulties in the field of logic-mathematics"; a "pupil successful in practical activities," and a "pupil successful in the area of logic-mathematics who has difficulties with language." Elements 5 and 4 had a matching score of 91 and a matching score of 93 with element 8. The third cluster was that of elements 7 and 2 (a "pupil with learning difficulties" and a "pupil who is not very intelligent") with a matching score of 93. Element 6, a "mediocre pupil," is placed between the last two clusters with the same matching score (86) with each of them (see Table 3). As can be seen, there is a clear distinction, even polarization, between the positive elements (1 and

Table 3. Nursery School Teachers' FOCUSed Mean Grid: Element Clusters

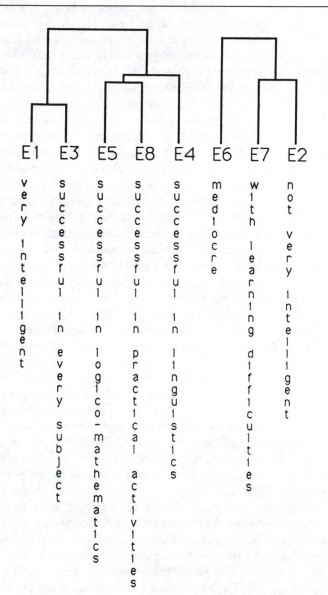

3) and the negative ones (2 and 7). The elements describing pupils excelling in a single area were placed between these two poles. The reason for this polarization becomes clear if the construct clusters are considered.

The FOCUS analysis disclosed two large clusters. The first clearly differentiated the elements according to a subcluster of cognitive abilities and a second subcluster that combined verbal and cognitive abilities. Elements 1 and 3 were rated at the positive pole of the constructs. They were seen to be capable of good to excellent verbal expression, memory, and so on. Elements 2 and 7 were rated at the negative pole of the same constructs with a very high rating. Finally, elements 5, 8, and 4 were located in an intermediate position but nearer the positively rated elements as they were mostly assigned to the positive pole of the constructs.

The second cluster differentiated among the elements on the dimension of relational behavior (first subcluster) and on that of motivation for learning and pace of learning (second subcluster). All the elements in this first subcluster were rated at the positive pole, although those types of pupil who were considered positive elements showed these characteristics more clearly. Moreover, in the second subcluster, the differences among the elements were less marked. Element 2 was set apart from the others because this was a pupil who takes a long time to learn and is not very accurate, so s/he needs many explanations and much support.

The FOCUSed mean grid of the primary school teachers showed a different cluster structure of the elements from that of the nursery school teachers' mean grid. Among the primary school teachers, the positive and the negative elements are polarized, but relations with the other elements were diverse. Two clusters were apparent; the first consisted of elements 1 and 3 with a matching score of 96. The second was subdivided into three subclusters. The first subcluster grouped elements 2 and 7 with a matching score of 97, the second included elements 6 and 8 matched with a score of 93, and the third included elements 4 and 5 with a matching score of 90. The last subcluster was the nearest to the positive element cluster (see Table 4).

Differences and similarities among the elements were clearly illustrated by the clustering of the constructs. Constructs were organized into two large clusters and further divided into two subclusters, with an additional small cluster of only two constructs remaining. This last included the constructs "isolated / mingles with the group" and "liked by all / disagreeable." This applied to all the elements at the positive pole. One subcluster incorporated motivational aspects and family background; the second included cognitive abilities and constructs relating to

Table 4. Primary School Teachers' FOCUSed Mean Grid: Element Clusters

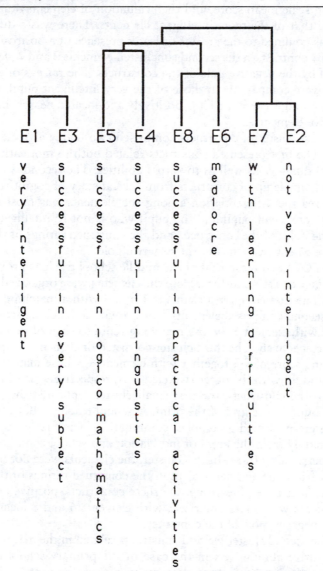

E1	E3	E5	E4	E8	E6	E7	E2
very intelligent	successful in every subject	successful in logico-mathematics	successful in linguistics	successful in practical activities	mediocre	with learning difficulties	not very intelligent

the pace of learning. In the former, elements 2 and 7 were located around the rating scale mean score, and the evaluation of elements 4 and 5 approached that of the more intelligent elements. There was a difference, but it was confined to the greater or lesser presence of a positive characteristic. By contrast, in the second subcluster, elements 2 and 7 were characterized by the negative pole of the constructs. The ratings of elements 4 and 5 were comparable to those of the very intelligent pupil, whereas elements 6 and 8 were rated less positively and located nearer the cluster of negative elements.

The last cluster of constructs comprised two highly articulated subclusters. The first presented constructs related both to motivational and relational qualities as well as to verbal abilities. The second was almost completely made up of constructs from the category of cognitive ability. In this area the differentiation among the elements was most marked. The very intelligent pupil and the pupil who is not so intelligent represented the poles of the constructs, and the construed ratings of the intermediate elements were nearer the negative pole.

The FOCUSed mean grid of the middle school teachers provided yet a different set of relationships. Here the elements were organized in three clusters. The first comprised elements 1 and 3 with a matching score of 97; the second comprised elements 5 and 4 with a matching score of 93, together with element 8, whose matching score to each of them was 88 and 86, respectively. The third cluster consisted of elements 2 and 7 with a matching score of 96, together with element 6, whose matching score was 91 and 90 with the other two elements, respectively (see Table 5).

As to the constructs, the first small cluster replicated the structure already found in the grid of the primary school teachers. Both the other two clusters presented a complex combination. The first grouped constructs mainly from the areas of motivation and school commitment, as well as personality traits. In this cluster, the elements were not markedly different from one another, except in the construed ratings of their cognitive skills or pace of learning. On these constructs, positive and negative elements were more polarized, with elements 6 and 8 located at or near the negative pole of the constructs.

In the second cluster we find constructs related in the main to verbal and cognitive abilities. As in the case of the primary school teachers, here, too, the distance among elements increased. Elements 2, 7, and in part 6, were characterized by poor verbal and cognitive abilities. On the other hand, elements 1 and 3 were considered good information processors, creative and capable of deriving procedures and strategies for solv-

Table 5. Middle School Teachers' FOCUSed Mean Grid: Element Clusters

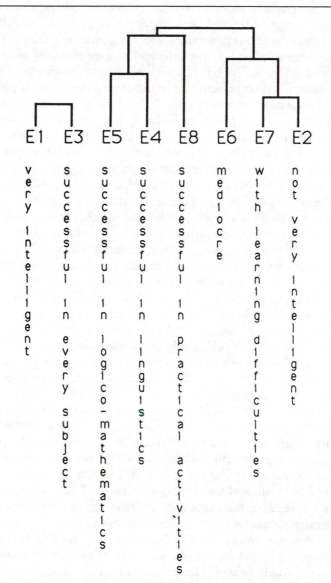

ing problems and for applying them on their own. Moreover, they are construed as being able to express original opinions precisely and articulately. It is interesting to note that element 5 (a pupil successful in the field of language study) is generally rated more positively than element 4 (a pupil successful in the logico-mathematical area of study) not only on constructs of verbal ability but also on constructs of cognitive ability.

Significant differences were also found among the teachers' constructions of intelligence when we considered the mean grids in light of the subjects taught by the respondents in the primary and the middle school. Among the primary school teachers, the clustering of the elements in the grids of the class teachers and the teachers of social studies was the same as that obtained for the mean grid for the entire primary school sample. The relationships that resulted from the grids of teachers who deal with language and with the area of logic and mathematics showed two clusters: a cluster with the elements 2 and 7 and another cluster with all the rest of the elements. Furthermore, all the teachers, except those who deal with the field of logic and mathematics, judged element 5 ("a pupil successful in language, but not in mathematics") to be more similar to the very intelligent pupils, regardless of the cluster in which it was placed. The teachers who teach subjects in the field of logic and mathematics, on the other hand, considered element 4 ("a pupil with difficulties in language but successful in mathematics") one of the more intelligent pupils.

The differences in the clustering of the elements were linked to differences in the relationships between the constructs. In this connection it is illuminating to examine the differences between the ratings of elements 4 and 5. In general, element 5 was rated higher in verbal ability and element 4 was rated higher in cognitive abilities. But the gaps between the ratings of the elements on these constructs were assessed differently by subgroups of teachers. There was a variation of 0.5 to more than 1.0 on the 5-point scale. While these differences were usually more favorable to element 5 in the realm of verbal ability and more favorable to element 4 in the area of cognitive ability, the grid that summarized the ratings of the teachers who specialize in logic and mathematics showed that they rated element 4 more positively in both areas.

The differences among the elements were more marked between the whole group and the subgroups of teachers from the different subject areas within the middle school. The grouped ratings of teachers whose subjects are the humanistic studies—Italian, history, and geography— yielded clusters of elements that were similar to the mean grid of the whole group at this level of schooling. As among the teachers of primary school, here, too, elements 1 and 3 are in a cluster separate from the others. However, although elements 5 and 4 were placed in the same cluster in the grid of the entire group, these teachers considered element 4 to be similar to element 8 ("a pupil who is most successful in practical activities"), with the ratings of element 5 placing outside the cluster in a position showing a more positive evaluation.

The teachers of technical subjects and of mathematics construed elements similarly, and they differed from both the whole group and from the teachers of humanistic subjects. The teachers of technical subjects provided two clusters of elements. In one there is a subcluster grouping of elements 5, 4, and 8 near elements 1 and 3. In the other, elements 6 and 7 were considered more similar to each other and related to element 2. The first cluster of the teachers of mathematics placed elements 4 and 5 near the subcluster containing elements 1 and 3, with the "pupil who is successful in the field of mathematics" rated nearer the positive elements.

The clusters of constructs were similar to those of the primary school teachers. In the mean grid of those who teach subjects connected with the humanities, the difference between the ratings of elements 4 and 5 on their verbal abilities is often more than two points. The distance between them as related to cognitive abilities is only about 0.5 points (in favor of element 4). In the mean grid of the teachers of technical subjects, the distances in favor of either one or the other element were generally confined to 0.5. And in the mean grid of the mathematics teachers, the ratings for cognitive abilities were consistently higher for the pupil who is successful in the field of logic and mathematics, with no important difference between them in the ratings of verbal abilities.

DISCUSSION

The two stages of the research reported here supply a rather complex picture of how teachers construe intelligence, or rather how they construe the traits that distinguish the very intelligent pupil from the one who is not very intelligent and from other identifiable types of pupils. Let us first consider the traits used as bases for the Repgrid. The respondents supplied highly varied sets of constructs. Furthermore, in addition to the constructs that all the teachers shared, there are diverse constructs idiosyncratic to the different levels of school. Our findings replicate those of Fry (1984) in that the traits representing the common core of the teachers' theories of intelligence relate to: cognitive abilities (especially the ability to reason, think logically, and recognize essential elements in different situations), verbal abilities (especially fluency, accuracy, and complexity), skills in social relations (mixes well, is sought after by his/her classmates), and motivation and participation in school activities.

But we found that teachers in our research related to intelligence in a way that was not identical to those in Fry's study. The following differences were found:

1. Emphasis on the ability to manipulate language was found chiefly among primary school teachers. Fry found this emphasis to be typical of secondary school teachers.

2. In our research, middle school teachers emphasized the centrality of cognitive abilities. In Fry's findings, these considerations were most salient among college teachers.

3. Only nursery school teachers related to motor and manual abilities in their construal of intelligence.

4. Teachers from the nursery schools and the middle schools considered social relationships with classmates as central to intelligence. This was not central to the construals of the teachers in the primary school.

   This finding is anomalous unless we take into account some of the factors that affect the teachers' construals in the primary school. Since 1985, the Italian government has implemented a New Program for Primary Schools. This program has led to a more scientific and a less artistic and affective view of the teaching-learning situation by encouraging a view of the educational situation almost exclusively in a cognitive perspective. In addition, teachers in the province of Verona have undergone intensive in-service training in connection with this program—training that has reinforced changed attitudes towards teaching. The social values in education have assumed secondary importance.

5. Finally, the area of commitment to and involvement in school differentiates the positive from the negative elements only in the characterizations of the teachers from postnursery education.

The analysis carried out on the repertory grids supports the conclusions outlined above only in part. For example, all the teachers construe verbal and cognitive abilities as characteristic of the very intelligent pupil. Similarly, all the teachers agree that the intelligent pupil has greater social awareness and involvement than the one who is not so intelligent. In addition, although the difference in scores is not very large, motivation is construed more often in the very intelligent pupil than in the one who is not so intelligent. Similarly, the very intelligent pupil is characterized by involvement in school activity, interest in studying, and accuracy in task performance, whereas the not so intelligent pupil is generally rated low on these qualities.

The element clusters obtained by the FOCUSed Mean Grids confirm that teachers identify intelligence with school success. At every school level, the pupil who succeeds in everything is also construed as a very intelligent pupil. A further interesting result is connected to the subject matter. We found that a pupil who succeeds in the subject taught by the interviewed teacher, no matter what difficulties s/he has with other subjects, is generally construed in a positive light. The construal is more positive than that of the pupil who is poor in the teacher's subject even if s/he is successful in other subject areas. In both primary and middle schools this was found in the construals of the language teachers on the one hand and among the teachers in the field of logic and mathematics on the other. As Sternberg (1985b) has asserted, the implicit theories of intelligence that these teachers articulated are deeply affected by the structural characteristics of the subject they teach. For the teachers in the area of language, the verbal and cognitive abilities linked to the comprehension and production of written and oral texts were decisive in characterizing the intelligent pupil. For teachers in the field of logic and mathematics, on the other hand, it is the ability to solve problems that signals the major distinction between the intelligent pupil and the pupil who is not so intelligent.

Studies that attempt to investigate how experts and laypersons construe intelligence are important in demonstrating different responses in differing contexts. In addition, they contribute to heightening people's awareness of how they use these construals in everyday life and in their professional behavior. This is important because, as Sternberg said, "Whether or not implicit theories are 'right' (and it is not always clear what *right* means in this context), they are our main bases for evaluating the competence of others" (1990, p. 145). Teachers who are responsible for evaluating pupils' achievements have an obligation to understand the bases for the assessments. I am convinced that the conversational technique used in this research to elicit teachers' construals of different types of pupils has enhanced their insight into the implicit theory of intelligence that underlies their assessments of pupils.

ACKNOWLEDGMENTS

The research was supported by a grant from the Ministero dell'Università e della Ricerca Scientifica (Ministry of University and Scientific Research), 1990. I would also like to thank the following people for their help in data collecting: Emanuela Antolini, Ombretta Cecchinato, Armando Pajola, Gianni Pontara, Marina Scipioni, and Raffaela and Battista Tamellini.

REFERENCES

Bannister, D., & Fransella, F. (1971). *Inquiring man. The psychology of personal constructs.* Penguin: Harmondsworth. [Italian translation, *L'uomo ricercatore. Introduzione alla psicologia dei costrutti personali.* Firenze: Martinelli, 1986].

Calegari, P. (1990). La rilevanza attribuita a tratti del carattere e della personalità nella rappresentazione dell'intelligenza elevata [The relevance attributed to character and personality traits in high intelligence]. *Studi di Psicologia dell'Educazione, 3,* 22–31.

Carugati, F. F. (1990). Everyday ideas, theoretical models and social representations: The case of intelligence and its development. In G. R. Semin & K. J. Gergen (Eds.), *Everyday understanding: Social and scientific implications* (pp. 130–150). London: Sage Publications.

De Bernardi, B. (1991, August). *Construing intelligence: A developmental study.* Paper presented at the IXth International Congress on Personal Construct Psychology, Albany, New York, USA.

Dweck, C. S., & Bempechat, J. (1983). Children's theories of intelligence: Consequences for learning. In S. G. Paris, G. M. Olson & H. W. Stevenson (Eds.), *Learning and motivation in the classroom* (pp. 239–256). Hillsdale: Erlbaum.

Fry, P. S. (1984). Teacher's conception of students' intelligence. In P. S. Fry (Ed.), Changing conceptions of intelligence and intellectual functioning: Current theories and research. *International Journal of Psychology, 19,* 457–474.

Guilford, J. P. (1967). *The nature of human intelligence.* New York: McGraw-Hill.

Kelly, G. A. (1955). *The psychology of personal constructs.* Vols. 1 and 2. New York: W. W. Norton.

Mugny, G., & Carugati, F. F. (1989). *Social representations of intelligence.* Cambridge: Cambridge University Press.

Nicholls, J. G. (1978). The development of the concepts of effort and ability, perception of academic attainment and the understanding that difficult tasks require more ability. *Child Development, 49,* 800–814.

Nicholls, J. G. (1980). The development of the concept of difficulty. *Merrill-Palmer Quarterly, 26,* 271–281.

Nicholls, J. G. (1984a). Conceptions of ability and achievement motivation. In R. E. Ames & C. Ames (Eds.), *Research on motivation in education Vol. 1* (pp. 39–73). New York: Academic Press.

Nicholls, J. G. (1984b). Achievement motivation: Conceptions of ability, subjective experience, task choice and performance, *Psychological Review, 91,* 328–346.

Nicholls, J. G. (1990). What is ability and why are we mindful of it? A developmental perspective. In R. J. Sternberg & J. Kolligian (Eds.), *Competence considered* (pp. 11–40). New Haven: Yale University Press.

Nicholls, J. G., & Miller, A. T. (1984). Reasoning about the ability of self and others: A developmental study. *Child Development, 55,* 1990–1999.

Salmon, P. (Ed.). (1980). *Coming to know.* London: Routledge & Kegan Paul.

Salmon, P. (1986). Personal construct psychology and education, *Documenti n. 1.* Dipartimento di Psicologia dello Sviluppo e della Socializzazione, Università di Padova.

Salmon, P., & Claire, H. (1984). *Classroom collaboration.* London: Routledge & Kegan Paul.

Shaw, M. L. G. (1979). Conversational heuristics for eliciting shared understanding. *International Journal of Man-Machine Studies.* 11, 621–634.

Shaw, M. L. G. (1980). *On becoming a personal scientist.* London: Academic Press.

Snyderman, M., & Rothman, S. (1987). Survey of expert opinion on intelligence and aptitude testing. *Amcrican Psychologist, 42,* 137–144.

Spearman, C. (1927). *The abilities of man.* London: Macmillan.

Sternberg, R. J. (1985a). *Beyond I.Q.: A triarchic theory of human intelligence.* Cambridge: Cambridge University Press.

Sternberg, R. J. (1985b). Implicit theories of intelligence, creativity and wisdom. *Journal of Personality and Social Psychology, 49,* 607–627.

Sternberg, R. J. (1990). Prototypes of competence and incompetence. In R. G. Sternberg & J. Kolligian (Eds.), *Competence considered* (pp. 117–145). New Haven, CT: Yale University Press.

Sternberg, R. J., Conway, B. E., Ketron, J. L., & Bernstein, M. (1981). People's conceptions of intelligence. *Journal of Personality and Social Psychology, 41,* 37–55.

Thomas, L., & Harri-Augstein, S. (1985). *Self-organised learning. Foundations of a conversational science for psychology.* London: Routledge & Kegan Paul.

Thurstone, L. L. (1938). *Primary mental abilities.* Chicago: University of Chicago Press.

Tschudi, F. (1988). *Flexigrid 4.4 manual.* Oslo: University of Oslo.

Tschudi, F. (1989). *Notes on Multigrid Vol. 1.1b.* Oslo: University of Oslo.

Yussen, S. R., & Kane, P. T. (1985). Children's conceptions of intelligence. In S. R. Yussen (Ed.), *The growth of reflection in children* (pp. 207–241). New York: Academic Press.

CHAPTER 11

Group Construing:
The Impact of Professional Training

BARBARA TOOTH

Working as a professional with dual qualifications has provided me with a unique opportunity to observe some of the relationships between the many groups that comprise mental health services in Australia. During my employment as a psychologist it became clear to me that my colleagues somehow viewed me as different from them. I had the same experience while employed as a nurse. Even the administration of the regional health service had problems accommodating a professional with dual qualifications and ruled that I should confine my provision of services to the profession in which I was employed at the time.

It became clear to me that there was a common assumption that the members of each of the mental health professions are similar yet different from the others. This assumption is in turn based on a further assumption that training can and does change an individual's construing. To my knowledge these assumptions have not been researched to any great extent. The philosophy of modern day mental health services challenges these assumptions by advocating the breaking down of professional boundaries through the introduction of the generalist mental health worker. The introduction of this category of worker acknowledges the overlap of the services provided by many professionals in the mental health field. It is my experience that each professional group is becoming more committed to establishing its uniqueness in the services it provides. Each profession has developed its own culture that makes the introduction of new policies that challenge these cultures particularly interesting.

This chapter presents my exploration of the issue of group construing among members of the mental health professions of psychiatry, psychology, and nursing to determine how they are similar to yet different from one another. My particular interest is in the role training has played in this process. The major problem that arises when exploring these issues is the question whether it is the professional's attitudes/personality that are fundamental determinants of their behavior or whether it is the training that each professional receives. The logical answer is that it is an interaction of both of these factors. However, this also raises more questions that require answers. First, given this interaction, why do our training programs fail so miserably in bringing this to the attention of their trainees? Next, in this view it is likely that commonality among group members may transcend professional boundaries to include all types of professions in a single specialist field. Such an assumption implies that as members of one profession we may be far more similar to members of other professions than we care to consider. To entertain such ideas goes against societal forces that demand our individuation in terms of professional groups. Finally, researchers in this area assume they know what the differences are among professional groups and what causes them, and they do not set out to test if this is true or not. The use of questionnaires that have predetermined specificity (Viney, 1987) in this type of research supports this argument. We have not undertaken the first step. We need to find out what similarity and difference exist within and between groups and set out to answer this question by asking those involved to share their experiences with us. My research was designed to fill this gap.

How each profession forms its own culture can be understood within constructivist theory. The sociality corollary extends the commonality corollary because not only do members of a group need to have some degree of commonality with other members, but in order for them to interact effectively, it is important to construe from the other members' outlook. The validation of a person's construct system is important if closer relationships are to be developed. It is more likely that the validation of a professional's construct system will occur within the person's own professional group both because of greater availability and the greater likelihood of construct similarity.

In this chapter I provide a brief summary of mental health service delivery. Then I review some of the nonconstructivist literature on training and professionals' constructions of their work with clients. Next, I shall review what other constructivists have reported about the training of professionals and present my current research. Finally, an overview of the usefulness of personal construct theory (PCT) to understand group construing among the various mental health professions is discussed and the implications for training described.

MENTAL HEALTH SERVICES

Over the past 20 to 30 years, major changes have occurred in the delivery of mental health services. These changes have involved a movement away from the traditional medically dominated hospital services to services provided in the community by many more mental health professionals. This "scientifically" based shift in the emphasis of care has not been accompanied by the expected improvement in the quality of care for people who have serious mental health problems. Many reasons for this less-than-successful transition have been put forward, and these are concisely summarized by Glick, Showstack, Cohen, and Klar (1989). They conclude that the major obstacles to providing quality care are training factors, treatment factors, economic and administrative factors, patient and family factors, and political and social factors.

However, training has been seen to be the major reason why the new approaches to mental health have failed to be implemented (Glick, Showstack, Cohen, & Klar, 1989). The authors propose that this is due to the difficulty in training professionals when the biases toward treatment vary markedly both within and among trainers, trainees, and even society. The proposed strategy to "fix" this problem, as put forward by these authors, is to provide a wider range of experiences for trainees so they can incorporate new treatment modalities into their work. Such an argument is based on many assumptions that may or may not be correct.

Implicit in the assumption that many professions are necessary for the effective treatment of mental health problems is an acceptance that each profession has something unique to offer in the treatment of clients. Logically this makes sense as each profession undertakes training that identifies them as having specific and unique skills enabling them to work in the mental health field. Another conclusion that can be drawn from this assumption is that the training process for each profession leads to a similar way of construing clients and treatment approaches. However, the role of training in forming clinicians' constructions of their work is complex and little studied. First, many studies start from the viewpoint that professions will vary from one another, without first establishing if this is true. This is important as we may have far more in common than we choose to acknowledge. Second, professionals, it appears, are reluctant to look at themselves and the role their thoughts and feelings play in the treatment process. It is also ironic that at a time when cooperation and understanding among mental health professionals is more important than ever before, each profession is becoming more territorial about its role and that each profession feels threatened by the others for survival (Soni, 1989).

The above viewpoints assume that training can, and does, change an individual's fundamental beliefs about mental health problems and their treatment. In terms of PCT, this would imply that training can change people's core constructs or at least their superordinate constructs rather than more subordinate and peripheral ones. This is an important issue and I expand on it later in this chapter.

TRAINING AND PROFESSIONALS' CONSTRUING

In the nonconstructivist literature there appear to be four major themes that refer to similarities and differences among mental health professional groups. The first focuses on the difference in the nature of science for each professional group. The second focuses on the impact of professionalization on the different groups. The third focuses on both clinical and theoretical training programs. The fourth concerns itself with staff attitudes and the personality factors of different professional groups. At this point it is important to point out that most of the available literature on group construing in the field of mental health is based on questionnaire data. As I have already noted, the limitations of this type of research are acknowledged because of the predetermined specificity of questionnaires; however it does provide some relevant information.

Diverse Views on the Nature of Science

Kingsbury (1987) argued that rivalry exists between psychologists and psychiatrists because neither profession shares the shaping experience of the other, rather than the more popular belief that rivalry is due to power struggles. It may be argued that nurses are similar to psychiatrists in their shaping experience, and Kingsbury's point about psychiatrists and psychologists has relevance for the nursing profession as well.

Kingsbury (1987) maintained that psychology views science as a method of inquiry with facts less important than the developing theories that guide thinking. In contrast, medical science is viewed as a set of facts, a body of knowledge and procedures, with literature reviews providing more facts with no room for how they were derived. In this paradigm science teaches a logical method for approaching clients, making it easier in medical emergencies, for example, to act immediately and contemplate and critique performance later.

Professionalization

Professionalization is another important factor in understanding the differences that exist among professional groups. The main influence of professionalization is the use of power by the more advanced professions to control those that are less advanced (Tooth, 1984). This in effect mitigates against the close working alliance needed in provision of mental health services. For example, professions such as nursing and psychology have a natural alliance as the two professions share many common interests and problems, yet they are reluctant to work together (DeLeon, Kjervik, Kraut, & VandenBos, 1985). According to DeLeon et al., the main reason for this is best understood at the educational level as nursing has only recently begun university-level qualifications in many countries. This is accompanied by a fundamental lack of understanding and respect for each other's professional skills and scientific knowledge base. Other reasons put forward are: the difference in the allocation of research money, an academic structure traditionally not affording cross-fertilization, the interprofessional competition for the shrinking mental health dollar, and the resistance of nurse practitioners to defer to another profession because they have traditionally deferred to the medical profession and this is under challenge. The authors conclude it is a luxury neither profession can afford any longer, whatever the reason. These arguments could apply equally to all of the health professional groups.

Clinical and Theoretical Training

The importance of both clinical and theoretical training in relation to professional attitude change has also been addressed by numerous authors within their disciplines. Some authors (Altrocchi & Eisdorfer, 1961; Creech, 1977; Gelfand & Ullmann, 1961) have found that theoretical training has not been enough to change professionals' attitudes about their work, with change occuring only when it included clinical experience. Other authors (Slimmer, Wendt, & Martinkus, 1990) have studied the effect of the site of the clinical experience on attitude change and found that while professionals did not change their attitudes as a result of the clinical site, their attitudes changed as a result of the clinical staff to whom they were exposed. Slimmer et al. (1990) concluded that it is necessary to provide exemplary role models to effect attitude development in students.

The different use of clinical experience by professions has also been noted, with some professions using it to reinforce learning about theories while other professions view clinical experience as primary (Kingsbury, 1987). From Kingsbury's work, the differences in attitudes among various professions are seen to be a direct result of both theoretical and practical training. This conclusion is in agreement with my suggestion at the beginning of this chapter that training changes attitudes and beliefs within a profession. It is not unreasonable to assume that if this is the case, then the instutionalization of different professions with differing training will result in similar attitudes and beliefs within the professions, but differences will exist among professions. However, not all training programs for each profession have the same theoretical orientation or provide similar clinical experience (Peterson, Eaton, Levine, & Snepp, 1982). Therefore, different kinds of training within the one profession may also result in differences in attitudes and beliefs within that same profession.

Theoretical training programs designed to emphasize the interdisciplinary process have been studied by Moffic, Blattstein, Rosenberg, Adams, and Chacko (1983). They found one group of students consistently more enthusiastic, with a greater preference for interdisciplinary training than another. Interestingly, the students' responses were in line with those of their faculty. These findings indicated that attitudes of the faculty appear to be a crucial factor in training professionals and that educators need to examine not only their training programs but their own conscious and unconscious attitudes and values. Again, the importance of the professional trainer as role model was highlighted.

Staff Attitudes and Personality Factors

The fourth major theme in the literature on similarities and differences within and among professions centers on professionals' attitudes and their personalities. In an extensive review of the literature on professionals, Roskin, Carsen, Rabiner, and Marell (1988) concluded that the observed differences among professions could be accounted for by the personality characteristics of individuals in a given field on the one hand

and training and clinical experience on the other. They postulated that the unconscious paradigms/models in professions attract certain types of individuals. Some authors (Krasner & Houts, 1984; Smyrnios, Schultz, Smyrnios, & Kirkby, 1986) suggested that behavioral scientists separate their beliefs about their discipline from other beliefs they hold, whether they openly claim to hold them or not. Krasner and Houts (1984) found systematic differences among psychologists' political, social, and philosophical values. They suggested that broadly culturally determined values can be compatible with different discipline-specific assumptions. Furthermore, it is possible that behavioral scientists select and value different assumptions about their discipline and that these choices are unrelated to their stands on broader value issues. In constructivist terms, the position of these authors would suggest that professional training influences an individual's more peripheral set of constructs, or that those constructs relating to their profession are contained within a separate subsystem of constructs.

In contrast, Winter, Shivakumar, Brown, Roitt, Drysdale and Jones (1987) found that the approach professionals take to treatment reflects their more general attitudes about life. It is assumed that these attitudes reflect the individual's central constructs and as such would be very difficult to change. Indeed, the influence of a professional's attributions in determining how they interact with clients and how they make treatment decisions has received attention from a few authors (Brickman, Rabinowitz, Karuza, Coates, Cohen, & Kidder, 1982; McGovern, Newman, & Kopta, 1986; Wills, 1978). All of these authors conclude that the therapists' attributions either complement or supersede their professional training. The research presented so far and the conclusions drawn can be accommodated within a constructivist framework.

A PERSONAL CONSTRUCT PERSPECTIVE

Some important issues were raised in the preceding section. First, there is evidence to suggest that each profession obtains its knowledge differently; hence, differences would be assumed to exist among them. Second, it would appear that clinical rather than theoretical training is more likely to change attitudes and beliefs. Third, there appears to be some conflict about whether training changes professionals' peripheral constructs or their more central constructs. Fourth, the question remains whether professionals' attitudes and values supersede their training or whether they take from their training those aspects of it that can be accommodated within their existing construct system. Fifth, the importance of role models in shaping these beliefs and attitudes in professionals needs to be explored further. These issues take us away from the logical assumption I presented at the beginning of this chapter that training accounts for the similarities and differences among professions to a much more important question of the impact the training process has on trainees.

I begin this section by clearly stating my argument. I believe our attitudes/constructs supersede our training, and we take from our training those aspects that are consistent with our more central constructs. I would argue that clinical training is more influential on attitude change because there is more flexibility in the clinical setting to use those aspects of our training with which we are more comfortable. By contrast, theoretical training requires learning sets of facts that are thought to be important for our professional development. There is often little room to diverge from these. In general, it is my belief that one of the most significant purposes of training is to serve the process of socialization into the culture of the profession; that is, to know the appropriate facts and role of someone in that profession. Having stated my argument, I now present the work of other constructivists in an attempt to support my view. Then I present the views of Kelly and aspects of personal construct theory that are relevant to this argument.

Relatively few personal construct studies address the impact of training on mental health professionals, and those that do exist were mainly conducted in the mid-1970s. However, while not interested in training per se, Winter (1985) researched professional attitudes and replicated the work of earlier researchers (Caine, 1975; Caine & Smail, 1969; Pallis & Stoffelmayer, 1973; Panayotopoulos & Stoffelmayer, 1972) who found that professionals' attitudes to treatment reflected their more fundamental constructions of the world. Winter, Shivakumar, Brown, Roitt, Drysdale, and Jones (1987) also noted differences among professional groups in how they viewed mental health problems, either in terms of psychosocial or illness contexts. The authors hypothesized: "Group differences of this order would suggest that interdisciplinary conflicts, ostensibly focusing on clinical issues, may in fact reflect divergences in more basic assumptions, values, and social and political attitudes" (p. 237).

The importance of professional attitudes prior to training has been reflected in the type of training chosen by professionals. Stone, Stein, and Green (1971) found that the orientation of psychiatrists at the time of entry to their training was strikingly similar to that of their chosen training center. Similarly, Soldz (1989) found that psychotherapists used constructs that were more concerned with emotional stability-instability. These findings are consistent with those of Winter and his colleagues (1987) that the construction of clients reflects the individual's personal style. Psychotherapists would be expected to be more psychologically oriented in their constructions than psychiatrists. Therefore, training per se is less likely to be the only variable influencing the treatment orientation of professionals. These results suggest that although the effect of training should not be minimized, it is likely that the attitudes the person holds prior to training are important in selecting treatment.

However, there is also a body of research that indicates that training influences professionals' more peripheral constructs. The common thread throughout these studies appears to be that constructs relating to client characteristics are more likely to be peripheral, whereas constructions about treatment appear to be more central. How professionals treat clients is more likely to be influenced by their values. As Walker (1992) noted, inherent in Kelly's writings is the importance of the values of both the researcher and participant and the proposition that values form a superordinate construct system. I suggest that the more personal nature of treatment accounts for its more central nature, whereas the more impersonal nature of labels for clients is more peripheral. The work of the following authors supports this view.

Tully (1976) found constructs used for clients were more isolated. He noted that the development of extended construct systems that are capable of being elaborated further when necessary is not a guaranteed outcome of professional training. Neither is the development of a sensitive open way of construing clients. Tully suggested there may be a split in conceptual systems that developed through training between professional and personal functions, a situation he attributed to resistance among professionals to change their constructs from the classification of disease. Fransella (1983) and Soldz (1989) suggested that the separate subsystems for clients and acquaintances is in fact a way of alleviating therapist anxiety.

Similarly, Bender (cited by Tully, 1976) found that the construing of clients involved significantly more psychiatric terminology and that these constructs had a limited range of convenience, suggesting that some evidence does exist for two languages, a professional one and a personal one. Soldz (1989) is in agreement with those who claim that psychiatric nosology results in stereotyping (Sarbin & Mancuso, 1980) and an automatic attribution of a wide range of characteristics. In Kellian terms, this is referred to as *constellatory construing*. It is of interest to note that age, gender, profession, years of experience, and theoretical orientation made no significant difference to the outcome in this study.

Agnew and Bannister (1973) agreed that there is a subsystem of specialist language in psychiatry, but that it is too poorly structured to be looked on as a professional language. The problem for these authors was that the language used may have similar labels but not similar meaning. Soldz (1989) advocated more research to clarify the exact nature of the differences in construals of clients and the possible implications these differences have both clinically and socially.

Apart from education, professional training also fulfills the purpose of socialization (Tully, 1976). Training not only develops competence through learning skills and understanding, but also the person's professional identity and professional values. According to Applegate (1990), people respond to others because they want to understand the immediate implications their behavior has for their own goals rather than to understand why others behave as they do. The rather intransigent nature of professional roles has also been noted by Ryle and Breen (1974). They found that those constructs relating to their role were more stable throughout training, while constructs relating to affect were less stable. These latter findings were not expected by these researchers; however, I believe they indicate the power of the perceptions of the professional role. This socialization process is also evidenced in Lifshitz (1974), who found that professional social workers differed in their constructions of clients as a result of the amount of training they had undergone. Specifically, there was a change in their values and approach to people as a result of training. Winter (1992) pointed out that this could be because the social workers were older than the trainees. However, it is also likely that the socialization process has had an impact, imparting what is expected in the role of social worker for the more experienced social workers.

Therefore, there appears to be considerable support for the view that training is a socialization process that influences the way mental health professionals interact with their clients. This training often leads to a change in the professional counselor's worldview, a shift from the more spontaneous gut reaction to a knowledge-based process. As Viney pointed out, this shift moves the professional counselor away from a shared worldview with the client (Viney, 1983). This must have implications for the relationship between client and professional.

Professionals may well have to develop a system of constructs they believe they are expected to have in order to survive in a system that does not meet their personal ideology. That is, professionals soon learn what role they are expected to perform; however, they appear to have difficulty fitting clients into categorizations in ways that are expected of them. A statement by Button (1985) exemplifies this: "In the language of Kelly's choice corollary, a society preoccupied with definition at the expense of extension may lead to a neat order and security in the short-term but pose severe restriction on societal members and be ill-prepared for eventual inevitable and possibly catastrophic change in the longer term" (p. 353). Professions to some extent may be viewed as societies in the mental health setting, each seeking to define its role or view of mental health or ill health without extending to meet the needs of the client population.

It might be timely then to address the theoretical side of training and how we learn and accumulate facts. Thomas and Harri-Augstein (1977) argued that "the source of a person's attitudes is their personal knowledge and past experience evaluated within a personal system of beliefs and values" (p. 85). So people do not necessarily learn from experience, only from reviewing the meaning they attribute to it. In this context the authors defined learning as "the construction and exchange of personally relevant and viable meanings" (p. 86). I believe the work of these authors provides some insight in understanding the greater impact of clinical training on professionals. In the clinical setting they are more likely to review the meaning they attribute to their experience because they are engaged in the process of interaction with their clients and the larger treatment setting.

Kelly (1970) argued that we spend a long time hoarding facts and would not be happy at the prospect of their being converted to rubbish. We would more likely want to see them preserved as truths. This clinging to truths alleviates the professional's responsibility for the conclusions they may draw. Kelly (1955) believed that professionals come to training with their own psychological processes, follow their own personal constructs, and learn those things that are frequently repeated. He considered that what is learned is mediated by what the person chooses to attend to and can build into their preexisting construct system. Kelly was cynical of formal education for he saw it as limiting the process of inquiry (Button, 1985). Kelly (1970) went on to state that the expression of new ideas can be both distressing to ourselves and disturbing to others, leading to new ideas being kept to ourselves. Ideas are therefore not likely to be shared and become part of a culture. Indeed, if the person has the view that authority is important, then they are likely to accept the knowledge of teachers as right, their theorizing is likely to be limited, and the development of new knowledge is stunted (Pope & Gilbert, 1985).

Mair (1979) was also critical of the theoretical training process because he was of the opinion that academics insist that students want to know more than they really do. He suggested that most people want to know only what they need in order to survive, with additional information being irrelevant and disturbing. For Mair, students are also socialized at universities only to ask those questions that lead to knowledge that is not troublesome to academics and therefore acceptable. He suggested that students dutifully learn which questions they are supposed to ignore, and this situation leads to what he calls "appropriate ignorance." These views are in accordance with those of Kelly on the culture of the education system.

Kelly's concepts about learning are gaining increasing recognition among educators (Pope & Gilbert, 1985). Bannister (1979) proposed that the most important aspect of Kelly's essay on social inheritance was that education should be about the personal meanings people give to their education (a theme taken up by Kalekin-Fishman in chapter 9). At present the role of the learner is that of "impotent reactor," but if we take the view that professionals construct their own worldview, then it may be more comfortable for many educators to prefer to believe that professionals' views are imposed on them by the way things really are (Pope & Gilbert, 1985).

As I have begun to demonstrate, personal construct theory lends itself to theorizing about the influence of training on professionals' constructions of their work, their interaction with other professionals, and the role of their training in both of these. Kelly's (1955) commonality corollary has been seen as crucial in providing a constructivist framework for understanding professions. The commonality corollary claims that to the extent that one person employs a construction of experience that is similar to that employed by another, the psychological processes of that person are similar to those of the other person. This corollary has important implications for understanding the behavior of groups. Kelly stated, "People belong to the same cultural group, not merely because they behave alike, nor because they expect the same things of others, but especially because they construe their experience in the same way" (1955, p. 94). Training seems to be the important factor in influencing members of the same professional culture to construe their experiences in the same way.

The sociality corollary is also important because professionals need to interact with members of other professions and construe from their outlook if they are to find common ground. At present, many mental health services are insisting on this by the use of multidisciplinary teams. The difficulties with these teams and their multiple problems are well documented. If a major impact of training is socialization into a role/culture, then multidisciplinary teams are likely to be threatening. Yet there may still be quite a degree of commonality among professions apart from those aspects that determine role. The threat and anxiety may well be proving to be a barrier to finding this commonality. Button (1985) noted: "Behavior and experience which may be labelled disordered, emerges within, gets 'treated' within and may even change within a social context. Patients, their families and their helpers all live in a shared world within which there are problems, possibilities, hopes and expectations" (p. 351).

CURRENT RESEARCH

My research aimed to identify how mental health professionals were similar to yet different from one another in their constructions of their work with clients. I also wanted to identify what role they perceived their values and training had played in this. In the remainder of this chapter I shall report on that aspect of my research identifying what professionals thought about the role of training in their work. I shall, as well, present how the professional groups were similar to one another. This inquiry was conducted in the spirit that Kelly recommended. Therefore, I simply asked these professionals to share their experiences with me.

Assessing Mental Health Professionals' Constructions of their Clients

My participants included 20 people from each of the professions of psychology, psychiatry, and nursing in a Regional Health Service in the state of New South Wales, Australia. They were asked to complete a repertory grid called the *Working with Clients Grid*. The grid allowed for the assessment of the content of the constructs professionals used about their clients as well as how they used the constructs. The elements included 12 different types of clients who could be identified as belonging to certain diagnostic categories. These categories were as follows:

Working with a person:

1. who has psychotic experiences

2. who is suicidal

3. who has exaggerated fears of being harmed

4. who has problems with drug abuse

5. who has many problems with moods

6. who has a great deal of anxiety

7. who has problems with sexual behavior

8. who is preoccupied with physical complaints

9. who has problems with daily living

10. who cannot control his or her behavior

11. with whom you feel comfortable

12. with whom you feel uncomfortable

The G-Pack computer program (Bell, 1987) was used to randomly select element triads. The participants were asked to tell me how working with two of these clients was similar to but different from the third. I recorded their first construct pole and then asked for the opposite meaning of that construct. The participants then rated on a 7-point scale each of the elements (types of clients) using the constructs they had provided, with 1 being the initial construct pole and 7 being its opposite.

Two methods were employed to analyze the grids. The first was designed to explore the content of their construing and the second to examine the ways they used them. The first method used a coding system I devised to analyze the content of the constructs elicited on the repertory grid. The second method applied the Sociogrid Analysis of the Rep Grid Program (Shaw, 1989) that allowed for the analysis of the ways constructs are used by groups of people. This information was used to determine the commonality within and among the groups by comparing the rating on the constructs for each of the elements to determine the percentage of constructs that are matched over the 80% cutoff. It also determines those individuals in each group who are the most closely linked with one another in the way they use their constructs. It is argued that the content of the constructs was not important for the determination of commonality within a group, only the way in which the constructs were used. This is in accordance with the commonality corollary.

In the next phase of my research I asked my coresearchers to tell me what role their training had played in their work with clients. Their responses were audiotaped, transcribed, and coded using the coding system devised by the researcher,[1] which enabled the themes to be detected (Tooth, 1993). To analyze the qualitative data, the coded transcripts were analyzed using the NUDIST computer program (Richards & Richards, 1991), which provided a means to group the transcribed accounts into categories. The major categories had various subcategories that were scored if the participant responded to them. The responses were recorded only once, regardless of the number of times the participants used them. This enabled me to obtain a clearer picture of usage of particular categories.

Commonality of Construction for Each Professional Group

The results of my research using the *Working with Clients Grid* indicated that the content of the construct systems of the psychologists, psychiatrists, and nurses was not significantly different statistically. However, inspection of Figure 1 indicates that the most frequently used categories for all three groups could be identified as those relating to their professional role. For example, the most frequently used category of construct content used by the psychiatrists and nurses was client symptoms. The most frequently used category for the psychologists was assessment.

The analysis of the usage of the constructs for the three groups by the Rep Grid program indicated that the psychologists and psychiatrists were significantly different, with the nurses not significantly different from either group but closer to the psychiatrists. This analysis indicated that as a group the psychiatrists had more commonality in their usage of constructs than did the psychologists. However, further analysis of the data yielded quite a different picture. The socio-grid program allows the most closely linked individuals in the group to be identified in a hierarchical fashion. I decided to form a group for analysis that consisted of

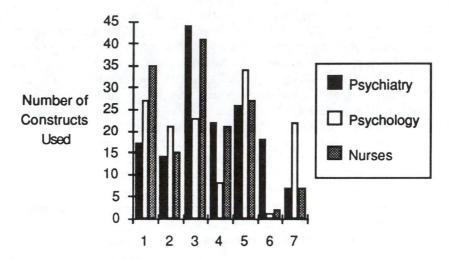

Figure 1. Most frequently used construct content for each profession

Note: 1 = Professional ability, 2 = Professional inability, 3 = Client symptoms, 4 = Negative reactions of clients, 5 = Assessment, 6 = Medical intervention, 7 = Cognitive intervention.

the seven most closely linked people within each group. In effect I created my own pseudo multidisciplinary team of 21 people.

The results were surprising because they showed that this new group had far more commonality in construct usage than any of the other groups. In the professional groups, the highest degree of commonality of construct usage was only 53%, yet in this new group the degree of commonality of construct usage increased to 78%. That is, the members of this new multidisciplinary group of professionals were far more likely to be able to understand the construing of the members of this group than they were of their original professional group because they used their constructs in similar ways. This suggests that commonality within groups is far more likely to be due to agreement among individuals rather than to belonging to a group whose training experiences have been similar. It is important to point out that there were no significant differences for the three professional groups on the variables of age, gender, or years of experience.

Significance of Training for Each Professional Group

The next phase of the research involved interviewing the participants. I asked them to tell me what they thought influenced their work with clients and what role their training had played in this. In response to the role their training had played in their work with clients, the trends were similar for all groups. The results indicated that the participants viewed their theoretical training as a negative rather than a positive experience, with participants referring to it more in terms of providing basic knowledge. In contrast, half of the respondents reported their practical training to be very positive.

One of the most important themes that emerged in the research for the professionals was the importance of their own personal characteristics rather than the importance of their training in determining how they made sense of their work with clients. When I asked the participants what they thought were the most important factors that influenced the way they thought about clients, only 2 out of 60 made any reference to their professional training. The results to this question are presented in Figure 2.

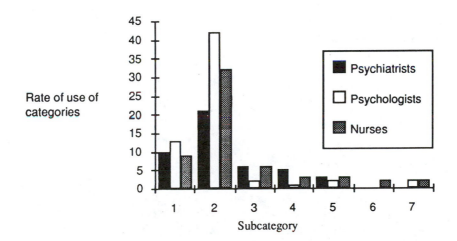

Figure 2. Rate of use of influential factors in categorizing work with clients for each professional group.

Note: 1 = therapeutic relationship, 2 = therapist's personal character, 3 = intervention, 4 = prognosis, 5 = client's personal character, 6 = negative social factors, 7 = positive service factors.

My results suggest that when professionals are asked more specific questions about their work with clients, as with the *Working with Clients Grid*, they are more likely to tap into a subsystem of constructs they developed during their training. However, when they are asked about what they thought were the most important factors that determine how they work with clients, they do not talk about professional roles but refer to their own personal characteristics. There may be two systems of constructs that professionals use to describe their work with clients; one relates to their professional role and one taps into constructs about themselves. This finding agrees with other constructivist researchers who have suggested the existence of two construct systems that professionals use. The results support the need for constructivists to extend their methodologies beyond the sole use of grids in their research because a grid is similar to a questionnaire if the elements are supplied, in that it is the researcher who determines the domain of discourse (B. M. Walker, personal communication, January 23, 1994).

The most plausible explanation of why professionals view their theoretical training as a negative experience may be that they have not been trained in ways that allow them to function effectively with those clients who have more serious mental health problems. It may also be that training programs are set up primarily to meet the criteria laid down by each professional group. The process of professionalization and the increasing push for specialization make this so. Increasing specialization may not be meeting the needs of trainees, let alone the needs of their clients. If this is the case, professionals working in mental health services may well be experiencing considerable conflict in their work because of the forces described above.

SUMMARY AND CONCLUSIONS

The study of the constructions of the groups of various mental health professions is a complex issue. Many factors need to be considered if any attempt is to be made to understand how these constructions occur. Personal construct theory promises to offer a great deal in the understanding of the many findings that often are in conflict in this endeavor. Kelly's (1955) notion of constructive alternativism allows for individuality in construing, while his concept of commonality and sociality highlights the sharing of meaning among groups of people.

From this research I have reached a number of conclusions. First, as professionals we have far more in common with other professions than we are prepared to acknowledge, and this occurs for a number of reasons. Professions as groups strive to make sense of their individual worlds in much the same way as individuals do. Under optimal conditions each profession strives to expand and revise its construct systems, providing a self-characterization of the profession. Like individuals, professions may become threatened when seeking validation for the expansion of their construct systems. Further imposed on this situation are the constraints that derive from the mental health system. The mental health budget is shrinking and the promised advances in community care of clients have not been realized. Such a situation imposes threat from larger societal groups. These forces mitigate against the close liaison that is needed among the various members of the mental health system.

Second, given all of the above, the values each individual brings to training are more important than the training itself (that is, if the individual's values are not taken into account). My justification for this conclusion is twofold. The research evidence appears to indicate that an individual's personality is more likely to influence his or her approach to their work. Also, the participants in my research largely reported their theoretical training to be a negative experience, whereas their practical training was viewed far more favorably. A possible explanation for this difference is that theoretical training requires the trainee to take on facts and concepts that may not be consistent with their worldview, whereas clinical training gives the individual far more freedom in using their own values and those acquired in training that are salient to them. There is also greater freedom in clinical practice to work with clinicians who are more like-minded. Naturally, such comments have implications for how educators should approach their work.

The process of socialization into a profession is of central importance. It would appear from my work and from the work of others that a major impact of training is imparting to trainees an understanding of what is expected of them in their professional roles. Professionalization to a large extent works toward increasing the specialization of members of a profession. Yet in mental health services at least, there is pressure to break down professional barriers by the introduction of generalist mental health workers. This is a move that causes great anxiety among professional bodies. A healthier approach may well be for professions to view the mental health system as their culture rather than for each profession to try to foster its own. My research supports the view that mental health professions have much in common and are more alike than they are different from each other. It is now time that attempts were made to work together for the benefit of our clients.

ENDNOTE

1. The major category of training had three subcategories, which had further subdivisions. The first subcategory referred to formal training with the divisions of positive, negative, and basic theoretical experiences, and positive and negative practical experiences. The second subcategory referred to informal training and had no subdivisions. The last subcategory was used when respondents referred to their own experience as important in training and the divisions in this category were personal experience, personal growth, and personal values.

REFERENCES

Agnew, J., & Bannister, D. (1973). Psychiatric diagnosis as a pseudo-specialist language. *British Journal of Medical Psychology, 46*, 69–73.

Altrocchi, J., & Eisdorfer, C. (1961). Changes in attitudes toward mental illness. *Mental Hygiene, 45*, 563–570.

Applegate, J. L. (1990). Constructs and communication: A pragmatic integration. In G. J. Neimeyer & R. A. Neimeyer (Eds.), *Advances in personal construct psychology*. Greenwich, CT: JAI Press.

Bannister, D. (1979). Forward to social inheritance. In P. Stringer & D. Bannister (Eds.), *Constructs of sociality and individuality* (pp. 1–3). London: Academic Press.

Bell, R. C. (1987). *G-Pack: A computer program for the elicitation and analysis of repertory grids*. Distributed by Personal Construct Group, University of Wollongong, NSW, Australia.

Brickman, P., Rabinowitz, V. C., Karuza, J., Coates, D., Cohen, E., & Kidder, L. (1982). Models of helping and coping. *American Psychologist, 37*, 368–384.

Button, E. (Ed.), (1985). *Personal construct theory and mental health: Theory, research and practice*. New York: Croom Helm.

Caine, T. M. (1975). Attitudes to patient care in OT students. *Occupational Therapy, 38*, 239.

Caine, T. M., & Smail, D. J. (1969). *The treatment of mental illness: Science, faith and the therapeutic personality*. London: University of London Press.

Creech, S. K. (1977). Changes in attitude about mental illness among nursing students following a psychiatric affiliation. *Journal of Psychiatric Nursing and Mental Health Services, June*, 9–14.

DeLeon, P. H., Kjervik, D. K., Kraut, A. G., & VandenBos, G. R. (1985).

Psychology and nursing: A natural alliance. *American Psychologist*, 40, 1153–1164.

Fransella, F. (1983). Threat and the scientist. In G. M. Breakwell (Ed.), *Threatened identities*. Chichester: John Wiley & Sons Ltd.

Gelfand, S., & Ullmann, L. P. (1961). Attitude changes associated with a psychiatric affiliation. *Nursing Research*, 8, 201–203.

Glick, I. D., Showstack, J. A., Cohen, C. & Klar, H. M. (1989). Between patient and doctor: Improving the quality of care for serious mental illness. *Bulletin of the Menninger Clinic*, 53, 193–202.

Kelly, G. A. (1955). *The psychology of personal constructs*. Volumes 1 and 2. New York: Norton.

Kelly, G. A. (1970). A brief introduction to personal construct theory. In D. Bannister (Ed.), *Perspectives in personal construct theory* (pp. 1–39). London: Academic Press.

Kingsbury, S. J. (1987). Cognitive differences between clinical psychologists and psychiatrists. *American Psychologist*, 42, 152–156.

Krasner, L., & Houts, A. C. (1984). A study of the "value" systems of behavioral scientists. *American Psychologist*, 39, 840–849.

Lifshitz, M. (1974). Quality professionals: Does training make a difference? A personal construct theory study of the issue. *British Journal of Social and Clinical Psychology*, 13, 183–189.

Mair, J. M. M. (1979). The personal venture. In P. Stringer & D. Bannister (Eds.), *Constructs of sociality and individuality* (pp. 35–47). London: Academic Press.

McGovern, M. P., Newman, F. L., & Kopta, S. M. (1986). Metatheoretical assumptions and psychotherapy orientation: Clinician attributions of patient's problem causality and responsibility for treatment. *Journal of Consulting and Clinical Psychology*, 54 (4), 476–481.

Moffic, S. H., Blattstein, A., Rosenberg, S., Adams, G. L., & Chacko, R. C. (1983). Attitudes in the development of public sector clinicians. *Community Mental Health Journal*, 19 (3), 211–218.

Pallis, D. J., & Stoffelmayer, B. E. (1973). Social attitudes and treatment orientation among psychiatrists. *British Journal of Medical Psychology*, 46, 75–81.

Panayotopoulos, D. J., & Stoffelmayer, B. E. (1972). Training preferences, social attitudes and treatment orientation among psychiatrists. *Journal of Clinical Psychology*, 28, 216–217.

Peterson, D. R., Eaton, M. M., Levine, A. R., & Snepp, F. P. (1982). Career experiences of doctors of psychology. *Professional Psychology*, 13, 268–277.

Pope, M. L., & Gilbert, J. (1985). Constructive science education. In F. R. Epting & A. W. Landfield (Eds.), *Anticipating personal construct psychology* (pp. 111–127), . Lincoln: University of Nebraska Press.

Richards, L., & Richards, T. (1991). The transformation of qualitative method: Computational paradigms and research processes. In N. Fielding & R. Lee (Eds.), *Using computers in quatialitative research* (pp. 38–53). Beverly Hills: Sage.

Roskin, G., Carsen, M. L., Rabiner, C. J., & Marell, S. K. (1988). Attitudes toward patients among different mental health professional groups. *Comprehensive Psychiatry, 29,* 188–194.

Ryle, A., & Breen, D. (1974). Change in the course of social-work training: A repertory grid study. *British Journal of Medical Psychology, 47,* 139–147.

Sarbin, T. R., & Mancuso, J. E. (1980). *Schizophrenia: Medical diagnosis or moral verdict?* New York: Pergamon.

Shaw, M. L. G. (1989) Interactive elicitation and exchange of knowledge. *International Journal of Personal Construct Psychology, 2,* 215–238.

Slimmer, L. W., Wendt, A., & Martinkus, D. (1990). Effect of psychiatric clinical learning site on nursing students' attitudes toward mental illness and psychiatric nursing. *Journal of Nursing Education, 29* (3), 127–133.

Smyrnios, K. X., Schultz, C. L., Smyrnios, S. M., & Kirkby, R. J. (1986). Values: A pervasive issue in psychotherapy research. *Australian Journal of Sex, Marriage & Family, 7,* 91–98.

Soldz, S. (1989). Do psychotherapists use different construct subsystems for construing clients and personal acquaintances? A repertory grid study. *Journal of Social and Clinical Psychology, 8,* 97–112.

Soni, S. D. (1989). Multidisciplinary teams and line management: Practical problems and areas of conflict in clinical psychiatry. *Psychiatric Bulletin, 13,* 657–661.

Stone, W. N., Stein, L. S., & Green, B. L. (1971). Faculty and resident commitment to varieties of psychiatric treatment. *Archives of General Psychiatry, 24,* 468–473.

Thomas, L., & Harri-Augstein, S. (1977). Learning to learn: The personal construction and exchange of meaning. In M. J. A. Howe (Ed.), *Adult learning: Psychological research and applications* (pp. 85–106). Chichester: John Wiley & Sons.

Tooth, B. A. (1984). *Psychology, medicine and the health system: Impli-*

cations of professionalization. Unpublished manuscript, The University of Wollongong, Wollongong, NSW, Australia.

Tooth, B. A. (1993) *Mental health professionals' constructions of their clients*. Unpublished manuscript, The University of Wollongong, Wollongong, NSW, Australia.

Tully, J. B. (1976). Personal construct theory and psychological changes related to social work practice. *British Journal of Social Work, 6*, 481–499.

Viney, L. L. (1983). Experiences of volunteer telephone counsellors: A comparison of a professionally orientated and a nonprofessionally orientated approach to their training. *Journal of Community Psychology, 11*, 259–268.

Viney, L. L. (1987). *Interpreting the interpreters: Strategies for a science of construing people*. Malabar, FL: Krieger.

Walker, B. M. (1992). Values and Kelly's theory: Becoming a good scientist. *International Journal of Personal Construct Psychology, 5*, 259–270.

Wills, T. A. (1978). Perceptions of clients by professional helpers. *Psychological Bulletin, 85*, 968–1000.

Winter, D. A. (1985). Personal styles, constructive alternativism and the provision of a therapeutic service. *British Journal of Medical Psychology, 58*, 129–136.

Winter, D. A. (1992). *Personal construct psychology in clinical practice: Theory, research and applications*. London: Routledge.

Winter, D. A., Shivakumar, H., Brown, R. J., Roitt, M., Drysdale, W. J., & Jones, S. (1987). Explorations of a crisis intervention service. *British Journal of Psychiatry, 151*, 232–239.

CHAPTER 12

Explorations of Constructivist Approaches in Continuing Professional Education:
Staff Development for Changing Contexts

PAM DENICOLO
(with contributions from
Sandra Tjok-a-Tam and Catherine Baker)

In the last decade, teachers worldwide have increasingly been urged to become more adaptable. As a result of demographic shifts, student profiles have changed. The advent of new technology (at least in the prospective workplaces of their students, if not in the classrooms) and the challenge to educate flexible lifelong learners has produced new curricula specifically demanding new teaching/learning techniques. Postcompulsory education in the United Kingdom has not been immune to changes in the social context, and the teachers in this area have accordingly been pressured to change. This is an opportunity for dynamic evolution. However, the forward movement of the teaching profession in response to the needs of the society within which it is embedded may seem to the individuals involved like random motion in reaction to pressure. It is proposed that a process that allows teachers to share their personal constructions of their professional roles can both raise their consciousness of the forward propulsion and enable them to take a more active part in advancing the profession.

Examples from two research projects will illustrate how teachers in groups can be enabled to work effectively and comfortably in the changing milieu. The studies described in this paper are set in an environment with the following general characteristics. The students that teachers in postcompulsory education will be meeting now represent diverse age groups and life experience (Department of Education and Science, 1989). The previous differentiated educational experience of these students gives rise to different expectations about their new experiences. Some demand didactic teaching from experts in the new facts, while others may be familiar with project work and anticipate methods of independent learning (Denicolo, Entwistle, & Hounsell, 1992).

Moreover, the world of work for which they are preparing demands more than a good subject knowledge base. It requires additional transferable skills of problem solving, communication, interpersonal interaction, and initiative (National Foundation for Educational Research, 1990). In their prospective employment, students will also be required to demonstrate a willingness and an ability to continue to substitute new understandings for old as the knowledge explosion continues to reverberate. It is commonly estimated, for example, that the life expectancy of the specialist knowledge of a medical graduate is between 5 and 10 years, while the specialist knowledge of graduates in electronics and computing becomes obsolete even more quickly. The disparity between the teaching/learning milieu in which students first learned a craft and the current one in which they practice it means that many teachers, if not most, are required to increase the range of their professional skills and their understanding of the process of learning.

The first of the two studies, which illustrate how teachers' professional expertise can be advanced when teachers engage in group construing, is abstracted from a doctoral research program on the management of learning in management education (Tjok-a-Tam, 1993). In recent years there has been widespread concern about British competitiveness in industry and commerce. This concern provided a trigger for action that instigated a number of reports (for instance, Handy, 1987 and Constable & McCormick, 1987) and national initiatives (for instance, the 1990 project for the Accreditation of Prior Learning). The implications for postcompulsory education were axiomatic. Appropriate resources, structures, and facilities that offer potential participants wider access routes than have been previously available, and flexible learning programs that acknowledge current competence, needed to be embedded in colleges and curricula. The recognition of this need for change resulted in the establishment of a plethora of national committees, reports, and initiatives in the arena of management education. The scene is described in the opening paragraph of a journal article as remarkably like a circus. All round the Big Top . . . teachers of management are calling attention to their latest tricks like so many jugglers . . . (I)n the ring . . . a couple of hundred captains of industry are endeavoring to raise an enormous pyramid on the backs of a team of cantering ponies. This particular feat has never before been attempted, even on a more stable platform, and its success is by no means assured. (Foster, 1988, p. 72)

This paper reports the part of the Tjok-a-Tam study that focuses on lecturers' attitudes toward the effectiveness of learning methods currently in use in management education.

The second illustration, abstracted from a doctoral study by Baker (1992), is set in further education where once again a wealth of new, mainly government supported, initiatives have demanded a change in curriculum approach. Among these are the Technical Vocational Educational Initiative (TVEI) and the Youth Training Scheme (YTS). One significant divergence from tradition is in the delivery mode, involving a move away from teacher- or subject-centered education to student- and skill-centered education.

This approach involves a concept of learning as an integrated, holistic activity in which a range of skills and knowledge from different disciplines that have traditionally been perceived as separate are brought together. Thus, lecturers were urged to collaborate to establish a network of interlocking provisions. The aim was to offer students a variety of opportunities to plan individually relevant programs of educational and personal development (cf., Further Education Unit document, 1985). This approach to course delivery implies a need for a strong team. The staff has to work together closely and supportively in order to coordinate the identification and facilitation of skills and competencies. No skill could remain the province of one staff member or any one subject area. The effectiveness of these courses therefore depends on the ability and willingness of staff members with different types of subject expertise, educational philosophy, and habitual teaching style to weld themselves together as a team.

Although most teachers would subscribe to a view that values the integration of ideas and a more student-centered emphasis to education, other factors detract from a wholehearted commitment to the required style of organizing instruction.

Calls for more accountability from the teaching staff together with the introduction of staff appraisal mechanisms, cuts in budgets, increased workloads, and uncertainty of tenure created a climate that undermined individual perceptions of professional freedom. When new courses demand different working patterns and threaten subject specialism and there is little or no budget for staff development, then a degree of resentment can be expected (Everard & Morris, 1988). Those staff members who have established a stable occupational identity tend toward inflexibility in the face of new conditions that require new approaches (Weathersby, 1980). Lecturers in this situation are encouraged to share and elaborate their views on course goals and how they can be achieved as part of a team-building exercise.

Both the studies I present concern the facilitation of group construing in a continuing professional education/staff development context and use similar methods to achieve their aims.

THE PROJECTS

Participants in the studies were experienced teachers who had been attempting to establish new curricula but had found themselves experiencing difficulties related to the modes of teaching/learning used. In each case, participants had been invited to join a workshop, as a form of staff development, in which these salient issues would be explored.

For the Tjok-a-Tam study, the group consisted of seven lecturers who had had practical experience within their respective profession or specialism and who now taught and/or led a course in the business school (BS). For the Baker study, the group was composed of a team of eight volunteers charged with implementing a return to study core course in further education (FE). Each member had formerly been a subject specialist teacher of award-bearing courses. The guidelines for each workshop were derived from a combination of personal construct theory (Kelly, 1955) and action research as described by Grundy and Kemmis (1982). The common thread linking these two is that both are participant-centered. Kelly believed it was essential to focus on an individual's definition of his/her problem. Indeed, he was "skeptical of any piece of human research in which the subjects' questions and contributions have not been elicited or have been ignored in the final analysis of results" (Kelly, 1969, p. 132).

Similarly, Grundy and Kemmis (1982) felt that all participants were equal in the research process and needed to be involved at every stage: defining the problem, reflecting on practice, planning and implementing action, and evaluating its effects. Action research facilitates a process of engagement in self-evaluation that can provide the means to help teachers to revise their constructs and "open their eyes (so) they can see how to choose and fashion their own version of reality" (Diamond, 1985 p. 34).

Kelly (1955) developed a method called the repertory grid to help people open their eyes so as to become more aware of their own construing. One of the main advantages of this technique lies in its flexibility as a research methodology (Pope, 1980). The version of the technique used in these studies was based on a process that allowed for ready comparison of individuals' grids so that commonalities and differences in construing of some aspect of the world-in-focus could be easily identified (cf. Stewart & Stewart, 1981). When the process was being described at the beginning of each workshop, care was taken to emphasize that individual differences are inevitable since our constructs derive from different experiences and diverse opportunities to test their validity. By exploring each other's perceptions, the team or group could evaluate individual differences either as creative resources for problem solving or as areas with a potential for producing conflict. Joint acknowledgement of the latter would be a fruitful start for further investigation to identify conciliatory activities. Initial clarification of the process using dummy grids as demonstration devices proved invaluable not only for smoothing the procedure but also for illustrating the above caveat. Thus, an example of a dummy grid is worth describing here.

First, a universe of discourse is identified as suitable for the purpose of the exercise. If the purpose is to identify a suitable range of biscuits to provide for the group's coffee break, the universe would be the range of biscuits with which all the members of the workshop were familiar. Agreement would be reached on a selection of these (about nine for convenience), and these would form the elements for the grid. The element order is randomized and then noted on each grid form for each individual to construe. At first participants are encouraged to view the biscuits/elements in threes (the method of triadic sorting), identifying a similarity between two that makes them contrast with the third. Later, we move to the full context to produce bipolar constructs such as "like to dip in my drink. . . . . unsuitable for dunking." The elements are then rated on each construct in turn, receiving a tick if a construct fits the left-hand description and a cross if it is nearer the right-hand description (see Figure 1).

Once each individual had produced a few rated constructs they were asked to share these with colleagues. By this point much interested (and

✓ Similarity	shortbr ead	wafer	ginger	Chocol ate half- coat	etc.	x Difference
like to dip in my drink	✓	x	✓	x		unsuitable for dunking

Figure 1. Part of a dummy grid

frequently amazed) discussion will have taken place concerning the initial choice of representative elements, the kinds of constructs members have in common, and the strange ones that individuals have. Comparisons of ratings of individual elements on particular constructs then illustrate that we often perceive even relatively simple parts of our worlds differently. (How could anyone rate shortbread as crunchy?!)

The original disclosed purpose of the grid would then be met by identifying which biscuits received ratings near the positive poles of their constructs for most people. The covert purpose of valuing individual differences would be served by noting the benefit of including some biscuits that only some people like (more for those who do) and the sharing/learning to be achieved in discovering that someone knows the calorific value of each or that another is allergic to chocolate.

Only imagination limits the choice of an element set that is relatively easy for a group to construe but serves the covert purpose well.

To return to the research cases, the purpose of the BS group was to review the learning methods that were perceived as effective for today's managers, so the elements used in the main part of the workshop were a representative range of learning methods. In their attempt to develop their own effectiveness as a team, the main goals of the FE group, derived from the published course aims and from individuals' views of the intent of the course, were elicited and negotiated as elements.

Procedures similar to those used for the dummy grid were then used to elicit individual constructs, followed by discussions about the constructs themselves. In an additional step, the groups chose a set of par-

	Integrating the course	Developing the course	Developing a shared philosophy	Communicating within the team	Supporting the students	Sharing responsibility	
Everybody is committed to							Only some members are committed to
This is our main focus							This is a peripheral focus
Everybody supports this and takes part							Very few members participate
This is within our control							This is not within our control

Figure 2. An example of an uncompleted grid with negotiated elements (group goals) and negotiated constructs.

ticularly salient constructs for all to rate individually to produce a new grid. Figure 2 is an example from the FE team. This time it was drawn up on transparencies. Blocking out of half the cell for each element/construct intersection was substituted for ticks and crosses. Figure 3 illustrates how the top left segment can be used for ticks and the bottom right segment for crosses.

This procedure allowed for direct comparisons between pairs and groups of grids. By overlaying them and noting where blocked segments coincided, we could see the general commonality of construing. Where a totally blocked-in square was apparent, we could discern that an element was rated dissimilarly on a construct, although the same words were used to denote it. An example is provided in Figure 4.

Several blocked-in boxes along a horizontal line would indicate that the wording of the construct conveys different meaning to individuals or that they apply it differently to those elements. Several blocked-in boxes

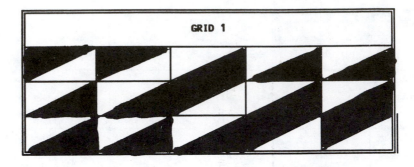

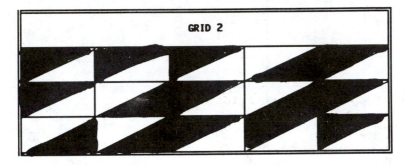

Figure 3. Stylized versions of grids using blocked in segments instead of ticks and crosses.

in a vertical column suggest that an element (learning method or goal) is construed differently.

These data were then the provocation for more informed discussion among the members of the respective groups. It may be of interest to note that, with some of the participant groups in the main body of each piece of research, Tjok-a-Tam and Baker used a more detailed method of grid analysis using more traditional grids in which elements were rated on a scale (e.g., 1 to 5) against the constructs. The analysis involved using a computer program, FOCUS (Shaw 1990), which produces single-linkage clustering of city block distances between elements and constructs when each set of ratings is compared, each with every other of its kind. The individual grids could then be compared in terms of similarities and differences in the content of clusters. Further, by using the SOCIOGRID part of the same (software) package, complete grids could be compared

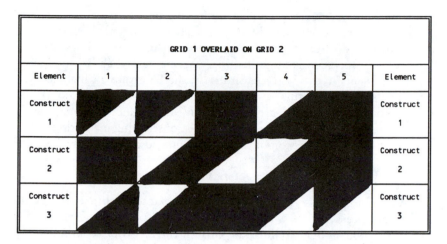

Figure 4. An example of overlaid grids

between individuals so that degrees of commonality of construing the whole group of elements could be estimated. This method, while providing rich, detailed data for research, is seldom practical for staff development workshops since it requires access to hardware, software, and, most important, time. Thus, it will not be elaborated on here though interested readers are referred to the respective theses and to Shaw (1980).

ILLUSTRATIONS FROM THE RESULTS OF THE EXEMPLAR STUDIES

With both groups the stage of eliciting and then negotiating the elements proved valuable in itself. This stage highlighted the fact that sometimes different words are used to denote the same things, while in other instances participants thought they were discussing the same thing because they used the same word but later discovered that they were not. In the BS group, for example, *systematic reflection* and *evaluating past experiences* were used to describe similar activities, though the person who used the latter viewed the former as academic jargon. In contrast, listening to speakers was a relatively passive activity for several people, while for one person it involved an active mental interaction following preparation.

The goals/elements produced by individual members of the FE group that were not derived directly from the documented course aims demonstrated divergent emphases: student-focused or course-focused. However, all included communicating, sharing responsibility, and supporting students in their choice. Similarly, the BS group all included listening to speakers, writing, and discussing issues, while some contributors mentioned particular learning methods (for instance, sculpting) with which others were not familiar. The final list of teaching methods did not include these, but discussion of them was pursued after the workshop.

Constructs

When individuals' constructs were compared within each group there were indeed some that seemed common to all participants and some that were unique. To illustrate this for the BS group, common constructs related to the degree of activity that was engendered in the students while learning and the amount of ownership or control the students had over the process of learning. One unique construct was the extent to which a learning method would tend to validate or confront previous understanding. The members of the FE group all tended to use constructs concerned with degree of commitment to the goals that the group shared and with the amount of control the group had over the achievement of shared goals. Perhaps not surprisingly, part-time staff, who were nevertheless members of the core team, included constructs demonstrating their perceived marginalization. An example is the construct "feel enabled to contribute—feel restricted in what I can contribute." In this instance similarities were highlighted within subgroups, while differences between subgroups emerged.

Overlaid Grids

The overlaid grids (see Figure 4) produced more thought-provoking results, some of which demonstrated similarity of construing while others invoked some concern because of the conflicting views revealed. All members of the FE group felt there were insufficient resources allowed for them to develop a shared philosophy. Although the team leader felt that everyone shared responsibility for all the goals, the rest of the group felt that responsibility rested with very few members. The BS group universally agreed that listening to speakers was not a particularly effective learning method, coming towards the negative side of most constructs, while discussing issues with others was viewed by some teachers as helping to clarify ideas and by others as creating confusion.

DISCUSSION BASED ON THE RESULTS USED FOR ILLUSTRATION

Elements

One particular product for all of the teachers involved in the studies described here was the realization that speaking the same language is not necessarily synonymous with communicating. The process of selecting the elements and then negotiating them first alerted them to this, and the recognition was amplified as constructs were compared. In a group of professionals whose main purpose is communication this was particularly salient as it has ramifications for interchanges among themselves and with their students. The exercise had included both common words and technical terms, and confusion was encountered with both. Members of the staff were accustomed to explaining technical terminology to students, but not to clarifying it with one another. Common words had gone unchallenged by partners to all kinds of conversations.

In sum, the particular character of each of the groups was illustrated by the goals produced individually by members of the BS group and the mix of commonly agreed learning activities with some relatively unique contributions produced by the FE group. The differences in emphasis ultimately provided two positive learning experiences for the participants: common ground was identified and opportunities to learn from one another were found. This outcome confirms the importance of the introductory session using dummy grids to stress the value of individual differences. The differences in professional construals were made less threatening by the opportunity to find that there are often very different ways of construing trivial elements (such as the biscuits we used in the demonstration). Given the tensions within the professional culture described in the introduction to this chapter, it would not have been surprising if such differences had given rise to fault/blame/conflict scenarios. Instead, these groups discussed the value of having a range of interest and expertise within courses so that students may have a wider resource to draw on. This then led to discussion about how that range might best be utilized to gain maximum effect.

Constructs

Similarly, the identification of common constructs used to rate the elements further enhanced the feeling that there was some stability and a conjoint basis from which to work. This was founded on the recognition of shared problems and mutual interests. Agreement that some learning experiences left the students feeling disengaged or not owning the process led to decisions by the BS group to minimize these activities in the course. In addition, ways to improve discussion sessions in lessons were explored.

As a result of the workshop, the FE group decided to concert its efforts when they discovered the shared commitment to a goal. The members of the group felt much less isolated.

Overlaid Grids

The full-time members of the FE group expressed surprise about the part-timers feeling marginalized, but the part-timers were relieved to find they were not alone in their feeling. Various procedures were discussed to help alleviate this problem. Plans were made to set aside time for discussing ideas and sharing philosophies.

A lengthy discussion took place concerning the disparate views about responsibility held by the team leader and the other members. This revealed a misunderstanding on both sides. The members of the staff were convinced the leader wanted responsibility to rest with her, while she thought they were reneging on theirs. In other circumstances this could have been a heated and unproductive exchange of views. But, by this stage in the process, the participants reported being intrigued by the exploration of other viewpoints and felt personally challenged to understand them. In this connection, an additional meeting was arranged to facilitate a more democratic distribution of responsibility.

Further Discussion

A particular benefit accrues from spotlighting these two case studies. Since they were abstracted from larger, complex research studies, we can report on the longer term influence of the workshops and on postintervention evaluation by the participants. Plans of action were devised by the groups as a result of their being alerted to shared constructions as well as to hitherto undisclosed contradictions in assumptions and perspectives. These were indeed implemented. Some of the plans had very practical outcomes: expertise was used more efficiently to revise course designs and information and workloads were perceived to be more fairly distributed. But perhaps the most important outcomes were those that were less tangible. Participants felt their individual viewpoints were valued while they recognized they had much to learn from each other. Reports that the two groups have used the grid process again to clarify issues as a basis for planning and action is a measure of how valuable it was to them. The FE group generated a set of elements to elicit possible criteria for building student profiles. The BS team used the process to review the roles of the different contributors to the learning experience: course teachers, line managers, mentors, assessors, employers, other students, colleagues at work, and the students themselves. A more general evaluation of this process of joint construing is included in the next section.

GENERAL REVIEW AND DISCUSSION

The feedback from the participants has confirmed the value of this particular form of grid technique in providing a structured way for people to recognize and explore their own perceptions, attitudes, and beliefs and those of others within a bounded context. Further, these studies confirmed the worth of the grid as a catalyst of positive action for these professionals at a critical time.

Before considering its potential in other spheres, the constraints and caveats should be weighed against the reported benefits. The input of practical and human resources into these workshops was considerable. Given an insight into the educational scene reviewed in the introduction to this paper, it will not come as a surprise that, with teachers struggling with subject autonomy erosion, increasing workloads, and externally produced edicts challenging their professionalism, there was a latent predisposition to disharmony. Rather than opening a possible Pandora's box by sharing individual viewpoints with colleagues, it would be understandable if participants felt it would be safer to retreat into the isolation and insulation of their respective personal shells. Thus, the workshops demanded careful planning and managing, incorporating sensitive interpersonal skills along with an emphasis on the creative benefits of sociality, i.e., being able to construe the constructs of others and appreciate their contextual worth without necessarily agreeing with them. Therefore, there are extraordinary demands on the facilitator (particularly when the workshop is the first of its kind for a group) in managing feedback. Demands on the participants include the challenge to take the risk of self-revelation while suspending judgment of others. Needless to say, this is time consuming. For instance, reflection on the time it took simply to negotiate an agreed element set in the illustrative examples led Tjok-a-Tam and Baker to recommend a half day as the minimum time to devote to the whole exercise. For already pressured professionals, this is no mean commitment. Potential participants need to be convinced that benefits will outweigh the costs.

This is not an enterprise to be undertaken lightly, either, in terms of its emotional demand. If the exercise is to be more than the cathartic release of opinion, if it is to be an exercise in self and collaborative reflection that engenders personal and group growth, then it is not likely to be a comfortable experience. As Pope and Denicolo (1991) pointed out, strategies that do not challenge a person's implicit theories are unlikely to lead to any deeper reappraisal of current theory or practice.

As demonstrated earlier, it is seldom that such workshops fail to heighten awareness of the limitations of the language we have previously believed to be our main mode of communication. Immediately after the workshop, participants frequently feel compelled to explain, elaborate, and reiterate in other forms everything they say. Fortunately, this effect soon accommodates to the normal exigencies of conversation, leaving a residue that reminds them to check their understanding of others and vice versa when misinterpretation is likely to have unfortunate consequences.

The cases cited exemplify how previously tacit tensions were shared and acted upon. It is only fair to alert the reader to the further possibility that some problems may come to light that are not readily resolvable. In exploring their interaction as a group, for example, another group of teachers involved in further education recognized that a main inhibiting factor was physical distance. Some aspects of their work required them to work on distant sites. The obvious practical difficulties involved in meeting regularly, which would have ameliorated other problems, could only be partially addressed. As a result, participants had to be content with fewer steps forward than they would have wished. This emphasizes that the repgrid technique described here serves first and foremost as an illuminative instrument and as a catalyst to action rather than as a provider of easy solutions.

These difficulties confirm, however, that the use of the grid can highlight critical features of programs, interactions, and so on, that have not hitherto been identified. It can provide a forum for the consideration of perspectives and opinions that may not otherwise receive a fair hearing and demonstrate connections among features that might otherwise be viewed in isolation. It can provide vicarious experience, a metaphorical walk in another's moccasins, that challenges the hypotheses and models that individuals have formed about their professional worlds. In this way, people may discover that they actually wear the same size.

If, as we suspect, inflexibility of professional practice is a concomitant of constraining constructs, then the elaboration of constructs together with the consideration of alternative interpretations may provide the key to developing the adaptability required for professional survival. The techniques described in this paper, or suitable modifications designed to fit other contexts, are proffered as means to potential liberation.

REFERENCES

Baker, C. (1992). *A model for teamwork in further education: The narrative of a methodological journey*. Unpublished PhD thesis, University of Surrey, England.

Constable, J., & McCormick, R. (1987). *The making of British managers*. London: B.I.M. & C.B.I.

Denicolo, P., Entwistle, N., & Hounsell, D. (1992). What is active learning? In *Effective learning and teaching in higher education*. Sheffield: USDTU/Department of Employment. Module 1.

Department of Education and Science (1989, March). *Student numbers in higher education—Great Britain 1975–1987*. D.E.S. Statistical Bulletin.

Diamond, C. T. P. (1985). Becoming a teacher: An altering eye. In D. Bannister (Ed.), *Issues and approaches to personal construct theory* (pp. 15–35). London: Academic Press.

Everard, K. B., & Morris, G. (1988). *Effective school management*, 2nd edition. London: Paul Chapman Publishing.

Foster, G. (1988). A degree of confusion. *Management Today*, July, 72–76.

Further Education Unit (1985). *Working together: Towards an integrated curriculum*. London: F.E.

Grundy, S., & Kemmis, S. (1982). Educational action research in Australia: The state of the art. In S. Kemmis (Ed.), *The action research reader* (pp. 83–97). Victoria: Deakin University Press.

Handy, C. (1987). *The making of managers*. London: M.S.C. & N.E.D.C. & B.I.M.

Kelly, G. A. (1955). *The psychology of personal constructs*: Vols. 1 & 2. New York: Norton.

Kelly, G. A. (1969). Ontological acceleration. In B. Maher (Ed.), *Clinical psychology and personality* (pp. 7–45). London: Wiley.

National Foundation for Educational Research. (1990). *Evaluation of E.H.E.: Student Questionnaire*. Slough: N.F.E.R.

Pope, M. L. (1980). *What is the repertory grid?* Occasional paper, Institute for Educational Technology, University of Surrey.

Pope, M. L., & Denicolo P. (1991). Developing constructive action: Personal construct psychology, action research and professional development. In O. Zuber-Skerrit (Ed.), *Action research for change and development* (pp. 93–111). Aldershot: Gower.

Shaw, M. L. G. (1980). *On becoming a personal scientist*. London: Academic Press.

Shaw, M. L. G. (1990). *Rep grid manual, version 2 release*. Centre for Person Computer Studies, Alberta, Canada.

Stewart, V., & Stewart, A. (1981). *Business applications of repertory grid*. Maidenhead, Berks: McGraw-Hill.

Tjok-a-Tam, S. (1993). Learning-in-Action in management development: The facilitation of self-created learning opportunities. Unpublished Ph.D. thesis, University of Surrey, England.

Weathersby, R. P. (1980). Educating learners of all ages. In E. Greenberg, K. O'Donnell, & W. Bergquist (Eds.), *New directions for higher education no. 29*. London: Jossey-Bass.

CHAPTER 13

The Construing of Teaching Microcultures in Eastern Europe:
A Dialogue in Three Voices

A. DEVI JANKOWICZ

THE KRAKÓW CONSORTIUM PROJECT AND AN APPROACH TO ITS ANALYSIS

The account that follows is an attempt to make sense of my own experiences during a 3-year period in which I helped to organize a series of training courses for managers in Polish organizations as part of the Kraków Consortium Project, a program funded under Joint European Program 0771 of the TEMPUS scheme coordinated by the European Community. The project involved four academic institutions, two Western and two located in Kraków, Poland, together with several associated companies, in a two-step procedure. First, the Western academics trained their Eastern colleagues as trainers, and second, both Western and Eastern partners acted as teams providing training jointly, using interpreters as necessary, to a number of companies in the Kraków region. Jankowicz and Pettitt (1993) offered a more detailed account of the objectives involved and the procedures followed.

This scheme is one of several in which Western European governments and intergovernmental agencies have attempted to convey management expertise to a number of Eastern European countries that have recently eschewed communism as an economic system and turned to

Western capitalism as a preferred alternative. Despite substantial expenditure of governmental fund aid (the TEMPUS program alone has had a grant aid budget totaling 181.3 million ecu over the last 3 years) and enormous personal commitment on the part of the thousands of academics involved in this transfer of knowledge, the metaphor underlying the activity remains relatively crude. We have been seen as involved in the delivery of management know-how as if it were a commodity that can be packaged in crates and shipped by container loads to be unloaded at an ultimate destination.

Occasional authors have acknowledged the cultural relativities involved in the whole endeavor (see, for example, Auerbach & Stone 1991; Porket 1991; Tittenbrum 1991), but these have been academic discussions of cultural and economic differences as constraints and have not explicitly influenced the practices of people involved in knowledge transfer on the ground. Consequently, it is arguable that the transfer has been less effective than it might have been. Very few Westerners (e.g., Millman & Randlesome, 1993) are beginning to realize and educationally confront the practicalities of the massive inertia of a status quo that has its roots in national cultures whose significant causes go back for 500 years rather than simply for the past 50 years of Communist rule. On their part, the Eastern European partners have yet to face the epistemic challenges raised by Western training methods, most of which demand personal change on the part of the learner (Jankowicz, 1994).

I will illustrate and justify these statements by presenting a conversation occurring within a community of three selves. I describe a number of incidents that occurred during the 3 years of the Kraków Consortium Project, events occurring on the ground with the Polish managers who were participants in our training activities. First, in my English voice, I draw on constructs familiar to the Western academics involved in the aid effort to describe my reactions at the time. I then reply in the voice of our Polish academic partners and trainee managers to account for the same incidents in a Polish voice, articulating Polish constructs. This I am able to do since my first language is Polish, my cultural background is that of a first-generation emigré, and recently the bulk of my time (including 120 of 226 working days during the last year) has been spent in Poland, *inter alia* discussing these very events. I also comment on this dialogue in a third, authorial, voice, leaving the reader to form an opinion about the status of the last as it attempts to cast light on the reactions previously presented, an issue of epistemology to which I shall return in conclusion.

BASIC ASSUMPTIONS ABOUT THE PROCESS
OF MANAGEMENT

It is 8.00 A.M. on a dull day in a heavily polluted southern Polish town. A group of 22 middle-aged men sit round a table facing the accoutrements of Western-style management training: a team of two lecturers, a flipchart, and an overhead projector. They have assembled on the first day of an 8-day course that has been announced to them by their employer as offering training in the basics of strategic management, marketing, financial management, and human resource management. The course is staffed by people from the local university and (presented in words designed to be perceived as an attraction) some Western academic experts.

The starting time is normal for a Polish working day. The introductions, a brief statement of who we are and what we hope to do by the two lecturers (the English lecturer speaking through an interpreter), are followed by a similar round-robin by the course participants. This is a normal beginning to a Western-style management short course of this kind. The participants appear to be very senior; all have titles in which the word *director* takes prominence. The activities begin, with the Western lecturer outlining the course objectives and presenting material on the basic assumptions of the training techniques used. Active learning techniques such as case study work, simulations, and role plays, all of which are appropriately chosen to focus on management as an active process are used. In the course of subsequent discussions, the emphasis on action is questioned by the participants. They ask, "Why is there an obsession with participation and action in the didactic methods used? In the Western approach to training about the supervision and control of staff, is there no time in which to pause for thought?"

Voice I. "Well, you see, we in the West tend to take as a point of departure
. . .

the difference between accomplishing a simple task oneself, and managing a group of people so that a more complex goal can be achieved. That difference is one of the control of action and, more subtly, how the actors involved construe the control. Managers become socialized into the role through a process of on-the-job apprenticeship, sometimes supported by a formal educational or training course and sometimes not. In either case, the wherewithal to control others (and particularly, the legitimization of such control) is developed during a period in which one's actions are controlled by a supervisor. The degree and nature of this influence varies, from the gentle hinting that tentatively but purposefully suggests improvements in decisions taken under circumstances of maximal delegation to the rigid dominance involved in the fulfillment of a set of instructions in circumstances of constant monitoring and interference. In either case, the style adopted by the supervisor provides an important role model for the manager-to-be, as the trainee learns to construe phenomena as the supervisor and the organization construe them.

A person with a generalist educational background who enters an organization as a junior line manager will typically be posted to several different departments in succession for periods of 3 months at a time. S/he will learn three things from the experience of action: organization-specific knowledge, the social and technical skills required to complete a given task, and an awareness of the organization's formal and informal culture (Eden & Sims, 1981). S/he may then additionally seek a management qualification through part-time study. A person entering the organization in a professional capacity does so at a junior level, either with a qualification giving membership in a professional body or with a compulsory commitment to obtain one by qualification through part-time study during the early years of employment. In the meanwhile, managerial status is earned during a period in which the same things are learned by doing the job itself.

During the formal qualification program of study, the same emphasis on action under supervision can be found. Since management is about making decisions by using the services of other people, every opportunity is taken to practice the behavioral skills involved. Techniques such as simulations, role plays, the analysis of case studies, business games, and group decision-making exercises are used to reproduce the situation within the organization as fas as possible. The emphasis is on doing rather than listening, skills rather than knowledge, principles experientially induced rather than propositionally deduced, and competency in action rather than wisdom in repose. Indeed, the two most influential Western movements in management training, the Organizational Development technique developed in the United States (Beckhard 1967; Argyris, Putnam, & Smith 1985) and the Action Learning technique of the United Kingdom (Revans 1983), both emphasize learning by doing. The Organizational Development technique emphasizes training through the solution of work-based problems in real time by the intact working

group. The Action Learning technique emphasizes personal development, with its swapping of trainee managers among organizations so
that each must learn by doing someone else's job. This emphasis is particularly marked in the very common short (1- to 8-day) management
training course.

In all of these various approaches to management socialization, the
learning strategy emphasizes action, while the teaching strategy involves
the creation of situations in which this guided action can take place. The
epistemology involved is quite straightforward and is intended to answer
the following question as expressed in the words of the prototypical
management trainee:

> My machinery's down and I'm losing money every second. Now, I appreci-
> ate what Maslow and all the rest of them are saying about motivation, but
> tell me, and tell me quite clearly in words of one syllable, how does this
> help me to handle the bloody minded maintenance foreman who's coming
> to see me tomorrow morning at 10:30 precisely? Never mind the knowl-
> edge; what am I to do?

We do not know by simply knowing about. We know things, by the gut
feeling that comes from having acted successfully or unsuccessfully along
similar lines in similar situations in the past. This is the sense of knowing
written about in Genesis chapters 3 & 4 whereby the "knowledge of
good and evil" is gained through an act of finding out for oneself, rather
than through obeying God's didactic command. In other words, we anticipate events by construing, not their exegeses but their replications."

> **Voice II.** "Hold it, hold it. I can follow your rationale for the methods you
> use in training, but let's pause a while, since we first need to examine some
> very basic assumptions about management itself. For a start, it is actually
> quite difficult for us in Eastern Europe to find a word that corresponds to
> your word manager. Could that mean that we don't do the same thing? . . .

The nearest words in Polish, for example, to the English word *manager*
are *zarządca* or *kierownik*, which translate into English as governor/
ruler or director, respectively. (There is a word *menedżer*, but this is simply the English word, recently introduced, with an orthography that re-
produces its Polish pronunciation. Its meaning is entirely foreign to the
culture of recent times. Thus, its dictionary definition is simply "the director of a large capitalist enterprise" (Kopaliński, 1967) and reflects no
more than the last 50 years of Communist command economy.) Etymology is worth a glance. After all, if words as symbols gain their meaning

as much from their relationships to other words and the ideas they represent as they do from their relationship to the object being signified, it is worth exploring these relationships. The web of associations by which meaning is engendered includes the history of the words and their usage, associations that are particular to a culture and representative pointers to it.

The Polish etymology of the native words *kierownik-director* and *zarządca-governor/ruler* emphasizes the directive, commanding role that is an aspect of some forms of control. For example, a very early use of these two Polish words for *management* occurs in Tarnowski's legal codex of 1579, in which the military flavor of these Polish words for *management* is apparent: "The Grand Marshal should so arrange things that no cohort requires his active **direction**; rather, that each should know how to turn in place on the word of command." And an 18th-century translation of Homer's Iliad into Polish gives a good example of the immediacy involved in governing/ruling: "Neptune, whose tridentine sceptre shaketh the earth, who **ruleth** the fathomless seas." We're talking a very directive form of control here; if I manage, I must tell my subordinate what s/he's to do."

> Voice I. "I see. Well, yes, the English connotations of the word manager also involve control . . .

However, these carry an implication of administration ("The provisions . . . had been managed without economy"; Sir Thomas Smith, 1609, see OED, p. M105, vol. 6) and the exercise of skilled technique to cope with problems ("Her estate therefore requir'd both a discreet manager to husband it, and a man well furnish'd with money, to disengage it"; Cotton, 1670, see OED, p. M106, vol. 6). Its derivation relates to wielding and to training, as in the careful husbandry of activity, almost the manual shaping of behavior, involved in the training of the action and pace of the horses stabled in the 16th-century Italian *maneggio* from which the word *manager* descends. And so there are etymologies such as Disraeli's 1826 (see OED, p. M106, vol. 6) "Managing mankind, by studying their tempers and humouring their weaknesses" and, somewhat older, Dryden's charming note of 17th-century social husbandry as expressed in "She manages her last half-crown with care, and trudges to the mall on foot for air" (see OED, p. M105, vol. 6). (The derivation techniques used for these etymological comparisons are given in Jankowicz [1994]; the sources are Linde [1951] in the case of the Polish ones, and the OED

[1961] and Burchfield's Supplement [1972], together with Onions et al. [1966] in the case of the English.)"

> **Voice II.** "Yes. In contrast, for a Pole the manager is one who commands and governs . . .

You should realize that the flavor of apparent autocracy that pervades these terms lies deep in the Polish culture, originating well before the last 50 years of Communist economics (Jankowicz & Pettitt, 1993). Remember that since 1573 our aristocratic landowners elected all our kings, and the country was governed largely by the local lords' small parliaments rather than by the national parliament (Leslie, 1971). Well-meaning Westerners should know a great deal about the last 200 years before attempting to train the Polish manager. The industrial revolution occurring in the West in the early 19th century came somewhat later to Poland, but it came not to a sovereign state but a territory partitioned between Prussia, Austria, and Russia. The management function between 1797 and 1918 when the state was reconstituted took its nature from two predominant cultures: Prussian directive *ordnung* (with, in the south of Poland, a dash of Austrian *gemütlichkeit*) and Russian *eksploatacia tcherez uprawlienie*, the cruel and blatant exploitation which, especially after the failure of the January 1863 uprising, exported the wealth created by Russian-managed Polish enterprises to Russia at Polish expense.

The German occupation of 1939 to 1945 took directive exploitation to an unparalleled level while once again removing native Poles from substantial positions of authority in business enterprises. The Communist economic model of the succeeding 45 years crystallized the function into commanding and governing, as an annual plan of some 8 million constituent decisions was handed down from the Politburo to various government ministries, through industry federations to individual enterprises (Krysakowska-Budny & Jankowicz, 1991). In the socialist system, industrial enterprises had no responsibility for purchasing, promotion, or sales, and so had little familiarity with their own market. The executives had no responsibility for profits or losses, simply for the completion of the assigned plan.

A manager operating in these circumstances received no training. His or her responsibility was to fulfill the plan at any cost, at a time of irregularities of supply of raw materials, spare parts, and fuel. Hoarded labor was used as a buffer; do it or lose the bonuses promised for over-fulfillment of the annual plan."

Voice I. "Little wonder, then, that with such a cultural and political background, from a Western perspective . . .

When assessed by the Vroom-Yetton leadership exercise, a standard, Western decision-making measure, Polish managers were found to have a much more autocratic leadership style (Mączyński, 1991; Vroom, Yetton, & Jago, 1976)."

"If you say so . . .

In that case, you will probably see the relationship between teacher and learner in Poland as also somewhat autocratic, although we would prefer the term *directive*. You must understand that the same processes that created directive managers also created directive academics. A professorial system modeled on the Prussian *cathedra*, together with long periods of deprivation in the 19th century when native-language teaching was forbidden; privation during the 1939–1945 period when university-level teaching was punishable by death; and shortages of accommodation, textbooks, and equipment during the immediate postwar years, all reinforced the primacy of the individual academic as the sole owner of that scarce resource, knowledge."

INTERJECTION BY VOICE III

The constructs the Westerners enact seem to be as follows:

Management by doing	vs.	Inaction and passivity
Training by apprenticeship	vs.	Formal education
Education while working	vs.	Education prior to work
Training by simulation and practice	vs.	Teaching of principles and theory

Notice that the Polish constructs involved in this discussion are different. Here we have not just the simple oppositions of meaning engendered by a choice of opposing poles of the same constructs, but rather entirely different constructs.

Ingenuity and business survival	vs.	Profit-making and growth
Instruction	vs.	Laissez-faire

(indeed,

Directive steering and wise   vs.   Individualist anarchy
     governance
and NOT!
Autocratic management style   vs.   Democratic style)
Legitimate authority   vs.   Political & social helplessness

THE LEARNING CONTRACT: THE DEGREE OF INVOLVEMENT EXPECTED

A day and a half into the course, the English staff members are a little worried. The exercises in which participants have been asked to engage have not seemed to go down very well. To be sure, the managers have taken part, although the level of discussion in their groups has, as far as can be judged across the linguistic barrier, been restrained. There is a feeling that the participants may not be getting the point of the experiential activities arranged for them.

Voice I. "Our Western assumptions about the training process . . .

presuppose a learning contract, in which the varying expectations of participants and staff can be made explicit and a mutually satisfactory procedure for learning can be negotiated.

The expectations the participant brings to the course will typically set a limit to his or her openness to change during that course by defining the actions on the part of the trainer, and other trainees, which the participant will see as appropriate or inappropriate to his or her learning experience. Some topics, like those that explore the ways in which managers relate to other employees as people, imply greater involvement in personal growth and change and a greater level of personal intervention than others like accountancy of marketing where people are viewed as resources or consumers. And in this case, we need to involve the participant in role plays, simulations, and group exercises in order to personalize the material being taught and to turn abstract principles into subjective experiences in which the opportunity for real personal change can be offered to participants and in which skills, rather than principles, can be learned."

Voice II. "But we don't want any of this . . .

In our circumstances, it should be appreciated that principles are what matter. You have been here long enough to have heard the phrase "the

Polish Reality." Here's what it means. We have a time of turbulent change as a set of strange, foreign, and very underspecified rules for a market-driven economy come to replace the official certainties of the command economy in a period during which administrative instruments implementing government legislation are not yet complete and radical changes of ownership from the State to the employees are undertaken. (Privatization here in Poland is as much post-socialist "employee participation" as it is your Thatcherite "popular capitalism".) We are extremely careful about taking responsibility because systemic and bureaucratic inefficiencies make it very difficult to succeed at the most trivial tasks. In such times the manager turns to the academic and expects an expert, directive style, a complete statement of the economic precepts following which some degree of certainty might be regained. Our situation is too unpredictable to do anything but attempt to survive, and when we want to learn how management should be done, as there is no training department in our organizations, we approach academia and go to sit at the feet of the wise. Why are you so shy of being called wise? It is your expertise that we're paying for, after all. Our recourse is to first principles, to identify those certainties in the knowledge base of academic theories about management from which the certainty needed to control action can be derived."

Voice I. "Yes, we can appreciate your position . . .

but consider, real management on the ground is not a matter of applying principles. It's about negotiating an appropriate set of objectives and finding a way to achieve those objectives with the only people, employees, through whom they can be achieved. In this part of the course, we are frankly trying to influence attitudes toward the management role, and to do this we need to engage your feelings as well as your intellect. Our way of managing the learning situation is to enter into this negotiation with you, to see what freedom of movement you will allow us in moving away from your preferred style of ex-cathedra lecturing. Our expertise as educators is that we have to personalize learning if it is to be effective. So we ask participants to contemplate the personal practical implications of ideas we introduce during the course as we ask them to engage in activities that put these into practice. Systemic change is impossible without a degree of personal change."

Voice II. "But we find the very notion of a learning contract, of negotiating learning, very strange . . .

The purpose of a course is to listen, as a set of distinct individuals, to an *authoritative* presentation of academic principles and findings. (Never mind the ex-cathedra, thank you very much; not all lecturers are full professors!) This is intellectual property of which you Westerners have ownership, which we seek to obtain from you. We are surprised, for example, when you make statements like "There are five different kinds of situational factors to take into account when you think about the leadership role, but we want to focus attention this morning on two." If the textbooks, as repositories of that scarce resource, knowledge, mention five theories, then we want to hear about all five. This issue should not be negotiable!"

> Voice I. "The difficulty is perhaps that we don't see ourselves as educators but as trainers. In the West, the view is that . . .

we aren't purveying knowledge in a representative sampling of the content, but that we're trying to create a learning situation or, in Novak's words, "construct a community of inquiry in the classroom" (Novak, 1990, p. 247). And for the purposes of the next exercise, we only need to consider two theories to get our point across.

There is indeed room for theory and for principles. But in addition, we seek to create opportunities for you to deduce the implications; test them out through some practical exercise, discussion, or activity; personalize the learning outcomes; and reintegrate the experience in the form of personally validated principles, following the Kolb cycle (Kolb, 1984) of abstract conceptualization, active experimentation, concrete experience, reflective observation, and personalized conceptualization, respectively. Where skills are being taught, some practice of simple technique is mandatory; where the skills are the interpersonal ones involved in management, the need for you to mull over the personal implications is also essential."

> Voice II. "This makes us feel uncomfortable . . .

As you conceptualize it, *management* is in practice somewhat strange. Yes, we understand the term but see its implications differently as we discussed earlier. Consequently, in thinking through the implications of the principles you present, we must fall back on the assumptions in which we have been trained, whether as engineers, accountants, or economists. By definition, these involve disparate perspectives on the questions you are asking us to address, and so someone in the group will inevitably "come up with the wrong answer." We are different people with different professional backgrounds, we experience different feelings, and, after all, all of these different viewpoints cannot be right at the same time."

Voice I. "So what you want us to do is to use our authority . . .

to tell you what this mystical management perspective is so that you can all be right, and in the meanwhile, spare you the embarrassment of acting out your misconceptions. What you're saying is that mistakes can be tolerated in intellectual debate that cannot be handled in the more personalized forms of learning experience in which your feelings, emotions, and personal values are publicly engaged. Novak was right, "the 'wisdom of practice' is often more difficult to grasp than the 'dogma of convention' " (Novak, 1990, p. 247).

Left at this level, our interactions will be reduced to a fearful exchange of diplomatic notes. What we must do is to vary the level of personal involvement demanded, recreate a "safe space," so that learning can progress. It is precisely this opportunity to air the disparate viewpoints characteristic of the different job functions (marketing, personnel, production, finance) which training of this kind can provide; its value will lie precisely in the opportunity to compare distinct and, at times, competing constructions of the same events. The objective here is to clarify your understanding of one another's point of view, since it is this kind of debate which helps you to form an effective management team rather than a group of people who without realizing it compete, because each has competing or at least incompatible understandings of the issue in question. We ask you to accept that in training, the group of participants are as much teachers as the staff!"

AND VOICE III

The Western constructs seem concerned with

Having a surface impact	vs.	Engendering deep personal change
Negotiating mutual needs	vs.	Dictating a viewpoint
Developing a community of inquiry	vs.	Directive teaching

while the eastern constructs concern

| The certainty that principles bring | vs. | vulnerability to turbulent change |

Being authoritative and   vs.   Having little knowledge to
  knowledgeable   offer
Intellectual vulnerability   vs.   Emotional vulnerability

TEACHING AND EMPOWERMENT

Doing a rating scale exercise, one group of participants showed considerable reluctance in working out the implications of their scores for themselves. "You're the expert; tell us what this psychological test actually means" was the view expressed. Test-naive participants in any culture might make the mistake of thinking that a simple set of 5-point scales used to describe their reactions during a structured exercise is not a psychological test. It was surprising that the exercise, which called for some intuitive insights, fell flat.

Voice I. "We can't help thinking that . . .

while acknowledging the impact of a political system that discouraged the thinking through of implications in ways that were not sanctioned from a higher echelon, the participants were being a little passive in requesting our expert pronouncements. If this were a course at the more experiential end of the academic-experiential dimension, like a T-group- or encounter group-based personal development program, we would at this point be processing issues concerning unwillingness to take personal responsibility. We would try to understand the reluctance to interpret scores as arising from uncertainties about the subsequent use we might make of the personal information involved and worry that we had not created a sufficiently safe space in which the learning could proceed. Perhaps the participants were taking the exercise too seriously, as a test-based diagnosis of personal traits analogous to the visit to a doctor for one's ills to be tested. Its purpose was simply to stimulate thinking, feeling, and discussion. Much management knowledge, especially in the management of the human resource, is nonprescriptive unlike the graphs and formulae of the engineer or the econometrician. Treatment and cure are not possible by the application of a favored nostrum, the medicine of choice."

Voice II. "What you should realize is that . . .

the nature of responsibility and its discharge in a Polish organization is complex. We're not saying that the autocracies of the command economy prevented habits of personal responsibility from being developed by

Polish managers. On the contrary, as the command economy fell apart through the manifold ills of overstaffing, irregularity of supply, insufficiencies of spare parts, localized corruption of state funds in the nomenclatura companies, and the collapse of markets for finished goods (Krysakowska-Budny & Jankowicz, 1991), Polish managers demonstrated extreme ingenuity and a level of entrepreneurship greater than any the West has ever known simply to keep their companies afloat.

But we are the products of a system in which power is important, and knowledge, of course, is a form of power. We are not accustomed to the Western view, much advocated by organizational development trainers, that power can be distributed; that it need not flow downhill from the upper reaches of the organization but can puddle at various levels of the hierarchy; and that, far from being a nonrenewable resource, empowerment empowers the giver as well as the recipient. In any case, until a substantial proportion of Polish managers accepts these assumptions, they will by definition be untenable. The powerful cling to power and do not share it readily.

With this perspective, it is more familiar for us to view the lecturer as the possessor of knowledge to be learned, and thereby, the individual with the greatest power—not because he or she uses sophisticated training methods with doubtful value. Of course, power sharing in education is possible. One becomes a student; works as an assistant lecturer; completes a PhD (without which a full lectureship is not possible); does one's *Docentura*, which conveys the right to tutor other PhDs; and then gains a professorship. At some stage along this route, one gains knowledge. There is a sense in which the style of authoritative knowledge dissemination with which we normally address trainee practitioners is a courtesy, a symbolic simulation of the real personal journey toward empowerment that a professional academic undertakes. Or, shifting the field of application, it is a simulation of the real empowerment that the manager's fight to climb organizational ladders engenders."

AND VOICE III

The Western constructs seem concerned with

Personal responsibility	vs.	Diffuse/unspecified responsibility
Power hoarding	vs.	Personal empowerment

while the Eastern constructs concern

| Personal initiative and entrepreneurship | vs. | Submission to autocracy |
| Knowledge as power | vs. | Knowledge as neutral |

AN ANALYSIS IN VOICE III

Every formally organized learning experience, whether as short as a conference or a training course or as long as a 3-year qualification program, brings together a group of people who, over the time they spend together, develop a temporary society, and hence a microculture pro tem, in which some of the norms created by both lecturers and participants might be internalized. Writing from a Kellian perspective, Novak has called this a "community of inquiry" and has noted that "special skill is needed to construct communities of enquiry in classrooms" (Novak, 1990, p. 247). We might add the caveat that the characteristics of the broader culture, and the intentions brought to the situation by the participants themselves, are also involved in determining the nature of the community.

It would be possible to analyze this broader, Eastern culture within which we sought to build our community of inquiry in the following categories:

- an epistemology based on the propositional rather than the experiential

- a style based on a preference for autocratic role relationships in teaching and learning, with a lack of awareness that alternatives are possible

- unfamiliarity with the concept of a learning contract, and unwillingness to negotiate it

- an economy based on knowledge as a scarce resource

- a model of learning as a process of intellectual accretion rather than one of restructuring and absorption at both cognitive and affective levels

- a climate based on a deep feeling of seriousness rather than experimentation and play

- an avoidance of personal responsibility by an avoidance of delegation
- discomfort with the idea of power equivalences in the teacher-participant relationship

As soon as this is articulated, two fundamental issues arise. First, am I, writing in the third voice, right in making these assertions? (For "right" read convincing, plausible, possible to agree with; all because the reader would arrive at the same characteristics from the same evidence as presented earlier.) The second issue is more fundamental and concerns the general issue of validity in constructive alternativism; this will be dealt with later.

Regarding the first matter, the answer is most likely "yes, if one chooses to view things Western-style and identifies oneself, voice three, with voice one." As one might predict from Kelly's sociality corollary, the reader making this statement may not necessarily use these analytic categories him- or herself (I'm avoiding calling them "metaconstructs" of any kind, not wishing to commit myself as to their status for the moment), but s/he could understand how I arrived at them from the incidents described, assuming I were English voice one.

Equally, the answer is likely to be "no, if one were to identify with voice two. Your very analysis of linguistic and cultural differences is powerful evidence to suppose that the description afforded by the analysis would be unrecognized by your Polish clients and colleagues. You demonstrate the low commonality, and so it is very difficult for sociality to emerge. Therefore, from their perspective, such an analysis would be somewhat arrogant."

Very well, but here is my difficulty. If I am to take further action in these circumstances, it is awkward and distasteful to run with two sets of incompatible constructs. It is awkward because some of the utterances made by the two voices are incompatible, and distasteful because my personal values include a commitment to the notion of a learning community, which I find difficult to apply in voice two. Therefore, my actions are constrained.

Consider the fact that the notion of a learning culture in a management group would be quite foreign to the participants. First, on culture itself, Czarniawska (1986) has remarked on the lack of distinct organizational cultures in the various organizational units making up Polish industry and administration. This is not surprising given the Communist polity of a "worker state," which in this regard does not distinguish between the societal and the occupational. Second, on the notion of a learning culture (and here the reason is deeper-seated, antedating the communist state), the Polish language itself does not distinguish between *teaching* and *learning*. It provides just one word-stem, *uczyć*, meaning "to teach" and *uczyć się*, defined by the dictionary as "learning," but with an active meaning of "to be taught" to a Pole, where English, French, and German have two separate roots for the two separate meanings (Jankowicz and Pettitt, 1993). This use of *-się* is similar to the French *se-*. It is a syntactical rather than a semantic reflexive, and therefore does not indicate reflexivity of agency so that there is, for instance, a separate form for teaching oneself (*uczyć siebie*), with much the same connotations as the English phrase.

But that learning (as opposed to teaching oneself) can be an active process of personal development and growth and that what the teacher can best do is create a situation in which this can happen is linguistically strange in Polish and foreign to voice two.

Third, the notion of a teaching strategy as distinct from a learning strategy, the notion that the student can have different goals from his or her teacher and still be serious about the endeavor, is difficult to construe in voice two.

None of the above represents idiosyncracy, faulty learning, or some aberration from a global norm; it *is* reality as the Pole construes it and has construed it for generations. According to the ideas of Hofstede (1991; see also Inkeles and Levinson, 1969), it represents a particular cultural resolution to the classic dilemmas facing any society, with the Polish culture being one of large power difference, both in the workplace and outside it. These classic dilemmas include:

- social equality versus inequality, including the relationship with authority as indexed by the power difference between leaders and led

- individualism versus group dependence

- masculinity versus femininity

- control versus expression of aggression and feelings.

Further, if Hofstede (1991, pp. 182–183) is correct when he says that the core of a national culture lies in shared values while the core of an occupational culture lies in shared perceptions of daily practices, then any ideology that includes an experience of communism is going to be resistant to change because the command economy sought to guide daily practices by universal values and in effect to elide the values-practices distinction. Of course, it is easier to change daily practices than it is to change universal values or actions informed by such values.

It may be, then, that there are limitations to the effectiveness of the learning situation or community of inquiry model, and that such approaches are possible only in situations of small power difference as in the United States and United Kingdom, from which many of the curriculum ideas expressed in this paper have originated. Western trainers have a materially more-developed training technology because their culture and language allow for this. They are better able to engage in teacher-learner relationships that involve negotiation of the joint construing, entered into on a basis of near equality, that is required for the creation of a learning situation or community of inquiry.

Very well, that is the argument for my wish to identify voice three with voice one and make use of the notion of a learning community. But voice two will not understand what I'm doing. What status is voice three to ascribe to voice two?

First we turn to the analysis offered by a constructivist writer, Applegate (1990). In his terms, the Polish teacher-learner relationship represents a traditional communication system. Applegate (1990, pp. 207–208) listed the characteristics of nontraditional, person-centered communication systems (messages that are more responsive to partner aims, are relatively personal, and are encouraging of reflection about the circumstances in which they are exchanged) and suggests that these represent more sophisticated message behavior. Clearly, there is a need for this kind of comparative analysis, if only to distinguish more sensitive from less sensitive communicators within a given culture. However, it would be very dangerous to conclude that such a comparison is appropriate between cultures so that the voice two understanding of the teacher-learner relationship is seen as a less advanced system than the supposedly more sophisticated Western learning community approach.

Voice two does not understand what I'm doing with my learning community, and I lose the effectiveness that I claimed earlier for my subscription to this way of looking at the world. One way out of the resultant dilemma is to conclude, as many current Western and Eastern educationalists activists in Eastern Europe have concluded, that it is more effective to organize long staff exchanges of 6 to 12 months' duration between East and West, rather than relying on short 3- to 8-day management courses (Jankowicz, 1994; Dietl, personal communication, 9th February, 1993) for management development and training. Let both parties learn the other's general culture and values by total immersion over a relatively long period, and then let them come together to devise entirely new ways of looking at the world of teaching and learning in order to transcend the difficulties in applying the Western learning community model.

Finally, there is the fundamental issue that underlies the analysis presented above and that is surely problematic for any discussion of communicated construction. How does one decide which of two incompatible constructions is more appropriate in a given situation? A first reaction might be to evade the question. The individuality and choice corollaries suggest that a system of construction should be judged only with reference to its usefulness in elaborating the freedom with which a particular individual can act with respect to his or her own goals, and, faced with a second individual's incompatible constructs for the same shared goals, all one can do is acknowledge the value of constructive alternativism.

This doesn't take us very far, however. If those individuals must work together, there will inevitably be situations in which efforts toward sociality and commonality carry an implicit evaluation that some constructions are a more effective way of proceeding toward shared goals than others. Applegate (1990) is surely right in asserting the superiority of the learner-centered, nontraditional, learning community model of the learning process within our single Western culture; for example, if the alternative is a traditional ex-cathedra didacticism without activity on the part of the learner. The therapist has the same problem if, in understanding his or her patient's goals, s/he feels (in the analytic voice three) that a more useful construction, a voice two, is available for issues construed in the patient's voice one. To return to the question left in abeyance when introducing the idea of voice three earlier in this paper, what is the epistemological status of voice three?

It is dodging the issue, I think, to invent a set of superordinate, therapeutic, or educational meta-goals according to which voice three can make a preference choice between any voice two or voice one. After all, voice three is still simply another utterance spoken by a fallible human being doing his or her best to construe a situation that both therapist and patient, trainer and trainee, share: just another alternative attempt at construction.

This issue can be resolved by offering an analysis in terms of power. Voice three gains primacy over voices one and two and can sanction the greater validity of either if it offers a statement of its power to do so and (a crucial simultaneity) voices one and two accept, or indeed, in the case of those therapeutic relationships in which there is a cry for help, seek out this assertion. According to this analysis, the power resource (French & Raven, 1959) used cannot be coercion. Expert and (given the existence of the phenomenon of transference) referent power are clearly important, and it is very likely that in the case of the educational relationship described above, reward power plays a part in the sense that an important aspect of the Eastern participation is a wish to reap the perceived material benefits of a capitalist economy.

This gives no special primacy to any one voice, either still and small or pitched loudly at some metalevel or other. It suggests that we search for truth or, if you prefer it, validity, by negotiating temporary primacies for the voice that emerges as most likely to achieve our aims at the time. The Kuhnian paradigm shift is what occurs when a sufficiency of voices resolves Babel to agree to cohere for a time on one new voice in particular. It is then a Kellian value to see the emergence of health and the success of the educational endeavor as the restoration of a situation in which the possibility of choice, of continuing elaboration of the system, are restored.

"And now, (very quietly, whisper who dare) . . .

This is what voice one was trying to say by its adherence to a learning community model. But then, for all my knowledge of Eastern Europe and all my efforts at sociality, I am a product of Western culture, the culture that produced George Kelly too. It would be fascinating to speculate what an Eastern constructivism would look like."

REFERENCES

Applegate, J. L. (1990). Constructs and communication: A pragmatic integration. In G. J. Neimeyer & R. A. Neimeyer (Eds.), *Advances in personal construct psychology* Vol. 1 (pp. 203–230). London: JAI Press.

Argyris, C., Putnam, R., & Smith, D. McL. (1985) *Action science: Concepts, methods and skills for research and intervention*. London: Jossey-Bass.

Auerbach, P., & Stone, M. (1991). Developing the new capitalism in Eastern Europe: How the West can help. *Long Range Planning, 24,* 3, 58–65.

Beckhard, R. (1967). Optimising team-building efforts. *Journal of Contemporary Business, 1,* 23–32.

Burchfield, R. W. (Ed.), (1972). *A Supplement to the Oxford English Dictionary.* Oxford: Clarendon Press.

Czarniawska, B. (1986). The management of meaning in the Polish crisis. *Journal of Management Studies, 23,* 313–331.

Eden, C., & Sims, D. (1981). Computerised vicarious experience: The future for management induction? *Personnel Review, 10,* 22–25.

French, J. R. P. Jr., & Raven, B. H. (1959). The bases of social power. In D. Cartwright (Ed.), *Studies in social power* (pp. 150–167). Ann Arbor: University of Michigan Press.

Hofstede, G. (1991). *Cultures and organizations: Software of the mind.* London: McGraw-Hill.

Inkeles, A., & Levinson, D. J. (1969). National character: The study of modal personality and sociocultural systems. In G. Lindzey & E. Aronson (Eds.), *The handbook of social psychology* (pp. 977–1020). Reading, MA: Addison-Wesley.

Jankowicz, A.D. (1994). The new journey to Jerusalem: Mission and meaning in the managerial crusade to Eastern Europe. *Organization studies, 15*(4): 479–507.

Jankowicz, A.D., & Pettitt, S. J. (1993). Worlds in collusion: An analysis of an Eastern European management development initiative, *Management Education and Development, 24,* 93–104.

Kolb, D. A. (1984). *Experiential learning: Experience as the source of learning and development.* Englewood Cliffs, NJ: Prentice-Hall.

Kopaliński, W. (1967). *Słownik wyrazów obcych i zwrotów obco-języcznych* [Dictionary of Foreign Words and foreign-language phrases]. Warsaw: Wiedza Powszechna.

Krysakowska-Budny, E., & Jankowicz, A.D. (1991). Poland's road to capitalism. *Salisbury Review, 10,* 28–31.

Leslie, R. F. (1971). *The Polish question: Poland's place in modern history.* London: Historical Association.

Linde, M. S. B. (1951). *Słownik języka Polskiego*—3rd ed. [Dictionary of the Polish language]. Warsaw: Państwowy Instytut Wydawniczy.

Mączyński, J. (1991) *A cross-cultural comparison of decision participation based on the Vroom-Yetton model of leadership, Report PRE no. 23.* Wroclaw: Institute of Management, Technical University of Wroclaw.

Millman, T., & Randlesome, C. (1993). Developing top Russian managers. *Management Education and Development, 24,* 83–92.

Novak, J. M. (1990). Advancing constructive education. In G. J. Neimeyer & R. A. Neimeyer (Eds.), *Advances in personal construct psychology* Volume 1 (pp. 233–255). London: JAI Press.

OED. (1961). *The Oxford English Dictionary*. Oxford: Clarendon Press.

Onions, C. T., Friedrichsen, G. W. S., & Burchfield, R. W. (1966). *The Oxford Dictionary of Engish Etymology*. Oxford: Clarendon Press.

Porket, J. (1991, September). Tensions in post-communist economies. *Proceedings of the conference on international privatisation: Strategies and practices.* University of St. Andrews, Scotland.

Revans, R. (1983). *The ABC of action learning*. Bromley: Chartwell-Bratt.

Tittenbrum J. (1991, September). Privatisation in Poland: Peoples' capitalism? *Proceedings of the conference on international privatisation: Strategies and practices*, University of St. Andrews, Scotland.

Vroom, V. H., Yetton, P. W., & Jago, A. G. (1976). *Problem Set No 5.* New Haven, CT: Yale University School of Organization and Management.

PART THREE

Extending the Theory in New Directions

INTRODUCTION

Part Three, "Extending the theory in new directions," consists of four chapters that indicate how discoveries of group construals lead to extensions of Kelly's theory. In these papers, the findings of research are reintegrated in theoretical principles that yield a basis for further investigation and additional therapeutic applications. They all relate to a pervading issue in psychological theorizing: how to describe the interrelationships between the person and the environment. Personal construct psychology attempts to allow full regard for individual agency without detracting from the impact of circumstance and history.

In chapter 14, Franz Epting, Shawn Prichard, Larry M. Leitner, and Gavin Dunnett draw on the contrast between traditional role(s) and those based on the construing of others' construing (the latter delineated in Leitner's work as ROLE) in order to extend the application of personal construct theory to the sphere of social action. They discuss how definitions of social phenomena arise and how these definitions imply opportunities as well as limitations. In this light, personal construct psychology can be interpreted as a practical theory that facilitates social action and furnishes a moral framework for living one's entire life.

Larry M. Leitner, Ellen A. Begley, and April J. Faidley use personal construct theory to examine the dynamics of social relationships and their theoretical underpinnings. In chapter 15 they view intimate (ROLE) relationships as the basis for determining a person's bond with one's social group. Beyond this, the authors deal with the processes that establish the group locations of individuals and the experience of social locations. In this context, the authors show that marginalization and distancing from the social center is experienced when core ROLE constructs are consistently invalidated by a dominating group. Release from such social irrelevancy can be attained through organized protest. A dilemma that can be resolved with the help of a personal construct perspective is the paradox that social movements seemingly depend on strong individuality for their success.

Ulrike Willutzki and Lothar Duda take up the thread of domination. In chapter 16 they explore extending personal construct theory into the realm of the political. A case study of faculty meetings in a German university provides insights into microstrategies that institutionalize relations of domination and subordination. As the authors point out, the verbal and nonverbal constructs that work for the powerful in this milieu hint at how macrostructures are generally filtered into face-to-face relationships.

In the final chapter of this part, Harry Oxley and Linda Hort take the stand that the study of personality and the study of culture are two branches of a single area. In their view, the basis in personal construct psychology is the premise that Kelly's person is a meaning maker. Since what we understand as culture is centrally a compendium of meanings negotiated by individuals, there is no alternative but to study them as a united field. By adopting the metaphor of ecology for their discussion, the authors demonstrate the inescapable bonds between the individual and the society in which s/he lives.

CHAPTER 14

Personal Constructions of the Social

FRANZ R. EPTING, SHAWN PRICHARD,
LARRY M. LEITNER,[1] AND GAVIN DUNNETT[2]

The purpose of this chapter is to examine some of the aspects of personal construct psychology and psychotherapy that bring one's attention to the social world. These are components of personal construct psychology we believe need further elaboration and extension. While various understandings of the social world have been discussed in the theory, there is a need to extend this discussion in areas where there is an intimate and passionate interchange between the person and the social world. In particular, we hope to illustrate some of the ways that personal construct theory, rather than being a theory of techniques to understand and treat disorders, is first and foremost a theory about values or fundamental principles for living one's entire life.

The relationship between the person and the social world can be seen as like the relationship between a construct and an event or element. There would be no construct with nothing to construe, and there would be no meaning to an event if that event had not been embraced in a personal construction. Keen (1972) provided a dramatic example of this in his report of an experiment in which a person is imagined to be surrounded by robots that only resemble humans. A close reading of Keen's description suggests that under such imagined conditions, the meaning of both the world and the person disappears. The person would be empty and incomprehensible without a social surround; the social surround would be barren and even nonexistent if it were not for the personal action of constructing a meaning. Yet there has been far too little said about this unbreakable bond and what is offered by approaching the social world from the viewpoint of the person.

In fact, there is evidence to suggest that we are too ready to abandon any active and creative role for the person when considering the nature of social influence. For example, Rychlak (1990) critiqued the current trend toward offering a social constructionist analysis, operating from the position that the "human mind takes its origin in the social world and especially in the structure of language" (p. 15), as abandoning the active, meaning-making person in psychology. Giorgi (1992) made a similar point when he stated:

> . . . certain recent movements, such as social constructionism, deconstructionism, certain types of postmodernism affirm human subjectivity, but then leave it so powerless that, in the end, there really is nothing to affirm. The contextual elements are so potent that the human subject is not so much de-centered as rendered centerless. (p. 428)

In social constructionism, the social situation is used to define the person; the person is considered a more or less passive participant in life's great events. Essentially, the individual disappears into the collective with little room for the passionate heart and body of the person to meaningfully exist outside some abstract social group. We believe that personal construct theory has a much more active role to offer the person in this process.

In this chapter we attempt to cover three central themes. First, we examine how the other is defined in relation to the person. This is a concern with the invitation extended to view the other in specifically personal ways rather than as just another object of concern. Second, we discuss the way the social world becomes defined and the nature of the constraints and opportunities that are held therein. This is a concern for the nature of power and influence in the social world. Finally, we elaborate on the implications of personal construct psychology for social action and involvement.

THE OTHER AS PERSON

Much of what we say in this chapter centers on the sociality corollary of the personal construct theory: "To the extent that one person construes the construction process of another, he [or she] may play a role in a social process involving the other person" (Kelly, 1955, p. 95). In many ways, this corollary provides the foundation for the heart and spirit of the theory (e.g., Landfield & Leitner, 1980; Leitner, 1985). It also has profound implications for structuring relationships with others, as well as how we experience the other in our lives. Thus, we discuss this corollary in some depth. The sociality corollary clearly defines a "role" in terms that are at odds with the traditional sociological definition. A role (which we refer to in all capitals—ROLE) involves interpersonal actions based on one's understanding of the inner meaning-making process of another. Relationships based on an attempt to construe the other's process of creating meaning, termed ROLE relationships, are viewed as absolutely essential for engaging life. Life is experienced as empty and meaningless if the person surrenders to the temptation to retreat from ROLE relationships. Although elaborations of this viewpoint can be found elsewhere,[3] we provide a brief overview of this work in order to illustrate the ways in which the interpersonal resides at the heart of personal construct psychology.

First, in this corollary, Kelly stated that ROLE relationships involve understanding the other's process of construing more than the content of constructs. Since content and process are intimately intertwined, we are confronted with the paradox of attempting to understand the process of creating meaning through a knowing of the specific contents of the meanings. Thus, we are left with the theoretical challenge of understanding what meaning contents govern the meaning-making process. Kelly (1955; see Leitner, 1985) suggested that one's core constructs, the most central dimensions of a person's identity, govern the process of meaning making.

Core constructs, particularly those involved in our process of relating to others (core ROLE constructs), are defined as those constructs that govern our maintenance process. In other words, the invalidation of core constructs can result in physiological upheaval due to their role in regulating our biology. In a ROLE relationship, then, we allow the other access to meanings that centrally define our constructions of ourselves as persons. Such intimacy, while potentially rewarding, also carries substantial risks. The possibility of having core ROLE constructs invalidated leaves us open to experiencing a conglomeration of threat, fear, anxiety, hostility, and guilt termed terror. As a matter of fact, such devastating disconfirmation may be expected in relationships. Even if we can get beyond disconfirming one another in the present, there is no guarantee we will grow in compatible ways in the future. Thus, ROLE relationships are both vitally necessary yet potentially terrifying.

This theoretical viewpoint contains strong implications for how the other should be treated. ROLE relationships are a meeting of persons, not of objects necessary for the meeting of needs. Within a ROLE relationship, each person has access to the other's most central meanings, those that govern the very process of being in the world. If someone affirms those central meanings, the other can experience emotions such as love, joy, and reverence (Leitner & Faidley, in press; Leitner & Pfenninger, 1994; McCoy, 1977). Should these vital meanings be disconfirmed, the other will experience a conglomeration of emotions (e.g., pain, anger, anxiety, panic, devastation) that may be most upsetting. As a matter of fact, life itself could be threatened if these most central of meanings, the core ROLE constructs, are disconfirmed (Kelly, 1955; Landfield, 1976). Of course, one person may very well choose to deny another access to these most central of meanings without knowing something about the central meanings of the other. In other words, each person comes to know the most central meanings of the other as each person is simultaneously known. This position of reciprocity, inherent in most ROLE relationships, implies that all persons risk the joys as well as the pain of intimate relating.

Leitner (1988) has conceptualized symptoms and psychopathology in terms of the retreat from such relationships. The potential for disconfirmation is too terrifying for the person. The person opts for the safe-yet-empty world of treating others as objects over the risky-yet-meaningful world of persons. Rather than trying to appreciate your hopes, dreams, aspirations, areas of greatest fear, devastations, etc., I objectify you. You become someone to meet my needs for companionship, sex, conversation, etc. To paraphrase the existentialists, if I am retreating from a ROLE relationship, I love you because I need you; I do not need you because I love you. A broad retreat from ROLE relating has been linked to the experience of emptiness and meaninglessness (Leitner, 1985).

Psychotherapy involves engaging the person over the dilemma of retreating from versus engaging in ROLE relationships. In so doing, the relationship between therapist and client forms a crucible for the struggle over ROLE relating (Faidley & Leitner, 1993; Leitner & Dill-Standiford, 1993; Soldz, 1993). In the living relationship with the therapist, the client has an opportunity to mourn devastating injuries associated with the invalidation of central meanings as well as to find the courage to relate in profoundly open and creative ways once more. However, such a process can only occur with a therapist who values and affirms the client's personhood, not a therapist who views clients as collections of symptoms to be treated. The latter approach, by definition, is a retreat from ROLE relationships (Leitner, 1990; Leitner & Pfenninger, 1994). Clients will wisely refuse to risk a ROLE relationship with a therapist who tends to objectify them.

Thus, Kelly's sociality corollary, with its theory of ROLE relationships, places us in the position of mutually engaging one another in the most highly intimate of connections. Such reciprocally intimate relationships place extensive personal demands on us. In addition to the potential for devastating disconfirmation, all ROLE relationships take time and effort. We must take the time and energy to understand one another in meaningful ways currently as well as be willing to commit ourselves to this process in the future (Leitner & Pfenninger, 1994). Thus, we live with potential terror over an extended period of time.

Not surprisingly, we limit the number of reciprocal ROLE relationships we are actively elaborating at any one time, such that most of our days are consumed with non-ROLE relating. However, even here we have a choice. On the one hand, we can retreat into the objectification of others. In so doing, others lose their subjectivity, their individuality, their aliveness. On the other hand, personal construct psychology reminds us that even these more distant others are meaning-making creatures. Like us, they hope; they fear; they love; they hate; they live; they die. We do not have to allow the fact that we cannot understand their vital individual meanings to lead us to the conclusion that we do not have to appreciate them as meaning-making creatures.

In other words, even though I lack the time, inclination, energy, or even the courage necessary to form a ROLE relationship with you, I still can grasp that you, by virtue of being human, need meaning. Such a position implies a profound respect for the will to meaning felt by all persons. In so doing, I recognize that the meanings you have created have been those that have allowed you to most meaningfully grasp the realities you have faced. While I may not understand or agree with them, I can respect the fact that you created these meanings for the best of reasons: the need to engage and transcend the events of life. Further, this position leads me to actions to increase the affirmation of the process of meaning making for all persons (Leitner & Pfenninger, 1994). Without such transpersonal affirmation of the process of meaning creation, all persons ultimately wind up objectified and made less than what they are.

POWER AND INFLUENCE

Having discussed the profound ways in which the interpersonal can be seen as at the center of personal construct theory, we can now address the important topic of social power and influence. In her assessment of Kelly then and now, Salmon (1990) was concerned with the seeming individualism of the theory. She called for a clearer way for the theory to handle issues of inequity, privilege, coercion, and oppression. Appreciating the perspective offered by discourse analysis and critical deconstruction, she is concerned that social influence is ignored in personal construct theory in favor of imposing a "purely private and individual solution on problems that are essentially social and cultural in character" (p. 12). This led to responses by Dunnett and Leitner (1990) and Walker (1990). This section of the paper can be seen as our attempt to extend this discussion.

Efran (1991) provided an opportunity to further examine this issue and bring it into clearer focus. Efran was asked to respond to the needs of "a young, depressed, single mother on welfare trying to keep her kids from dropping out of school and becoming part of the local drug scene" (p. 51). In his response he emphasized the idea that, even in dire circumstances, there is the possibility of choice. In his response, Efran adopted the position taken in personal construct theory that the external conditions of life do not directly control one's life. The person is capable of making some sense out of a situation other than that which appears to be dictated by the immediate external circumstances. In fact, leaders like Mohandas Gandhi and Martin Luther King, Jr. based their models for social change on changing the consciousness of their followers in order to enable them to take some action to change their life conditions.

Personal construct theory would hold that the greater danger lies in allowing the bare facts to dictate the choices (or the lack of choices) a person has. In his article, Efran examined how the mother is living her own life as well as how she is then modeling that life for her children. This is an excellent example of Kelly's (1970) notion that

> Men [persons] change things by changing themselves first, and they accomplish their objectives, if at all, only by paying the price of altering themselves—as some have found to their sorrow and others to their salvation. (p. 16)

This position in no way diminishes the fact that social conditions can have a very significant effect on a person's life. It does, however, place the person in an active stance in relationship to just how much influence the social condition will be allowed to have. It allows the person to exercise a transcendent consciousness in order to create a reality other than the one presented. Stojnov's letter (in chapter 4) provides a particularly poignant illustration. The welfare mother does not have to surrender her constructions to the conditions around her and can choose to live in a way that might just provide pathways out for both her and her children. This in no way prevents her from joining in with others in social action groups and protest in order to effect social change. In fact, exercising such transcendent consciousness in order to reach alternative constructions could make it possible for her to form her own action groups to deal with her neighborhood conditions. In no way does it prevent that mother from realizing her victimization by the conditions of her world. However, rather than inviting her to merely view herself as a victim of the conditions around her, it points to a way of seeing beyond the decay of her neighborhood. The construal may help her find the courage to take action that might free her and her family from such conditions.

This is not far removed from the position Fromm (1973) took when he advocated changes in social structure in order to change individual lives. He, too, started with helping the individual to change so that she or he would be able to envision the changes that would be needed on the more abstract social level. In addition, this position is quite similar to the radical movement in psychotherapy (Steiner, 1981) where the explicit aim of the therapy is to enable the individual client to prepare for direct participation in social action groups designed to bring about social change. The aim is to help persons create a new social order that would come closer to meeting the explicitly human needs of every individual in the society.

Further clarification of this complex issue was provided by Dorothy Rowe (1991) in her book *Wanting Everything*. Addressing the concept of power and influence even more directly, she examined what we can and cannot have as well as how power fits into our happiness. She argued that "Power is usually represented as position, wealth and military strength, but this is not what power ultimately is. Power is the right to define reality" (p. 28). She further elaborated that "Power is the ability to get other people to accept your definition of reality" (p. 29). In other words, power is the ability to have an impact on the other's creation of reality (see chapter 15).

The personal construct position is well represented in that Rowe placed the ultimate control in the power debate in the hands of the person. Persons have accepted a definition of a situation that then has profound consequences for them. Rowe (1991, p. 163) made this even clearer later in the book when she asserted that "Power is an illusion because it is no more than a meaning the powerful have created and which the powerless accept as reality." She went on to examine in some detail the illusions the powerful create and the subtle ways various aspects of the social order are arranged so that this definition of what is real is never challenged.

Rowe integrated this view of power with a challenge to understand the nature of the limits to one's ability to obtain everything that might be desired. Some limitations, which she calls *Category One*, include those things that we could potentially obtain. However, we (or other people) withhold those things from ourselves (or us) "by the way we each choose to define ourselves and our world" (p. 33). Other limits, called *Category Two*, are excluded from us by the nature of human life. Our challenge is to accept Category Two limits while recognizing that, with Category One, we are able to exercise our own choices (if we can bear to make them) and get what we want. Not only are we forever making mistakes in distinguishing these two categories, those in power have a great deal invested in keeping us confused and in convincing us that Category One is really Category Two. This confusion ensures the present advantage of the power elite; the rest of us have a way to excuse limits, thereby ensuring the status quo and reducing the threat of change.

Integrating these types of limitations with an understanding of social power allows us to examine social influence from a personal construct perspective. It provides a way to talk about that which is open to change in terms of social and personal construction as opposed to those things that have to be provided for outside of personal choice. While one cannot choose not to die, one can choose how to live. It is a way of talking about the "givens" in personal construct theory. It also provides a way to deal with the issue that a construct system is operating in a way that allows for both personal constructions to be real and for there to be an external world to be reckoned with.

Smail (1987) expressed a similar view when he stated that "Human suffering arises from our embodied interaction with the world whose reality, though it cannot be known, cannot be wished away" (p. 11). While it is not possible for us to live in what is known as the "wish world," we cannot just receive it as any one thing. This analysis provides us with the notion that we need to understand the differences between what we can and what we cannot choose. It provides a way to begin to recognize those things that are construed as possessing certain influence, as if they were given in the world, when in fact they are not. Not allowing ourselves to perform this analysis of determining which things belong to Category One and which belong to Category Two is almost always just a way to keep us confused and to convince us to give up our own reality for what others say it should be.

This is consistent with the introduction of the concept of subscription, a concern with the factors that must be understood in order to account for our adopting the constructions of others as our own, proposed by Epting and Prichard (1993) with respect to psychotherapy. In this process, we accept as reality the constructed meanings that others have provided for us. Such bamboozling commonly occurs between parents and children (Rowe, 1991). While much more needs to be done in understanding this process, this is a way that power and influence can be seen to operate in a personal construct psychology. If one has subscribed to certain meanings, it is possible for those subscriptions to be canceled, although the terms and costs of this cancellation may need to be understood. Such an analysis, however, places the person in an active role that challenges her/him to understand how influence takes place and empowers the person to struggle with what can and cannot be done about it.

IMPLICATIONS FOR SOCIAL INVOLVEMENT

It is our opinion that holding to the central tenets of personal construct psychology predisposes one to certain kinds of social involvement and action. In the spirit of exploration we now undertake the task of seeing how clearly such implications can be shown. This is offered in the invitational mood of personal construct psychology, which is a way of talking about the possibility of such implications rather than asserting some absolute truth concerning these matters.

Perhaps there is no better place to start this exploration than with the very foundation of the theory, constructive alternativism, the fundamental philosophical assertion:

> ... the assumption is that whatever nature may be, or howsoever the quest for truth will turn out in the end, the events we face today are subject to as great a variety of constructions as our wits will enable us to contrive (Kelly, 1955, p. 1).

Such a position makes it very difficult for a person to accept the word of authority in an unquestioning manner. If the person is placed in the position of creating meaning and events in life can be viewed in a number of different ways, it would be very difficult for one to assume a dogmatic position concerning social issues. Dogmatism demands to be maintained; personal constructivism is always open to alternative understandings (see chapter 5).

On a more practical level, assuming such a position implies that a great deal of toleration would be expressed for alternative lifestyles. There is no one way to live; in fact, there might be any number of quite productive and constructive lifestyles. This approach also stands in opposition to prescribing any particular family structure or sets of values as if they were the only way to organize reality. In short, this position leads to the acceptance of pluralistic conceptions of society.[4]

Another example of implications for social action might be found in the case that could be made for nonprejudice against all others. After all, as meaning-making creatures, they are like the self in very important ways. In this regard, Leitner and Pfenninger (1994) speak of transpersonal reverence, in which "the degradation of any race, sex, nationality, etc. becomes a problem for the entire human race" (p. 29). This point was also covered in greater detail in the first part of this paper discussing ROLE relationships. We only want to point out here that the issues discussed in that section can be seen to hold clear implications for social action.

The stance we are assuming in personal construct theory is far from value neutral. Although many psychologists will be distressed at such a value laden position, Kelly (e.g., 1980) viewed values as an intrinsic part of any theory of persons (Walker, 1992). Rather, the initial question—the point of departure for the genuinely adventuresome person—is:

> What should he try to be? Or simply, what ought he to be. I am well aware of the allergy psychologists have for 'oughts'. This is because many of them regard all commitments as coercive. (Kelly, 1980, p. 20)

Hopefully, our essay, rather than pretending to be value-neutral—an impossibility according to personal construct theory—contains many values stemming from the position that the world is not an absolute. In fact, it is more consistent with enabling people to tolerate the unknown and to be able to handle uncertainty and insecurity rather than the opposite side where things are collected, pinned down, and known for certain. It is a position of not investing too much in tradition or set ways without giving yourself a chance for reconstruction. It is our position that this theory leads one to welcome social change if not actively to engage in it. Change is, after all, seen as inevitable from this point of view.

CONCLUDING STATEMENTS

We have undertaken in this paper to cover a lot of territory in a very short amount of space. In addition to elaborating specifically on some of the social implications of personal constructivism, we have attempted to invite you to extend your own imagination into the boundary that appears to separate theory and values, as well as that which seems to separate fact from value. We believe this dividing line is an arbitrary one at best, perhaps nonfunctional in this day and time. Every theory has some value position to take; we have tried to trace some of these in the social direction for personal construct psychology. Like Maslow (1971) when he examined the "fusion of facts and values" (p. 105), we are concerned with the fusion of is and ought. He believed that what you should do about something becomes clearer once you begin to find out more and more about what it is like. Thus, further knowledge leads to clearer values.

We are extending an invitation to you, the reader. We invite you to think about this attempt of ours to take the facts or isness of personal construct psychology and try to trace out the social value implications the theory has. Further, we extend the invitation to come along and see just where it all might take us.

ENDNOTES

1. This chapter was written while the third author was on a Faculty Improvement Leave from Miami University.
2. Dr. Dunnett, formerly of the Redcliffe Centre for Community Psychiatry, Kettering, Northants, U.K., is deceased.
3. See Faidley & Leitner, 1993; Leitner, 1985, 1987, 1988; Leitner & Dill-Standiford, 1993; Leitner & Faidley, 1993, in press; Leitner & Pfenninger, 1994 for a discussion of this previous work.
4. See Epting, 1984 and Epting & Leitner, 1992, for fuller discussions of this point.

REFERENCES

Dunnett, G., & Leitner, L. M. (1990, July). Commonality, sociality, and validation. Paper presented at the North American Personal Construct Network Conference, San Antonio, TX.

Efran, J. S. (1991). Constructivism in the inner city. *Networker*, September/October, 51–52.

Epting, F. R. (1984). *Personal construct counseling and psychotherapy.* New York: Wiley.

Epting, F. R., & Leitner, L. M. (1992). Humanistic psychology and personal construct theory. *The Humanistic Psychologist, 20,* 243–259.

Epting, F. R., & Prichard, S. (1993). An experiential approach to personal meanings in counseling and psychotherapy. In L. M. Leitner & N. G. M. Dunnett (Eds.), *Critical issues in personal construct psychotherapy* (pp. 33–59). Melbourne, FL.: Krieger.

Faidley, A. J., & Leitner, L. M. (1993). *Assessing experience in psychotherapy: Personal construct alternatives.* Westport, CT: Praeger.

Fromm, E. (1973). *The anatomy of human destructiveness.* New York: Holt, Rinehart & Winston.

Giorgi, A. (1992). Whither humanistic psychology? *The Humanistic Psychologist, 20,* 422–438.

Keen, E. (1972). *Psychology and the new consciousness.* Monterey, CA: Brooks-Cole.

Kelly, G. A. (1955). *The psychology of personal constructs* Vols. 1 and 2. New York: Norton.

Kelly, G. A. (1970). A brief introduction to personal construct theory. In D. Bannister (Ed.), *Perspectives in personal construct theory* (pp. 1–30). London & New York: Academic Press.

Kelly, G. A. (1980). The psychology of the optimal man. In A. W. Landfield & L. M. Leitner (Eds.), *Personal construct psychology: Psychotherapy and personality* (pp. 18–35). New York: Wiley Interscience.

Landfield, A. W. (1976). A personal construct approach to suicidal behavior. In P. Slater (Ed.), *Explorations of intrapersonal space* (pp. 93–108). London: Wiley.

Landfield, A. W., & Leitner, L. M. (1980). Personal construct psychology. In A. W. Landfield & L. M. Leitner (Eds.), *Personal construct psychology: Psychotherapy and personality* (pp. 3–17). New York: Wiley Interscience.

Leitner, L. M. (1985). The terrors of cognition: On the experiential validity of personal construct theory. In D. Bannister (Ed.), *Issues and approaches in personal construct theory* (pp. 83–103). London: Academic Press.

Leitner, L. M. (1987). Crisis of the self: The terror of personal evolution. In G. J. Neimeyer & R. A. Neimeyer (Eds.), *Personal construct therapy casebook* (pp. 39–56). New York: Springer.

Leitner, L. M. (1988). Terror, risk, and reverence: Experiential personal construct psychotherapy. *International Journal of Personal Construct Psychology, 1*, 261–272.

Leitner, L. M. (1990, April). *Sharing the mystery: A therapist's experience of personal construct psychotherapy.* Paper presented at the Second British Conference on Personal Construct Psychology, York, England.

Leitner, L. M., & Dill-Standiford, T. (1993). Resistance in experiential personal construct psychotherapy: Theoretical and technical struggles. In L. M. Leitner & N. G. M. Dunnett (Eds.), *Critical issues in personal construct psychotherapy* (pp. 135–155). Melbourne, FL: Krieger.

Leitner, L. M., & Faidley, A. J. (1993). Validation of therapist interventions in psychotherapy: Clarity, ambiguity, and subjectivity. *International Journal of Personal Construct Psychology, 6*, 281–294.

Leitner, L. M., & Faidley, A. J. (in press). The awful, aweful nature of ROLE relationships. In G. J. Neimeyer & R. A. Neimeyer (Eds.), *Advances in personal construct psychology* (Vol. 3). Greenwich, CT: JAI.

Leitner, L. M., & Pfenninger, D. T. (1994). Sociality and optimal functioning. *International Journal of Personal Construct Psychology, 7*, 119–136.

Maslow, A. H. (1971). *The farther reaches of human nature.* New York: Viking Press.

McCoy, M. M. (1977). A reconstruction of emotion. In D. Bannister (Ed.), *New perspectives in personal construct theory* (pp. 93–124). London: Academic Press.

Rowe, D. (1991). *Wanting everything: The art of happiness.* London: Harper Collins Publishers.

Rychlak, J. F. (1990). George Kelly and the concept of construction. *International Journal of Personal Construct Psychology, 3*, 7–19.

Salmon, P. (1990, April). Kelly, then and now. Paper presented at the Second British Conference on Personal Construct Psychology, York.

Smail, D. (1987). *Taking care.* London: Dent.

Soldz, S. (1993). Beyond interpretation: The elaboration of transference in personal construct therapy. In L. M. Leitner & N. G. M. Dunnett (Eds.), *Critical issues in personal construct psychotherapy* (pp. 173–192). Melbourne, FL: Krieger.

Steiner, C. (1981). Radical psychiatry. In R. J. Corsini (Ed.), *Handbook of innovative psychotherapies* (pp. 724–735). New York: Wiley.

Walker, B. M. (1990, September). *Individualism and personal construct theory*. Paper presented at the Fifth Australasian Personal Construct Conference, Adelaide, SA, Australia.

Walker, B. M. (1992). Values and Kelly's theory: Becoming a good scientist. *International Journal of Personal Construct Psychology, 5*, 259–269.

CHAPTER 15

Cultural Construing and Marginalized Persons:
Role Relationships and ROLE Relationships

LARRY M. LEITNER, ELLEN A. BEGLEY, AND
APRIL J. FAIDLEY

The relationship between the person and the external world is complex and poorly understood. On the one hand, the history of psychology has contained theories/worldviews (e.g., some forms of existentialism, some interpretations of traditional psychoanalysis) emphasizing dynamics within the person so extensively that the external world seems to have little impact. On the other hand, there are other theories/worldviews (e.g., behaviorism, cognitive behaviorism, social constructivism) in which the external contexts of our lives are emphasized to the point that the choosing agentic person seems lost within the constraints of external forces.

The field of psychology has lacked theories that combine a respect for the creative, choosing power of the person with a complex appreciation of the role of the external environment, particularly the social/cultural environment, in determining personal actions. It is our contention that personal construct psychology (Kelly, 1991a, b) provides such a theoretical framework, but that this framework, like much of Kelly's theory, has yet to be explored. In this chapter, we elaborate personal construct theory in the direction of realizing its potential for integrating the person and the social world. In so doing, we pay particular attention to the experience of persons who are marginalized within their culture. As Kelly often emphasized, theoretical development that is useless for understanding and improving human lives is of little use to psychology. Thus, an elaboration of the social and cultural aspects of personal construct psychology should touch the lives of those persons most injured within contemporary social systems. We begin this discussion by talking about the nature of the person within personal construct psychology.

A PERSONAL CONSTRUCT UNDERSTANDING
OF THE PERSON

According to Kelly (1991a, b), each of us creates dimensions of personal experience and meaning (termed *personal constructs*) that we use to understand the events confronting us in life. Further, we use our personal constructs as foundations for future actions and understandings of the world. Rather than being merely the sum total of constructs, the person is viewed as the active creator of the meanings of one's life. In this regard, Kelly (1991a) talked about carefully choosing every word in his fundamental postulate and corollaries. In these fundamental theoretical assertions, he carefully distinguished the person who is creating the dimensions of meaning from the meanings themselves. However, since one can only know another through understanding his or her personal meanings (i.e., personal constructs), the other lies enshrouded in mystery, forever just beyond our grasp. We have to struggle with the paradox of understanding the creative mystery of the other (Mair, 1977) through understanding his or her creations (Leitner, 1988).

At a superficial level, Kelly's emphasis on understanding the person's created dimensions of experience may seem to focus on the the inner person to the point that external reality is de-emphasized. However, such an interpretation of Kelly would be seriously in error. Kelly (1991a, p. 5) said quite clearly that the external world plays an important role in his theory:

> We presume that the universe is really existing and that man is gradually coming to understand it. By taking this position we attempt to make clear from the outset that it is a real world we are talking about, not a world composed solely of the flitting shadows of people's thoughts. But we should like, furthermore, to make clear our conviction that people's thoughts also really exist, though the correspondence between what people really think exists and what really does exist is a continually changing one.

In other words, both the inner person and the outer world are important to personal construct psychology.

Persons use the dynamic interplay between inner self and outer world to create the meanings that govern their lives. Personal constructs are neither formed in a vacuum nor dictated to us by the realities we face. All of our constructions are tested against the environmental realities that confront us. However, we also maintain a role in how we experience even the most oppressive of environmental circumstances. This can be seen quite clearly in Kelly's discussion of the role of validation. In this discussion, the person creates the constructs that are tested against challenging world events. The world provides validating or invalidating feedback on the person's creation. The person, however, also decides what evidence is seen as validation and what is seen as invalidation as well as what is done with the constructs that are invalidated. The world provides confirmation or disconfirmation of these decisions. As these cycles continue infinitely, it becomes very difficult to distinguish clearly between the ways the person and the world affect the evolution of personal meanings.

Clearly, then, Kelly saw the "between" as the ground where constructs are formed, tested, validated or invalidated, reformed, hostilely clung to, and so on. Both poles (person and world) are central in the formation of the dimensions of meaningful experience, which is the essence of engaging the world. Discounting either side of this dynamic tension between self and world distorts the very heart of personal construct psychology. Of even more importance, it will result in attempts to understand persons that dishonor those being understood. For example, arguing that those persons exposed to similar oppressive realities are choosing to experience pain or invalidation discounts the effects of prejudice and discrimination on the meaning-making person. On the other hand, arguing that persons exposed to very similar oppressive realities have to see the world in a particular way discounts those persons who have creatively and courageously found other ways of understanding the world. It further discounts the possibility that persons may in the future find creative alternative constructions of these events. In summary, then, the person uses the events of life to create systems of meaning for understanding self and world. In so doing, the person, the world, and the interplay between the two are critical to the process of meaning making. This theoretical reasoning is particularly important when considering the social world. Understanding the critical nature of the social world provides the foundation for understanding the process and the power of cultural construing.

SOCIAL AND CULTURAL CONSTRUING

Kelly was clear that the social world is the most important validator of most psychological construing. This can be seen most profoundly in his sociality corollary: to the extent that one person construes the construction process of another, he or she may play a role in a social process involving the other (Kelly, 1991a, p. 66). Kelly emphasized the importance of this corollary for understanding persons:

> Here we have the take-off point for a social psychology. By attempting to place *at the forefront* of psychology the understanding of personal constructs, and by recognizing, as a corollary of our Fundamental Postulate, the subsuming of other people's construing efforts as *the basis for* social interaction, we have said that social psychology *must be* a psychology of interpersonal understandings, not merely a psychology of common understandings (1991a, p. 67, emphasis added).

According to Landfield and Leitner (1980), "This corollary is so important that Kelly almost entitled his theory 'role theory' " (p. 10). Similarly, Stringer and Bannister (1979) stated "But for Kelly, the person, which is all that his psychology deals with, was only constituted in relations with others; constructs were chiefly available through interaction with others and obtained their meaning in the context of that interaction" (p. xiv).

Kelly elaborated the importance of the relational aspects of the person when he called our most important constructs *core role constructs*: "One's deepest understandings of being maintained as a social being is his concept of his core role" (1991a, p. 370). He later stated "Our constructions of our relations to the thinking and expectancies of certain other people reach down deeply into our vital processes. Through our constructions of our roles we sustain even the most autonomic life functions. These are indeed *core role structures*" (1991b, p. 246, emphasis in original). These statements clearly imply that those scholars (e.g., Salmon, 1990) who construe personal construct theory as being individualistic and lacking an appreciation of the social nature of the person have greatly oversimplified the depth and complexity of Kelly's thought (Dunnett & Leitner, 1990).

Given the vital nature of the interpersonal world for Kelly, it follows that the social world provides the validational contexts for our most important constructions. In a very literal sense, we are alive because of our constructions of our relationships. In an empirical test of Kelly's (1961) hypotheses concerning lethally suicidal individuals, Landfield (1976) found that highly lethal persons use suicide as a means of protecting core role constructs from further interpersonal disconfirmation. Less literally, the affirmation of our most central meanings leads us to the experience of love, contentment, meaning, and reverence (Leitner & Faidley, in press; Leitner & Pfenninger, 1994; McCoy, 1977).

The sociality corollary, so central to Kelly's thought, has a number of specific implications for our interpersonal world. We focus on its implications for the struggle over forming highly intimate relationships (called ROLE relationships) with others. These relationships involve mutually understanding one another's processes of meaning making, not just the content of the constructs. Previous works (Faidley & Leitner, 1993; Leitner, 1985, 1987, 1988; Leitner & Dill-Standiford, 1993; Leitner & Faidley, 1993, in press; Leitner & Pfenninger, 1994) have discussed both the vital necessity and the potential terror (defined as a conglomeration of threat, fear, anxiety, hostility, and guilt; Leitner, 1985) of ROLE relationships as an avenue for meaningfully encountering the world.

Thus, there is a paradox within the struggle over ROLE relationships. On the one hand, the formation of intimate relationships in which each person is affirmed in the uniqueness of his or her process of meaning making is essential for authentically engaging life. On the other hand, since the formation of ROLE relationships is an arduous, time consuming, and potentially terrifying task, most persons spend a great deal of their time in non-ROLE relationships. As a matter of fact, society probably would not be able to function if people engaged exclusively in ROLE relationships. (Think of the implications of having to get to know the unique construing processes of each service station attendant every time you fill up your car.)

Thus, we are challenged with the necessity of forming both intimate and nonintimate understandings of others. These nonintimate understandings are facilitated if groups of us can agree on specific ways of understanding one another. Further, if those of us in a culture develop general, common, agreed-upon meanings, we will have some readily available understandings of others that may provide at least some sense of intimacy. However, in so doing, we begin to construe in a more constellatory fashion, assuming that because we know where an element falls on one construct, we also know where it falls on others. Although these meanings may contain some truth when applied across large numbers of people, we err when we begin to apply these general meanings to the personal others in our lives. Since each person is uniquely situated in his or her approach to the world, these common understandings, by definition, distort the other's experience.

Such stereotypical construing may be particularly common in the initial formation of constructs. When faced with an interpersonal situation for which no (or few) meanings are available, the person is confronted with potentially massive anxiety. For example, children, when initially attempting to construe the social world, have a very limited number of personal meanings, most of which have little to do with the complex personalities of other human beings (Barratt, 1977; Klion & Leitner, 1985). Thus, a child may be faced with two options: either (1) admit to overwhelming anxiety (an awareness that the meanings created to understand one's life are not adequate to the events one is facing) or (2) assume that his or her few interpersonal understandings account for the other's experience. Generalizing beyond the meaning making of children, our protections against such anxiety may invalidate others as they try to elaborate their uniqueness in the face of common cultural constructions. In other words, constellatory construing, while having an important function, serves to limit the formation of ROLE relationships.

As persons search for meaning in the world, they inevitably struggle with deciding how much to protect themselves from the potentially devastating invalidation of others versus how much to risk potential disconfirmation in order to form more meaningful relationships. All of us strive for a middle ground between protection versus risk. A culture functions both to reveal aspects of others to us as well as to protect aspects of others from us. However, culture can only provide common meanings; since each of us is also unique, culture is destined to fail as the sole arbiter of meaning. Further, to the extent that cultural meanings validate us for forming stereotypical relationships, we feel less need to risk the terror of establishing truly intimate relationships. By settling for the validation within the common, we miss others' uniqueness, thereby impoverishing ourselves and others.

SOCIAL VALIDATION

To facilitate our total evolution, the culture would not just validate common meanings; it also would provide opportunities for the validation of our uniqueness. There is an inherent conflict here as the assumptive nature of constellatory cultural construing limits our ability to understand the uniqueness of individual persons. All cultures probably place their citizens in such double binds. While we cannot relate in Western culture without certain shared understandings, to the extent that we, or the others in our lives, deviate from these common understandings, we may be injured by the culture. In addition, we may be injured by the value the important others in our life place on these common understandings.

Thus, as in personal ROLE relationships, each person is charged with the task of looking at the mix of confirmation and disconfirmation given by shared cultural constructs (see Leitner & Faidley, in press). All other things being equal, cultures that provide for the confirmation of more of our personal meanings will be better for us than those that provide for the affirmation of fewer meanings. Further, cultures that confirm our more superordinate (important) constructions will result in greater satisfaction than those that invalidate our more central meanings. However, in contrast to personal ROLE relationships, persons who are extensively invalidated by the culture may not be able to relocate to a culture that will be more affirming. Instead, they may attempt to challenge the culture to evolve greater abilities to affirm different meanings.

However, cultures do more than merely confirm or disconfirm our personal meanings. Through a validational process involving the individuals within it, cultures play a major role in the actual creation of our meanings. For example, parents, teachers, ministers, and so forth can be powerful validating agents (Landfield, 1988) in the development of a child's construing. They may have the power to confirm or disconfirm so many meanings that they literally cocreate, with the child, core constructs that will govern the child's entire life. In other words, through their validational feedback, they play a potent role in the formation of meanings for the child.

This position places these potent validating agents in a predicament. Parents, teachers, and so forth want what is best for those young persons under their care. In particular, they want their children to grow into happy, well-adjusted adults. However, they also know from firsthand experience the unhappiness associated with social invalidation. Thus, although sympathetic to the unique meanings of children, they may be prone to validate more common meanings that are at odds with the child's uniqueness. In other words, even though they may personally desire a child to be free to develop his or her uniqueness, they also are concerned with the pain society might inflict on the child for deviating too much from the shared group meanings. Interestingly, this paradox may have the effect of making parents, teachers, and others agents of the common cultural constructs more than agents of unique individual constructs. In so doing, they act as conservative agents, validating the status quo of a culture more than the unique needs of the person. (Halleck, 1971, makes a similar point about the process of psychotherapy.)

Parents, teachers, and other validating agents can do this to us because they have power. We define power as the ability to act as validating agents for others (i.e., the ability to influence the construction processes of others). It should be pointed out that people with the power to validate our meaning-making process also have the power to invalidate us as persons. In some relationships, the power to validate may be freely given (as in the love relationship). In other relationships, this power may be derived by virtue of social position (e.g., a slave owner). In many relationships, there is some blend of personally given and socially derived power One example is a landlord. We are free not to pay rent to some specific landlord, but since we need shelter and safety, some landlord will have power over us. However, in all cases, the more powerful person can influence the construing process of the less powerful person. (Please note that we are not saying that because these two types of power have the same effect, they are equally good or bad.)

There are both personal and social implications to this definition of power. First, with regard to the personal, each of us gives certain others more power to influence our process of meaning-making. Ideally, we will carefully discriminate between those persons who are more versus less likely to injure our process of construing and only award such power to those most likely to affirm us (Leitner & Pfenninger, 1994). However, even then, we have to deal with the awful experience of sometimes giving power to those who injure us (Leitner & Faidley, in press). Once we give others such power, they codetermine with us what meanings are affirmed and retained or disconfirmed and altered. Thus, they play a major role in the continuing evolution of our process of meaning-making.

The shared meanings defining a culture also result in others having the ability to act as validating agents to us. In this regard, given the constellatory nature of cultural construing, others may be granted such power simply by being members of certain constructed social groups (e.g., men, Caucasians, etc.). As with individuals to whom we grant such power, these groups determine with us what meanings are retained or discarded by the culture, as well as by ourselves as a part of our culture. Members of constructed social groups who possess less power in creating the meanings of the culture can be thought of as marginalized persons.

Cultures, like the persons who participate within them, are not static entities. The shared personal meanings defining a culture continue to evolve. The more powerful constructed groups play a major role in determining the evolution of the culture. Because of the differential assigning of power by the members of a culture, some persons will construe events of having experiences attended to by the culture more than other persons. By way of contrast, marginalized persons may be construing more events around their experiences as discounted. These different events (and, more important, the meanings created to understand these events) can result in the culture evolving in the direction of even greater affirmation of the more powerful members. If greater credence is given to our experiences, we may create meanings based on the assumption that our experience will be attended to. Alternatively, if we are members of marginalized groups, we may create meanings based on the assumption that our experience will be discounted. Thus, the shared personal meanings of the culture may evolve toward even greater affirmation of the powerful and even greater marginalization of the neglected. Members of marginalized groups may not only experience themselves as less powerful, they may experience the more powerful as not understanding their experience of the world, resulting in even greater marginalization.

MARGINALIZED PERSONS' EXPERIENCES OF GUILT AND INTEGRITY

As discussed above, our relationships to our cultures can be construed as mixtures of personal validation and invalidation. A culture that is made up of ROLE relationships for a person is bound to be a dynamic blend of validation and invalidation by virtue of those relationships alone. However, Kelly (1991a) went further in his discussion of culture by asserting that there are "group expectancy-governing constructs" that act as "validators of one's own ROLE constructs" (p. 124). In other words, we not only conceive of our core constructions in the context of our ROLE relations with individuals, but we also form them in accordance with our construal of our surrounding culture as a whole. What we construe to be the shared constructions of our place and time are part of what is assumed in any relationship. These implicit meanings are often left unspoken. Our construction of culture provides a framework for making meaning out of our lives and the lives of others. Thus, our construction of culture mediates all of our relationships. In our human attempts to construe the process of our culture, we invariably experience much validation and invalidation.

Members of a community who do not have a part in the creation of the criteria for validation are in a potentially perilous position in that community. Although the community is set up to validate these members to the degree that they conform to the values of the group, for these people conforming may be experienced as invalidating. If the criteria for validation in that culture requires that the person act against core ROLE constructs, the person may feel painfully bound by two kinds of choices: to conform and give up core ROLE structures or to risk abandonment by acting in conflict with the cultural rules. While people's choices are often a mix of conforming and not conforming, we will discuss these alternatives as though they are more clear-cut in order to describe the bind the person experiences.

For the person in this position, conforming to the expectations of the community may result in experiences of both guilt (the experience of acting against core ROLE constructs) and integrity (the experience of acting consistent with core ROLE structures). A woman who is born into a community that has proscriptions for the behavior of women inconsistent with her core processes may find herself in a terrible bind. To live in a community of shared constructions that invalidate her core ways of engaging the world demands that she compromise on the very dimensions in which she feels most alive.

For example, let us consider a girl who is born into a home and community in which gender roles are rigidly defined. Becoming a woman means eventually becoming the wife of a man. According to the shared construals of her community any elaboration of *woman* that is inconsistent with that construction automatically lies outside of that community. This culture construes preemptively on this matter.

For the most part, in her early years, this girl conforms to and actively participates in the traditional construction of gender. She acquires the appropriate knowledge and skill in anticipation of her prescribed future as a woman. In early adulthood, she experiences love and physical attraction for another woman. The experiences of love and affection in this relationship are profoundly validating to her as a person. She feels alive in this relationship in ways that she does not feel in any other. At the same time, these feelings are tied to total alienation from all of her other current existing ROLE relationships. If she attempts to construct an alternate vision of a woman, she will not be able to exist in her community. She knows that she would be effectively exiled from her family and current community if she lived in a lesbian construction of romantic love.

This woman could attempt to reconstruct what being a woman means and not conform to her culture. This might mean abandoning the only community she has ever known. Instead of facing that exile, she chooses to conform to the proscriptions of her culture. In making this choice she maintains the important, validating relationships that bring ongoing meaning to her life while sacrificing deeply passionate romantic relationships.

This decision is experienced as both validating and invalidating. This woman has the validation of many of the most important people in her life. However, conforming to the culture is also invalidating to her because in order to gain validation as a woman, she has compromised on other core constructs. This compromise is compounded by the realization that she has less say in creating the criteria for validation in her community. As a result, she may not experience her decision as having been as freely chosen as the choices of the people in nonmarginalized positions.

In choosing not to conform, one may also be risking life itself. Kelly (1991b) wrote of how a member of a community who commits a "taboo" behavior "may not be able to sustain life" as a result of this dislodgement from core ROLE structure (p. 246). When core ROLE structure is on the line, one's basic biological processes may be threatened. To elaborate core ROLE constructions outside of socially sanctioned boundaries requires that one attempt to live outside of the cultural story that sustains much of social life. Acting outside of the cultural norms may validate some core ROLE constructs but also result in the loss of relationships that act as important validators for other core ROLE constructs. The marginalized person who chooses *not* to conform to the prevailing culture may also experience integrity and guilt at the same time.

For example, if the woman in our earlier example chose to act on her desire to be romantically involved with a woman, she would experience integrity with regard to acting consistently with this core construction of herself as well as guilt around not meeting the expectations of her community. If her constructions of her romantic love relationships are central to how she sees herself as an evolving relational being, she may choose to act in accordance with these constructs. In so doing, she may be making the choice to be alive in her relationships and risk even more of herself in those relationships than she would if she followed the proscriptions of her culture. This experience of integrity may be continually validated in a relationship that affirms this woman as a lovable human being.

She may also experience guilt over acting against the constructions that she once shared with her community—the constructions of what a good daughter, sister, wife, lover, mother, and female friend are. Until she can fully reconstrue her idea of what a woman is she may feel, in some ways, incongruent with her own vision of herself. Such total reconstruction may take a very long time. Years later, she may still experience guilt upon realizing, at some heretofore unseen level, that she has invalidated the core constructions of the people closest to her. The knowledge that who she is has fundamentally threatened the personal meanings of important others can be devastating. If she leaves her community, she will experience the loss of the relationships in which most of her constructions of herself have grown.

BRAKES ON THE AFFIRMATION OF
THE MORE POWERFUL

There are some brakes on this tendency of cultures to evolve toward the even greater affirmation of the more powerful. First, people as members of different constructed social groups continue to interact with one another. These interactions must be understood as they are events in our lives. Due to the relational nature of the person for Kelly, persons will strive toward some understanding of others as meaning-making creatures. In so doing, they will begin a process of construing one another's construing process, the natural tendency toward forming ROLE relationships (Leitner, 1985). Since ROLE relationships cannot be extensively developed in the presence of highly constellatory construing based on social groupings, both persons in a ROLE relationship must be able to transcend the common social meanings in order to reach the person of the other.

Another brake on the unchecked evolution of cultures toward affirming the more powerful can be seen in the need for contrast, inherent in personal construct psychology. One can only create meanings through the simultaneous experience of generalizing and contrasting. Contrast is essential; each pole of the dialectic derives some meaning due to its relationship to the contrasting pole (Kelly, 1991a, b). Due to constellatory cultural constructs, the members of more powerful groups within a culture have the experience of others invalidating them. Although these experiences are not as pervasive as those experienced by members of marginalized groups, they can be extremely useful in highlighting the horrors of such disconfirmation. As most therapists who work with traumatized persons know, a person who has been more consistently invalidated actually may be more numb to the pain than someone who has been more affirmed by life. Thus, paradoxically, there are ways in which members of constructed social groups with more power may be more empathic to the despair of marginalized persons than some marginalized persons themselves. It should be emphasized that this possibility cannot occur unless the member of the more powerful group uses the disconfirmation to understand more fully the experiences of those who have been marginalized.

These brakes notwithstanding, marginalized persons still engage a culture in which the construction of social groups results in their experiencing more disconfirmation than others in the culture. Further, the continued objectification of others through cultural constellatory construing impacts the potential to develop ROLE relationships for all persons in the culture. In so doing, opportunities for experiencing transpersonal reverence (reverence for all persons), an important aspect of optimal functioning (Leitner & Pfenninger, 1994), is limited. However, since the more powerful members of a culture play a major role in determining what is affirmed, change, no matter how necessary, can be difficult to effect.

CHANGE MOVEMENTS

Alternative cultural groups are one way of affirming parts of us that are different from the shared meanings of the broader culture. These groups, which are also socially constructed, can validate meanings ignored by the larger culture. In so doing, they are a vital step in the transition of the larger culture toward one that affirms more personal meanings. We discuss three ways in which this transition might be understood, recognizing that there are innumerable other ways of construing this process (Kelly, 1991a): (1) the affirmation of parts of our uniqueness, (2) contrast reconstruction, and (3) the demand for social validation and reintegration into the larger culture.

The Affirmation of Parts of Our Uniqueness

Due to our inherent sociality, we need others to validate central parts of our process of meaning-making. Others who have created meanings like ours are more likely to validate us than those whose meanings differ markedly (e.g., Duck, 1973). Meanings that are affirmed become tighter, clearer, more strongly held, and more critical to our identity. As we become more confident in these meanings, they can play a more central role in governing life. Further, due to their being more validated, these meanings are associated more with emotions like pride and joy than with shame and disgust (McCoy, 1977). For example, the formation of civil rights groups in the 1960s and 1970s led to movements like Black Pride and Black is Beautiful in the United States. As we take more pride in some of our unique meanings, we often experience contrast reconstruction.

Contrast Reconstruction

Contrast reconstruction, or slot change (Kelly, 1991b), is simply changing from one pole of a construct to the contrasting pole. The system itself is not reorganized. Rather, elements are rearranged. For example, assume someone has two constructs (African-American versus Caucasian and superior versus inferior) that have been organized for them such that African-Americans tend to be inferior and Caucasians tend to be superior. Slot change might occur by the person now seeing African-Americans as superior and Caucasians as inferior. Neither the constructs themselves nor the relationships between the constructs have changed. Thus, the construing system is unaltered; only the placement of the groups within the system has changed. Since most painful psychological issues are challenges to our system of construing, such simple change tends not to be very effective in leading to optimal relationships.

Contrast reconstruction often is the first type of change persons risk when reconstruing. It makes use of the hostility and anger that can be associated with the experience of being marginalized. Further, since it is easier to accomplish, this type of change can be less threatening than more fundamental reorganizations of the entire system (Kelly, 1991b; Leitner, 1985). Further, the placing of the self on the contrasting poles of constructs may be a useful precursor to more fundamental change. After experience has been gained on both poles of a construct, new superordinate structures may be created in which both poles of the preexisting construct are subsumed by the newer meaning.

With regard to persons in marginalized groups, contrast reconstruction often shows itself in terms of members viewing everything associated with their group as good and everything associated with the more dominant culture as bad. Thus, whites cannot be trusted, Eurocentric worldviews are the bane of the planet, Afrocentric worldviews are the key to the planet's salvation, etc. In this way, they have reversed the placement of self and other on this basic dimension, although they still are using the same construct system. One negative impact of this contrast reconstruction is that some members of the dominant culture will retreat from engaging the marginalized person due to their feelings of distress at being construed so negatively. If the members of the dominant culture and the members of the marginalized group are to continue relating, both will need courage. They will need to believe that the members of both groups respect one another, want to deal with one another, and have the entire group's best interests at heart. The members of the dominant group will need the courage to construe the pain of the marginalized person. The marginalized person will have to find the courage to construe the members of the dominant group in nonconstellatory ways.

Demand for Social Validation and Reintegration

As we become clearer about personal meanings, we can begin the process of asking the larger culture to validate the parts of us that have not been confirmed before. After all, despite the validation from our particular subgroup, we still are part of a larger culture that will continue to play a powerful role in our ongoing meaning-making activities. With greater clarity about the meanings that need to be affirmed, a more constructive dialogue can now take place among different members of the culture. Malcolm X, for example, after initially railing against all Caucasians, eventually grew to see the value of working with persons of all races in his quest (Haley, 1990). The marginalized person can educate others about the personal meanings in need of greater social affirmation. A new social consensus is built.

THE MISSING PERSONAL—PERSONAL RESPONSIBILITY

Without the person, there would be no social protest. In educating members of a culture as to how cultural assumptions affect us deeply, it is important that we do not neglect the power of the person. The tendency of people to simplify the individual and the world results in constellatory construing. Change movements, for example, may conceptualize social construing as the driving force in the world. Great emphasis may be placed on the social nature of the world while the individual nature of the world may be downplayed. In the same way, the excessive individual emphasis of the culture has resulted in the marginalized person feeling greatly misunderstood. Thus, the new social constructs, like all cultural constructs, may be applied in a more constellatory manner. Cultural constructs tend to get reified, particularly because they are learned relatively early in life, at a time when it is believed people are discovering the nature of the world, not realizing that with their constructions they are creating a world with a given nature. As such, the new cultural constructs created out of the dialogue between a change movement and the larger culture tend not to be used with an appreciation of the power of the person to use the social world to create meanings that have not been seen before. Thus, fundamentally, each of us is ultimately responsible for the meanings we create in dialogue with the others in our culture. Until the person, as an integration of the individual and the social, is understood and respected more, cultures will marginalize and alienate groups.

ACKNOWLEDGMENTS

This chapter was written while the first author was on a Faculty Improvement Leave sponsored by Miami University. We extend our appreciation to Kim Collier for offering comments on an earlier draft of the manuscript.

REFERENCES

Barratt, B. B. (1977). The development of peer perception systems in childhood and early adolescence. *Social Behavior and Personality, 5,* 351–360.

Duck, S. (1973). *Personal relationships and personal constructs.* London: Wiley.

Dunnett, N. G. M., & Leitner, L. M. (1990, July). Commonality, sociality, and validation. Paper presented at the North American Personal Construct Network Conference, San Antonio, TX.

Faidley, A. J., & Leitner, L. M. (1993) *Assessing experience in psychotherapy: Personal construct alternatives,* Westport, CT: Praeger.

Haley, A. (1990). *The autobiography of Malcolm X.* New York: Ballantine.

Halleck, S. (1971). *The politics of therapy.* New York: Science House.

Kelly, G. A. (1961). Suicide: The personal construct point of view. In N. L. Farberow & E. S. Schneidman (Eds.), *The cry for help* (pp. 255–280). New York: McGraw-Hill.

Kelly, G. A. (1991a). *The psychology of personal constructs* (Vol. 1). London: Routledge & Kegan Paul.

Kelly, G. A. (1991b). *The psychology of personal constructs* (Vol. 2). London: Routledge & Kegan Paul.

Klion, R. E., & Leitner, L. M. (1985). Construct elicitation techniques and the production of interpersonal concepts in children. *Social Behavior and Personality, 13,* 137–142.

Landfield, A. W. (1976). A personal construct approach to suicidal behavior. In P. Slater (Ed.), *Explorations of intrapersonal space* (pp. 93–108). Chichester: Wiley.

Landfield, A. W. (1988). Personal science and the concept of validation. *International Journal of Personal Construct Psychology, 1,* 237–249.

Landfield, A. W., & Leitner, L. M. (1980). Personal construct psychology. In A. W. Landfield & L. M. Leitner (Eds.), *Personal construct psychology: Psychotherapy and personality* (pp. 3–17). New York: Wiley Interscience.

Leitner, L. M. (1985). The terrors of cognition: On the experiential validity of personal construct theory. In D. Bannister (Ed.), *Issues and approaches in personal construct theory* (pp. 83–103). London: Academic Press.

Leitner, L. M. (1987). Crisis of the self: The terror of personal evolution. In G. J. Neimeyer & R. A. Neimeyer (Eds.), *Personal construct therapy casebook* (pp. 39–56). New York: Springer.

Leitner, L. M. (1988). Terror, risk, and reverence: Experiential personal construct psychotherapy. *International Journal of Personal Construct Psychology, 1,* 261–272.

Leitner, L. M., & Dill-Standiford, T. J. (1993). Resistance in experiential personal construct psychotherapy: Theoretical and technical struggles. In L. M. Leitner & N. G. M. Dunnett (Eds.), *Critical issues in personal construct psychotherapy* (pp. 135–155). Melbourne, FL: Krieger.

Leitner, L. M., & Faidley, A. J. (1993). Validation of therapist interventions in psychotherapy: Clarity, ambiguity, and subjectivity. *International Journal of Personal Construct Psychology, 6,* 281–294.

Leitner, L. M., Faidley, A. J. (in press). The awful, aweful nature of ROLE relationships. In G. J. Neimeyer & R. A. Neimeyer (Eds.),

Advances in personal construct psychology (Vol. 3). Greenwich, CT: JAI.

Leitner, L. M., & Pfenninger, D. T. (1994) Sociality and optimal functioning. *International Journal of Personal Construct Psychology*, 7, 119–136.

Mair, J. M. M. (1977). Metaphors for living. In J. K. Cole & A. W. Landfield (Eds.), *Nebraska symposium on motivation* (vol. 24, pp. 243–290). Lincoln: University of Nebraska Press.

McCoy, M. M. (1977). A reconstruction of emotion. In D. Bannister (Ed.), *New perspectives in personal construct theory* (pp. 93–124). London: Academic Press.

Salmon, P. (1990, April). Kelly then and now. Address to the Second British Conference on Personal Construct Psychology, York, England.

Stringer, P., & Bannister, D. (1979). Introduction. In P. Stringer & D. Bannister (Eds.), *Constructs of sociality and individuality* (pp. 1–3). London & New York: Academic Press.

CHAPTER 16

The Social Construction of Powerfulness and Powerlessness

ULRIKE WILLUTZKI AND LOTHAR DUDA

In this chapter we discuss the concept of power and describe how, from a social constructionist perspective, power is exerted in specific contexts. We begin with a description of our basic premises and relate them to the ideas of G. A. Kelly (which we aim to develop further by our contribution). After application of this perspective in three different realms of social life, implications for the use of the concept of power are discussed.

THE CONCEPT OF POWER FROM A SOCIAL CONSTRUCTIONIST PERSPECTIVE: AN INTRODUCTION

What does a social constructionist perspective—in this case on power—mean? Like other constructivists, social constructionists do not perceive reality as a duplicate of the outside world or an image that corresponds (more or less correctly) to the world around us but as our construction of (a) reality. In contrast to a number of other approaches (for example, Maturana, 1985; Richards & von Glasersfeld, 1979; Roth, 1992), they are not as concerned with justifying the assumption of a construed reality by referring to individual mechanisms and processes at work. Instead, social constructionists are interested in the communal aspects of reality constructions, that is, their social nature. By studying such concepts as love (Averill, 1985), aggression (Averill, 1982; Gergen, 1984), emotions (Lutz, 1988; Potter, 1988), or the self (Gergen, 1991), and the social practices connected with them, social constructionists focus on interpsychic processes, namely, the form and content of the dis-

341

course between individuals. According to this view, whatever we seem to know of the world is determined by the constructions available in specific cultures at certain times: "The terms in which the world is understood are social artifacts, products of historically situated interchanges among people" (Gergen, 1985, p. 5). In everyday interaction, in a kind of "conversational apparatus" (Berger & Luckmann, 1966), the individual's world views are supported, validated, challenged, and also changed.

Therefore, the discourse, the way people talk about certain subjects, is of primary significance. Following Weingarten (1991), several aspects are important in this context:

1. Discourse comprises the ideas, practices, and values related to a certain topic that are common in a given historical situation.

2. Every discourse reflects, constructs, and reconstructs a particular worldview.

3. Discourse changes continually. These changes can be conceptualized as the transformation of culturally available dominant narratives about people's lives and the world by collective conversations. In interaction, ideas that contrast with currently influential discourses emerge and in a way challenge the respective world construction. Such contrasts may be rather minute (just introducing a peripheral differentiation, such as distinguishing a further source of power as do Raven & Rubin, 1983) or may apply to basic premises (for example, characterizing power as a myth as in Bateson, 1972).

4. A discourse can be looked upon as dominant (that is, widely accepted as the proper world construction) or as, following Foucault (1992), subjugated. (Note that even subjugated discourse can be locally dominant.) The dominant discourse defines and constrains what we can feel, think, and do.

5. That which is not part of the discourse (be it only implied, tabooed, or just nonexistent) shapes our experience as critically as the discourse itself.

Implicit in this characterization of features of discourse is a specific construction of power. Power is not produced by individual intentions or a ruling class, a power elite, particular institutions, or specific systems of repression. Instead, "power is everywhere; not because it embraces everything, but because it comes from everywhere" (Foucault, 1980, p. 94). Power is seen as exerted in and through discourse. Thus, discourse analysis can be regarded as the analysis of power relations. These relations are not to be understood as static, unchanging forms of domination or submission, but characterized as dialogic (Foucault, 1980, pp. 29ff.). Subjects and their domains, intentions, and behaviors are constituted rather than caused by power relations. To study power relations means to analyze the discourse because both of these condition and constitute each other: "There are manifold relations of power which permeate, characterize, and constitute the social body, and these relations of power cannot themselves be established, consolidated nor implemented without the production, accumulation, circulation and functioning of a discourse" (Foucault, 1980, p. 93). Discourse is not just a translation of the systems of domination and the struggle for power into language; rather it is when the fighting takes place and what is fought for. "The discourse is the power one attempts to seize" (Foucault, 1972, p. 11). Thus, the issue of power is to establish a dominant discourse that defines a certain world perspective and challenges or constrains others. To have power means to define reality (Portele, 1989).

Recently, related definitions from a personal construct perspective have been proposed by Walker (1990); Rowe (1991); Epting, Prichard, Leitner and Dunnett (chapter 14); Leitner, Begley, and Faidley (chapter 15); and Kalekin-Fishman (1995). While we share their emphasis on the construction of reality as a power issue, we think these definitions focus too much on the powerholder and thus are in danger of reifying the power concept. The ability to get other people to accept my definition of reality, or in Leitner, Begley and Faidley's terms, to "act as a validating agent for others," depends not merely on my specific behavior, but ultimately on the powerless person and his or her construct system. Following Kelly, the person him- or herself has to construe my (re)actions as a challenge to his or her worldview or at least as somehow relevant in order to have an impact. Thus, we'd like to emphasize the relational or coconstructive aspects of the power issue.

Moreover, as constructivists, we do not think of Foucault's view on discourse as representing the world as it is. Even though we find his position very useful in order to analyze power, we keep in mind the warning of Bateson when he characterized power " . . . as a myth, which, if everybody believes in it, becomes to that extent self-validating" (1972, p. 487). Following Bateson, the ascription of power and powerlessness just amounts to a specific punctuation of the flow of interactions that creates or constructs a certain relation. And there may be ample reason to construe it differently. Consequently, in the framework of Kelly's concept of constructive alternativism, "all of our present interpretations of the universe are subject to revision or replacement" (Kelly, 1991, p. 11).

By applying Kelly's recursive and self-reflexive stance to power, we hope to move the discourse onward with our analysis of the topic, so as to at least seize the chance for change—without assuming naively that we can altogether step out of this circle.

Thus, to use the concept of power means to construe power-thematic relationships, to anticipate respective behavior for oneself and others, and to act accordingly, or from a Kellian perspective, to assign the construct powerful-powerless a central role in one's construct system. Other constructions would open other possibilities.

Our position can be summed up as follows: No such phenomenon as power exists independently of an observer in the real world. Power is rather a communal construction with implications (possibilities as well as dangers) specific to a social context. It is a concept that people use to describe their inferences about persons and situations within the framework of their communal subsystem and its language games (Wittgenstein, 1953). As there is no such entity as power, any interaction can be constructed as power-thematic, and any bringing up of the topic of power can be denied.

In the following sections we illustrate this approach by looking at the way the concept of power is dealt with in everyday life before turning to discourse patterns that we construe as power-relevant.

Power in Everyday Use

In general, it seems to us that power as an explicit topic has almost vanished from everyday discourse. In comparison with the late 1960s and early 1970s when from an egalitarian and civil rights perspective power relations were often regarded as a primary subject, people now seem to avoid or even reject the word power as an appropriate description of relationships.

For example, politicians or executives represent themselves as having responsibility and influence, as having the legitimate right to make far-reaching (and often irreversible) decisions. They construe themselves as fighting for truth, caring about the citizens' welfare, and carrying the heavy burden of responsibility. Yet they still do not see themselves as having power, but rather as being powerless and forced by circumstances beyond their control, or simply the facts, to do what has to be done.

If anybody at all is explicitly supposed to have power, it is the people, the voters. This position is expressed pointedly in the saying: All power rests upon the people. But in most cases, when the people speak up (for example, when demonstrating for nuclear disarmament, for peace, or against abortion laws), politicians explicitly characterize these claims as illegitimate or irrational pressure that has to be resisted. So, in contrast to the perspective taken particularly in sociology (e.g., Weber, 1964), politics and power are not consistently associated in everyday discourse. Likewise, the word *power* is not accepted as applicable by many people in authority (e.g., politicians or university administrators). They regard themselves as fulfilling their responsibilities or following the rules and hardly ever focus on the selection processes, the granting and denial of chances that is a central feature of their jobs.

Politics and administration are just examples of hierarchically organized fields where people have different degrees of influence in the system because of the organizational design. Such organizational structures are an important avenue to attaining status. Still, the power that is exerted this way is kept hidden if possible. Why does it seem to be so problematic to describe blatantly asymmetrical relationships such as power relations? What happens once someone brings up the term *power* to describe a certain relationship? What do people mean when they talk about powerful and powerless persons?

As power is a bipolar construct whereby we differentiate between those in power and those who are powerless or dominated, we will look at both sides consecutively. First, what does it mean if someone describes others or him- or herself as powerless? Interestingly enough, such descriptions can have two apparently contradictory implications. On the one hand they may imply a reproach against those who are thought to be in power and thus dominate others. The powerless person doubts whether the powerful person has the right to decide upon a controversial topic. S/he makes it clear that s/he is not willing to accept what is going on, that at least s/he will not regard it as a collaborative decision. The topic of power in these cases is raised in order to change the relationship, to challenge the decisions and the status of those who are in power. On the other hand, people often characterize themselves (and others) as powerless in order to explain why they do not try to change relationships and decisions they regard as illegitimate, unjust, or irrational. In these cases, talking about being powerless reflects a stance of resignation and at the same time a denial of any responsibility for the current state of affairs. Ultimately, it leads to the stabilization of a specific situation by blocking access to resources for challenging it. Steiner (1981) described this attitude as relying on a myth: the myth that in principle and ultimately everybody is powerless.

Characterizing someone or oneself as powerful can also be interpreted in different ways. On the one hand, those described as powerful, often by others, may construe it as a challenge to their status, opinions, and decisions, as an attack that asks for changes in their behavior or at least calls for a more elaborate legitimation. Engaging in legitimation implies a certain risk for the powerful as they cannot be sure their line of reasoning will be accepted. In such situations we therefore often find efforts by the powerful to challenge the use of the word *power* altogether.

On the other hand, those described as powerful may gladly accept that characterization. They may regard it as an acceptance of their superior position, as the ascriber's insight into their legitimate and rational dominance, be it by birth or because of their rewards. They may feel like an elite and see those who describe them as powerful as clear-sighted realists. With this stance they institutionalize or even ontologize the status quo.

Looking at the implications of the ascription of powerful- or powerlessness, we thus find an ambiguous picture. The concept can be used (and understood) as a challenge to or critique of a certain state of affairs, and it can also be used and understood as an acknowledgment or verification of the same constellation.

These patterns can be interpreted in a framework originally proposed by Lukes (1982) for scientific conceptualizations of power. According to Lukes, concepts of power tend to describe either a symmetrical relation between power-holders and the powerless by assuming that the consensus between them is reached unanimously such that both are in agreement on the goal-state they want to attain (see for example Weber, 1964, and Raven & Rubin, 1983). By contrast, the second interpretation features an asymmetrical relation: The powerless are forced to consent, which means that their own goals are attained only in part or not at all. If the powerless agree with the goals set by the agent exerting influence, they do so as a result of the power held and exercised by that agent. The first perspective supplies a conception of power in terms of cooperation and consensus; the second one gives a picture of power in terms of hierarchy and domination. The first perspective also implies a notion of stability and homeostasis, whereas the second one is more easily associated with change and perturbation. In the explicit discourse on power, interlocutors often disagree on whether the symmetrical or the asymmetrical concept depicts reality. It is difficult as well to ascertain what implications the powerful-powerless construct really has.

Since the ethos of democratic industrial countries (or at least of the subculture we live in) does not favor an explicitly asymmetrical power theory, people in power tend to avoid the term *power*. Its critical potential can thus be brushed aside and the image of cooperation, rationality, and shared responsibility can be maintained.

As the reader may have noticed, we do not accord a privileged status to symmetrical power concepts. We are interested in the ways by which one world perspective is established at the expense of another. Therefore, in the next section we will analyze a rather common strategy for gaining superiority before turning to a specific setting that we construe as particularly power-relevant. The following observations were collected and systematized by the *Bochumer Arbeitsgruppe, für Sozialen Konstruktivismus und Wirklichkeitsprüfung* within the framework of what we have called *Wirklichkeitsprüfung*, that is, the study of reality as the study of the ways reality is depicted in discourse. (For a more detailed discussion of the methodological and epistemological background, see Bochumer Arbeitsgruppe, 1990, 1991.)

The examples presented in the next sections are looked upon as behavioral experiments (Kelly, 1970) following from the construct powerful-powerless. Even though we presume our construction is quite understandable and common—or from a social constructionist perspective, communally anchored—we would like to draw the reader's attention to the fact that we as participant-observers have construed these instances as means for dominating and invalidating other constructions.

PSYCHOLOGIZING AS A STRATEGY TO EXERT POWER

A widespread strategy that interests us particularly—maybe because of our professional affiliation as psychologists—is psychologizing. This is the use of psychological concepts, metaphors, scripts, or structures in order to achieve definitional power/superiority. Motives, values, powers, dispositions, deficits, or pathologies are attributed or interpreted because of some observable behavior (or the lack of some behavior). For example:

- "You're only avoiding that because you're afraid of anything new!"

- "Somehow it's strange that you cannot accept that . . . "

- "I think John wasn't arrogant but only shy."

- "Why is that a problem for you . . . ?"

This discourse strategy rests upon the common assumption that behavior can be looked at as a sign, as something with a surplus meaning, determined by some psychological cause. Laypersons are not the only ones to hold this assumption. Influential scientific psychological theories, for example dispositional and psychoanalytic theories, are also grounded in it. Whereas Kelly (1991) ridiculed scientific theories that rely heavily on psychologizing, it seems important to note that the strategy is widely used in everyday interaction and often has rather harmful or vicious consequences. Thus, a more comprehensive analysis seems appropriate.

For those who psychologize, the underlying psychological dimension becomes much more interesting than the behavior itself as it explains and ultimately qualifies the behavior. It can lead to a favorable interpretation of what is at first sight highly unpleasant behavior or to the unfavorable interpretation of what to a naive observer is acceptable behavior. Someone who beats his children/wife may do so "only because he wants them to get along well in life." Or someone who is friendly to you maybe "only wants you to support his/her aims." The overt behavior itself becomes quite uninteresting, highly ambiguous, and even deceptive. Doing something or not doing it can be interpreted as indicating the same underlying psychological reason ("He did not talk because he is so shy" or "He talked all the time because he's so shy").

Two dimensions of these discourse patterns seem particularly important to us. First, the cause of the behavior can be thought to be closer in time to the actual behavior ("he did that because you just offended him") or more deep-rooted ("he did that because he always thinks he has to fight"). Additionally, the underlying cause can be characterized as known, in principle knowable, or unknowable to the person who is driven by it. In a kind of popularized psychoanalysis, the psychologizing person says that the analyzed person would never admit "it" because s/he could not tolerate "it" ("it" would hurt him/her too much).

The latter dimension is particularly interesting in order to discount the other person's perspective. When someone regards the reasons for another person's behavior as in principle not knowable to that person, there is no basis for disputing the interpretation or engaging in a dialogue about it. Furthermore, in many cases denying the attributed interpretation is even seen as a confirmation of the interpretation. The person thus has no chance to escape. A very vivid example of this strategy is Rosenhan's field experiment. People who pretended to have delusions were admitted to mental hospitals. They had a very hard time getting out again because their claim that they did not have the delusions any more was judged as a lack of insight into the severity of their disease. On the other hand, still talking about delusions could not be accepted as a sign of mental health either (Rosenhan, 1973).

Psychologizing is a widely used discourse strategy because it is a very potent means to get control. The person who introduces any kind of psychological interpretation sets the stage and defines a new context. The person whose behavior is subjected to these interpretations has to react, be it to refuse the use of such strategies altogether, be it to defend him- or herself, or be it to correct the interpretation. The strategy often serves to turn a socially relevant request or problem into an unfounded opinion that can be attributed to the individual's deviant, deformed, or pathological structure and therefore should be dismissed, neglected, and ignored. Thus by psychologizing, at least the claim or request that was made is discredited; in many cases the attack also serves to devalue the whole person.

What can the attacked person do to cope and still get her or his point across? S/he may try to ignore the turn altogether and hope that her or his status in the contextual field is high enough so that the strategy will not be regarded as acceptable by the rest of the audience. The situation becomes more complicated when the relationship is formally more or less symmetrical or, even worse, when the person making psychological assessments has a somewhat higher status. In these cases the victim has to react to the attack, invalidate it or prove his or her sanity, and provide proper reasons for holding such an opinion. Then s/he may eventually return to the point s/he wanted to make. The problem is: Will her or his explanation be accepted? If s/he is generally unable to know the true causes of her or his behavior, how can s/he explain inconsistencies that the knowing beholder has noticed?

If the attacked person is not supported by anybody or if the interlocuters agree on the importance of a specific psychologizing theory, it is quite unlikely that her or his request will survive the strategy. Group settings are particularly dangerous in this context. The psychologizing challenge can be validated directly by the others' approval (quite likely when it comes from a person with a higher status, e.g., the faculty board), thereby turning it into a communal myth that is supposed to represent the world as it is.

Ascribing psychological motives has to be accepted in the given communal subsystem. That is why the strategy is so popular in professionally proficient subcultures. There is psychoculture in which it is generally acceptable to interpret oneself and others as quite complicated, psychologically determined persons. Another such subculture is a human services context where professionals are regarded as superior knowers of psychological functioning. Still, psychologizing is not restricted to these subcultures as in almost every sphere of modern life it is common to interpret behavior and look for underlying motives. Good examples are the TV commentators on sports and armchair analysts of the workings of the economy.

Whereas we analyzed a general strategy to dominate other world perspectives in this section, we now turn to a concrete setting and show how different power strategies complement and support each other.

POWER IN A SPECIFIC SOCIAL SETTING: THE FACULTY BOARD

We now present an example of how power—as we would like to feature and accentuate it—is communally constructed in the specific setting of a faculty board meeting.

In a field project we conducted systematic observations in order to characterize how the powerful and the powerless act and interact in faculty board meetings. While doing this, our intention was of course not to come up with a true representation of reality but to illustrate how the use of the power construct can be helpful in organizing specific instances of power in action. We start by describing the organizational constructs relevant to the expression of power in this context and then move to an account of verbal and nonverbal indicators of power-thematic constructs provided by the powerful and the powerless during their interactions. Finally, we discuss coping strategies that could be adopted by the powerless.

Power-relevant organizational constructs

We conducted our observations during a number of board meetings at a West German university over a period of several months. Such a committee typically consists of members of the four groups that live, struggle, and survive in a university community: students, nonacademic employees (e.g., secretaries), academic employees, and professors.

The number of representatives of each group does not directly correspond to its actual size but is determined by the relevant administrative laws that ensure a majority of professors on all important bodies.

In our study the faculty board consisted of:

- 2 persons representing about 1,000 students

- 2 persons representing about 50 nonacademic employees

- 2 persons representing about 50 academic employees

- 9 persons representing 14 professors.

This means that roughly 70% of the professors (the powerful) are members of the board; i.e., each professor speaks practically for him/herself. The nonacademic and the academic employees are represented by roughly 4% of their groups and the students are represented by roughly 0.2% of their members. Members of these three groups (the powerless) are therefore forced to agree on positions of compromise among themselves before each meeting in order to protect their interests. On the other hand, the powerful discuss their strategy during an informal get-together a week before the actual board meeting and therefore have usually already reached agreement on how to handle the items on the agenda.

The agenda and the rules of procedure are something the powerless (are expected to) stick to, whereas the powerful do not have to stand for that. Throughout the course of events, most of the powerful sit next to one another at the upper half of the table (close to the chairperson). They are allowed to structure the whole meeting, plan the course of the discussion (who is allowed to talk, when, and for how long), and determine when it is time to come to a decision. The powerful do not have to stick to the order of speakers and may speak after the discussion has already been closed, while at the same time pointing out to the powerless that the discussion has been closed. Not only can the powerful interrupt and talk when someone powerless is speaking, but they are even allowed to interfere with an ongoing vote if a result that is not in their favor can be foreseen.

On the other hand, the powerless, who sit close to each other in pairs, often ask to speak but are often not allowed to do so. During one meeting they made 22 requests but were given the floor only 9 times. They begin to speak without being addressed only if they have been overlooked very pointedly. Otherwise, they do not cut in or interrupt while others are talking.

Behavior of the powerful

Let us start with the verbal behavior demonstrated by the powerful. The powerful:

- speak slowly and distinctly.

- do not present their ideas and opinions on certain items as suggestions, but as generally binding and valid statements such as "As has already been discussed . . . " "Of course we ought to. . . . " However, if the powerless nevertheless try to start an argument about such a topic, the powerful simply move on to the next point on the agenda: "This fruitless discussion is not getting us anywhere!" "Let's leave it at that and move on to the next item!" "Please stop interrupting the meeting!"

- are allowed to determine once and for all what actually makes sense and is important, what is possible, even what is "true." The naive-realistic matter-of-fact statements made by the powerful are short, firm, and definitive: "These are the facts!" "That idea is senseless!" "I never said that!" Interrupting comments made by the powerful are "That's it!" "Precisely!" "Right on!" "Ridiculous!"

- are allowed to deal with contributions made by the powerless in any way they wish without interference. The powerful may evaluate, analyze, and classify suggestions made by the powerless; treat them with irony; or generally discredit them: "Well, this idea doesn't lead us anywhere!" "Thank you for elaborating my argument!" "This is irrelevant!" "That won't make your work any easier, remember that!"

- point out how limited their time is. Ample statements are: "I've got another appointment after this!" "I'm expected at this other meeting!" "I'm expecting an outside visitor!"

- define the meaning of formulations and terms to be used. They talk about "restructuring the library facilities," for example, instead of "reducing the library facilities."

- are allowed to criticize the others who hold power. When this happens, criticism is regarded as stimulating and encouraging: "Thank you for your suggestions!"

These verbal expressions of constructs of powerfulness are supported by a number of nonverbal self-presentational constructs. To start with, the powerful come to the meeting with only a few papers and documents (with the exception of the chairperson). Most of the time they lean back in a relaxed position. They are calm and friendly and smile or grin almost constantly. Their gestures and their manner of speaking are firm and confident or are meant to seem that way.

Behavior of the powerless

In our observations of the representatives of the other three faculty groups, the following verbal expressions could be noted. The powerless:

- speak redundantly, quickly, in a low voice. They tend to get muddled, sounding rushed and excited.

- restrict their own contributions by using phrases such as "Maybe I can read this aloud . . . " "Actually I find it kind of a pity that . . . " "Maybe we could . . . " "I guess . . . " "Well, we kind of figured this might be a way of . . . " "Perhaps you misunderstood me there." Generally the powerless use a lot of qualifiers such as "maybe," "kind of," etc. Their formulations are not expansive but restrictive, sometimes to the point of retracting their own statement.

- limit interaction among themselves to short whispers. When doing so they still concentrate on the general talk and look up immediately if there is any turn in the ongoing discussion.

We were also able to observe some indicators of complementary nonverbal self-presentational constructs. Unlike the powerful, the powerless come to the meeting with vast amounts of papers and documents that they busily read, write on, and generally fumble with, especially when another one of the powerless is speaking. Most of the time they keep their arms on the table and do not lean back. While doing this they often cross their forearms and sit bowed forward for rather long periods of time. With their elbows resting on the table, the powerless frequently touch their faces, shade their eyes, narrow their visual field, and hide the mouth with their hands. Notably, while speaking the powerless try in vain to find a pair of eyes looking at them; otherwise they look around the room with a blank face, staring into space or gazing at the floor. If a vote results in a clear majority against the powerless, they smile.

Interaction between the powerful and the powerless

In this section we report observations that illustrate the ongoing interaction and discourse. Which verbal and nonverbal constructs define interaction if the opposite side begins to speak? What changes in behavior occur? What happens when one side and the other alternate during the discussion?

First, what happens if one of the powerless speaks after one of the powerful has had the floor? The powerful restrict themselves to two kinds of reactions: On the one hand, they deny any kind of support or reinforcement. They avoid eye contact with the powerless when the latter are speaking. They look down, read the few papers they have in front of them, talk to their powerful colleagues, laugh, and stroke their chins with their hands in a bored or turned-off manner. They look out of the window, stare into the room, or hide their faces in their hands. They do not nod approvingly to the powerless as they did when one of the powerful was speaking. A second type of reaction is to attack. They lean forward, fixing their eyes upon the powerless speaker with arched brows and grimaces. They shake their heads and interrupt with formulations such as "Now that's enough!" "Let me tell you . . . " "But that's completely unfounded!"

If the powerless speak calmly at some length (which happens very rarely), they are usually not interrupted by the powerful. Instead, the powerful will listen restlessly in a distracted and impatient manner, making asides, whispering, laughing, and so on.

On the other hand, the powerless themselves seldom affirm contributions made by their powerless colleagues. While one of the powerless is speaking, the others will hardly ever look at her or him or nod approval. Only very few supporting and reinforcing gestures or looks are exchanged among the powerless, and if such gestures occur, they are inconspicuous and of short duration. If student members of the public audience act irreverently, the powerless prefer to stare at the table or fumble with their papers.

Second, what happens if one of the powerful speaks after one of the powerless? The powerful start their reply with phrases like "Let me tell you that . . . " "But that's utterly unfounded!" "Now that was ve-ry con-vin-cing!" "Obviously this is irrelevant to the issue!" "I really believe you're not interested in the issue, you just want to cause some trouble!"

While a member of their group is speaking, moreover, the other powerful signal their support by looking for and establishing eye contact, smiling at each other, nodding, and emitting words like "Precisely," "Exactly," and "That's it." Furthermore, they show signs of relief when one of the powerful takes a turn to speak. They lean back if they had not already done so, laughing and joking.

The powerless, too, almost always keep eye contact with powerful speakers. While doing this, the powerless have a serious mien and rarely smile. When controversies become heated, the powerless intensify their bowed postures. Their faces are shaded even more and their visual field is narrowed. During lengthy discussions the above gestures increase in frequency. Only in moments of general amusement will the powerless lean back and sit in a relaxed manner.

In sum, the powerful occupy, define, state facts, and attack while the powerless concede, relativize, retract, and withdraw.

Power under pressure

Over several months, the faculty board we observed had to deal with challenges that threatened to upset the smooth and easy-going way board meetings had been run in former years. In one challenge, the legitimation of the board was fundamentally questioned. Since the faculty groups were obviously not represented equally, and because the powerful always a priori hold the power, talk of pseudodemocracy began to circulate. Observers were allowed to attend the meetings. The presence of a large public audience, consisting of other powerless persons, caused a certain uneasiness during the meetings. Most members of the public audience showed disapproval in their facial expressions. The number of pejorative comments increased as well. Disunity developed among the powerful; new communal subgroups emerged from within.

In this new situation of power under pressure, a number of changes took place. The powerful increased the intensity and frequency of their behavioral strategies that had been so successful previously. They chose the approach of more of the same. The hard-liners among the powerful intensified their efforts in order to maintain the legitimization and structures of power enforcement that had been effective in the past. The powerful tried to justify and convince the powerless of the justice in their 9 to 6 majority by referring to the long and hard route they had had to take in order to gain the status of professor. The fact of having become a professor was meant to indicate that a person was qualified (himself, seldom herself) and should be recognized as an expert.

In this changing situation, the powerful referred more and more to formal legitimation: rules of procedure, higher authorities, the rector, and so on. A long discussion was held on whether the public audience should have the right to speak and what meaning this had for a society as a whole in a democracy. The right to speak was first denied but granted at the next meeting. An increasing number of votes took place. Because of their overall 9 to 6 majority, the powerful sustained their power. At the same time, they were meant to demonstrate how democratically and tidily the procedures are handled in the faculty board.

In this new and unusual setup, some of the powerful actually lost their temper. They started to speak out loudly, they pointed at misbehaving participants, they tore up papers dramatically, and they threatened to take leave or resign.

Summary

The strategy demonstrated by the powerful members of the faculty board can be characterized as oscillating between a symmetrical and an asymmetrical interpretation of the power construct. On the one hand, the powerful try to persuade the powerless that power is a symmetrical and legitimate relation and demand that they participate in the democracy game. On the other hand, the powerful immediately punish the powerless for any active participation, for any intrusion that does not fit into the scheme of the powerful. If the representatives of the powerless actually act on behalf of the powerless, they are silenced and distracted by the powerful.

This approach makes it impossible for the representatives of the powerless to do what they intend to do: stand up for their interests steadily and successfully. Furthermore, powerlessness and the impression of complete failure is enhanced by the fact that the powerless do not validate each other's constructions as a counter to the powerful. It seems that each representative has to rely completely on her/himself and the ability to validate her/his own behavior as appropriate. Therefore, most of the powerless apparently regard their failure as their individual deficiency or even as a weakness inherent in their personality structure. So for hours after the meeting the powerless think about how they should have reacted in a better way at specific moments. It turns out to be hard to see that the game is about (in)validation and enforcing one worldview at the expense of another (Portele, 1989).

In our opinion, it is impossible for the powerless to behave appropriately or even correctly, or to deliver the expected complementary gestures of powerlessness without great personal expense and danger of self-damage.

But then, what chances do the powerless have to improve their situation? What sort of coping strategies can be suggested and what consequences can be anticipated if the powerless try to deal with the described variety of power gestures described above?

The first coping strategy, and the one actually pursued by some of the powerless we observed, can be summarized as "come to the meeting well prepared." Thus, the powerless intensively tackle the agenda items beforehand, study seemingly relevant papers extensively, look up former minutes and administrative regulations that might come in handy, and try to collect arguments and anticipate counterarguments that will sustain the courses of action they want to pursue in the meeting. All the while, they concentrate completely on the official program side of the meeting, and, as it turns out, thereby actually support and reinforce the power relations set up by the powerful. In our view, this attempt to cope with the situation is doomed to failure because it is based on the misconception that decisions are reached by the faculty board after a fair and unbiased exchange of arguments where the better argument wins. The powerful like to foster this illusion because by tabooing the power construct, the image of a democratic institution whose members reach conclusions and decisions solely on rational grounds can be maintained. What is not talked about is that goals and values of the powerful and the powerless are in fact quite different, and the aims of the powerless are constructed as irrelevant by the powerful.

A second strategy that could be used to move away from the pole of powerlessness is to reverse the usual sequence of interactions by adopting the gestures and utterances typically shown by the powerful. This striking back with the same weapons requires a great deal of preparation. The powerless must first of all learn what those specific power gestures are and then actually practice performing them. Furthermore, they need to be prepared for the reactions their changed behavior will arouse among the powerful who can hardly be expected to accept them without resistance. The whole power construct rests on the differences between what powerful and powerless are expected and allowed to do. Most likely, the powerful will immediately try to force the powerless back into their old behavioral patterns by either ignoring the deviant behavior completely or by more or less directly asking them to act normally again, i.e. in a way considered adequate for one of the powerless in this situation. Clearly, the powerful cannot allow a reversal of existing power relations and therefore will not tolerate any attempt undertaken by the powerless in this direction for very long. Such an attempt will be considered to be impudence, exacted under duress. On the other hand, the powerless will only become capable of demonstrating power gestures at all if they learn to support and reinforce each other.

Finally, the powerless can try to uncover the existing power relations by adopting a metaperspective and introducing it into the ongoing meeting. Thereby the implicit rules of procedure as well as the behavior shown by the powerful themselves become a topic of discussion and are challenged. If, for example, one of the powerless who wishes to speak is constantly ignored by the chair, or if when speaking s/he gets interrupted by one of the powerful, s/he can openly address these acts, thus returning power gestures to the sender on a metalevel instead of struggling to compete in vain. Under an ethical perspective, we find this coping strategy more acceptable than the former one of adopting behavioral acts and patterns normally shown by the powerful.

No matter what the powerless eventually decide to do (or not to do), there are three things they ought to keep in mind: First, whatever is said during a meeting is said by someone, and is therefore always to be regarded as a statement of opinion, not a statement of facts. Even though the powerful like to act as if they know the real truth, they too have only their constructions of reality at their disposal. Second, the powerless themselves cannot ignore responsibility for their constructions either, specifically the decision to behave the way they usually do, thereby supporting and maintaining the power relations within the faculty board. And third, whatever happens, the powerful can always rely on a 9 to 6 majority!

CONCLUSIONS

What conclusions can be drawn from our inquiry into power? We have suggested that the products of our observations and analyses (as social practices themselves) may be used as a basis or starting point to reflect upon social practices and eventually to change them. So, where do we stand now?

It seems important to us to differentiate between contexts where from our perspective it is more or less productive to bring up the topic of power. Thus, the range of convenience of the power construct (Kelly, 1991) is not defined by a specific constellation in reality, but is a constructive and pragmatic enterprise. What is my aim with respect to my partner(s) in the interaction? Do I plan to collaborate with others in order to reach a commonly agreed-upon goal? Do I see our interaction as a useful tool to bring about the structural changes I desire, or do I expect others to affirm the status quo by attesting to the legitimation of the power position I hold?

Krüll (1986) pointed out that our decision to construct relationships with the help of the construct of power should take into careful consideration the consequences for the specific context. She focused her discussion of the power metaphor on a feminist perspective. To her mind, it is appropriate to describe the economic, political, social, psychological, and physical relations between the sexes in terms of the power of men over women in order to be able to fight against oppression. As long as women's worldviews are not accepted and woman are mistreated, discriminated against, and handicapped within the patriarchy, the power construct can be a useful and necessary tool. With it we can achieve the aim of labeling and eventually changing these grievances, even against the will of the powerful.

If, on the other hand, we prefer to pursue other goals apart from criticism and protest, for instance to work cooperatively with friends, colleagues, or lovers on ways of living that are important to us, the construct of power becomes inconvenient and might even block this end. To construe my spouse as the holder of power in our relationship, for example, can easily lead me to overlook my own share in the construction of our relationship and at the same time restrict the chances for dialogue. In general, those who see themselves as powerless in an interaction ought to realize what part they are thereby deciding to play. Do they want to participate in the construction of stabilities that limit their resources and the possibility of further development? Do they construe so tightly on matters of power that they cannot anticipate any other types of relationships?

We would like to invite those who construe a relationship as power-relevant to reflect upon that construction in order to open new possibilities. Still, we do not claim that their construction is wrong; such an assertion would seem cynical to us in many cases.

As has been pointed out, "constructivism, taken seriously, implies the freedom to construct—together with other persons—any kind of reality that appears to be useful or adequate to achieve one's own personal or social goals" (Krüll, 1986, p. 226). Following Krippendorff (1989), we want to combine this freedom with a social and ethical imperative: Always strive to maintain or expand the number of choices possible— your own as well as those of others!

REFERENCES

Averill, J. R. (1982). *Anger and aggression: An essay on emotion.* New York: Springer.

Averill, J. R. (1985). The social construction of emotion: With special reference to love. In K. J. Gergen & K. E. Davis (Eds.), *The social construction of the person* (pp. 89–110). New York: Springer.

Bateson, G. (1972). *Steps to an ecology of mind.* New York: Chandler Publishing.

Berger, P., & Luckmann, T. (1966). *The social construction of reality.* New York: Doubleday.

Bochumer Arbeitsgruppe für Sozialen Konstruktivismus und Wirklichkeitsprüfung (1990). *Macht* [Power]. Bochum: Ruhr-Universität Bochum, Fakultät für Psychologie.

Bochumer Arbeitsgruppe für Sozialen Konstruktivismus und Wirklichkeitsprüfung (1991). *Methoden der Wirklichkeitsprüfung* [Methods for the study of reality]. Bochum: Ruhr-Universität Bochum, Fakultät für Psychologie.

Foucault, M. (1972). *Die Ordnung des Diskurses* (L'ordre du discours) [The order of discourse]. Frankfurt: Fischer.

Foucault, M. (1980). *Power/knowledge. Selected interviews and other writings.* Brighton: Harvester Press.

Gergen, K. J. (1984). Aggression as discourse. In A. Mummendey (Ed.), *Social psychology of aggression* (pp. 51–68). Berlin: Springer.

Gergen, K. J. (1985). Social constructionist inquiry: Context and implications. In K. J. Gergen & K. E. Davis (Eds.), *The social construction of the person* (pp. 3–18). New York: Springer.

Gergen, K. J. (1991). *The saturated self.* New York: Basic Books.

Kalekin-Fishman, D. (1995). Kelly and issues of power. *International Journal of Personal Construct Psychology, 8,* 19–32.

Kelly, G. A. (1970). Behavior is an experiment. In D. Bannister (Ed.), *Perspectives in personal construct theory* (pp. 255–269). London: Academic Press.

Kelly, G. A. (1991). *The psychology of personal constructs,* Vols 1 and 2 (2nd edition). London: Routledge.

Krippendorff, K. (1989). On the ethics of constructing communication. In B. Dervin, L. Grossbery, J. O'Keefe, & E. Wartella (Eds.), *Rethinking communication: Paradigm issues.* Vol. 1. Newbury Park, CA: Sage.

Krüll, M. (1986). Ist die "Macht" der Männer im Patriarchat nur eine

Metapher? [Is the 'power' of men within patriarchy just a metaphor?] *Zeitschrift für systemische Therapie, 4,* 226–231.

Lukes, S. (1982). Panoptikon. Macht und Herrschaft bei Weber, Marx, Foucault [Panoptikon. Power and domination in Weber, Marx, Foucault]. *Kursbuch, 70,* 135–149.

Lutz, C. (1988). *Unnatural emotions.* Chicago: University of Chicago Press.

Maturana, H. R. (1985). *Erkennen: Die Organisation und Verkörperung von Wirklichkeit* [Perception: The organization and embodiment of reality]. Braunschweig: Vieweg.

Portele, G. (1989). *Autonomie, Macht, Liebe* [Autonomy, power, love]. Frankfurt: Suhrkamp.

Potter, S. H. (1988). The cultural construction of emotion in rural Chinese social life. *Ethos, 16,* 2, 181–208.

Raven, B. H., & Rubin, J. Z. (1983). *Social psychology.* New York: Wiley.

Richards, J., & von Glasersfeld, E. (1979). The control of perception and the construction of reality. *Dialectica, 33,* 37–58.

Rosenhan, D. L. (1973). On being sane in insane places. *Science, 179,* 250–258.

Roth, G. (1992). Das konstruktive Gehirn: Neurobiologische Grundlagen von Wahrnehmung und Erkenntnis [The constructive brain: neurobiological fundamentals of perception and knowledge]. In S. J. Schmidt (Ed.), *Kognition und Gesellschaft* (pp. 277–336). Frankfurt: Suhrkamp.

Rowe, D. (1991). *Wanting everything: The art of happiness.* London: Harper Collins.

Steiner, C. M. (1981). *The other side of power.* New York: Grove Press.

Walker, B. M. (1990, September). *Individualism and personal construct theory.* Paper presented at the Fifth Australasian Personal Construct Conference, Adelaide, SA, Australia.

Weber, M. (1964). *Essays in sociology.* London: Routledge & Kegan Paul.

Weingarten, K. (1991). The discourses of intimacy: Adding a social constructivist and feminist view. *Family Process, 30,* 285–305.

Wittgenstein, L. (1953). *Philosophical investigations.* New York: Macmillan.

CHAPTER 17

Ecologies of Meaning

HARRY OXLEY AND LINDA HORT

In this paper we seek to relate the processes of personality and of culture. We derive our essential idea of personality from personal construct theory (PCT), but we give it a twist that allows us to base our model on a non-Kellian metaphor.

Kelly showed each person as having a·system of interrelated concepts (constructs) that he/she uses to understand the world of experience, especially in terms of what to expect from it. These systems are built up by personal experience in much the same way that the ideal scientist builds up systems of concepts and theories; this is why Kelly often spoke of "man the scientist."

But man [sic] the [applied] scientist does not pull concepts out of thin air or build all his or her own ideas from the ground up by pure reason. People are like scientists in getting their concepts from stores of ideas current in their groups to mix and match for their own particular needs. Interaction is not just a matter of mutual experimentation but is for most of the time a process of conceptual learning, a perpetual seminar. Through discussion and experimentation together, a body of concepts or constructs thus available—which is called a *culture*—is constantly being tested and developed by those who draw from it. Questions of how any individual thinks are thus inseparable from questions of the thoughts available to groups of individuals to which a person belongs. Kelly himself was not strong on this fact in his two 1955 volumes because he wrote them as a clinician. He was very strong on it in his 1962 paper *Europe's Matrix of Decision*, where he sought to contrast intergenerational developments of climates of thought internationally (see chapter 2).

There is practically nothing at all in culture itself except for the per-

363

sonal construct systems of its people in their interactions. The 'practically' caveat is to include written and other made symbols, but they themselves are only meaningless shapes without the meanings that the minds of interacting people attach to them. Cultural elements have intergenerational histories often starting many millenia before their users were born, but again they only have force at any one time through how they can appear to people currently alive. Cultural change is changes in the thoughtways of people. All other attributions to culture as a thing "out there" are, to us at least, reifications.

Thus, an overarching theme of this paper is that explorations of personality and of culture should not merely be more closely joined as cognate areas of study, but that they should be seen as two branches of a single area of study. They are branches of the study of systems of meanings—study areas which, far from merely needing to inform each other, are totally incomprehensible unless they are considered together.

In developing our argument relating personality and culture, we depart from the PCT tradition on the matter of constructs' integration.

It would be wrong to see Kelly as presenting a person's constructs as all nicely integrated. His fragmentation corollary (1955, p. 83) says that "A person may successively employ a variety of construction subsystems which are inferentially incompatible with each other." He saw the healthy personality as having to work that way if it is to adapt well to new experiences. Just so are many anthropologists now seeing cultures with overly tight integration as unviable because of their allowing no openings for necessary corporate adaptations to the new.

For all of that, however, Kelly's major focus is still on meanings' integration by internal systems of logic. Some incompatibilities are permitted by permeability or open-endedness of higher constructs to give pliancy. If a person can keep superordinate constructs sufficiently flexible, then "while [his] bets on the turn of minor events may not appear to add up, his wagers on the outcome of life do tend to add up" (1955, p. 88).

We certainly agree that man the applied scientist is not always careful about the integrating logic of all the middle-range theories and methodologies he or she uses for everyday contracts; else they would often never be completed on time. We know from experience that the same can often be said of the professional applied scientist. But, humanly or professionally, there is still an integrating process that goes two ways.

As in science where higher theories are made by induction from and tested through the lower, superordinate constructs are themselves shaped by those lower subsystems, just as the subsystems are shaped by immediate experiences. Mostly this process is one of unconscious drift rather than of agonizing reappraisal, but it still happens. And so those wagers on the outcomes of life that add up in the end often manage to do so only because the nature of the bet itself quietly changed while the race was being run. That bet will have changed its nature according to which of those inconsistent subsystems happened to work best.

Nor do we see inconsistencies as only lurking at the level of lesser subsystems of meanings; we see most people as maintaining inconsistencies at their very highest levels. Indeed, they do well to do so, for then they can place a number of different wagers on the outcomes of life simultaneously, and rejoice in those that happen to come off while putting the others out of mind.

For all of these reasons we see intermeaning inconsistencies not as things merely to be tolerated as necessary slack in their systems, but as of the very essence of those systems. To us the ideal model of a system of meanings is not primarily an organismically or mechanically or logically integrated whole, with or without slack. It is a jumble and a jostling in which some meanings relate mutually-supportively, others antagonistically, and yet others with varying kinds of ambivalence.

Our guiding metaphor for making sense of this situation is the ecological process, as our title says. In talking about *ecologies* we are not thinking of balanced ecologies or of particular entities' individual adaptations to their environments. Since the word is often used by others with connotations like those, it seems advisable to say what ecology does mean to us, what makes it so attractive to us for metaphorical use.

Ecology is what is found in any area where different flora and fauna grow together, most interestingly in the wild but anywhere. Here we observe a jostling of what we can conceptualize either as forms of DNA molecule or as plant and animal species. As with meanings, we do not see species as species, we only see their individual exemplars. But this is quite good enough for us to understand how the species characteristically relate. These exemplars we see variously competing, coexisting with others as parasites or in symbiotic relationships and/or keeping clear of others in special niches. Each species (we can say) lives in an environment which includes all the other species, as well as external forces affecting the system as a whole such as climate, soil, poisons or fertilizers floating downriver, the odd bushfire, and so on. When external impacts or internal battles advantage any one species, others parasitic upon or existing symbiotically with it are also advantaged, and species in direct competition with it, and their own parasites and symbionts, are correspondingly disadvantaged.

These changes cause new battle lines to be drawn, new alliances to be made (unconsciously, of course—we are not personifying), old niches' barriers of protective isolation to get broken down, and so on. Any new plant or animal introduced from outside or evolving within the system produces the same effects. Any initial effect reverberates with greater or lesser force through the whole system, the advantaged or disadvantaged entities of any change similarly passing on effects of their new position. The process goes on constantly in any jungle or backyard so that a truly balanced ecology is very unlikely and can only present the merest semblance of reality to a very short-term viewpoint.

This system/process is infinitely complex, like the subject of the human sciences, but it is not incomprehensible. The game for lawlike generalization from its observation is to find the linkages and see the kinds of things that happen over time as a result of all these interrelated changes and their effects. This rougher approach to what we are about will never give those certainties for dealing with new situations that the physical sciences can find in their simpler worlds. But it may articulate some of those lessons of history that benefit our guesses in the ongoing human experimentation with environments just a little better.

Unlike biological entities, meanings are often in the conscious minds of individual humans, which in turn may often be driven by needs to perceive logical relationships among them. This is a peculiarity of meanings' environments without parallel in those of natural species. There are other ways in which jostling meanings do not quite parallel jostling species of a wilderness ecology. But metaphors are only for starting thought, not for ruling it, and a lack of perfect parallels is only to be expected.

As a final note in this overview, let us say that we differ terminologically from Kelly in preferring to talk of *the self* or *self-concept* rather than of the *basic role*. Kelly objected to theoretical connotations of the self and self concept that did not fit well into his own approach. We accept all his arguments for that terminological distancing and most of what he had to say about the basic role in general. As with our preference for using *meanings* over *constructs*, we stick to the more common terms because they are the more easily recognizable across different disciplines.

MEANINGS

Anthropology is all about what things characteristically mean to people in various groups. For examples of meanings see any dictionary. Obviously, words are not the only things to have meanings, although they are perhaps the most important. Anything worth thinking about is worth talking about and soon gets a verbal label; thus, the Sapir/Whorf hypothesis (Whorf, 1956) that all of any culture (if not purely individual thought) is embodied in its language.

Meanings are not discrete entities, but they derive their very essence from relations to other meanings. For example, real lions remain lions without any other animals to eat, albeit hungry ones, but the concept *predator* is simply meaningless without the concept *prey*. Meanings also derive qualities from their inclusion (along with some additional meanings but without others) in higher order categorizations, and from the lower order categorizations they do and do not contain within them. And so on.

The meaning of anything, symbol or sight or whatever, must necessarily differ somewhat from person to person because personal construct systems are all different. But those that have public labels and are taught accordingly are in more or less large part shared within interacting groups. This sharedness is a major aspect of what the idea of culture is all about.

In our discussion of meanings, we restrict ourselves to labeled meanings. These can be seen in either of two ways according to the context of investigation. We can look at them as they are understood by particular individuals and/or we can look at them in the dimensions of their sharedness within a society at large or any one of its various subgroups. Historians concerned with the actions of particular movers and shakers will clearly have to look at both sides. Clinical psychologists are presumably most concerned with the first and cultural anthropologists with the second, but it seems to us that they need to be able talk to each other on each other's primary terms.

That distinction gives us the first of many dimensions along which meanings of symbols as culturally viewed can differ: the extent to which a common symbol does denote shared meaning and how much of the meaning is shared. Some of our most potent words (community, democracy, work, rationality, for example) can mean a lot of very different things to different people, a fact from which they no doubt derive a lot of that potency. Associated with this all things to all people quality is a question of how important the variations may be in generating or fostering or inflaming or justifying conflicts among groups of people.

Other dimensions of difference according to meanings' sharedness and/or power within groups include such obvious matters as:

1. Overall, how important is each one in directly ruling the practicalities of people's everyday lives—and of how many people and what kinds of people—through their acceptance of it?

2. How indirectly important is each one for general everyday living via the power within society of particular groups for which it (or certain of its particular variants) is important?

3. How consciously is each one held by people (and again by how many and what kinds of people), as against being taken for granted as going without saying?

4. How inextricably welded in how much common thought are each particular meaning's cognitive and emotive/evaluative sides?

5. What sacred or magical qualities are imputed to each one, by how many overall, and by how many of those endowed with special sociopolitical power?

6. How resistant is each one to questioning or change?

These six questions represent only a grab bag to show some of the many questions that might be used for classification. Without actually sorting such differences out under headings, Kelly's paper (see chapter 2) raises them—in cross-cultural historical/developmental perspective.

CULTURE

Culture is an analytical construct denoting a producer, a process, and a product. Each of those three aspects can only be comprehended fully in terms of the rest, but they can be introduced in order.

Culture is a convenient term to sum up the major thrusts of socializing and constraining forces upon any one person from all other people. Remembering for our terminology that we have repackaged evaluation along with cognition in our down-to-basics exercise, we call this summing up the *prevailing cognitive environment*. So long as one does not reify it, we think this to be as good a term as any for culture as producer. It is the producer of the basic construction kits and spare parts from which people make and remake themselves and each other as humans.

Viewed from the ideational standpoint, which leaves material artifacts and overt actions out in favor of the mental side of things, and of which Kelly would approve (1955, p. 93), culture is a system of meanings potentially available to a people viewed in the context of what is happening in it. We say "potentially available" rather than "shared" because a large group's culture includes many meanings that individuals do not encounter until a situation that calls for them comes up—and for many people that appropriate situation never arises. This is obviously so with conceptual skills especially attached to particular lines of work or other specialized areas of human endeavor. But it also applies to special living places, classes, and experiences. Having never been in trouble with the Australian police, for example, we never knew what *verballing* was until we encountered the term sociologically from people who had been.

Emergence from the realms of the potential into the actual through special experiences will be a matter of major concern in a later section on group and category cultures.

Some basic anthropology texts still in print present culture as a set of ideals within which counterrealities spring up like weeds. A favorite example is that of the common hobby of adultery flourishing beside our society's prescribed duty of marital fidelity. Malinowski (1926) similarly found actions following contradictions among accepted principles in a traditional Pacific society during the dawn years of British anthropology. He distinguished them as *crimes* versus *customs*, although all were equally customary. To us such conflicts following mismatching principles are not conflicts between culture and something else, but between different sets of prescriptions equally cultural but at war.

At the center of our own thinking is a view of culture not as an integrated whole but rather as a system containing some mutually supportive ideas and prescriptions, but also many inconsistent ones, often in conflict. This is the case for changing cultures as well as for cultures that anthropologists found in isolated places and generally presented as stable. Some basic texts are at one with us in seeing internal cultural inconsistencies as normal and in presenting them as having an important survival value as we noted in our introduction. Old prevailing ways of thinking can prove to be bad guides when circumstances change, and then notions and approaches equally old but not hitherto strong or wide-spread in popular thought can rise up to meet the need.

A people of a relatively stable culture need inconsistencies to maintain their very stability because contexts of their existence can alternate. For example, they may well have periods of peace and of war, which call for different virtues and inconsistent values to support them. Traditional anthropological accounts of intermittently warring tribes quite often showed ambivalent views of noted warriors—heroes in battle but remembered as killers in calmer days. Times of want and plenty can likewise call up different meanings and expectations. Because of these embedded inconsistencies, we see in cultural interaction a long battle of meanings.

Sometimes the battle involves individuals more or less consciously and very practically using particular meanings as weapons against others. People also use meanings for control. A definition of power as "the ability to influence the construction processes of others" has been quoted by the authors of chapter 15. This is the whole point of radical critiques of ruling class hegemony.

But battles of meanings do not always involve battles among people. Many are waged inside people without their even noticing it, much less making use of it. Any of us could give plenty of examples of inconsistent meanings of many kinds that we have learned.

For example, we all know of work as a vehicle for present or potential self-actualization. We also know it as a nasty chore best made palatable by importing as much play into it as possible, and even then done only for the sake of wages necessary for self-actualization after knock-off time. Sometimes it seems the one thing and sometimes the other. Later we pursue the obvious fact that quite small differences and changes in working conditions can raise either one or the other of those views up to predominance in particular work worlds.

Conflicting meanings can coexist in happy illogicality if they are kept isolated for special circumstances. Many of us have some only for (say) the church or community activities, some only for business, some only for family life, some only for intimacies with close friends. This may get mocked as hypocrisy, but it is perfectly normal. Different contexts call for different patterns of behavior, and diverse and often conflicting meanings grow up to validate them.

But conflicting meanings are always potentially at war even if they are not actually so at any particular time, and circumstances can always arise that turn potentiality into actuality. When battle is joined—and it is happening all the time—some meanings win and others lose.

Losing meanings may be killed off altogether, but their more usual fate is to get pushed more or less underground (an underground to be discussed later). In this context it becomes useful to make a distinction quite familiar to cultural anthropology under various labels between *culture in use* and *culture in store*. Culture in use is itself no integrated whole but is where the active battles are. Culture in store is all the other meanings, those that lost yesterday but still wait on the sidelines to join battle if circumstances change to favor them tomorrow.

We will have more to say about this battle of meanings. At this stage, let us just say that it is as good a way as we can imagine for seeing culture as process.

Winning meanings (and of course there are degrees of winning) go into the next round's battles strengthened. Here, viewed in time and change, cultures and subcultures are at once the (abstracted) coaches and scorers for individuals' personal construct systems. They are coaches insofar as they guide newcomers in first forming their personal construct systems and older members in their no less universally ongoing reeducation. They are scorers insofar as they do this according to which particular constructs prevailed in the last day's matches for construct supremacy.

If the process went on in discrete bouts, we would have times at which cultures could be frozen to give an ethnography or cue study that did not do violence to their fluidity. But, alas for neat analysis, it does not. The consequently ever-developing outcomes, when viewed as outcomes of earlier rounds rather than in their role as starting points for the next, represent *culture as product*.

CULTURE AS AN ECOLOGY OF MEANINGS

We see the system of meanings in culture as outlined so far as an ecological system because it has these characteristics:

1. It is not an integrated whole. Some culturally available meanings coexist in mutual supportiveness. A classic case would be superficially unrelated racisms, sexisms, anti-intellectualities, hard-nosed child-rearing ideas, magical beliefs, and so on, which are said to go together in many totalitarian cultures (see chapter 5). Some meanings

may be dependent upon others without giving support in return, parasitically. But many meanings do not agree and some are in open conflict. Some meanings coexist without actual conflict within particular niches discussed below, but still have the potential for conflict. Some others likewise coexist without conflict only because there are customary devices to reconcile their logical oppositions, like the myths and rituals of reconciliation often described by anthropologists.

2. Special meanings flourish in two kinds of special niches: group and contextual. Particular group cultures provide special niches for special meanings by making culture in (regular) use of what is for most of the populace only culture in store, or a set of alternative perceptions known but seldom evoked. Thus, we have special meanings in status groups, like the once well-described working-class culture or culture of poverty. Special meanings in professional groups have been widely documented; some of them annoy the wider society's law enforcers (cf., Grabosky, 1991; Tomasic 1991; and many more), but a whole industry has long worked under the banner of corporate culture to develop more generally approved forms. Meanings also have contextual niches such as in peace or in war, for being parents or friends or fellow officeholders, for being workers in our jobs or battlers fighting to keep our jobs, or for being good family members or good citizens.

3. These niches and the special advantaging of the meanings in them are created by the environment. For example, while all people have their moments of viewing work as a debilitating and meaningless chore or the police as licensed muggers out to cop the harmless, groups low in the social hierarchy are encouraged to see things in those ways more often than others, which strengthens for those particular groups their own interpretations of widespread ambivalences. Oxley (1975) described the peculiarities of the then-distinct lower class culture in those terms. Those writers noted above explained those higher status job culture differences in much the same way. Similar approaches can be taken to the contextual niches.

4. Broad social change, or changes in environments outside of the system of meanings as such, like a major population change or a natural disaster or a new invention, relatively advantage and disadvantage meanings in the same way. They can bring to the fore particular groups or

contexts of behavior where people always thought in particular ways. Or they can cause meanings hitherto widely taken for granted as appropriate and useful to become less so, to the advantage of alternatives. They can also bring into open conflict meanings that previously coexisted in only potential conflict, in which case some win and others lose out.

5. Developments of meanings within a culture according to their own intrinsic logic may bring about the same results, sometimes to their own ultimate disadvantage. This is when we talk of ideas and principles containing the seeds of their own destruction, but more regularly to the disadvantage of other meanings. The same consequences can result from climbs to societal power because of purely internal developments of hitherto less important groups with their own spectra of special preferences among available cognitions.

6. Winning meanings drag along with them any other meanings attached as symbionts or parasites, while meanings in opposition to all those are weakened. The opposite happens with meanings similarly attaching to or opposed by defeated ones. Social groups that go strong on the meanings concerned are also relatively strengthened or weakened in their commitment to all the ways they happen to think and see all things, whether the connections concerned are logical or not. Groups specially associated with winning meanings may rise in social power and in the ability to propagate all their favorite thoughtways, regardless of logical connection.

7. People use meanings to fight other people as well as to control the vanquished of past intergroup fights hegemonically, but only a very few of the battles among meanings involve opposed people. We have mentioned the two views of work because, as teachers of the psychology and anthropology of work and also as active unionists, it springs most immediately to our minds. But many phenomena of common social experience are subject to similarly ambivalent public conceptualizations, and a battle of meanings is implicit in any such ambivalence.

The introduction of human will in using meanings as weapons of attack or tools of control simply switches our metaphor from the wilderness to cultivated parks and gardens. But there is one respect in which our ecology of meanings differs from its biological inspiration. Nature's battles occur among species fairly clearly distinguishable; intermediate

forms that no doubt existed during the process of evolution are seldom
still around to confuse our observation. Cultural and conceptual evolution is a much speedier process than its natural counterpart, so much so
that there the natural metaphor is not nearly so useful. What this means
for our own metaphor is that in the world of ideas we keep all the intermediate forms around to confuse the issue. In fact, these are what our
ecologies of meanings are mostly about.

But metaphors are only metaphors, and it would be silly to expect
exact parallels all the time or to pursue them too hard. The point is that
we have here another ongoing (unconscious) struggle of entities jostling
for survival while pursuing their own developments—some in symbiosis
but many in opposition—in a wilderness with a changing environment
where any balance is rare and temporary. That is far more of an ecological than of any other sort of system.

GROUP AND CATEGORY CULTURES

Culture cannot be talked about very easily outside of the very sim-
plest societies in any way other than in the context of various groups.
Nobody in large-scale society ever encounters its culture as a totality, to
be socialized by it or to input directly into it. We live in groups, most of
us living a little of our lives in each of many of them. It is the special
variants of culture in those groups that form our personal thinking, and
it is only through groups—the same or different ones—that we can make
any inputs.

Groups within a larger society do not necessarily have anything culturally distinctive about them at all. Some students of organizational culture talk as if they did, and they are diligent in their search for the distinctive. But people in modern society carry culture into any group from
others, and most single groups (work group or other) would be able to
function well enough on the strength of meanings brought wholly from
the wider world without adding anything of their own. Thus, when we
were asked to investigate "The Culture of the X Faculty," we changed
the title of the project to "Culture in the X Faculty." That was because
we knew that a group could work without necessarily having any meanings of its very own worth talking about, and indeed the X Faculty
proved to be just such a group. What it showed was a nice jostling of
some meanings developed within its own subgroups and others brought
in from occupational and professional groups outside.

In group cultures, as with those of traditional anthropology's whole societies, any cultural peculiarities that arise come from peculiarities of environment and history, along with socialization to keep things going and relative isolation to weaken the importation of meanings from other groups. In group cultures of the larger society, the isolation is more often social than physical, as where people meet outsiders only impersonally and in limited contexts, and the environment is likely to be a social one created and maintained by the activities of other groups. In very few groups does socialization start as early as childhood. But all groups socialize, and most groups deliberately or accidentally select new members already presocialized into any special ways of thought with which their old members feel at home and so have an easier socializing job, like finishing schools.

Even a group that takes all the elements it needs from the wider world will take only those it needs. Managers of a work group will take in meanings involved in specialist skills to get the job done, useful ideas about the work ethic, obedience, cooperation, and many more things. Workers will no less automatically bring ideas from other groups and earlier socialization. They will bring ideas about identification with classes or resentment of exploitation, about "if you can't lick 'em join 'em" or maybe about confrontation for its own sake as proof of sturdy independence, about work as self-fulfilment or about that necessity to mix work with enough play to stomach its disutility, and again many more things. So likewise for any other kinds of group.

In their operations with particular meanings from the overall store of widely available culture, group activities strengthen those meanings in the minds of their members at the expense of other meanings. They also strengthen particular options from among generally permitted variants of those meanings. An earlier generation of investigators of groups among the lower strata (to which one of us belonged; see Oxley, 1975, for a list of others) never found any meanings in groups of that culture not shared in some degree by people of all strata. It was just that particular meanings were kept in more constant use at that economic level and so were more strongly reinforced and better elaborated there, while other conflicting meanings got a better run in the lives of the higher strata.

Categories are groupings of people who are socially defined in some way as special, but who never all come together as interacting groups. They are men, women, young people, entrepreneurs, particular professional categories, and so on, including those social strata just used as an example. It makes sense to speak of categories as having culture in them.

Some of them have elements of socialization in common, as with work categories trained in similar schools by groups of similar teachers or by category-specific rituals or writings. But without even the least sense of commonness of kind, category memberships often operate as boundaries within which interacting groups form, and they often go with characteristically special meaning-shaping experiences. These latter may include being treated the same way by people of other categories. Certainly there are other factors of which we have not thought, but those alone would be enough.

PERSONALITY

The personal construct system, noted as being what we mean here when we talk of personality, is very like the cultural system. It is at once product and process and producer. It also involves continuity and change such that neither is understandable except in context of the other.

Personalities' linkages to culture come on the one hand from the fact that they make and maintain and change it; personal construct systems in interaction are what culture is all about. On the other hand, although personal construct systems can never be exactly the same for any two people since no two can ever have had exactly the same life experiences for the building, there will be similarities among fellow members of groups and categories because of socialization and/or other characteristic (culturally mediated) experiences in common.

Personalities' parallels to culture are that here again we can and must focus upon the jostling of meanings, and here again we see an ecological system of the same kind as we saw before. Personality, the personal construct system, can be described in the following ways:

1. Personality is not an integrated whole. Many psychologists have liked to see it that way, at least as an ideal, just as earlier anthropologists liked to see cultures as an integrated whole. We suggest not only that the fully integrated personality is impossible but that, like the fully integrated culture, it would be unviable.

   We have noted Kelly's fragmentation corollary, and we fully agree with his view (1955, p. 89), paralleling the newer view of culture in anthropology, that too close an integration could wreck "the ability to adjust to the vicissitudes of life." In fact, we accept all the tenets of personal construct theory (PCT) except for the points we made in the introduction. Permeable constructs at higher levels of the personal science indeed let inconsistent subsystems of meaning enter at lower levels, and they keep doing so without regard for the finer points of their fit. But man [sic] the scientist engages in induction as well as deduction, so that higher level constructs are constantly being reformed according to the relative success enjoyed in facing life by use of the lower ones. Thus, people's middle-range theories constantly remake their higher personal theories and paradigms. And so we see the jostling not only among lower level constructs but as continuing to constructs' very highest levels.

2. Personality similarly contains meanings in use and in store. There are also some inconsistent ones coexisting peacefully in regular use for different circumstances, and those in store can get brought up for unfamiliar circumstances.

3. Personality again shows regular repetition of particular circumstances bringing particular meanings to the fore of thinking for general purposes beyond those which originally called them into use.

4. Personality is again kept in constant flux by its environment, of events and other people that again and similarly give victories and defeats to meanings. Here is where we see a process quite crucial to cultural change in process, for one of the things that personality as producer produces (along with actions) is interpretations of new inputs and reinterpretations of the old. This is not the only reason why small changes can produce large unforeseen consequences, but it can be a major one when massive reinterpretations get started.

5. Personality can also start and monitor directions through developments from within its own internal logic. The personality level is where this process has its roots for culture because people are unlike cultures in being pushed by what Festinger presented as an in-built force against cognitive dissonance toward just that internal logical consistency, a force inside people although not inside culture that makes sense of what often happens in culture. This force does not stop people letting themselves be ruled by logically inconsistent ideas for different contexts as long as they can keep those contexts apart, but it guarantees instant internal conflict when developments stop the segregation working. Clinicians may know cases of constructs developing to prove that they contained the seeds of their own destruction at the personality level too; new constructs can certainly contain

seeds of destruction of old ones, a process brought up earlier as keeping inconsistency and change boiling.

6. Personality again shows meanings raised up by victories or pulled down by defeats in internal battles dragging up or down along with themselves their symbiont and parasite meanings. Here again the relationship may be accidental rather than even internally logical, as when ideas get associated through a person's having first encountered them in the same learning package.

We cannot see anything in personality quite like a society's battles among individuals who whip up bystander support and hit each other over the head with meanings. In this respect, personalities do not contain armies but are the battleground. There is some resemblance to societies' ruling-class users of meanings (consciously or unconsciously) for their own survival in the idea of the self, to be considered shortly, but we would not want to carry this analogy too far.

We do not think that any such differences seriously hinder our seeing personalities in time and contextual change in the same ecological way as we see culture. When we moved from our biological ecologies to ecologies of meanings we were using metaphor; when we move between culture and personality we are talking identity—the same process operating at two interrelated levels.

THE SELF

The self or self-concept is that part of the personality within which people define who and what they are, their fundamental natures, where they fit into society and the universe, and (an imperative that seems to move some of the least intellectual people) how they justify a self-respecting existence. As such it is an ultimate guide and a most demanding master both for behavior and for interpretation of experiences, so that people can continue to see themselves in ways that let them feel best.

It was all that to Kelly too, although he called it the "basic role." It is the core, he said, of "one's deepest understanding of being maintained as a social being" (1955, p. 502), central to "the maintenance of identity" (p. 503). It is a monkey on one's back to direct, to produce guilt, and to threaten when it is denied. Its constructs "operate as rigorous controls upon his behavior . . . . much of [a person's] social life is controlled by [it]" (p. 131). "Perception of one's apparent dislodgment from his core role constitutes the experience of guilt" (p. 502). And "one can be threatened by the prospect of changing [it] . . . . by a new 'realization' of what he has been doing . . . . by mounting proportions of an alternative interpretation of himself" (p. 493).

Kelly gave us a nice example of a midlife crisis: "A childless husband [presumably one who had defined himself in fatherly terms] can be increasingly threatened as each year adds new weight to the evidence that he does not have what it takes to be a father" (p. 493). This will serve as a starting point to show where we feel we may be going beyond Kelly.

We see self-concepts as developing in youth and young adulthood as mixed bags likely to include too many ideals of excellence for any mere mortal's reasonable aspirations, including some that are incompatible with others. Over the years some of these ideals get lost, not so much weeded out as crowded out by those that get reinforced by experience of life pushing out those that do not. This process is generally quiet and scarcely noticed.

In a study of university academics' work orientations that we did some years ago (Oxley & Hort, 1987), we found older academics a little more likely to see themselves as teachers than their younger colleagues and less likely to see themselves as primarily researchers. Our explanation for this was that young academics came from their PhD studies seeing themselves as about to make their mark in life from their new ideas, but changed as the new ideas generally failed to make as much impact on the world's thought as they could see themselves making upon the thought in their students' minds. Thus, they tended to change self-definitions according to what had at least not been invalidated.

Crises arise if circumstances force conflicting ideals into open contradiction or if elements of the self-concept suddenly suffer denial after long and successful years of operation have raised them too high in a person's self-definition.

The self offers its own subsystems of meanings for bringing up in appropriate situations on a day-to-day basis. It is in this context that Miller Mair (1977) talked about the community of self from the PCT viewpoint. Although the internal pushes for logical consistency may make more of a problem at this most intimate of all levels, it is still possible to maintain one self for the office and another for the family and maybe another for friends, and maybe more than one for each of these for different kinds of situations according to special contexts.

For all of these reasons it seems to us that the self is best seen as yet another ecological system of meanings, containing the integrated subselves of Mair's community, but with even more muddle and inconsistency than that idea alone suggests. Here again there is an ongoing process of reordering those elements (and subselves) for importance in interaction with an environment. Here again we can get internal developments among elements and subsystems of elements that can contain seeds of their own destruction and/or grow to compete savagely where there was no competition before.

It also has parts in store in addition to the parts regularly in use; parts kept underground, as it were, but ready to spring up if environmental changes encourage them. Again, this means that quite small changes of impacts from without can bring about great crises of change within.

CONCLUSION

Some people in the social sciences object to the use of natural science metaphors, but we see nothing wrong in it. Sociologists of knowledge argue well that we derive our ideas of nature from our social experiences, so the practice can well be seen as simply bringing insights back home. The game is to bring the right ones back to the right places. Mechanistic and organismic metaphors do not work well for cultures or, we would argue, for the personality or the self. So far, the ecological one seems to be working for our own real-world sense makings.

The idea that instability and incoherence is normal and adaptive is gaining credibility in biological circles through the concept of ecology. By using that metaphor in the social sciences, we question the more traditional ways of viewing personality and culture but show more importantly that the two are inextricably linked. Practical issues about the nature of our behavior and our society follow from this view. In current research we are pursuing some of these issues.

REFERENCES

Grabosky, P. (Ed.). (1991). Complex commercial fraud. *AIC Conference Proceedings No. 10*. Canberra: Australian Institute of Criminology.
Kelly, G. A. (1955). *The psychology of personal constructs*. Vols. 1 and 2 New York: W. W. Norton.

Mair, J. M. M. (1977). The community of self. In D. Bannister (Ed.), *New perspectives in personal construct theory* (pp. 125–149). London: Academic Press.

Malinowski, B. (1926). *Crime and custom in savage society*. London: Routledge & Kegan Paul.

Oxley, H. (1975). The culture of poverty and beyond. *Mankind, 10*(2): 69–83.

Oxley, H., & Hort, L. (1987). The learner in higher education: Where are the teachers? In A. Miller & G. Sachse-Akerlind (Eds.), *The learner in higher education: A forgotten species?* (pp. 307–315). Sydney: HERDSA.

Tomasic, R. (1991). *Casino capitalism: Insider trading in Australia*. Canberra: Australian Institute of Criminology.

Whorf, B. L. (1956). *Language, thought and reality: Selected writings of B. L. Whorf* (J. B. Carroll, Ed.). Cambridge, MA: MIT Press.

Postword

When we began to look for material to include in this collection, we focused on the sources and expression of social construing. Through their work with individuals, most of the contributors to this volume concluded that construals are implicated in some way in group memberships. A few of the contributors became interested in individual construing as a result of a primary interest in group contexts. All of the papers demonstrate that personal construct theory (PCT) and personal construct research offer novel approaches and new understandings of the social. They point to "roads and avenues" (the Kellian phrase) that invite further exploration. These can be classified under four headings, all directions that Kelly hints at in chapter 2.

The first significant road leads us to find new uses for Kellian terms. Walker has found that Kelly himself was quite convinced of the centrality of society for individual functioning. Three papers in this collection specifically explore the possibilities in the theoretical terminology. Stojnov extends the meaning of hostility; Leitner, Begley, and Faidley elaborate on role relations; and Willutzki and Duda clarify the social construction of both verbal and nonverbal constructs related to power.

A second path is that of the exploration of culture. One approach has grown out of the cross between anthropology and personal construct psychology. Oxley and Hort discuss the parallels between culture and personality that are brought into prominence in personal construct psychology. Ross uses PCT analysis to highlight a specific culture. Further turns on this path are taken by Jankowicz, Denicolo, and Tooth, who each look at different professions, using Kellian methods, fortuitously in different countries. They show how PCT makes it possible to explore the dialectic of occupational cultures in interaction with national cultures.

The conversational orientation of Kelly's theory is a third strand that has led writers to describe the evolution of construals in definable face-to-face social units. A personal construct group can be a group that deliberately sets out to experiment together with personal constructs as Stringer and Thomas describe it. But even when the aims are quite different as in the friendship groups described by Neimeyer, Brooks, and Baker, and in the families that Procter has worked with, it turns out that the groups can be characterized in terms of shared constructs or shared ways of construing. Shared narratives also have implications for action as Kalekin-Fishman shows.

Finally, several of the papers exemplify and elaborate the principle of constructive alternativism. Paradoxically, these construals of constructivism provide heretofore unexplored nuances of what might be seen as a nonquestion in personal construct psychology: the idea that the person is central. De Bernardi demonstrates the importance of constructive alternativism in evaluating children's intelligence. Epting, Dunnett, Prichard, and Leitner detail alternative choices for ways of living. And while Warren draws out theoretical connections between constructive alternativism on the one hand and democratic ideologies and social egalitarianism on the other, Ross illustrates how a government can in fact make use of alternative constructs in order to reach an egalitarian policy.

Through the elaborations that contributors to this book have presented, foundation stones of personal construct theory have begun to map the complex network of paths between the individual and the society he or she lives in. Through its preoccupation with social constructs and the construction of the social, PCT will undoubtedly attract a wider audience and foster new interdisciplinary initiatives. Nor is this merely an academic peccadillo. The Kellian principle of constructive alternativism is, when all is said and done, not merely a guideline for academic probing. It is a principle that gives meaning to the theory in everyday life. An acceptance of constructive alternativism is a basis for insuring that people can indeed live together even though they construe the worlds they share differently.

Devorah Kalekin-Fishman
Beverly M. Walker

AUTHOR INDEX

385

SUBJECT INDEX

NOTE: Certain terms/concepts literally permeate each chapter in the book and are not indexed. These include construct (in its most general sense), construing as a process, group, interpretation, and personal construct psychology/theory.